PARALLEL MODELS OF ASSOCIATIVE MEMORY

Edited by

Geoffrey E. Hinton
M. R. C. Applied Psychology Unit
Cambridge, England

James A. Anderson
Brown University

LEA LAWRENCE ERLBAUM ASSOCIATES, PUBLISHERS
1981   HILLSDALE, NEW JERSEY

Copyright © 1981 by Lawrence Erlbaum Associates, Inc.
All rights reserved. No part of this book may be reproduced in
any form, by photostat, microform, retrieval system, or any other
means, without the prior written permission of the publisher.

Lawrence Erlbaum Associates, Inc., Publishers
365 Broadway
Hillsdale, New Jersey 07642

Library of Congress Cataloging in Publication Data
Main entry under title:

Parallel models of associative memory.

Bibliography: p.
Includes index.
1. Memory.   2. Human information processing.
3. Association of ideas.   I. Hinton, Geoffrey E.
II. Anderson, James A.   [DNLM: 1. Computers—
Congresses.   2. Information theory—Congresses.
3. Models, Psychological Congresses.   4. Memory—
Physiology—Congresses. WL 1026 P222 1979]
BF371.P27   153.1'2   80-28697
ISBN 0-89859-105-8

Printed in the United States of America

Contents

Preface

Most of our ideas about computing are derived from our experience with conventional digital computers. There is, however, a widespread feeling that these computers are not a good model for how cognitive processes are embodied in the brain. Tasks like arithmetic or flawless memory for large numbers of unrelated items are very easy for the computer and very hard for us. Tasks like perceiving the three-dimensional world or recalling items from partial descriptions come naturally to us but are very hard to implement in a conventional computer.

It seems that the computational processes in the brain are different in kind from those in the computer and that this difference may stem from the fact that the brain has billions of units that all compute in parallel, whereas conventional digital computers have to reduce every computation to a sequence of very simple primitive steps.

People in many different fields who are deeply puzzled by the question of how the brain computes have been struggling to formulate models of computation that are appropriate for parallel systems composed of large numbers of interconnected, simple units. In particular, they have been investigating a class of computational models in which memories are stored by modifying the interconnections between units. In June 1979, with help and guidance from Don Norman, we brought some of these people together at a small informal conference in La Jolla, California. This book is the result. We deliberately chose people from fields as diverse as neurophysiology, cognitive psychology, artificial intelligence, mathematics, and electrical engineering. Most of the participants had not met each other previously and in some cases were unaware of each other's work. Yet as things progressed, it became clear that there were large areas of agreement, as well as strong disagreement about details.

The field of parallel models is still in its infancy and is not yet ripe for a textbook. We hope, however, that this collection will serve as a source book for students and researchers in neuroscience, psychology, and computer science who, like us, feel that understanding this kind of model is the key to understanding how our minds are embodied in our brains.

In the first chapter we present the reasons for investigating parallel alternatives to the basic architecture of conventional digital computers, and we review some of the simpler parallel models. We also review the extensive evidence from neuroscience about the organization of neural functioning. The other chapters range in their concerns from neurophysiological details to experimental data on human memory. They are united, however, by the conviction that parallel interactions among relatively simple units provide a better metaphor for the basic operations of the mind than long sequences of simple steps.

Finally, we would like to thank the members of the Program in Cognitive Science at the University of California, San Diego, especially Don Norman and David Rumelhart. They created a wonderfully free working environment and a receptive but well-informed group of colleagues. This book would not have been possible without them. The conference, the Program in Cognitive Science, and our time there as Visiting Scholars were all made possible by grants from the Sloan Foundation.

Geoffrey Hinton
James Anderson

Introduction

David E. Rumelhart
Donald A. Norman
University of California, San Diego

This is a difficult book, difficult but important. To understand the articles requires knowledge of mathematics, neurophysiology, computer science, and psychology. But the novelty of the approaches and the substantive weight of the contributions makes the book worthy of considerable study. The aim of the book is to present a group of models of human processing structures built upon what is known of neurophysiological processing principles.

Investigation into the nature of the long-term memory system has been a central theme in cognitive science in general and cognitive psychology specifically for the last 10 or 15 years. The twin questions of how information is represented and of what kinds of processes operate on this information have formed the focal point of most of the theories of long-term memory. Many alternative systems have been considered. We have viewed long-term memory as consisting of vectors of components (c.f. Bower, 1967; Norman & Rumelhart, 1970), of multidimensional spaces (c.f. Henley, 1969; Shepard, 1962), of hierarchical tree structures (c.f. Mandler, 1967), of networks of semantic relationships (Quillian, 1968; Rumelhart, Lindsay, & Norman, 1972), of sets of propositions (c.f. Kintsch, 1975), of various collections of schemata, frames, scripts, and plans (c.f. Bartlett, 1932; Minsky, 1975; Rumelhart & Ortony, 1977; Schank & Abelson, 1977), of sets of productions (c.f. Newell, 1973), and of various combinations of the above (c.f. Anderson, 1976). In addition to these more or less specific proposals we have engaged in a more general debate about whether knowledge representation was best considered "propositional" or "analogical" (c.f. Kosslyn, 1976; Pylyshyn, 1973).

Now just when we are beginning to get some of these issues clear in our minds, and when we are coming to see how all of these various proposals interrelate, and perhaps when a consensus is arising, we find ourselves, in this book, facing yet another new array of proposals. Where do these fit in? Why should we bother to understand these systems?

The types of memory systems outlined in this book differ from those currently in fashion in at least three important ways:

1. These systems are closely tied to a neurophysiological foundation.
2. These systems offer an alternative to the "spatial" metaphor of memory storage and retrieval.
3. These systems assume a distributed parallel-processing system with no need for a central executive to coordinate processing.

In the following sections we discuss some of the consequences of each of these differences.

Neural Plausibility

Most of the proposals discussed in this book have been inspired by considerations of the hardware of the brain. This is a feature that clearly distinguishes these proposals from the more conventional memory representational systems of cognitive science. Of course we have always realized that someday our theories of memory would have to be brought into line with our knowledge of brain function, but we assumed that the hardware of the brain was general enough to support almost any proposal that we found useful to postulate. Thus neurophysiological considerations have largely been ignored in conventional accounts of memory phenomena. Instead we have begun by considering the kinds of information that must be represented and then developed our memory representations to be appropriate for the information stored. This has proven a demanding task in itself. In this book we see the question turned around. These models begin with a consideration of the brain, how it works, and how it is organized. The authors then reason from these considerations to their memory theories. Of course, it has not yet been demonstrated that the complex information-processing demands that stimulated the development of the more conventional systems is possible in these neural models. Hinton's demonstration that semantic networks can be implemented in terms of an associative memory is intended as one step along toward this demonstration. Still, these models are surely promising. Indeed some of their features promise to emulate aspects of human memory that have proven incredibly difficult to capture even in the most sophisticated models.

Thus, at the least, we should view these models as a challenge to the implicitly held assumption that not enough is known about the structure of the brain to offer a serious constraint on our hypotheses about the nature of memory representations. Perhaps the constraints *are* minimal. But the debate that occurred at the conference over whether there were enough neurons in the brain to implement Feldman's proposal is an instructive one. However such a debate is resolved, once such issues are seriously raised it becomes clear that there may be at least some neurophysiological constraints on our theory development. It may soon become a necessary exercise for those proposing particular memory representations to provide at least an argument to show that the brain could encode information in the way required by the theory.

Distributed Memories

A second dimension along which the present proposals differ from those previously developed involves the very nature of storage itself. We conventionally characterize memory in terms of storing information in some *place*. One piece of information is at one place; other pieces of information are at other places. The library, the filing cabinet, the modern digital computer, and the junk box have served as our metaphors for memory. In all of these cases information is stored in some particular place and retrieval involves going to where it is stored and finding it. Knowledge may contain references (pointers or associations) to other knowledge; and there may be various types of indexes and organizational structures to the knowledge; but the principle remains constant: Memory is stored by place. The process of retrieval has thus been characterized as "finding the right place in memory." In semantic network terminology we find this place by following the appropriate links in the network. In a multidimensional representation this amounts to "finding the right region of the space." In the language of the schema theories, this amounts to "finding the right schema." The notion that information is stored in particular places is an assumption that has gone almost unchallenged. Most of the papers in this book offer a completely different conception. On their view, information is not stored anywhere in particular. Rather it is stored everywhere. Information is better thought of as "evoked" than "found." Rather than imagining that particular neural units encode particular pieces of information, this view has it that information is stored in the *relationships* among the units and that each unit participates in the encoding of many, many memories. To an intuition tutored on the spatial metaphor this is a strikingly nonintuitive proposal. How can a simple memory unit reasonably participate in the encoding of a large number of memories? How can they be kept straight? The answer to these questions is, it seems, at the very heart of the conceptualization. In short, these *distributed* memories can retrieve individual memory traces from a complex of memory traces in much the same way that a filter can extract individual frequency components from a complex acoustic waveform. Even though the individual frequency components are completely intertwined with one another, the filter is able to detect the presence of whatever specific component it is tuned for. As long as the individual memory traces are sufficiently different from each other, there is no interaction among the stored traces. In these conditions a distributed memory system can operate as a perfect storage and retrieval device. This is not the most interesting result however. The most interesting aspect involves what happens when memories are not independent of one another. In these cases they do interact. Storing one memory can affect another. But herein lies the great strength of the system. Information that is related to, but different from, previously stored information tends to evoke the original pattern of activity—even though the inputs to the system may differ in many details. Thus these memory models, unlike the more conventional models mentioned previously, have similarity and the ability to generalize as a central component. Similar items of information interact with one another in such a way as to reinforce those aspects they have in common and cancel out those aspects on which they differ—this can lead to the building of a prototype representation that is most sensitive to information falling about the central tendency of the highly similar inputs.

Now that the spatial metaphor has been clearly pointed to as an assumption, it is clear that we have to reconsider our assumptions on this issue. If the brain really stores information through changes in synaptic efficacy distributed over large numbers of neurons with many memories encoded in the *same* set of neurons, what does that mean for our theories of memory? Do they really depend on the notions of spatially distinct memories? What features do spatially distributed memories have that the conventionally localized memories don't have? Can the theories developed within the place metaphor of memory be translated into a spatially distributed equivalent? We don't have answers for these questions, but after reading this book we submit that these are the questions that must be faced.

Parallel Processes

Perhaps a less controversial feature of the models presented in this book is their assumptions of parallel distributed processing. These assumptions have been increasingly apparent in most modern views of human information processing. Whereas modern high-speed computers operate with processing units which function on the order of 10s or 100s of nanoseconds, the brain consists of processing units that operate on the order of milliseconds. Yet the brain is unquestionably able in a few hundred milliseconds to perform processing feats that have proven impossible to emulate in hundreds of minutes of computer time. Clearly, the brain accomplishes this feat through the simultaneous operation of many, many processing units. The models presented here, by and large, assume that the memory system consists of many very simple units rather than a few relatively complex units. Gone are the executives of previous generations of models. Gone are the sequentially organized stages of processing. In their place, along with a distributed memory system, is a distributed processing system. Complex computations are assumed to be carried out through the concurrent action of an enormous number of independent processing units—each carrying out its own simple computations or reacting only to its own local set of inputs. According to these theories the upshot of these local responses by local computing units is a system capable of complex global goal-directed processing. In our opinion this remains a matter of faith for most of these proposals. It is relatively clear how Fahlman's proposals can be used to implement such global processing, but his system is under the control of an executive—only a small portion is under distributed control.

In spite of these reservations it is clear that we must give serious consideration to the models with parallel distributed systems of control. We have not yet had enough experience with models of this kind to understand fully the consequences of such a control system. It is only through exploration of these kinds of models that we will begin to understand the limitations and strengths of such a processing scheme.

A COMPARISON OF MODELS

It is interesting at this juncture to compare the kind of memory system being proposed in this book to one that we developed (following the work of Bower, 1967) just about 10 years ago (Norman & Rumelhart, 1970). Both in our model and in these associative memory models information is stored in terms of a vector of features; Both receive inputs in terms of partially specified perceptual vectors that are "filled out" in the process of perception; both represent similarity in terms of common values on common features; both have one specific representation for each feature in the memory system. But here the similarity stops. Our model was organized along much more conventional lines. Perceptual vectors were "matched against" a "sensory-memory" dictionary and a best match was found between the incomplete perceptual vector and the complete memory representation. (We were nonspecific about how this matching process occurred. It would of course have been possible to use an associative memory system to carry out this matching process.) The output of this process was then sent to "short-term" memory where these "memory vectors" resided for a time before they decayed. Information was stored by attaching relevant "context" tags to the features in memory. Retrieval occurred in our memory by accessing all of the features associated with a particular context and matching the partial memory vector against the possible set of memory vectors and thereby reconstructing the appropriate response. In the associative memory systems we encounter here the concept of short-term memory is not directly considered. However, long-term information storage occurs in a way very different from our approach. Information is not encoded in terms of external contexts; rather it is encoded in terms of a pattern of interrelations among the attributes themselves. If two features tend to co-occur, activity in one tends to cause activity in the other. Features which never co-occur tend to suppress each other. Context, rather than being an external tag associated with the memory units, is represented in terms of other memory units. The relations between context and a set of co-occurring units is of the same form as that among the units. Namely, the occurrence of one tends to cause the other to become active. This process elegantly solves a number of the problems we set out to solve with our model. The reason that the current models choose this particular mechanism for storage and retrieval, rather than the sort we chose, is clear enough. These authors take seriously the view that the attributes we are talking about are really neural units and note the obvious fact that neural units function through excitatory and inhibitory relationship with one another. The further assumption that storage involves the modification of the way one unit affects another leads directly to their solution. This then is one case study of a solution growing directly out of a consideration of a direct neural interpretation of the elements of a theory.

ACKNOWLEDGMENT

Preparation of this forward was supported by the Office of Naval Research under Contract N00014-79-C-0323.

REFERENCES

Anderson, J. R. *Language, memory, and thought.* Hillsdale, N.J.: Lawrence Erlbaum Associates, 1976.

Bartlett, F. C. *Remembering.* Cambridge: Cambridge University Press, 1932.

Bower, G. A multicomponent theory of the memory trace. In K. W. Spence and J. T. Spence (Eds.), *The psychology of learning and motivation.* New York: Academic Press, 1967.

Henley, N. M. A psychological study of the semantics of animal terms. *Journal of Verbal Learning and Verbal Behavior,* 1969, *8,* 176–184.

Kintsch, W. The representation of meaning in memory. Hillsdale, N.J.: Lawrence Erlbaum Associates, 1974.

Kosslyn, S. M. Can imagery be distinguished from other forms of internal representation? Evidence from studies of information retrieval times. *Memory & Cognition,* 1976, *4,* 291–297.

Mandler, G. Verbal learning. In G. Mandler, P. Mussen, N. Kogan, & M. A. Wallach (Eds.), *New directions in psychology: III.* New York: Holt, Rinehart & Winston, 1967.

Minsky, M. A framework for representing knowledge. In P. H. Winston (Ed.), *The psychology of computer vision.* New York: McGraw-Hill, 1975.

Newell, A. Production systems: Models of control structures. In W. C. Chase (Ed.), *Visual information processing.* New York: Academic Press, 1973.

Norman, D. A., & Rumelhart, D. E. A system for perception and memory. In D. A. Norman (Ed.), *Models of human memory.* New York: Academic Press, 1970.

Pylyshyn, Z. What the mind's eye tells the mind's brain: A critique of mental imagery. *Psychological Bulletin,* 1973, *80,* 1–24.

Quillian, M. R. Semantic memory. In M. Minsky (Ed.), *Semantic information processing.* Cambridge, Mass.: MIT Press, 1968.

Rumelhart, D. E., Lindsay, P. H., & Norman, D. A. A process model for long-term memory. In E. Tulving & W. Donaldson (Eds.), *Organization and memory*. New York: Academic Press, 1972.

Rumelhart, D. E., & Ortony, A. The representation of knowledge in memory. In R. C. Anderson, R. J. Spiro, & W. E. Montague (Eds.), *Schooling and the acquisition of knowledge*. Hillsdale, N.J.: Lawrence Erlbaum Associates, 1977.

Schank, R., & Abelson, R. *Scripts, plans, goals and understanding: An inquiry into human knowledge structures*. Hillsdale, N.J.: Lawrence Erlbaum Associates, 1977.

Shepard, R. N. The analysis of proximities: Multidimensional scaling with an unknown distance function, I & II. *Psychometrika*, 1962, *27*, 125–140 & 219–246.

1

Models of Information Processing in the Brain

James A. Anderson
Brown University
Geoffrey E. Hinton
M.R.C. Applied Psychology Unit
Cambridge, England

1.1. INTRODUCTION

This chapter introduces some models of how information may be represented and processed in a highly parallel computer like the brain. Despite the staggering amount of information available about the physiology and anatomy of the brain, very little is really known about the nature of the higher-level processing performed by the nervous system. There is no established theory about the kinds of neural activity that occur when we hear a sentence, perceive an object, or form a plan, though data on many fascinating and significant bits and pieces is now available.

An obvious feature of the brain is its parallelism (see Section 1.5 for a review of the neurophysiological evidence). This parallelism is a major reason for investigating computational models other than the conventional serial digital computer in our attempts to understand how the brain processes information. The concept of parallelism may need some explanation. A system which is parallel at one level of description may well be serial at a higher level. At the level of individual motor neurons, for example, the human motor system is highly parallel. The simultaneous actions of many muscles are necessary for coordinated movement. If, however, the pattern of activity of the whole set of motor neurons is used as a unit of description, the system is strictly serial because only one pattern can exist at a time. Similarly, in a conventional digital computer many electrical events occur in parallel when each machine instruction is executed, but the instructions, considered as units, are executed sequentially. The transition between the parallel and serial levels of description thus occurs at the level of the individual machine instructions.

If many computational operations are performed at once, a system can obviously operate faster. However, one part does not know what the other parts are currently doing because the parts operate simultaneously. This causes serious problems of coordination and lateral information transfer from one part of a parallel system to another. These problems have made it hard to program general purpose computers that execute many instructions at once though numerous special purpose systems have been developed for specific tasks.

We feel that problems of coordination and lateral information transfer are not merely irritating; they are fundamental. They determine the kinds of operations that are easy to implement at the level at which a machine is parallel. These may be much richer than the rather restricted set of primitive operations of a conventional digital computer. For example, the state of activity of a large set of feature-detecting units can determine the state of activity of another large set of units in a single step in a parallel machine.

The idea that a parallel machine may have a different and richer and much more powerful set of primitive operations constrasts sharply with the idea that parallelism should be added on top of existing programming techniques by providing message-passing facilities that allow communication between multiple processors, each of which is a fully fledged conventional computer. The latter approach is obviously a sensible way of extending existing computational techniques, and it is currently under investigation within computer science, but it takes for granted the primitive operations of a conventional digital computer, which are probably an inappropriate computational metaphor for the brain.

As an example of a task for which a conventional computer seems inappropriate, consider the problem of recalling an item when given a partial description of its properties or a description of its relationships to several other items (Norman & Bobrow, 1979). This appears to be a fairly basic human ability. If the partial description is sufficient to identify an item uniquely, the item often just "comes to mind," with no awareness of any deliberate searching. It is relatively easy to implement this kind of access to items in memory if all the partial descriptions that might be used for access are known in advance. However, human memory does not seem to require this. We can access items from partial descriptions that have not been anticipated. This kind of memory, in which the partial contents of an item can be used to retrieve the remaining contents, is called content-addressable memory. It is a desirable thing to have, but it is very hard to implement in a conventional digital computer (a von Neumann machine). The reason for the difficulty is that the von Neumann machine accesses items in memory by using their addresses (locations in memory), and it is hard to discover the address of an item from an arbitrary subset of its contents. As we shall see, if we abandon the idea that the basic method of retrieving items is via their addresses, we can use parallel computation in systems of interconnected simple elements to achieve content-addressable memory.

Von Neumann machines are based on the idea of a sequential central processor operating on the contents of a passive memory in which data-structures simply wait around to be inspected or manipulated. This conception of memory is shared by most psychologists and is embodied in the spatial metaphors we use for talking about the process of remembering. We think of memory as if it were a filing cabinet or warehouse, and the act of recalling an item is referred to as finding it in memory as if each item were in a specific place and could be found only by going to that place. How else could it be?

The memory models presented in this volume assume a very different basic architecture. Instead of a sequential central processor and a passive memory there is a large set of interconnected, relatively simple processors, which interact with one another in parallel via their own specific hardware connections. Changes in the contents of memory are made by forming new connections or changing the strengths of existing ones. This overcomes a major bottleneck in von Neumann machines, which is that data-structures or programs in memory can only have effects via the sequential central processor, so that it is impossible to mobilize a large quantity of knowledge simultaneously.

A consequence of replacing passive memory by simultaneously interacting units is that the addressing mechanism is replaced by specific hardware connections. The addressing mechanism allows the central processor of a von Neumann machine to access any piece of data, provided the address is known. It thereby allows complex data-structures to be stored in memory by simply making one piece of a data-structure contain the address of the next piece. If one piece contains several addresses, branching structures like trees can easily be stored. Such structures appear to be essential for the implementation of complex representations and computational procedures.

Feldman (Chapter 2, this volume) and Fahlman (Chapter 5, this volume) propose that addresses be replaced by specific hardware connections. Some of the other models in this volume also replace addresses by hardware connections but in a less direct manner. They do not replace a single address by a single hardware connection because they do not use the individual processing units to correspond to items in memory. Instead, items correspond to patterns of activity distributed over many simple hardware units, and the ability of an address to link one item to another is implemented by modifying the strengths of many different hardware connections in such a way that the pattern of activity corresponding to one item can cause the pattern corresponding to the other item (see Section 1.2.3 for details).

The idea that a pattern of activity could represent an item requires some explanation. We use the term *distributed representation* to refer to this way of coding information. Although the concepts of distributed representation and parallelism are quite different, distributed representation appears to be a particularly appropriate method of coding for a highly parallel machine.

Suppose we wish to build a system that can recognize any one of a number of items. One approach to this problem would be to have one internal unit that would respond when and only when its particular item occurred. An alternative approach would be to have each internal unit respond to many of the possible input items. Provided only one item is presented at a time, it will be represented by the pattern of activity of the internal units even though no individual unit uniquely specifies the input item. Thus a pattern of activity becomes the basic representation of the item. There is no necessary loss of precision or ability to discriminate; it is just that internal operations are now performed in a different way. Instead of a single unit causing particular effects on other internal representations or on motor output the pattern of activity of many units causes those effects. It is unnecessary to have a separate higher-level unit that detects the pattern of activity and causes the appropriate effects.

1.2. SYSTEMS OF SIMPLE UNITS WITH MODIFIABLE INTERCONNECTIONS

This section describes some models in which changes in the strengths of the interconnections in a system of simple units are used to implement category formation and associative memory. Before introducing these models, however, we outline the ideas about "formal" neurons that were largely responsible for the choice of the particular kind of simple unit used in these models.

1.2.1. The McCulloch–Pitts Neuron

Probably the best known, and arguably the most influential model of the nervous system, even today, is that proposed in 1943 by Warren McCulloch and Walter Pitts. They approximated the brain as a set of binary elements—abstract neurons which were either on or off—that realized the statements of formal logic. To quote the first sentence of the abstract of their paper (McCulloch & Pitts, 1943):

> Because of the "all-or-none" character of nervous activity, neural events and the relations between them can be treated by means of propositional logic. It is found that the behavior of every net can be described in these terms . . . and that for any logical expression satisfying certain conditions, one can find a net behaving in the fashion it describes [p. 115].

One finds in their paper much of the machinery familiar to those who study automata theory: binary elements, threshold logic, and quantized time where the state of the system at the $(n + 1)$th moment reflects the states of the inputs to the elements at the nth moment. The primary result of their paper was that nets of such neurons were perfectly general in that they could realize any finite logical expression.

This model obviously has practical implications: put together such neurons and you can make a powerful, general computing device. At about the time of the 1943 paper, exactly such a project was underway at the Moore School of Engineering of the University of Pennsylvania. This paper on brain modeling had an influence on John von Neumann when he sketched the logical outline of the first modern digital computer—the first machine with a program stored with the data.

In a famous technical report, von Neumann (1945) said:

> Every digital computing device contains certain relay like *elements* with discrete equilibria. Such an element has two or more distinct states in which it can exist indefinitely.... The relay action manifests itself in the emission of stimuli by the element whenever it has itself received a stimulus of the type indicated.... It is worth mentioning that the neurons of the higher animals are definitely elements in the above sense.... Following W. Pitts and W. S. McCulloch . . . we ignore the more complicated aspects of neuron functioning . . . [p. 360].

1.2.2. Perceptrons

The perceptron, originally developed by Rosenblatt, and related models such as MADALINE and ADALINE developed by Widrow were intensively studied in the early 1960s. These models have now become part of the lore of pattern recognition, and good short introductions are available in many books on pattern recognition, as well as in the classic books, *Learning Machines* (Nilsson, 1965) and *Perceptrons* (Minsky & Papert, 1969).

The basic element in these devices is the threshold logic unit (TLU), which is a particular type of McCulloch–Pitts neuron. The TLU has a number of inputs, say *n*, each associated with a real-valued weight that plays a role analogous to the "synaptic strength" of inputs to a neuron. The total input to the TLU is an *n*-dimensional vector, a pattern of activity on its individual input lines. Each component of the input vector is multiplied by the weight associated with that input line and all these products are summed. The unit gives an output of 1 if this sum exceeds its threshold. Otherwise it gives an output of 0. More formally, the output is the truth value of the expression

$$\sum_i f_i w_i > \theta \tag{1-1}$$

where f_i is the activity on the *i*th input line and w_i is its weight, and θ is the threshold.

A TLU divides the *n*-dimensional space of possible input vectors into two regions, separated by a hyperplane, one region being associated with an output of 1 and the other with an output of 0. The values of the weights determine the orientation and position of the hyperplane.

The Perceptron Convergence Procedure. Threshold logic units were advanced as adaptive pattern recognition devices (Rosenblatt, 1961; Nilsson,

1965). In the standard perceptron scheme each input line to the TLU is the output of a feature detector that responds to the presence of some feature in an input array. A perceptron can be made to discriminate instances of a particular class of pattern in the input array by associating appropriate weights with the feature detectors, provided any set of appropriate weights exists.

The main reason for the interest in perceptrons during the 1960s was the existence of an automatic procedure for finding a set of weights that would cause the perceptron to respond if and only if a pattern of a particular type was present in the input array. The procedure, known as the perceptron convergence procedure, works by adjusting the existing set of weights whenever those weights would cause the perceptron to give the wrong response to the current input array. If the perceptron would respond with a 1 and the pattern is actually absent, then all the weights of the active features are reduced equally, and the threshold is raised by the same amount. If the perceptron would respond with a 0 when the pattern is actually present, then all the weights of the active features are raised and the threshold is reduced. Some freedom is allowed in the magnitude of the alterations. One strategy is to make all alterations be of a small constant size. Another method is to make the alterations on each trial just large enough to ensure that the perceptron responds correctly to the current input pattern. If the feature detectors have real-valued levels of activity rather than just being on or off, the alterations in the weights must be proportional to the activity levels of the corresponding feature detectors. Proofs that the perceptron convergence procedure works, and precise statements of its conditions can be found in Nilsson (1965) and Minsky and Papert (1969).

The Limitations of Perceptrons. The perceptron convergence procedure cannot be applied to devices in which there is more than one layer of modifiable weights between the input array and the decision unit. The reason for this restriction is that there is no good way of deciding which layer of weights ought to be changed when a multilayered device makes an error. It is clear that devices with multiple layers of modifiable weights are more like the brain and are capable of more sophisticated discriminations, but they lack the automatic learning procedure which is the most important characteristic of the simple perceptron.

Certain limitations of the perceptron were apparent almost from the outset. It is incapable of performing the basic logical operation of exclusive-or. There is no way of setting the weights and the threshold of a perceptron with two inputs so that it will respond positively in just those cases where exactly one input is active. Despite this strong restriction, many people thought that perceptrons were a promising model of perception until Minsky and Papert (1969) produced a rigorous analysis of the limitations of perceptrons as pattern recognition devices.

One psychologically unrealistic aspect of the perceptron convergence procedure is that no learning occurs when the response is correct. Satisfactory psychological learning models incorporate what might be called "positive" learning; that is, learning when the organism is correct usually appears to be more important than learning when a mistake is made. Extensive experimental evidence supports this claim. Statistical learning theory behaves this way (see the collection of papers in Neimark & Estes, 1967). In the simpler versions of statistical learning theory, learning involves only having a correct response *increase* the probability of making that response in the future.

The Future of Perceptrons.   Human perception is an extremely complex activity involving multiple interacting representations at many levels. A simple perceptron is clearly an inadequate model. A similar but more complex device involving many layers of perceptrons and collateral and recurrent connections may be capable of perception, but there is no known procedure for learning the weights. A common conclusion has been that devices like perceptrons are not worth studying. This is may be correct if perceptrons are considered primarily as learning devices, but there is an alternative approach that has received little attention until recently (Hinton, Ch. 6, this volume; Minsky, 1977, 1980). This new approach is to consider how computation might be organized within a device consisting of many interconnected perceptronlike units. The emphasis is on programming and on ways of representing knowledge and implementing procedures rather than on finding a magic formula that will enable the machine to organize itself. The problem of how the machine learns is left until we have a clearer idea of what kind of organization needs to be learned.

1.2.3. Matrix Models of Associative Memory

By associative memory we mean the ability to get from one internal representation to another or from one part of a complex representation to the remainder. Association has been known to be a prominent feature of human memory since Aristotle. J. R. Anderson and Bower (1973) give a good historic review of the subject in Chapter 3 of their seminal work, *Human Associative Memory.*

Some associations seem to be relatively capricious and unstructured. Others seem regular and predictable. William James (1890-1962) commented that: "It will be observed that the *object called up may bear any logical relation whatever to the one which suggested it* [p. 284]."

We can easily associate random events, in fact, sophomores have been learning random verbal associations since the dawn of experimental psychology. Yet our awareness that black is the opposite of white or that Robert Kennedy was John Kennedy's brother are examples where two representations are connected by a specific relationship. Selz (1927-1964), in criticizing classical associationism, pointed out that such specific associations are necessary if thought is to be structured and directed rather than degenerating into a diffuse activation of multiple items through nonspecific, pairwise associations. For example, a system cannot retrieve the fact that the opposite of black is white on the basis of independent pairwise associations between black and white and between opposite and white. Night is just as strongly associated with black and with opposite, so simply combining pairwise effects would activate night just as strongly as white. The specific association needs to be stored as an integrated unit that can be aroused by the combined effects of black and opposite. The question of how integrated units may be stored is treated in some of the subsequent chapters. Here we simply show how pairwise associations could be stored in a parallel system like the brain.

The physiological basis of memory is still something of a mystery. However, there is considerable evidence suggesting that it depends on changes in connectivity between units in a set of interconnected elements. Most neurophysiologists accept that precisely specified changes in synaptic connectivity store memory (see Sec. 1.5). There is clear evidence for this in invertebrates (Kandel, 1976). The suggestion for precise modification that seems most commonly accepted (without detailed physiological evidence, be it noted) is some variant of one originally proposed by D. O. Hebb. Hebb's (1949) suggestion was stated as follows: "When an axon of cell A is near enough to excite a cell B and repeatedly or persistently takes part in firing it, some growth process or metabolic change takes place in one or both cells, such that A's efficiency, as one of the cells firing B, is increased [p. 62]."

This suggestion predicts that cells will tend to become correlated in their discharges, and a synapse acting like this is sometimes called a correlational synapse. As formulated by Hebb, this model was not suitable for mathematical development. However, in the past few years several groups have developed similar types of parallel, distributed, associative memory which incorporate, in various forms, a learning postulate somewhat like Hebb's. Our feeling is that the qualitative properties shown by existing systems of this kind may be typical of more realistic and complex parallel, associative, distributed systems, so it is worth developing one example of those models in a little detail, including some simple numerical examples.

The models were specifically developed as brain models and as psychological models and have not been used within systems as complex as those studied in artificial intelligence. However, attempts have been made to use the models to generate testable predictions in psychology (Anderson, J. A., 1973).

More detailed explications of parts of these models are available in the original sources and in other chapters in this volume. General references for this section are Kohonen (1977), Willshaw, Buneman, and Longuet-Higgins (1969), J. A. Anderson (1972, 1973, 1977), and Anderson, J. A., Silverstein, Ritz, and Jones (1977). Holographic brain models, which in some respects are similar to the models we describe are developed in Westlake (1970), Willshaw (1971), Cavanagh (1972), and Pribram, Nuwer, and Baron (1974). Willshaw (Chapter 3, this volume) discusses the relationship between holographic and matrix models.

The basic notion in all these models is the idea of a *state vector,* that is, that the currently active representations within the system are coded as patterns of activity simultaneously present on the set of elements that comprise the system. Elements are generally considered to be neurons or very closely related to neurons in these models, and activity is intended to correspond to firing frequency or something very close to firing frequency (e.g., deviation from spontaneous firing rate).

What we wish to store are associations between the state vectors that are the basic entities of the system. But state vectors are not localized in a single place. How can they be handled? Consider a quotation from Karl Lashley (1950) discussed at greater length in Section 1.5. "From the numerical relations involved, I believe that even the reservation of individual synapses for special associative reactions is impossible. [pp. 478–479]."

Lashley argues that there are no privileged sites in the brain for the storage of specific associations in isolation from each other. This idea seems superficially unpromising because it seems that individual associations between pairs of complicated state vectors would interfere with one another if every association used the same set of synapses. To show that interference need not be a problem, we sketch briefly a typical example of such a memory (see Anderson, J. A., 1970, 1972; Cooper, 1974). It is formally a simple linear associator. This model is very similar to those of Willshaw (1971) and Kohonen (1977), which were arrived at independently.

Suppose we have two sets of n neurons, α and β, which are completely convergent and divergent, that is, every neuron in α projects to every neuron in β. A neuron j in α is connected to neuron i in β by way of a synapse with strength α (i,j). Our first basic assumption, which we have partially justified previously, is that we are primarily interested in the behavior of the set of simultaneous individual neuron activities in a group of neurons. We stress pattern of *individual* activities because our current knowledge of cortical physiology suggests that cells are highly individualistic. For example, their activities at the times of interest to us are typically not correlated with their neighbors, and cell properties differ from cell to cell. We represent these large patterns as state vectors with separate components. We also assume (for this particular model) that these components can be positive or negative. This can occur because the relevant physiological variable in some cases seems to be the deviation in firing rate around a nonzero spontaneous activity level. In other parts of the brain, there may be two separate systems for positive and negative transduction, as in the mammalian visual system with parallel sets of on-center and off-center cells.

Suppose a pattern of activity, **f,** occurs in α. Suppose another pattern of activity, **g,** occurs in β. Suppose that for some reason we wish to associate these two arbitrary patterns. We assume a synaptic modification rule: To associate pattern **f** in α with **g** in β we need to change the set of synaptic weights according to the product of presynaptic activity at a junction with the activity of the postsynaptic cell. Note that this is information locally available at the junction. Thus if $\mathbf{f}(j)$ is the activity of cell j in α, and $\mathbf{g}(i)$ of cell i in β, then the change in synaptic strength is given by $a(i,j) = \eta\ \mathbf{f}(j)\mathbf{g}(i)$. We see that this defines an $n \times n$ matrix of changes $\Delta\mathbf{A}$ of the form $\Delta\mathbf{A} = \eta\ \mathbf{g}\mathbf{f}^T$ where $\mathbf{f}^T$ is the transpose of $\mathbf{f}$. Suppose $\mathbf{f}$ is normalized, that is, $\mathbf{f}.\mathbf{f} = 1$, and also $\eta = 1$ so that $\Delta\mathbf{A} = \mathbf{g}\mathbf{f}^T$. Suppose that instead of one association we have m of them, $(\mathbf{f}_1, \mathbf{g}_1), (\mathbf{f}_2, \mathbf{g}_2), \ldots,$ $(\mathbf{f}_m, \mathbf{g}_m)$, each having an incremental matrix $\Delta\mathbf{A}_k = \mathbf{g}_k \mathbf{f}_k^T$. Because there are only the n^2 synapses in the system, the same synapses participate in storing all the associations; that is, they are modified again and again. Suppose the overall connectivity is given by

$$\mathbf{A} = \sum_k \Delta\mathbf{A}_k \qquad (1\text{-}2)$$

By the linearity that, we argue, holds at the synaptic junction, when a pattern of activity, $\mathbf{f}_k$, occurs in α, it will cause a pattern of activity, $\mathbf{g}$, in β, which is given by $\mathbf{g} = \mathbf{A}\mathbf{f}_k$. Suppose, for the sake of illustration, that patterns $\mathbf{f}_k$ are orthogonal. This means that for any pair of patterns $\mathbf{f}_l^T \cdot \mathbf{f}_k = 0$ for $k \neq l$. If one of the $\mathbf{f}_k$ appears at α, the activity pattern of β is given by

$$\mathbf{g} = \mathbf{A}\mathbf{f}_k = \Delta\mathbf{A}_k\mathbf{f}_k + \sum_{l \neq k} \Delta\mathbf{A}_l\mathbf{f}_k$$

$$= \mathbf{g}_k + \sum_{l \neq k} \mathbf{g}_l(\mathbf{f}_l^T\mathbf{f}_k)$$

$$= \mathbf{g}_k \qquad (1\text{-}3)$$

Thus, for orthogonal $\mathbf{f}$'s, the system stores random associations between vectors perfectly.

The capacity of a linear system containing n units and n^2 connections is n different associations if the input vectors are orthogonal. If they are nonorthogonal, interference effects become severe as the number of associations approaches n. Because the number of neurons in the human brain is of the order of 10^{11} this need not be as serious a limitation as it may seem. A single region of the cortex, Area 17, say, may have 50–100 million cells.

Clearly, the activity of a single unit or connection is of little importance to the overall functioning of the system provided the vectors each involve the activity of many different units. On the average, removal of a single unit or connection will cause very slight degradation of many associations rather than complete destruction of a particular one. Wood (1978) has done a number of simulations demonstrating this point.

There is an important property that this simple linear associator has in common with more complicated, nonlinear models that also use a matrix to transform a state vector. It and its variants are *reconstructive*. This means that the system yields the entire output vector (or a close approximation to it) even if the input is noisy or only partially present, or if there is noise in the memory matrix. This reconstructive property can be used to make a content-addressable memory. First, each of a number of vectors is associated with itself. Then when an incomplete version of one of the stored vectors is used as the input, the output will be a complete or nearly complete version of the vector. So, from any sufficiently large part of the content, the system generates the whole content without using anything like a separate address or entry in an index.

A spectacular example of reconstruction using a linear matrix model is given by Kohonen (Chapter 4, this volume). He shows that the rest of a picture of a face can be reconstructed when the system is presented with a part of the picture. This is an impressive demonstration of the power of the model even if human memory for faces works quite differently. The nonlinear models presented by Willshaw, Hinton, and Anderson and Mozer (Chapters 3, 6, and 8, this volume) show that under certain conditions the output vector can be reconstructed exactly from an incomplete or degraded input.

A Numerical Example of the Linear Matrix Model.   Table 1.1 shows three input vectors that were chosen to be roughly orthogonal. A required output vector for each of these input vectors was chosen, and the matrix of connection strengths was determined by the three associations between an input and an

TABLE 1.1
The Input Vectors

Component Number	Input Vectors[a]		
	f_1	f_2	f_3
1	.00	.00	−.23
2	−.15	.00	−.23
3	−.29	−.06	−.23
4	.88	−.09	.14
5	−.29	−.30	.56
6	−.15	.00	.56
7	.00	.89	.14
8	.00	.00	−.23
9	.00	−.30	−.23
10	.00	−.15	−.23

[a] Correlation between f_1 and f_2 = .03
Correlation between f_2 and f_3 = .06
Correlation between f_3 and f_1 = −.02

output vector. The matrix, **A**, is shown in Table 1.2. Formally, it is given by

$$\mathbf{A} = \sum_k \mathbf{g}_k \mathbf{f}_k^T = \mathbf{g}_1 \mathbf{f}_1^T + \mathbf{g}_2 \mathbf{f}_2^T + \mathbf{g}_3 \mathbf{f}_3^T \qquad (1\text{-}4)$$

Table 1.3 shows three required output vectors, $\mathbf{g}_1$, $\mathbf{g}_2$, and $\mathbf{g}_3$, and also the actual output vectors, $\mathbf{h}_1$, $\mathbf{h}_2$, $\mathbf{h}_3$, which are slightly different. The difference is caused by the nonorthogonality of the input vectors, which leads to some interference between the different associations.

The effects of local damage or degraded input on this kind of system are illustrated by Kohonen (1977) and Wood (1978) who performed an extensive series of computer simulations of the effects of damage on systems of the type presented here. Wood's results show that, because of chance effects, some elements turn out to be important for particular associations while others are not particularly important to any one association. This corroborates the idea that the individual units in such a system will exhibit varying degrees of specificity.

Table 1.4 shows the effects of degrading the input vector, $\mathbf{f}_3$, by setting some of its components equal to zero.

A Comparison of Linear and Nonlinear Matrix Models. In the linear models the output of a unit is just a weighted sum of its inputs; whereas in the nonlinear models, the output is a more complex function of the weighted sum. The sum may be compared with a threshold to yield a binary value, for example, or it may be rounded up or down if it falls outside certain lower or upper limits. The linear models are easy to analyze and are a sensible and useful first step in the investigation of the whole class of matrix models. However, they have certain insuperable drawbacks that prevent them from exhibiting some of the more interesting properties of the nonlinear models.

If the input and output vectors have the same number of components, it is possible to recycle the output vector and add it to the vector of external inputs to

TABLE 1.2
The Matrix of Weights

.055	.055	.055	−.033	−.132	−.132	−.033	.055	.055	.055
.055	.077	.098	−.163	−.088	−.110	−.033	.055	.055	.055
.055	.098	.145	−.288	−.027	−.088	−.086	.055	.072	.064
−.033	−.163	−.288	.810	−.156	−.051	−.059	−.033	−.001	−.020
−.132	−.088	−.027	−.156	.491	.359	−.185	−.132	−.044	−.088
−.132	−.110	−.088	−.051	.359	.338	.079	−.132	−.132	−.132
−.033	−.033	−.086	−.059	−.185	.079	.811	−.033	−.297	−.165
.055	.055	.055	−.033	−.132	−.132	−.033	.055	.055	.055
.055	.055	.072	−.001	−.044	−.132	−.297	.055	.143	.099
.055	.055	.064	−.020	−.088	−.132	−.165	.055	.099	.077

TABLE 1.3
The Required and Actual Output Vectors

Component Number	g_1	h_1	g_2	h_2	g_3	h_3
1	1.00	1.00	.00	.03	.00	−.02
2	1.00	1.00	.00	.03	.00	−.02
3	1.00	1.00	.00	.03	.00	−.02
4	1.00	1.03	1.00	1.03	.00	.04
5	.00	.03	1.00	1.00	.00	.06
6	.00	.03	1.00	1.00	.00	.06
7	.00	.00	1.00	1.06	1.00	1.06
8	.00	−.02	.00	.06	1.00	1.00
9	.00	−.02	.00	.06	1.00	1.00
10	.00	−.02	.00	.06	1.00	1.00

form the next input vector to the system. So, given a constant external input vector, the system can run for many iterations. In a nonlinear system it is possible to perform complex computations on the external input vector by repeated iterations using this kind of feedback (see Anderson and Mozer, and Hinton, this volume). In a linear system, however, the result of many iterations through a matrix is just the same as the result of one iteration through some other matrix, so nothing is gained by the multiple iterations.

Implicit Rules and the Matrix Models. In their behavior some matrix models can be shown to act like "rule-governed" systems. There is, however, no explicit representation or application of rules within the system. Matrix models

TABLE 1.4
The Required and Actual Responses with Degraded Input

Component Number	Required Response to f_3	Actual Response to f_3	Response to f_3 with $f_3(6) = 0$	Response to f_3 with $f_3(7) = f_3(8) = f_3(9) = 0$
1	.00	−.02	.06	−.02
2	.00	−.02	.06	−.02
3	.00	−.02	.06	−.02
4	.00	.04	.13	−.15
5	.00	.06	.06	−.13
6	.00	.06	.06	−.13
7	1.00	1.06	.75	.74
8	1.00	1.00	.68	.87
9	1.00	1.00	.68	.87
10	1.00	1.00	.68	.87

have two significantly different types of entity: the active, explicit state vectors, which correspond to activations of the basic units, and the more passive implicit weights in the matrix. It is relatively easy to observe the active, explicit part of the system, but the bulk of the transformational structure is hidden in the implicit part of the system, in the matrices, which are difficult to study because any one weight lumps together many different associations and any one association is distributed over many weights.

It is possible to have complex systems of associations implicit in the matrix of connection strengths. This may cause the system to act in a very rule-governed manner even though there is no process of accessing and applying rules in the sense of a computer program. Because of the interactions between different associations in the implicit structure, adding a set of associations which "agree" in the way they modify a particular subset of the weights may well affect other similar associations. This transfer of effects to associations that are not explicitly represented may make it appear as if a new rule has been added even though there is no explicit representation of the rule within the system. The status of the rules used in conventional computer models of cognition is thus thrown into question. They may well be *descriptions* of regularities in the behavior of the system that do not correspond, in any simple way, to the representations that are explicit within the system. We return to this issue in Section 1.4.

1.2.4. Minsky's K-Lines Model

Minsky (1980) outlines a theory of the way in which computation may be organized in the human brain. His paper contains a great many speculative suggestions, but the main thrust of his theorizing is that instead of a central processor, which can access arbitrary memory locations by their addresses, the brain may consist of a "society" of fairly simple, local agents, each of which has direct access to a limited number of other agents. Locally, agents may be organized into mutually inhibitory sets, and more globally there will be partial mental states consisting of the currently dominant agents from each local group. Minsky identifies the patterns of active agents with particular mental episodes, and he argues that we need to be able to re-create previous patterns of activity that have proved useful in situations like the current one. To achieve this he proposes that we create a new agent that has connections to all the agents active within a particular mental state. By activating this new agent the old state can be recreated. Minsky elaborates this simple model in various ways to reduce the number of hardware connections required between agents and to allow the recreated state to differ from the old one in ways that make it more appropriate to the situation at hand.

In many respects, Minsky's model constitutes a break with the now-traditional artificial intelligence approach. The agents communicate by emitting excitation and inhibition rather than by passing symbolic expressions, and there is no mention of the problems associated with the creation of new and temporary object representations at run-time as opposed to just activating old ones. However, the model is an important advance because it takes the brain's hardware seriously. Minsky is particularly concerned with the hardware connections required between agents, a concern partly caused by the technological discovery that, in large-scale integration, it is the connections that cost, not the logical functions (Sutherland & Mead, 1977).

The central idea of the model, that partial mental states are re-created by activating particular agents that designate them, is an interesting intermediate position with respect to the issue of local versus distributed representations. It is the distributed pattern of active agents that is effective in generating the external and internal behavior appropriate to an episode or others like it, but a single local agent can create this pattern of activity. Thus other representations can cause the whole pattern by simply activating that agent. It seems that this combination of local and distributed representations would be effective for representing particular objects or concepts as well as for particular episodes. The advantage of the pattern of active agents as a representation is that new patterns can be created at run-time much more easily than new single agents which require their own specific hardware units and connections.

The real value of Minsky's model, will only be known when the model is specified in sufficient detail for it to be simulated, but the general approach of trying to implement sophisticated computational processes in parallel neuron-like hardware seems extremely promising.

1.3. SYSTEMS OF SIMPLE UNITS WITH FIXED INTERCONNECTIONS

The models reviewed in this section involve systems of interconnected simple units, but they deliberately avoid the issue of how interactions between the units are learned. Instead, the local interactions are specified in advance by the programmer, and the purpose of the model is to demonstrate the computational performance that can be achieved by a system that already has an appropriate set of local interactions between the individual units.

1.3.1. Relaxation Models

Relaxation models typically involve a constraint–satisfaction paradigm in which some input data must be given an interpretation that simultaneously satisfies a large set of local constraints. This interpretation corresponds to a pattern of activity over the units, and it is found by an iterative computation in which each unit affects many others until the whole system settles down into a stable state.

Many of the models are based on a detailed analysis of the computational structure of a specific task. The analysis provides a precise specification of the constraints that must be obeyed by any satisfactory interpretation, and these constraints are then implemented in the local interactions between units. Consequently, the models can only be fully appreciated in the context of the specific tasks that they perform.

Relaxation is best introduced by a classical example. A well-known problem in physics is to calculate the three-dimensional shape of a soap film that is bounded by a nonplanar wire hoop. The shape can be represented by associating a height with each element of a two-dimensional array. The wire hoop fixes the height of the elements at the edge of the soap film. The interior elements obey the constraint that the height of each element is the average of the heights of its neighbors. One way of calculating the heights of the interior elements is to give them arbitrary initial heights, and then to replace simultaneously every interior height by the average of its neighbors. This procedure is called relaxation, and after repeated iterations the heights will settle down to a stable state in which each is the average of its neighbors. This stable state will represent the shape of the soap film.

At least four distinct variations of relaxation have so far been proposed. First, Horn (1977) and Marr (1978) have pointed out that visual systems need to use the intensity information in a raw image to recover the objective characteristics of the surfaces that gave rise to the image. The intensity of each element in the image is the result of many local parameters of the corresponding surface elements. The reflectance of the element, its orientation to the viewer and to the light source, and the level of illumination all interact to determine the image intensity. These interactions can be described by physical equations. In addition, there are normally constraints between the parameters of neighboring surface elements. For example, reflectance usually remains constant, and surface orientation usually changes only slightly from one surface element to the next.

The relationships between local parameters are more complex than the simple neighbor-averaging constraint for the heights of elements in a soap film, but the same kind of relaxation technique can be applied to discover a consistent set of real values for the local parameters of the surface elements causing the image. The intensities in the image act as boundary conditions just like the heights of the elements attached to the wire hoop. The other parameters are given initial values which are successively adjusted to fit the constraints better and better until a stable state is reached. Barrow and Tenenbaum (1978) describe this type of relaxation in more detail.

A somewhat different type of relaxation model was used by Marr and Poggio (1976) to fuse pairs of random dot stereograms (Julesz, 1971). When each eye is presented with one of two random dot patterns, which are identical except for lateral displacement of some regions in one pattern, people see a number of surfaces at different depths. To do this they must decide which dot in one pattern to pair with which dot in the other. Because all dots are the same, there are many potential mates for each one. Each pairing, however, will give a different angular disparity and hence a different perceived depth for the dot. If the assumptions are made that each dot can only be paired with one other (based on the opacity of surfaces) and that neighboring pairings should have similar disparities and thus be at similar depths (based on the continuity of surfaces), it is possible to make the many potential pairings disambiguate one another.

Marr and Poggio showed that the computation of a good set of pairings can be performed by a machine consisting of multiple units, each of which was a threshold logic unit (see Section 1.2.2). Each unit represented a hypothesis about a particular pairing, and hence it corresponded to a piece of surface at a particular depth. Units corresponding to pieces of surface lying along a line of sight from an eye inhibited one another (the opacity assumption), and units corresponding to adjacent pieces of surface excited one another (the continuity assumption). A dot in a pattern excited all units corresponding to pieces of surface along that line of sight. At each moment a unit is either on or off, and the computation consists of multiple iterations during which units may be turned on or off by the combined effects of the external input and connected units. Whether or not this is a good model of human stereo fusion, it works well for fusing random dot stereograms. It differs from the previous relaxation model in that the values that are adjusted by the relaxation process are binary and correspond to the truth values of hypotheses rather than to continuous properties of surfaces.

A third type of relaxation was introduced by Rosenfeld, Hummel, and Zucker (1976). It is hard to extract information about the contours of objects from an intensity image because some edge segments are locally unclear. Because edges are generally continuous it should be possible to use information from one part of an image to clarify information from unclear neighboring parts. Rosenfeld et al. (1976) suggested that each hypothesis about a local edge should be given an association plausibility between 0 and 1. Initially the plausibilities are determined by how well the particular edge hypothesis fits the local data, but then a relaxation phase is applied during which each hypothesis is affected by its neighbors. The way in which the plausibility of one hypothesis affects the plausibility of another depends on how compatible they are. Rosenfeld and his co-workers have proposed a number of schemes for the interactions (Peleg, 1980), and they have applied their techniques to a number of problems in vision (Rosenfeld, 1978). It is hard to assess just how useful their relaxation technique is because the value of the relaxation phase depends on the extent to which the modified plausibilities are more useful to the higher levels of a vision system than the initial plausibilities. This can only be judged when higher levels exist.

Finally, Hinton (1976, 1977) has proposed a relaxation technique that also associates a value between 0 and 1 with each local hypothesis. Unlike the method of Rosenfeld et al. (1976), however, the hypotheses do not interact directly. Instead, the logical relationships between hypotheses are expressed as numerical constraints, which are implemented as negative feedback loops. Each loop measures the extent to which the constraint is violated by the current values of the hypotheses, and it "tries" to reduce the violation by exerting pressure on the values of the relevant hypotheses. Each value moves according to the net resultant of the pressures exerted on it by the violated constraints and by the local fit of the hypothesis to the input data. This method has been used to find optimal instantiations of a model in a picture. Unlike the method of Rosenfeld et al. (1976), it is possible to specify precisely what computation is achieved by the relaxation process.

The relaxation techniques are one way of organizing interactions in a parallel machine so that it settles on a good, consistent interpretation of some input data. The drawbacks of relaxation are that it often requires a large number of iterations to achieve equilibrium, and there may be no guarantee that it will find the best solution.

A Comparison of Relaxation and Nonlinear Matrix Models.   There are many similarities between the formal mechanisms used in relaxation models and those used in the nonlinear matrix models. We have already mentioned the major difference, which is that the relaxation models use weights fixed by the programmer, whereas in the matrix models the weights are determined by the system's experience. Apart from this, however, the main difference seems to reside not in the mechanisms but in the tasks to which they are applied and the interpretation given to the individual units.

Relaxation techniques have typically been applied to low-level vision where it is clear that a great deal of local computation is performed in parallel. The activity levels of individual units are then used to represent the existence of particular local entities or the values of local properties of the surfaces or edges in the visual field. The matrix models, on the other hand, have been applied to problems like recognition and memory, where there is no obvious correspondence between individual units and local properties of the world. Marr and Poggio's (1976) model of stereo fusion, for example, illustrates the close similarity between superficially different parallel models. They use threshold logic units just like perceptrons, and the whole system is equivalent to a nonlinear matrix model but with a sparse matrix.

1.3.2. Spreading Activation Models

Collins and Quillian (1972) and Collins and Loftus (1975) argue that the results of certain psychological experiments can be explained in terms of activation spreading along the links of a semantic network in which the nodes represent concepts and the links represent relations between them. They consider tasks like discovering how two concepts are related. The basic idea is that if two different concepts are activated, and activation spreads along the links, then nodes on the path between the two concepts will receive activation from both of them. These nodes will thus have particularly high activation levels.

Other experiments discussed by Collins and Loftus involve semantic priming effects in which activation of one concept tends to speed up reaction times for judgments involving related concepts. In their model similar concepts will have more short pathways between their nodes than dissimilar ones because there will be many other concepts to which both are linked. Thus when a concept is activated, more activation will spread to similar than to dissimilar concepts, and this will explain the priming effect.

The Collins and Quillian model has serious computational deficits. It is hard to use spreading activation effectively for the types of inferential processing for which semantic nets are typically used. There have, however, been two interesting and rather different developments from the Collins and Quillian approach. Fahlman (Chapter 5, this volume) has made it more computationally sophisticated by substantially modifying the idea of spreading activation. He uses discrete markers instead of undifferentiated numerical activation, and this allows him to generate combinations of markers at nodes instead of just activity levels. Fahlman shows that a great deal of computational power and control can be achieved by having a central controller that broadcasts marker-passing instructions to a whole network of nodes, which all obey the instructions in parallel.

In a quite different development McClelland and Rumelhart (1980) have kept the idea of real-valued activation levels, but they have applied it to perception rather than to inference and judgment, and they have been much clearer about the precise rules for propagating activation. Also they have shown how an appropriate scheme for propagating activation can remove the need for a central controller in the particular task domain they have studied. Whether the use of activation for control can be extended to the higher-level tasks that Fahlman tackles remains to be seen.

1.3.3. The Rumelhart and McClelland Model of Word Recognition

When a string of letters is presented very briefly, it is easier to recognize the letters if they form a word than if they form a nonsense string (Reicher, 1969). Letter strings which form pronounceable nonwords are intermediate in difficulty. McClelland and Rumelhart (1980) and Rumelhart and McClelland (1980) propose a model in which many simple, neuron-like units interact to produce these effects. For simplicity they restrict themselves to a three-layered system, and they omit feedback from the middle layer to the bottom one.

The bottom layer contains units that detect local features in specific positions within the word. A unit in this layer might, for example, be activated if there is a vertical stroke that could be the right-hand vertical of an H, M, or N in the second-letter position within the word. It is assumed that the feature units occur after some constancy mechanism so that changes in the retinal size, elongation, position, and orientation of the whole word do not affect the set of feature units that it activates.

In the middle layer a unit represents a specific letter in specific position within the word. Each letter/position unit receives excitatory input from all the feature detectors that fit it and also inhibitory input from feature detectors in the same position that do not fit it.

Units in the top layer represent specific words. Each word unit receives excitatory inputs from all the letter/position units that fit it and inhibitory inputs from the rest. Word units also provide excitatory and inhibitory feedback to the letter/position units. In addition to these interactions between layers there are inhibitory interactions between all pairs of word units and between those pairs of letter/position units that correspond to the same position within the word.

The activity level of a unit is a continuous variable constrained to lie between two limits, and the precise rules for the excitatory and inhibitory interactions and for the thresholds are fairly complex. They are chosen so that when the feature units are activated as they would be by a perceptually presented word, the system settles down into a stable state in which the appropriate word and letter/position units are highly active, and the other units are not.

The impressive achievement of the model is that the precise rules for the interactions can be chosen so that the model is in good agreement with the experimental data for a wide range of experiments. It can, for example, predict the way in which the probability of correctly reporting a particular letter depends on the precise time at which the other letters in the string are presented relative to the letter to be reported.

One intriguing aspect of the model is the way it accounts for the superior recognition of letters in pronounceable nonwords as compared with unpronounceable strings. Units corresponding to pronounceable digrams or trigrams appear to be unnecessary. Letters in a pronounceable string are helped by activity at the word level because there tends to be a whole gang of words which almost fit the string. The combined effects of this gang provide top-down support for each letter, even though every letter is inhibited by the few members of the gang that do not fit it. Although the words within the gang inhibit each other, each pair is in fairly good agreement about the letters, and this agreement causes the system to settle into a stable state in which many word units are slightly active. Thus, pronounceable nonwords are represented by distributed patterns of activity at the word level.

The Rumelhart and McClelland model is rare and promising because it explains experimental data with a computer model that can actually perform the task (given an assumed constancy mechanism). This contrasts with the majority of models in mathematical psychology which merely *describe* the relationships between various aspects of human performance without providing a mechanism for doing the task.

1.4. PARALLEL HARDWARE AND THE SYMBOL PROCESSING PARADIGM

Until recently, most researchers in cognitive psychology and almost all researchers in artificial intelligence have deliberately avoided any serious attempt to specify how their models might be implemented in the brain. There were a number of different reasons for this avoidance. The existing neural network theories were computationally weak—they were incapable of the complex computational tasks that humans routinely perform when they perceive or talk or solve problems. By contrast, computer programs were much more successful at these tasks (e.g., Newell & Simon, 1963; Roberts, 1965; Winograd, 1972).

The major effort in writing programs like these went into software considerations about the representations and processes needed to perform a task. These considerations were largely independent of the particular digital computer on which the software was implemented, mainly because the available digital computers were all extremely similar relative to the range of possible computational machines. Given the implicit assumptions about the computational primitives, the study of the computational properties of complex software was seen, correctly, as a science in its own right, and this distinction between software and hardware was identified with the distinction between the mind and the brain.

Computer programs then transcended their role as a mere tool for implementing theories, and they became metaphors for the mind. Intelligent processes could be implemented in a von Neumann machine, which operated by manipulating abstract symbols according to rules. The symbols themselves did not require any internal structure to give them meaning. Their meaning was determined by the rules for manipulating them, and these in turn were just more symbols. This solved the problem of how thought processes could exist in material objects, and it led to the view, now dominant within cognitive science, that people are symbol-processing machines (Newell, 1980; Pylyshyn, 1980). Conventional digital computers running high-level programming languages are, naturally enough, very good at this kind of processing (much better than people). Hence there is little incentive to investigate radically different kinds of computer architecture.

The symbol-processing approach is supported not just by the fact that computer programs exhibit intelligent behavior, but also by the fact that symbol-processing models provide a remarkably good account of certain human mental processes such as the errors that children make in simple arithmetic (Brown & Burton, 1978) or the verbal protocols that people produce while solving cryptarithmetic puzzles (Newell & Simon, 1972). Any critique of the symbol-processing approach needs to explain why these models work so well.

The models in this volume that use distributed patterns of activity as representations differ from the normal symbol-processing paradigm in an important way. The internal structure of a symbol is normally thought to be irrelevant to the way it interacts with other symbols. All that is normally necessary is that the symbol have an identity, such as a unique character string, so that it can be compared with others and seen to be either the same or different. The meaning of a symbol is determined by the rules or programs that contain it not by its internal structure.

It is important to realize that this is not the only possible way of organizing a symbol-processing system. It is quite possible for the symbols themselves to have internal structure and for the interactions between symbols to be causally determined by this internal structure rather than governed by stored explicit rules as in the normal symbol-processing paradigm. A symbol, for example, could be a pattern of activity in a large group of hardware units. Provided this pattern is reproducible and regularly causes other such patterns, it is possible to implement symbol processing by the interactions of these patterns.

The symbols in such a system are nonabstract in the following sense: The internal structure of a symbol determines how it interacts with others, so similar symbols tend to have similar interactions. The modifications in the strengths of the hardware connections that are required to alter the causal effects of one symbol will also tend to alter the effects of similar symbols.

Given this view of symbol processing, there are two rather different levels at which a system composed of multiple simple units can be described. At the high level, reproducible patterns of activity can be denoted by abstract symbols, and regular interactions between them can be captured by explicit rules. This kind of a *description* can be implemented rather directly on a conventional digital computer. The impressive performance of programs like those of Brown and Burton (1978) and Newell and Simon (1972) in modeling human behavior are, we think, the result of achieving this level of correspondence between the processes occurring in the brain and the abstract symbol manipulation occurring in the von Neumann machine.

However, because this level omits the internal structure of the symbols and because it captures regularities in causal interactions as explicit rules, there are aspects of cognition for which it is not a good model. For example, the development of the internal structure of the symbols (the specific patterns of activity used to implement them) may not be usefully describable at the same level. Because this internal structure determines how learned effects transfer from one symbol to another, aspects of cognition like the role of similarity and analogy in learning may be outside the appropriate range of the abstract symbol-processing metaphor. We do not mean to imply that these processes cannot be simulated on a von Neumann machine using abstract symbol processing. Indeed, many of the models in this volume are simulated in just this way.

What we are asserting is that the symbol-processing metaphor may be an inappropriate way of thinking about the computational processes that underlie abilities like learning, perception, and motor skills. The rather direct correspondence between the coarse-grained, high level description of our mental processes and abstract symbol manipulation (Card, Moran, & Newell, 1980), may not carry over to the fine-grained description of the highly parallel representations and processes that implement the individual symbols and steps in the coarse-grained description. Just because well-learned and regular interactions between patterns of activity can be captured as explicit rules governing the manipulation of abstract symbols, it does not follow that the emergence of these regularities can be fully captured by models in which explicit rules are added, deleted, or reordered. It is a fallacy to think that the kind of model which works well at one level *must* be applicable at all levels. Rational thought takes years to develop, and it is quite conceivable that it emerges as the highest level of organization of more basic processes that are quite different in character.

To summarize, we are not arguing against the idea that very complex information processing underlies people's ability to perceive, to act, and to learn. Nor are we arguing against computer simulation as a way of exploring such processing. What we are arguing against is the use of abstract symbol manipulation as a prototype for the fine-grained organization of this processing. There are alternative models that have a different computational flavor and that appear to be more appropriate for machines like the brain, which are composed of multiple simple units that compute in parallel.

There are already examples within Artificial Intelligence where hardware considerations have determined general organizational principles. In the early days of computer vision, it was found that it was very difficult to derive a clean line drawing of a scene composed of polyhedral blocks from the mass of gray-level data produced by a camera. Shirai (1973) showed how higher-level knowledge could be used to guide line finding so that the computer could restrict its slowest and most accurate line-finding techniques to areas of the image likely to contain lines. Shirai's program was used to support the idea that really competent vision systems require rich interactions between experts in different domains (like line finding and shape representation) rather than being restricted to a pass-oriented organization, in which each level of processing is uninfluenced by subsequent levels.

The application of this idea to the early stages of visual information processing was attacked by Marr (1976) who argued that the highly parallel hardware known to exist in the brain could produce much richer representations of edges and local surface elements than existing Artificial Intelligence programs without invoking knowledge of particular objects. The dispute has not been fully settled, but there seems no doubt that much of the plausibility of Marr's theory stems from the existence of a great deal of parallel hardware in the brain that is devoted to early visual processing.

The availability of parallel hardware drastically changes arguments about the relative efficiencies of different computational algorithms. The total number of computational operations becomes less important than the question of whether the operations can be performed in parallel or whether there is a necessarily sequential structure in which one operation cannot be performed until the results of others are known.

1.5. PARALLELISM AND DISTRIBUTION IN THE MAMMALIAN NERVOUS SYSTEM

This section outlines the anatomy and physiology of the mammalian neocortex. More details can be obtained from books such as Shepherd (1979), Brazier and Petsche (1978), and Kuffler and Nicholls (1976). Some striking themes are apparent even at the superficial level that we can discuss the system. There is clear evidence, for example, of parallelism and a degree of distribution.

Most of the visible bulk of the human brain is neocortex. Grossly, the cortex is a two-dimensional folded sheet, consisting of the gray matter, a 3-6 mm layer on the outside of the brain containing the cell bodies, and the white matter, a tremendous number of incoming and outgoing fibers. The surface area of the cortex is around 1 square meter, but the sheet is so folded and convoluted— presumably for compact packing—that only about a third of the cortex is visible from the outside; the rest is submerged in fissures.

There are two seemingly contradictory main themes that characterize cortical organization: differentiation and homogeneity. Although there are clear differences between different areas of the cortex, the basic cell types and the fundamental organization of all parts of the neocortex are surprisingly similar. The basic circuitry seems to be the same everywhere.

There are generally held to be two broad classes of neurons in the cerebral cortex: pyramidal cells and stellate cells, with the stellate cells containing a number of different subgroups. The two-dimensional sheet of gray matter of the cortex is itself strongly layered. Neuroanatomists generally identify six layers. The pyramidal cells send their axons to other parts of the cortex and to other regions of the central nervous system. They thus form the "output" cells of a region of cortex though there is no clear flow of information from input to output in the neocortex, a property that complicates analysis. The stellate cells are generally smaller and send axons to a circumscribed local region of the cortex, presumably being primarily short-range "intrinsic" cells.

Pyramidal cells can be very large, with a typical pyramid-shaped cell body and with a large "apical" dendrite, which runs to the surface of the cortex, through the layers, and perpendicular to the cortical surface (see Fig. 1.1). The cortex is a remarkably Cartesian system, with layers parallel to the surface and with fibers and dendrites running perpendicular to the layers and cutting across them. As has been pointed out on numerous occasions, this is in no sense a random network but is exquisitely structured, both anatomically and, as we are now discovering, physiologically.

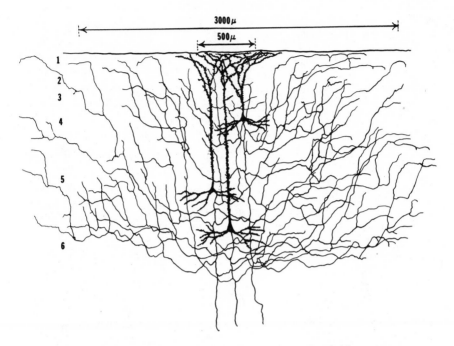

FIG. 1.1.   Three pyramidal cells in cerebral cortex, surrounded by recurrent collaterals. The thin, fuzzy processes on the pyramidal cell dendrites are dendritic spines. The outer surface of cortex is at the top; the apical dendrites run perpendicular to the surface. Drawn from several sections of 60-day cat cortex stained by a rapid Golgi variant. (Scheibel & Scheibel, 1970).

The apical dendrites run to the surface of the cortex and then branch. Other dendrites come off the base of the pyramid forming a number of "basal" dendrites. The extent of branching of these dendrites forms a cylinder which seems to be an important information-processing module of the cortex. The apical dendrite of large pyramidal cells whose cell body is in layer 5 may be several millimeters in length. This cell may receive extensive synaptic input over its entire length. Traditional estimates of numbers of synapses on cortical pyramids run from about 7000 in the visual cortex to 50,000 in the motor cortex.

A notable feature of pyramidal cells is the presence of small processes, a few microns in length, called "spines." At one time they were thought to be artifacts of the neuroanatomical staining methods used to visualize the cells, but now they are known to be real and important. All synaptic contacts outside the cell body are made on spines.

It has not been possible to show synaptic modification in vertebrates in detail or to have any idea of the quantitative form of the modification, if present, but the data and theory suggest that spine modification is one likely candidate for the detailed synaptic changes that almost certainly underlie learning in adults. The structure of the spine is ideally suited to the kind of correlational modification scheme proposed by Hebb (1949), in which synaptic changes depend on the conjunction of presynaptic and postsynaptic activity. The presynaptic element is at one end of the spine. A dendrite much thicker than the spine forms a low-resistance pathway to the cell body. Thus in close physical proximity, separated by only a few microns, we have presynaptic and postsynaptic activity. Rall and Rinzel (1973) have shown that the anatomy of the spines allows easy modification of synaptic coupling: Slight changes in length or thickness can cause substantial changes in degree of coupling between presynaptic and postsynaptic elements, and normal spines fall into the range where such sensitivity to modification is predicted theoretically.

In immature organisms considerable evidence suggests that change in the amount of dendritic branching is important as well, and dendrites and spines have been shown to respond to environmental influences in both the cortex and the cerebellum (Floeter & Greenough, 1979; Globus, Rosenzweig, Bennett, & Diamond, 1973; Pysh & Weiss, 1979; Volkmar & Greenough, 1972).

The axons of pyramidal cells branch extensively and reenter the cortex up to 3 mm away from the cell of origin. Szentágothai (1978) has suggested that such recurrent collateral connections are "quasi-random," synapsing with the first suitable candidate to be in their way. Such collateral connections generally contact other pyramidal cells and the contacts seem to be excitatory though this has been difficult to show physiologically (see Fig. 1.2).

At the level of the afferent connections of neurons, Szentágothai (1978) comments:

> There cannot be much doubt today that afferent input to cortex . . . is geometrically highly ordered. . . . The basic principle of order appears in many cases to be simply some parallel lamination of fibers of common origin or some other feature that they have in common. In other cases the ordering principle is more complex and may be the preservation of an almost complete isomorphism in the cortical representation of the periphery [p.p. 77-78].

> The picture emerging from such considerations is one of a very high degree of specific wiring both in distant and in local connections of the cerebral cortex . . . [pp. 81].

The one exception to this rule may be the collaterals which may exhibit a degree of 'randomization' that would give room for fortuitous connections. We can conclude that the cortex is a highly ordered structure with the possibility of some salutory local chaos.

A striking observation about cortical circuitry is that it is possible to speak about "cortical circuitry." The basic cell types and circuits seem, with relatively minor variations, to be similar everywhere in the neocortex. Variations exist in the thickness of the cortex, the number and arrangement of layer 4 stellate cells,

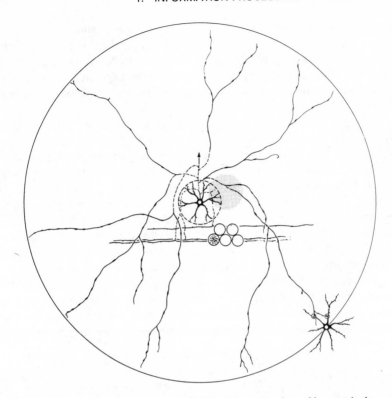

FIG. 1.2. Collateral system of a pyramid cell (center) as it would appear in the view from the surface (semidiagramatic reconstruction). The large circle having a diameter of 3 mm indicates the potential territory reached by the collaterals. The pyramid cell below right on the perimeter would be a potential recipient of synaptic contacts from the central cell. The small circles (100-μ diameter) correspond to the apical dendrite bundles containing 20–30 apical dendrites of a pyramid cell cluster. The round stippled area at right of central pyramid cell ($\pm$300-μ diameter) indicates width of an "arborization-column" of corticocortical afferents. (Szentágothai, 1978).

for example, or the occasional appearance of large and striking variants of a cell type, such as the giant Betz cells (pyramidal cell variants) in the motor cortex. However the basic plan, the arrangements in columns, in layers, and the same typical connections seem to be everywhere (Shepherd, 1979).

On the basis of rather small differences in structure Brodmann distinguished about 50 different cortical areas; other anatomists have made slightly different distinctions. Such distinctions are not mere parcellation. They often describe functional specialization. For example, Area 17 of the primate cortex is distinguished by a prominent fine white line called the "stria of Gennari." Area 17 is also called "primary visual cortex" (sometimes striate cortex) because the lateral geniculate body sends its most prominent projection to Area 17 in mammals. We should emphasize that these subareas of cortex and related subcortical areas are connected together in complex ways, in series, in parallel, and with potential loops. Figure 1.3 shows a partial picture of the earlier stages of visual system connectivity. The details of the projections of the visual system are of considerable interest because they illustrate an especially striking example of the precision of connection of the cortex.

Some levels of the visual system are intrinsically a two-dimensional parallel system: A layer of receptors in the retina projects, after intensive local processing involving important lateral effects, to a parallel array of retinal ganglion cells. The axons of the million or so ganglion cells go up the optic nerve to the lateral geniculate. The lateral geniculate is a six-layered structure in primates, with the projection from the ipsilateral eye (same side) occupying three layers, and the projection from the contralateral (opposite side) eye occupying the other three. The projection is not random but very precise, so that corresponding points in the visual fields of the two eyes, though still separate, are brought into register above each other in different layers, and a spatial map is maintained. A distorted (but not torn or dislocated) map of visual space is present in the geniculate. This projection maintains local continuity and topography. The projection from geniculate to cortex gives rise to a system that also has a precise map. The work

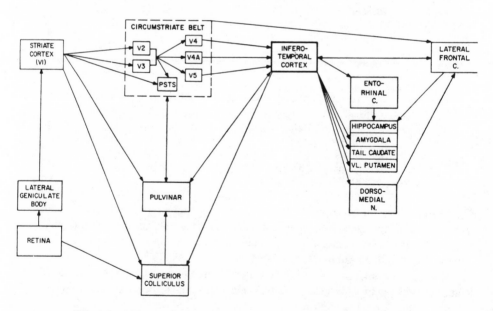

FIG. 1.3. Major ipsilateral afferent connections of inferotemporal cortex in macaque monkey, *Macaca mulatta*. This figure shows the complexity of pathways involved in a portion of the visual system connecting to the highest "visual" cortical region, inferotemporal cortex, which seems to be involved in complex visual function. (Gross et al., 1974).

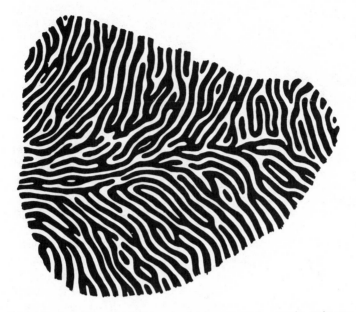

FIG. 1.4. Reconstruction of the ocular dominance pattern over the entire exposed part of the right primary visual cortex, from a series of sections stained by a reduced silver method developed by Simon LeVay. (LeVay, Hubel, & Wiesel, 1975). The left hand margin is at the medial edge of occipital lobe, where cortex folds downward; the area of cortex shown is roughly 2 cm in extent. (Hubel & Wiesel, 1979).

of Hubel and Wiesel and collaborators has shown that the different eyes project to what are essentially bands of eye dominance in cortical layer 4 which are brought together in the other layers so that cells outside of layer 4 are typically binocular. This is strikingly demonstrated in Fig. 1.4, which shows the alternating bands of eye dominance in cat visual cortex (Area 17).

As is well known, cells in Area 17 in the cat and monkey respond preferentially to oriented line segments. All the cells in a single cortical column seem to have the same orientation. The preferred direction of orientation shifts at a constant rate across the surface of the cortex. Bands of constant orientation intersect the bands of ocular dominance. Although there is precise mapping in that, at the scale of millimeters, there is a good average spatial map on the cortex, there is considerable noise and jitter in a small region, so a single cortical column may contain cells that respond to slightly different parts of the visual field (Albus, 1975). The diversity of single-cell response and the observation that nearby cells in the neocortex may be quite unlike each other in details of behavior, though corresponding in general properties such as (in the visual system) location in the visual field or orientation, seems well established (see Fig. 1.5). A

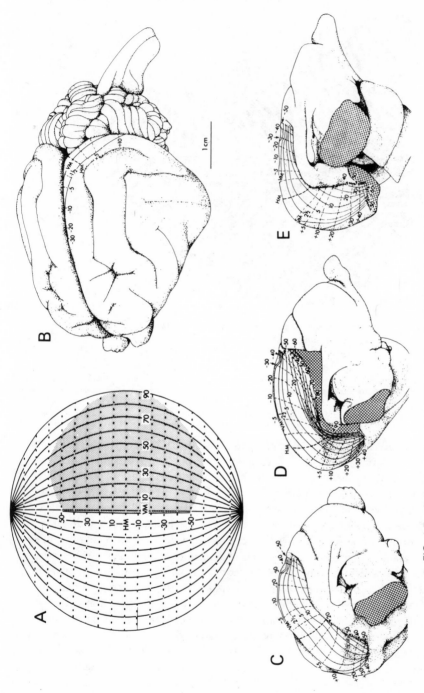

FIG. 1.5. Diagram of the representation of the visual field in Area 17.A is a perimeter chart showing the extent of the visual field represented in Area 17. The chart is based on a world co-ordinate scheme in which the azimuths are represented as solid lines and the elevations as dashed lines. The location of the visual field in Area 17 is illustrated in the four sketches of cat brain shown in B–E. (Tusa, Palmer, & Rosenquist, 1978).

fine discussion of the visual cortex with truly striking pictures is easily available (Hubel & Wiesel, 1979).

The precise topographic maps that are typical of visual inputs seem to be ubiquitous. At present we have many maps representing the sensory receptors on the body surface. For the motor cortex there is the famous "motor homunculus," a drawing of which is a staple of introductory psychology books, and for the auditory system there is a map in terms of frequency. These maps seem in general to conform to the rule of precision on the average but jitter in detailed local characteristics. Multiple and overlapping maps also seem common. At present multiple visual maps have been located in cats, all apparently analyzing the visual input in different ways (Zeki, 1978). An example has also been found of a case in the circumstriate visual cortex where a map of visual space and a map of auditory space are in register, so a cell might be excited by a visual or by an auditory stimulus if it is in the appropriate spatial location (Morrell, 1972).

Another aspect of these maps that is theoretically important is their distortions. The primate retina contains an area of relatively high optical quality that is very rich in receptors, the fovea. This area is highly overrepresented in number of receptors, retinal ganglion cells, and consequently nerve fibers associated with it. This preeminence is maintained all the way to the primary visual cortex, where over half of the cortical neurons are concerned with analyzing only the few degrees of visual space represented by the fovea and the area around it, and the remaining portion of the visual cortex is concerned with the remainder of visual space.

It seems to be a general rule that the more important a sensory system for the animal's behavior, the larger its relative cortical representation. A well-known example is the human motor homunculus, which has disproportionately large hands compared to the feet because hands are much more important in our behavior than feet. The rhesus monkey "monkeyunculus" has roughly equal-sized hand and foot representations. This "mass effect" is confirmed over and over in cortical organization. A particularly striking example is the bat auditory cortex. Often the distortions undergone by maps are apparently quite lawful; for example, a roughly logarithmic transformation seems to be found in both the visual system of the cat (Fischer, 1973) and in the tonotopic organization in the auditory cortex. However, telling exceptions occur. The mustache bat is an echo locator, and the maps of auditory space on its auditory neocortex seems to show clearly the use of map distortions and constructions as important aspects of information processing. The mustache bat emits cries with strong frequency components at 61.0 and 91.5 kHz. There are "disproportionately large" portions of this bat's cortex devoted solely to these two frequencies and a relatively small representation of other frequencies, causing a great distortion of the tonotopic map (Suga & Jen, 1976, as shown in Fig. 1.6).

The mustache bat uses a fairly complicated call (see inset on Fig. 1.7C). The call contains a previously mentioned constant frequency portion that allows a

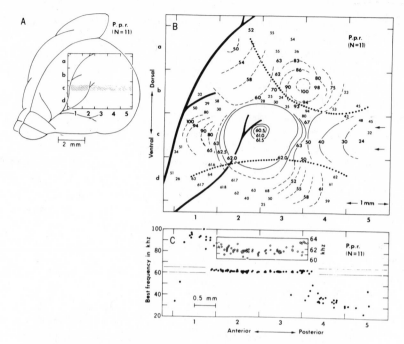

FIG. 1.6. (A) Dorsolateral view of the mustache bat cerebrum. The auditory cortices are within the rectangle. (B) Distribution of best frequencies in the rectangle shown in (A). The area between the dotted lines is the primary auditory cortex (AI). The areas dorsal or ventral to the AI are nonprimary auditory cortices. Orderly tonotopic representation is clear in the areas with sold contour lines, but it is vague in the areas with dashed contour lines. In the areas where contour lines are not drawn, the tonotopic representation, if present, is obscure. Some of the best frequencies obtained in the obscure areas are shown by small-print nos. (C) Distribution of the best frequencies along the anteroposterior axis in the shaded area in (A). Since the minor differences among the best frequencies in areas 2 and 3 cannot clearly be shown in (C), the distribution of best frequencies in this area is shown by the inset with a larger frequency scale and using open circles. P.p.r.: *Pteronotus parnellii rubiginosus* (species name). (Suga & Jen, 1976).

return echo to be analysed for Doppler shift to obtain relative velocity information. There is also a brief period at the end of the call where the emitted frequency suddenly drops several kilohertz in a few msec. This portion of the call, referred to as "chirp" by radar engineers, allows range information to be computed because the time at which a received signal was emitted can be computed from its frequency. Chirping is also an optimal technique for several other reasons having to do with the energy requirements of the emitted signal. However the computations required to obtain range information are not trivial, and in radar it can be computed with a dispersive delay line. It is remarkable that Suga and co-workers (Suga & O'Neill, 1979) have demonstrated that this bat has constructed, on the surface of its cortex, a map for target range, a derived quantity not immediately present in the signal.

The apparent importance, necessity, and universality of maintaining and even constructing a two-dimensional quasi-continuous representation of important aspects of the environment is a significant clue to the kind of parallel processing being performed by the cortex. We must emphasize, however, that maps continuous on the average and overall are *not* continuous in very small areas. Slabs of eye dominance intersected by orientation columns give rise to discontinuous

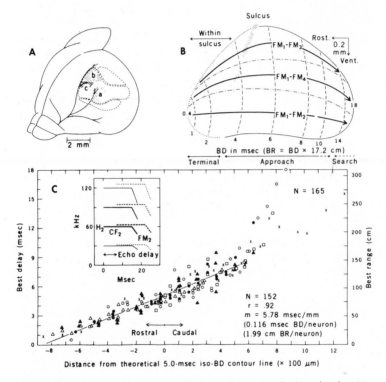

FIG. 1.7. (A) The left cerebral hemisphere of the mustache bat, showing (a) Doppler-shifted CF (= constant frequency), (b) FM (= frequency modulation), and (c) CF/CF processing areas. (B) The FM processing area consists of three major clusters of delay sensitive neurons: FM_1-FM_2, FM_1-FM_3, and FM_1-FM_4 facilitation neurons. Each cluster shows odotopic representation (i.e., topographical representation of target range). Range information in the search, approach, and terminal phases of echolocation is represented by activity at different loci in the cerebral hemisphere. (C) The relation between BD (best delay) and distance along the cortical surface. The data were obtained from six cerebral hemispheres and are indicated by six different symbols. The inset is a schematized sonagram of an orientation sound and a Doppler-shifted echo in the approach phase of echolocation. (Suga & O'Neill, 1979).

local representations of a continuous physical stimulus, a point emphasized by Hubel and Wiesel (1979).

Let us sum up the aspects of cortical neuroanatomy that are of importance to us here because they seem to be generalizations that may lead to approximations of theoretical interest:

1. The cortex is precise on the average in its connections both in terms of its incoming afferent projections (maps) and in terms of its internal connections. Topographic aspects of the external world may be maintained or reconstructed with considerable accuracy.

2. The cortex displays a very strong mass effect so that areas important in an animal's behavior are exaggerated proportionately.

3. The cortex displays precision on the average but imprecision in small areas, in that single neurons may deviate considerably from the average. A certain random component (i.e., Szentágothai's comments about the recurrent collaterals) may be present along with a more precise component. Neurons display considerable individuality, though partaking of some average similarities to neighbors.

4. The cortex is parallel in its organization from the initial afferent inputs, to its layered structure, to its topographically organized maps. Within a given region, such as Area 17, say, parallel organization is very striking. Serial connection of cortical regions, one region to the next, is present, but the individual cortical areas are highly parallel in their organization.

The evidence for parallelism of large aspects of cortical function is overwhelming. The evidence for distribution is also strong but more controversial. It is an experimentally testable area with extreme views on both sides present in the literature.

Neuron Specificity.   There are two extreme positions that one can take. One can claim great specificity and importance for single neurons. We can look at the physiological data and observe that single neurons respond to only a small number of stimuli; that is, they have considerable selectivity. We could then conjecture that when a neuron is active it signals very precise information about the sensory input. This point of view is held by Horace Barlow (1972), who summed up his position is a series of dogmas, three of which are particularly relevant here:

Dogma 2 states: "The sensory system is organized to achieve as complete a representation of the sensory stimulus as possible with the minimum number of active neurons [p. 371]."

Dogma 4 states: "Perception corresponds to the activity of a small selection from the very numerous high-level neurons, each of which corresponds to a pattern of external events of the order of complexity of the events symbolized by a word [p. 371]."

Dogma 5 states: "High impulse frequency in such neurons corresponds to high certainty that the trigger feature is present [p. 371]."

Thus: Single neurons are very important, very specific and signal certainty with increased activity.

The real virtue of this position is that it is easy to understand and makes good intuitive sense. When a cell fires, something specific and important happens, both because very few other cells are talking and because the cell is "meaningful." This position is held, deep in their hearts, by many practicing neurophysiologists because it seems to give a clear interpretation of what they observe with their microelectrodes.

Distribution. Karl Lashley, on the other hand, is identified with a strong statement of distribution. Although most of his work was concerned with the problem of memory, his ideas on distribution are quite general. To quote from the summary of his famous 1950 paper, "In Search of the Engram":

> It is not possible to demonstrate the isolated localization of a memory trace anywhere within the nervous system. Limited regions may be essential for learning or retention of a particular activity, but within such regions the parts are functionally equivalent. The engram is represented throughout the area.... Briefly, the characteristics of the nervous network are such that when it is subject to any pattern of excitation, it may develop a pattern of activity, reduplicated throughout an entire functional area, by spread of excitations, much as the surface of a liquid develops an interference pattern of spreading waves when it is disturbed at several points..... Consideration of the numerical relations of sensory and other cells in the brain makes it certain, I believe, that all of the cells of the brain must be in almost constant activity, either firing or actively inhibited. There is no great excess of cells which can be reserved as the seat of special memories. The complexity of the functions involved in reproductive memory implies that every instance of recall requires the activity of literally millions of neurons. The same neurons which retain the memory traces of one experience must also participate in countless other activities.
>
> Recall involves the synergic action or some sort of resonance among a very large number of neurons.... From the numerical relations involved, I believe that even the reservation of individual synapses for special associative reactions is impossible [pp. 477–480].

With this diversity of views, one can now look at the experimental literature and decide how the observed neuronal specificities agree with these two positions. Clearly, there is specificity. Cells do not respond to all conceivable stimuli or even a small subset of them but are quite specific in their responses. At the same time they are not, in our opinion, so specific as to be what Barlow's dogmas would lead one to expect. In fact, we conjecture if this were the case that single unit neurophysiology would be hopeless once beyond the very lowest levels of cortex because it would be almost impossible to ever find the precise stimulus required to drive any given cell. What we seem to observe in actuality is a spectrum of response types from quite specific and narrowly tuned to quite general and broadly tuned. As one well-known example, in inferotemporal cortex, a higher level visual center, many cells are quite broadly tuned, responding to orientation over many degrees of visual angle. Yet some cells (e.g., the famous "monkey hand" cell) seem to be very specific. Yet even the "monkey hand" cell can be driven by other stimuli such as some geometric shapes, while reserving its highest frequency discharge for the shape corresponding to a silhouette of a monkey hand (Gross, Bender, & Rocha-Miranda, 1974).

We suggest that truth lies somewhere in the middle of the two extreme views and that there is a moderate amount of distribution in the cortex, so that any single cell responds to many things but nowhere near all things. It seems to us both experimentally observed and sensible from the point of view of information processing that there be a considerable range of specificities from quite specific to quite broad.

Singer (1978), in an analysis of the visual cortex, comments that:

> The data . . . suggests that the result of any higher level integrative operation is presumably not encoded in the specific responses of a few but highly selective cells. . . . This might indicate a cooperative principle of encoding whereby the message about the presence of a particular combination of features is conveyed by the graded, mutually dependent responses of a large number of cells within a functional matrix of cells [p. 377].

One of us has discussed this question of single-unit specificity elsewhere (Anderson, J. A., et al., 1977), and Singer's remarks seem to us to capture the actual situation.

1.6. SUMMARY

We have presented a necessarily limited selection from among the wide range of models in which computation is performed in parallel by multiple, rather simple units. We feel that such models are worth further study for several quite different reasons.

First, the neocortex is clearly highly parallel in the arrangement of its basic elements. A single cortical area contains many millions of neurons arranged and connected with a high degree of parallelism. It seems entirely reasonable that such pronounced structure should have implications for cognitive function.

Second, there are a number of functional attributes of cognition, ranging from memory access and concept formation to stereopsis and visual perception, that seem to be very hard to explain with more traditional serial models. The existing models using parallel systems of simple units have already had some success in these areas and more can be expected as we gain further insight into the properties of this kind of computation. We feel that distributed representations are a very promising idea and that a successful cognitive theory, when it comes, may take the form of a calculus of state vectors where the psychological level of description will correspond to the permutations and interactions of the state vectors.

Finally, there are purely technological reasons for studying parallel systems, outside of their scientific interest, because they may be the best way to increase the speed and power of computation in the future. Recent developments in Very Large Scale Integration (VLSI) and in Computer Aided Design (CAD) make it relatively easy to implement parallel models directly in the hardware, expecially if the models use simple units and regular interconnection schemes.

Many of the systems we have discussed are still somewhat unfamiliar and difficult to work with. Parallel models tend to have intrinsic characteristics of their own, and the nonlinear ones are often very hard to analyze. Considerable experience with them may be needed before our ideas about parallel computation are adequate to allow us to exploit the enormous potential of this class of systems both as computational devices and as models of the mind.

ACKNOWLEDGMENTS

We would like to thank Stu Geman, Don Macleod, Jay McClelland, George Mandler, Don Norman, Dave Rumelhart, Tim Shallice, and Aaron Sloman for inspiration and for helpful comments on the manuscript. The chapter was written while we were Visiting Scholars at the Program in Cognitive Science, UCSD, supported by a grant from the Sloan Foundation.

REFERENCES

Albus, K. A quantitative study of the projection area of the central and paracentral visual field in Area 17 of the cat. I. The precision of the topography. *Experimental Brain Research*, 1975, *24*, 159–179.

Anderson, J. A. Two models for memory organization using interacting traces. *Mathematical Bio-Sciences*, 1970, *8*, 137–160.

Anderson, J. A. A simple neural network generating an interactive memory. *Mathematical Biosciences*, 1972, *14*, 197–220.

Anderson, J. A. A theory for the recognition of items from short memorized lists. *Psychological Review*, 1973, *80*, 417–438.

Anderson, J. A. Neural models with cognitive implications. In D. LaBerge & S. J. Samuels (Eds.), *Basic processes in reading.* Hillsdale, N.J.: Lawrence Erlbaum Associates, 1977.

Anderson, J. A., Silverstein, J. W., Ritz, S. A., & Jones, R. S. Distinctive features, categorical perception, and probability learning: Some applications of a neural model. *Psychological Review,* 1977, *84,* 413-451.

Anderson, J. R. & Bower, G. H. *Human associative memory.* Washington, D.C.: V. H. Winston, 1973.

Barlow, H. Single units and sensation: A neuron doctrine for perceptual psychology. *Perception,* 1972, *1,* 371-394.

Barrow, H. G., & Tenenbaum, J. M. Recovering intrinsic scene characteristics from images. In A. R. Hanson & E. M. Riseman (Eds.), *Computer vision systems.* New York: Academic Press, 1978.

Brazier, M. A. B. & Petsche, H. (Eds.). *Architectonics of the cerebral cortex.* New York: Raven, 1978.

Brown, J. S. & Burton, R. R. Diagnostic models for procedural bugs in basic mathematical skills. *Cognitive Science,* 1978, *2,* 155-192.

Card, S. K., Moran, T. P., & Newell, A. Computer text-editing: An information-processing analysis of a routine cognitive skill. *Cognitive Psychology,* 1980, *12,* 32-74.

Cavanagh, P. Holographic processes realizable in the neural realm: Prediction of short-term memory performance (Doctoral Dissertation, Carnegie-Mellon University, 1972.) *Dissertation Abstracts International,* 1973, *33,* 3280B.

Collins, A. M., & Loftus, E. F. A spreading activation theory of semantic processing. *Psychological Review,* 1975, *82,* 407-428.

Collins, A., & Quillian, M. R. Experiments on semantic memory and language comprehension. In L. W. Gregg (Ed.), *Cognition in learning and memory.* New York: Wiley, 1972.

Cooper, L. N. A possible organization of animal memory and learning. In B. Lundquist & S. Lundquist (Eds.), *Proceedings of the Nobel symposium on collective properties of physical systems.* New York: Academic Press, 1974.

Fischer, B. Overlap of receptive field centers and representation of the visual field in the cat's optic tract. *Vision Research,* 1973, *13,* 2113-2120.

Floeter, M. K. & Greenough, W. T. Cerebellar plasticity: Modification of Purkinje cell structure by differential rearing in monkeys. *Science,* 1979, *206,* 227-229.

Globus, A., Rosenzweig, M. R., Bennett, E. L., & Diamond, M. C. Effects of differential experience on dendritic spine counts in rat cerebral cortex. *Journal of Comparative and Physiological Psychology,* 1973, *82,* 175-181.

Gross, C. G., Bender, D. B., & Rocha-Miranda, C. E. Inferotemporal cortex: A single unit analysis. In F. O. Schmitt & F. G. Worden (Eds.), *The neurosciences: Third study program.* Cambridge, Mass.: MIT Press, 1974.

Hebb, D. O. *The organization of behavior.* New York: Wiley, 1949.

Hinton, G. E. Using relaxation to find a puppet. *Proceedings of the A.I.S.B. Summer Conference,* University of Edinburgh, 1976.

Hinton, G. E. *Relaxation and its role in vision.* Unpublished doctoral dissertation University of Edinburgh, 1977.

Horn, B. K. P. Understanding image intensities. *Artificial Intelligence,* 1977, *8,* 201-231.

Hubel, D. H. & Wiesel, T. N. Brain mechanisms of vision. *Scientific American,* 1979, *241*(3), 150-162.

James, W. *Psychology: Briefer course.* New York: Collier, 1962. (Originally published, 1890).

Julesz, B. *Foundations of cyclopean perception.* Chicago: The University of Chicago Press, 1971.

Kandel, E. R. *Cellular basis of behavior.* San Francisco: W. H. Freeman, 1976.

Kohonen, T. *Associative memory: A system-theoretical approach.* Berlin: Springer, 1977.

Kuffler, S. W. & Nicholls, J. G. *From neuron to brain.* Sunderland, Mass.: Sinauer Associates, 1976.

Lashley, K. In search of the engram. In Symposia of the Society for Experimental Biology, No. 4., *Physiological mechanisms in animal behavior.* New York: Academic Press, 1950.

LeVay, S., Hubel, D. H., & Weisel, T. N. The pattern of occular dominance columns in macaque visual cortex revealed by a reduced silver stain. *Journal of Comparative Neurology,* 1975, *159,* 559-575.

McClelland, J. L. & Rumelhart, D. E. *An interactive activation model of the effect of context in perception: Part 1.* (Tech. Rep. 91). San Diego: University of California, San Diego, Center for Human Information Processing, 1980.

McCulloch, W. S. & Pitts, W. H. A logical calculus of ideas immanent in nervous activity. *Bulletin of Mathematical Biophysics,* 1943, *5,* 115-133.

Marr, D. Early processing of visual information. *Philosophical Transactions of the Royal Society. Series B,* 1976, *275,* 483-524.

Marr, D. Representing visual information. In A. R. Hanson & E. M. Riseman (Eds.), *Computer vision systems.* New York: Academic Press, 1978.

Marr, D. & Poggio, T. Cooperative computation of stereo disparity. *Science,* 1976, *194,* 283-287.

Minsky, M. Plain talk about neurodevelopmental epistemology. *Proceedings of the Fifth International Joint Conference on Artificial Intelligence,* Boston, Mass. 1977.

Minsky, M. K-lines: A theory of memory. *Cognitive Science,* 1980, *4,* 117-133.

Minsky, M. & Papert, S. *Perceptrons.* Cambridge, Mass.: MIT Press, 1969.

Morrell, F. Integrative properties of parastriate neurons. In A. G. Karczmar & J. C. Eccles (Eds.), *Brain and human behavior.* New York: Springer, 1972.

Neimark, E. D. & Estes, W. K. (Eds.). *Stimulus sampling theory.* San Francisco: Holden-Day, 1967.

Newell, A. Physical symbol system. *Cognitive Science,* 1980, *4,* 135-183.

Newell, A., & Simon, H. A. GPS, a program that simulates human thought. In E. Feigenbaum and J. Feldman (Eds.), *Computers and thought.* New York: McGraw-Hill, 1963.

Newell, A., & Simon, H. A. *Human problem solving.* Englewood Cliffs, N.J. Prentice-Hall, 1972.

Nilsson, N. J. *Learning machines.* New York: McGraw-Hill, 1965.

Norman, D. A., & Bobrow D. G. Descriptions: An intermediate stage in memory retrieval. *Cognitive Psychology,* 1979, *11,* 107-123.

Peleg, S. A new probabilistic relaxation scheme. *I.E.E.E. Transactions on Pattern Analysis and Machine Intelligence,* 1980, 362-369.

Pribram, K. H., Nuwer, M., & Baron, R. J. The holographic hypothesis of memory structure in brain function and perception. In D. H. Krantz, R. C. Atkinson, R. D. Luce, & P. Suppes (Eds.), *Contemporary developments in mathematical psychology* (Volume II). San Francisco:W. H. Freeman, 1974.

Pylyshyn, Z. Computation and cognition: Issues in the foundations of cognitive science. *The Behavioural and Brain Sciences,* 1980, *3,* 111-169.

Pysh, J. J. & Weiss, G. M. Exercise during development induces an increase in Purkinje cell dendritic tree size. *Science,* 1979, *206,* 230-232.

Rall, W. & Rinzel, J. Branch input resistance and steady attenuation for input to one branch of a dendritic neuron model. *Biophysics Journal,* 1973, *13,* 648-688.

Reicher, G. M. Perceptual recognition as a function of meaningfulness of stimulus material. *Journal of Experimental Psychology,* 1969, *81,* 274-280.

Roberts, L. G. Machine perception of three-dimensional solids. In J. T. Tippett, D. A. Berkowitz, L. C. Clapp, C. J. Koester, & A. Vanderburgh (Eds.), *Optical and electro-optical information processing.* Cambridge: MIT Press, 1965.

Rosenblatt, F. *Principles of neurodynamics: Perceptrons and the theory of brain mechanisms.* Washington, D.C.: Spartan, 1961.

Rosenfeld A. Iterative methods in image analysis. *Pattern Recognition,* 1978, *10,* 181-187.

Rosenfeld A., Hummel R. A., & Zucker S. W. Scene labelling by relaxation operations. *I.E.E.E. Transactions on Systems, Man and Cybernetics,* 1976, *SMC-6,* 420-433.

Rumelhart, D. E. & McClelland, J. L. *An interactive activation model of the effect of context in perception: Part 2.* (Tech. Rep. 95). San Diego: University of California, San Diego, Center for Human Information Processing, 1980.

Scheibel, M. E. & Scheibel, A. B. Elementary processes in selected thalmic and cortical subsystems—the structural substrates. In F. O. Schmitt (Ed.), *The neurosciences: second study program.* New York: Rockefeller University Press, 1970.

Selz, O. Die Umgestaltung der Grundanschauungen vom Intellektuellen Geschehen. *Kantstudien,* 1927, *32,* 273–280. Translated as: The revision of the fundamental conceptions of intellectual processes. In J. M. Mandler & G. Mandler (Eds.), *Thinking: From association to Gestalt.* New York: Wiley, 1964.

Shepherd, G. M. *The synaptic organization of the brain* (2nd ed.). New York: Oxford University Press, 1979.

Shirai, Y. A context sensitive line finder for recognition of polyhedra. *Artificial Intelligence,* 1973, *4,* 95–119.

Singer, W. The functional organization of cat striate and parastriate cortex: A correlation between receptive field structure and synaptic connectivity. *Experimental Brain Research, Supp. 1.* O. Creutzfeldt (Ed.) *Afferent and intrinsic organization of laminated structures in the brain.* Berlin: Springer, 1978.

Suga, N. & Jen, P. H. S. Disproportionate tonotopic representation for processing CF-FM sonar signals in the mustache bat auditory complex. *Science,* 1976, *194,* 542–544.

Suga, N. & O'Neill, W. E. Neural axis representing target range in the auditory cortex of the mustache bat. *Science,* 1979, *206,* 351–353.

Sutherland, I. E. & Mead, C. A. Microelectronics and computer science. *Scientific American,* 1977, *237*(3), 210–228.

Szentágothai, J. Specificity versus (quasi-) randomness in cortical connectivity. In M. A. B. Brazier & H. Petsche (Eds.), *Architectonics of the cerebral cortex.* New York: Raven, 1978.

Tusa, R. J., Palmer, L. A., & Rosenquist, A. C. The retinotopic organization of Area 17 (striate cortex) in the cat. *The Journal of Comparative Neurology,* 1978, *177,* 213–235.

Volkmar, F. R. & Greenough, W. T. Rearing complexity affects branching of dendrites in visual cortex of the rat. *Science,* 1972, *176,* 1445–1447.

von Neumann, J. First draft of a report on the EDVAC, June 30, 1945. In B. Randall (Ed.), *The origins of digital computers: Selected papers.* Berlin: Springer, 1975.

Westlake, P. R. The possibilities of neural holographic processes within the Brain. *Kybernetik,* 1970, *7,* 129–153.

Willshaw, D. J. *Models of distributed associative memory.* Unpublished doctoral dissertation, University of Edinburgh, 1971.

Willshaw, D. J., Buneman, O. P. & Longuet-Higgins, H. C. Nonholographic associative memory. *Nature,* 1969, *222,* 960–962.

Winograd, T. *Understanding natural language.* New York: Academic Press, 1972.

Wood, C. C. Variations on a theme by Lashley: Lesion experiments on the neural model of Anderson, Silverstein, Ritz, and Jones. *Psychological Review,* 1978, *85,* 582–591.

Zeki, S. M. Uniformity and diversity of structure and function in rhesus monkey prestriate visual cortex. *Journal of Physiology,* 1978, *277,* 273–290.

2 A Connectionist Model of Visual Memory

J. A. Feldman
Computer Science Department
University of Rochester
Rochester, NY 14627

2.1. INTRODUCTION

Despite a long and vigorous history of research on human memory (Anderson & Bower, 1973), very little is known about how it actually works, and it is often treated as a mystery. This paper consists mainly of well-known results from psychology, biology, and computer science arranged in a way that appears to hang together. There are still many gaps, some of which get bridged with constructs of varying quality. For the sake of concreteness, we will be mostly concerned with visual memory and will present a fairly detailed distributed information-processing model of its function. In an effort to avoid both jargon and long explanations, I have come to adopt an informal conversational style often associated with content-free ramblings; bear with me.

There has been a great deal of experimental work on visual memory, some of which presents striking results that will have to be accounted for in our model. We are initially concerned with the set of experiments that are usually presented along with the statement "visual memory is infinite." In a typical experiment, Standing (Standing, 1973) presented subjects with 10,000 quite different images at exposures of 5 sec (with an interstimulus interval of 600 msec), and tested the subjects' ability to recognize later which one of a stimulus pair had been in the training set. Even after an interval of 2 days subjects would get over 90% of the forced choices correct. Related experiments indicate that the recognition involves a coherent structural representation of the remembered images. (To store 10,000 raw images, at 1000×1000 resolution and 10 bits/point, would require 10^{11} bits—about the number of neurons in the brain.) For example, Freedman and Haber (1974) did this kind of experiment with Mooney face pictures (Fig. 2.1).

FIG. 2.1.   Mooney Faces.

Images that were reported as being perceived as faces were matched at the 90% level and those that were not were recognized at chance.

The ordinary functioning of visual memory is no less remarkable. Consider the following situation from daily life. You are walking through a crowded airport, thinking about a problem. You pause, look back over your shoulder, and recognize a friend from a remote place. This example will be used informally to introduce the major conceptual tools that will be needed later.

As the example suggests, we are more concerned initially with the uses of memory than with its acquisition. Of particular concern are the interactions between memory and perception. Memory is assumed to be distributed and active; there is no homunculus to compare the features of the input with static memory lists. The term *knowledge* is used to encompass innate and developed capacities (neural connections) in addition to *memory*. *Learning* refers to any change in knowledge. According to the model, you do not *have* a store of knowledge; you *are* your knowledge, among other things.

Several important questions are totally suppressed, beginning with all phenomenological issues including the mind–brain problem. There is no attempt to trace the origins of the ideas presented nor any serious comparison with alternative formulations.

What we attempt to do is provide a plausible and relatively detailed "distributed information-processing model" of visual memory function that is consistent with the current state of knowledge in biology, psychology, and computer science. The fundamental viewpoint is that of information processing in a distributed, highly parallel, flexible system. An additional claim implicit in this work is that this kind of abstract model is appropriate for expressing detailed theories of biological function. The information-processing abstractions underlying our development are presented briefly in the Appendix to this chapter and in more detail in Feldman (1979). They are somewhat unusual in that they are neither linear nor (necessarily) binary. Closed loops are used heavily and the formalism permits encapsulating an arbitrary network as a single unit of the same type.

One fact that is essential to this entire enterprise is the remarkably small number of computational time steps involved in complex mental acts. After training, people can recognize and respond to quite complex visual scenes in less than 300 msec, which is about 100 times the firing rate of neurons. Current machine perception programs require millions of computational time steps. This suggests massive parallelism, not just in the visual system but throughout the brain. The question is how could an active, highly parallel network carry out the functions of visual memory in so few steps. From a communication standpoint, we can see that the firing frequency of a neuron cannot transmit more than six bits of information in 300 msec, so that signals from cell to cell cannot be very complex. Computational theories of parallelism and of complexity have made great strides since the last round of attempts to model brain function, and we can now formulate sharp technical questions of how known behaviors could be accomplished by the available circuitry.

The basic structure of permanent memory should be thought of generically as a conventional *relational network* of labeled links between concepts. There are many open questions in the details of how to encode knowledge in such networks, but the basic model has been explored extensively and is generally accepted in computer science and cognitive psychology. But for biological verisimilitude we must envision the net to be active rather than being just data that are interpreted (by the homunculus). There is no direct evidence justifying our identification of links between concepts with neural connections, but neither is there any reason to reject this obvious possibility. The network can be "doing" more than one thing at a time, and in fact there is considerable evidence that there are several anatomically separate "memories." But the number of resulting physical actions at a given instant is extremely limited. We can only do one thing at a time with a hand, with speech, etc.

The problem of multiple cogitation and singular action is addressed by postulating a very general mechanism of *lateral inhibition*. Lateral inhibition at lower organizational levels is one of the most ubiquitous information-processing mechanisms in animals: It is essential that opposing action systems do not execute simultaneously. Low-level visual processing makes very heavy use of mutual lateral inhibition, and this appears to be true for other sensory systems as well. We say much more about lateral inhibition later, but for now the crucial point is that the multifaceted activities of memory normally have at most one controlling link to a major input or output system. The selection of which section of the memory controls an input or output system (e.g., head turning) at a particular time can be done by mutual inhibition without central (attentive) control.

We are now in a position to consider (albeit still very crudely) the relation between memory and perception. The fundamental idea here is one of a continuous interplay between memory and the features extracted from images. Expectations, goals, and context affect the way we see an image and are, in turn, affected by what is seen. We call this accommodation process *relaxation* following the usage in computer science. Networks representing alternative readings of the input compete with each other until one of them dominates. Mutually consistent interpretations at various levels reinforce one another and inhibit rival nodes. One way to view this is to imagine cone-shaped (as in Fig. 2.7, p. 65) coalitions of units at various levels of abstraction competing to produce the best fit to the image. It is also reasonable to view this process as a very general "correlation" of input and memory.

In the airport scenario, we assume that the main context used with the vision system is a navigational one—treating people as objects to be avoided. But there must also be a considerable amount of (parallel) relaxation of the input with other contexts such as the appearance of friends or celebrities. Should some inputs fit well enough with something of sufficient importance, the dominant context will change. Often, as in the airport scenario, a person will pursue an information-gathering strategy (here turning and looking more closely) with no conscious notion of why he is doing so. At our current crude level, we can also understand why we often notice someone who resembles a friend and why these experiences often seem to be deferred responses. Finally we note that incomplete relaxation of new perceptions with memory could be the basis for assimilating information.

Recapitulating, the information-processing concepts that we employ include: (1) parallel operation of subunits; (2) generalized lateral inhibition; (3) active semantic net; (4) feedback, both positive and negative; and (5) generalized matching and relaxation.

Our goal is to develop a biologically plausible information-processing model of visual memory that could be used to integrate results from experiments of many kinds. The major point of departure from conventional information-processing models is the explicit adoption of a *connectionist* framework as opposed to assuming that symbolic information is transmitted along some general channel. These two fundamentally different information-processing strategies give rise to radically different views of how memory works.

For example, when we see an apple and say the word "ap'l" (or "pomme"), some information must be transferred, however indirectly, from the visual system to the speech system. Either a special *symbol* that denotes apple is transmitted to the speech system, or there is a special *connection* to the speech command area for the word "apple." Figure 2.2 is a graphic presentation of the two alternatives. The path on the right described by double-lined arrows depicts the situation (as in a computer) where the information that an apple has been seen is encoded by the visual system and sent as an abstract message (perhaps frequency-coded) to a general receiver in the speech system which decodes the message and initiates the appropriate speech act. I have not encountered anyone who will defend this model as biologically plausible.

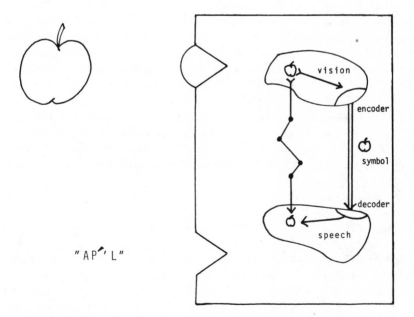

FIG. 2.2. Connectionism vs. symbolic encoding. Double-width path assumes some general encoding. Single-width path assumes individual connections.

The only alternative that I have been able to uncover is described by the path with single-width arrows. This suggests that there are (indirect) links from the units (cells, columns, centers, or what-have-you) that recognize an apple to some units responsible for speaking the word. The connectionist model requires only very simple messages (e.g., stimulus strength) to cross a channel but puts strong demands on the availability of the right connections. Current ideas in computing appear to be adequate to develop plausible connectionist models of memory and of other higher mental functions. This requires a significant departure from traditional information-processing models which have been based on sequential, symbolic, deterministic computation. Natural language is obviously a symbolic system and internal language is generally considered to play a role in thought. But there does not appear to be any general symbol transport mechanism besides inner speech, and one should not assume symbolic processing is needed for tasks accomplished by subprimates.

Information-processing models based on conventional digital computers have become the dominant paradigm in cognitive psychology and are becoming more influential in other disciplines. Artificial Intelligence (AI), the branch of computer science concerned with mental function, is almost totally bound to sequential processing models. The overwhelming strength of information-processing models is that they state explicitly the computations that are supposed to underlie the behavior being studied. A secondary advantage of information-processing models is that they can, to some extent, be embodied as computer programs. The most serious drawback of conventional information-processing models as a theory of higher mental function is that the brain doesn't seem to be much like a digital computer. Most workers in the field assert that we are not yet ready to worry about this problem because nothing relevant is yet known about the brain. If we *do* take the brain seriously in theorizing about the mind and also require explicit statements about the mechanisms that are hypothesized, there appear to be two main ways to proceed. Either one attempts to show how the brain (as it is understood) carries out the primitives of a digital computer, or one attempts to show how computations like those prominent in AI models would be carried out by neural nets.

Both of these research programs appear to be very difficult but well worth the effort. A central question, as Fig. 2.2 points out, is the role of symbolic information (cf. Newell, 1980). The other major conceptual problem in mapping current theories from AI (and philosophy) onto the brain is the nature of variables, pattern matching, and substitution. Equally profound issues arise in attempting to work directly from the computational principles apparently operating in the brain towards algorithms for carrying out mental activities. The ''distributed information-processing model'' is my notion of how to approach this enterprise. The following two sections are an initial exploration of the technical problems involved in a strictly connectionist paradigm. We attempt to show that visual memory can be modeled in detail and suggest that the results could be of value in interpreting and designing a wide range of experiments.

2.2.   THE MODEL: EXAMPLE AND DISCUSSION

One of the reasons that studying memory is difficult is that there is no way to examine it directly—there are always interactions with other modalities. In order to be specific about our memory hypotheses, we examine their consequences in a realistic but simplified environment. The environment we have chosen is the blocks-world of simple robotics where the tasks involve perception, motion, language understanding, and planning. This domain has been extensively examined by workers in artificial intelligence over the last 15 years and a great deal is known about it. Figure 2.3 is an example of a typical blocks-world task (Winograd, 1972).

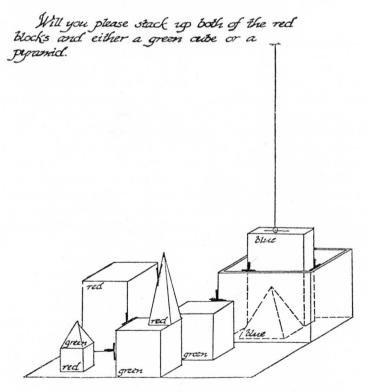

FIG. 2.3.   A blocks world task. From (Winograd, 1972).

We first consider in some detail how memory nets could function in the visual perception of simple blocks-world scenes. We begin (as was done historically) with the problem of recognizing the two-dimensional image of a single view of an isolated cube against a contrasting background. Our distributed information-processing model will be specified by describing the internal structure and connectivity patterns of the individual active elements that are postulated to carry out each function. All questions of learning and plasticity of the network are deferred to Section 2.3. At first we assume that each element gives an all-or-none response and is always correct. The extension to more realistic cases will follow shortly. The specific details of the example are much too simple to be correct, but it will suffice for introducing some conceptual tools.

We assume that there is a set of elements that detect local discontinuities (edges) in the image (Kuffler & Nicholls, 1976; Hanson & Riseman, 1978). We describe how constructs to detect longer lines, corners, and other visual features could be built up from the local edge data. The computations suggested are similar to ones commonly employed in machine perception research but are simplified and have been adapted to the computation mechanisms provided by the neural networks under investigation.

We model the perception of the cube as requiring four distinct levels of analysis. The edge data (level 1) are used to form lines (level 2), which are then used to compute vertices (level 3), which in turn are used to compute the location of a cube (level 4), if any, on the internal representation maintained by the perceiver. The computations at each level are done by simple retinotopic networks, using many more elements than necessary in order to simplify the presentation. Figure 2.4 depicts the computations graphically.

In part A of Fig. 2.4 there is a segment of a network for computing longer lines where present. Recall that we are assuming for now that all computations are reliable and yield one of two values, say 0 or 1. Each element in the array on the left detects the presence or absence of an edge. There is one element on the right for each possible length and orientation of a dark-to-light edge at each point in the image. For concreteness, one could imagine each active link contributing +1 to the sum computed by the elements on the right and the maximum of these being found by a tournament algorithm. Under our assumption of perfect information, the longest line at each orientation will be the correct one. (Cognoscenti will recognize this as a Hough technique from Ballard, 1979.)

Part B of Fig. 2.4 depicts some of the computations needed to recognize different kinds of possible vertices where lines meet. The boxes in the center represent elements that could respond to three different kinds of vertices at the point (18, 23). Machine perception research has shown that this kind of vertex classification provides a powerful set of visual features for understanding blocks-world scenes like Fig. 2.3. Part C of the figure shows how the three vertex types can be useful in evaluating the presence or absence of a cube. The connections in Part B include some inhibitory links, marked with circular end-

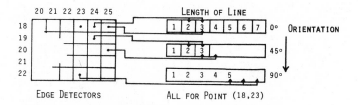

A) TESTING FOR LONGER LINES AT ONE POINT

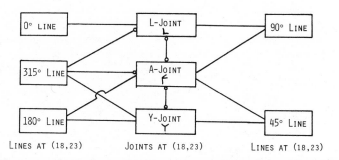

B) SOME VERTEX TYPE-COMPUTATIONS FOR POINT (18,23)

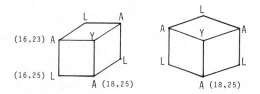

C) THE STANDARD VERTEX TYPES FOR CUBES
(A-VERTICES HAVE ALL THREE LINES IN THE SAME HALF-PLANE)

FIG. 2.4. Detection of lines and vertices.

ings. There would be many other inhibitory links in the complete network because no other lines can be present if one of these vertex types is to match. (The vertex-classifying elements are not parameterized by the length of the lines forming the vertex because this information is not useful in our example. The lengths of the lines appears in the computation of the relative position of the vertices at the next level.)

The elements responsible for the fourth (and final) level of cube detection are indicated in Fig. 2.5. In 2.5A we assume there is a separate element for each size cube at each point in the image; the elements shown detect the view of a cube given on the left in Fig. 2.4C. Still assuming perfect computations and a single

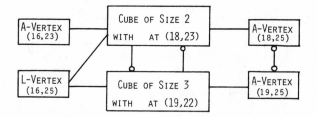

A) Fragment of a Particular Cube Network

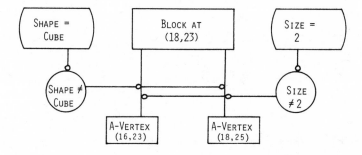

B) More Compact Representation for Information about Views of Simple Objects

FIG. 2.5.   Networks that describe a cube.

cube, exactly one level 4 element would have all six of its inputs activated and thus the entire network would be able to detect an isolated cube. Before continuing the examination of this example, we should notice that it would be natural to have a connectionist mapping from the location of the cube (in three-dimensional body-centered coordinates) to the set of joint angles required to get a hand to that location, as well as mappings to speech and other centers. Although it is well beyond the scope of this paper, the fundamental assumption of the model is that *every* mental use of the recognized object is by direct or indirect connections.

The perception of an isolated cube was the simplest realistic example I could concoct; yet even the crudest model of the task involved considerable complexity. An adequate model of cube perception would have to include a large number of other vision primitives dealing with color, texture, lighting and other sources of information (cf. Barrow & Tenenbaum, 1978). A theory of visual perception would also have to integrate variations with time. It is not hard to see how we could add networks dedicated to each vision subtask, but it is hard to decide how their results would be fitted together. As a first step towards doing this, we abandon the fantasy that all the image features are computed perfectly.

Error and uncertainty are fundamental issues in visual perception for some very basic reasons. The response of the retina to single quanta and the apparently random background firing rate of neurons establish low-level bounds on the possible determinacy of the system. It is also true that we see a cube outline like Fig. 2.4C even when some of the local edges are totally missing because of lighting effects. (This phenomenon is sometimes called *subjective contour.*) In scenes of multiple objects we usually see only a small fraction of the surfaces present—a single view never shows more than half of even an isolated object. Despite all these factors animals move through a visually complex world with great confidence and reliability.

The underlying basis for this reliability in the presence of noise and incomplete data is knowledge (memory plus innate) of the general laws of image redundancy and particular knowledge of the appearance of objects. We concentrate on the latter and discuss how we suppose memory and sensory processing to interact in visual perception. The networks depicted in Fig. 2.4 and 2.5 still apply; we simply drop the assumptions of perfect reliability and binary output.

The extended model is easy to describe in terms of the abstract information-processing elements specified in the Appendix. Each element is assumed to issue a *signal* whose strength is related (often proportional) to the internal *potential* of the element. Each edge, line, vertex, and cube-detecting element computes its potential by combining (e.g., summing) the results of its input signals. This is all terribly conventional and the first model one would think of in this context. But this model is also fairly powerful—especially when we add mutual lateral inhibition, as shown in the middle of Fig. 2.4B. At each level (edges, lines, vertices, objects) the computational units representing alternative interpretations of the activities of the preceding level act to diminish the potential of their rivals. For example, rivals at the vertex and object levels are shown in Fig. 2.5. The combination of hierarchical structure, mutual inhibition, and multistate elements provides a computational structure that is a much richer computing mechanism than that provided by perceptrons (Minsky & Papert, 1969). One could build systems along these lines that would quite reliably detect the "best match" of visual input to a fixed set of possibilities. Such systems could adapt by changing their computations of potential and of signal strength like a perceptron but are nonlinear and require different analysis techniques (see the Appendix).

In computer science, a system like the one described above would be called "bottom-up" because the information processing proceeds directly from detailed sense data through various levels of abstraction. The contrasting term "top-down" refers to processes where some conceptual goal (e.g., find a cube) drives the information processing. We are all familiar with cases where set and setting have a marked effect in visual perception. In terms of the models in Fig. 2.4, this means that each link should be thought of as representing a pair of connections, one in each direction. Mutual positive feedback occurs frequently in nervous systems, both as two-way electrical synapses and in more complex interconnec-tion patterns. The assumption that signals flow in both directions along the links in Fig. 2.4 and 2.5 is an abstraction of these phenomena. Thus, for example, if five of the six inputs to a particular cube-recognizer are strongly active, this raises the chances that an ambiguous sixth vertex will be interpreted as fitting into that cube (and seen as a subjective contour). Assuming ground–plane or other depth estimates to be available, one could build a quite robust and effective recognizer for blocks-world scenes by recoding existing AI programs in terms of the computational units of the Appendix and relaxation networks like Fig. 2.4.

This mutual interaction of lateral inhibition, top-down and bottom-up process-ing is what we referred to as relaxation in the introduction. In systematic terms, there is always an interplay between (active) elements expressing the internal information-processing goals of the organism and (active) elements computing properties of input stimuli. If time were stopped for an instant, the system could be seen as relaxing ("settling down") to a consistent interpretation of the sensory input. *Relaxation is the mechanism suggested here as the fundamental computa-tional principle of neural networks.* The main reason for developing the cube example in such detail was to provide a concrete example of relaxation computa-tion in visual recognition. Most people are able to get an intuitive feel for the relaxation process when attempting to perceive reversible figures like the Necker cube (Fig. 2.7) or recognize trick images like the Mooney faces of Fig. 2.1. (If you have not yet picked out the face in the lower left of Fig. 2.1, it might help to know that only the upper half is relevant and that it is the image of a woman, facing to her right and down.) Because nature often requires decisions to be made in haste, the relaxation process is assumed to have a mode that we will call "hyperconvergent"; it settles down to answers quickly rather than allowing enough time to be certain of the best overall answer (Ratcliff, 1978). Mutual inhibition quite rapidly selects the maximum of a set of contenders; global influences that are "distant" may be too late to affect the outcome. It is also important to remember that the relaxation process only works well for a limited set of contenders. The connection structure of the net and top-down priming are assumed to keep the relaxation computations in a feasible range. A more techni-cal consideration of these issues is given in Feldman & Ballard (1980).

On Imaging as Simulation

The model gives us a particularly simple way to describe visual imaging. It is what happens when the perceptual net operates top-down without sensory input. This same capacity could also be used to prime the visual system with expecta-tions for the next fixation. The priming of visual perception networks (along with directed eye movements) provides for an elegant way of using context to facili-tate the relaxation of new image input and its integration with existing percepts. There is a great deal of evidence that appropriate imaging instructions can aid or impede visual perception tasks (Cooper & Shepard, 1973; Neisser, 1976). This is explained in our model by the fact that the net is facilitated or competed for by the preset image. Notice that a visual image (just like a percept) is a state of activity of the network and the issue of iconic versus propositional representation (Kosslyn & Schwartz, 1978) doesn't arise. There is considerable evidence that visual images are mostly reconstructed from highly abstracted internal descriptions (Kosslyn & Schwartz, 1978), again consistent with our model. Visual imagery is just one instance of the ability of neural networks (in this model) to be operated with input and output connections suppressed. We refer to this as *simulation* and posit it as the fundamental mechanism underlying memory reorganization, planning, and other higher mental activities. It would be inconsistent with our connectionist viewpoint to postulate some metacognitive process that manipulated an abstract representation of, for example, visual memories. What is consistent (and seems plausible) is a higher-order network (cf. Edelman & Mountcastle, 1978) with input and output connections to the visual memory network, among others. Goals of the organism, both long- and short-term, find expression as top-down biasing of perception and action networks.

On Grandmother Cells

The cube-recognition example works out fairly neatly because we assumed separate units for each perceptual entity at each point in the visual space. Ignoring for now the fact that retinal images undergo continual change, we consider the question of whether one could really have a separate unit for each perceptual entity or whether some more diffuse representation is needed. This is our version of the classical issue of whether or not there is a specific (or pontifical) cell which fires exactly when a person recognizes his grandmother.

Consider the status, in a net like Fig. 2.5B, of the concept "a cube of size 2 at (18, 23)." It is technically correct to say that this concept does not exist except as a pattern of activity in the network. But there is nothing mysterious in this statement that should lead us into waveform processing or other occult practices. It simply turns out that the memory organization being employed doesn't happen to have a single element dedicated to that collection of attributes. We should not be surprised when pontifical cells tuned to a particular object are found or when they are not found. As we see later in the discussion of learning, the particular organization differs among individuals.

There is a reformulation of the question that appears to help: "Does each cell carry out a specific computation that can be characterized directly?" This is meant to separate direct, connectionist views from those which postulate that (higher) mental events appear only as mass properties of neural activity. Even if we decide this question in favor of specific units (which we do), we have to resolve the issue of whether the specific computations always partition the perceptual space in a way that makes it meaningful to talk about a "grandmother cell.'' The distinction can be made sharper with a simple example. Suppose there were three units that mutually fired one another and between them exactly captured some concept (e.g., apple or Granny Betty). Any magic of neurophysiology that identified one of these units would surely show that it was a pontifical cell, but of course if one of the other two units failed, there would be major deficits. In our formulation the group of three cells could be treated as a conceptual unit that would not be externally distinguishable from a single cell. A consortium of five cells with overlapping functions provides a perfectly plausible model (cf. Barlow, 1972) of individual function that overcomes the problem of cell death. (Approximately 10^5 of our 10^{11} cerebral cells die each day; the probability of losing even two of the five collaborators in a lifetime is negligible.)

Redundancy is not, however, the major problem with models based on pontifical cells. A more basic issue is the representation of complex concepts. Suppose we agree that the cube of Fig. 2.4 represents a die of purple velvet with green spots showing the numbers 1, 2, 4. Do you now have a cell dedicated to this bizarre concept? If not, how is the new concept retained in memory?

We first propose a special purpose solution to this problem for the perception of cubes and then extend it to more general situations. The central idea is spatial *coherence* of the (real or imagined) image. We suggested earlier that separate (but interacting) computations of color, texture, lighting, etc., are feasible and appear to be present in animal visual systems. If these are kept coordinated through spatially specific connections, all the properties of a given point in visual space will automatically be grouped together. Figure 2.6 gives an extremely crude schematic view of how this could work. Obviously enough the relaxation computations in the various modalities would interact, leading to all sorts of useful and exotic perceptual rivalry effects.

Still remaining with the cube example, we can see (Fig. 2.5B) that there are a large number of equivalent representations for the information about a purple velvet die of size 2 at (18, 23), for example, depending on which collections of properties happen to be explicitly represented in a single unit. There is some evidence (Paivio, 1975) that shape and position are computed together (i.e., Fig. 2.5A is right) as our example, ordinary intuition, and traditional philosophy would suggest. But it seems likely that reflectance, texture, and other image properties are associated with an object (indirectly) by being in corresponding positions in appropriate internal spatial frames.

The general idea is that each cell (or unit) carries out a computation that can be sharply defined but may only be meaningful as part of a larger unit. Exactly the same condition applies to individual components of an electronic circuit. In addition, each unit will be involved in more than one kind of computation. This has already shown up repeatedly in the example. For instance, in Fig. 2.4B, a 90° line is part of the support for either an L- or an A-joint. More generally, a unit like an edge detector could be involved in the computation of texture, color, and

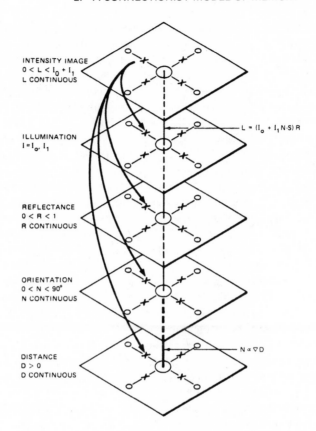

INTENSITY IMAGE
$0 < L < I_0 + I_1$
L CONTINUOUS

ILLUMINATION
$I = I_0, I_1$

$L = (I_0 + I_1 N \cdot S) R$

REFLECTANCE
$0 < R < 1$
R CONTINUOUS

ORIENTATION
$0 < N < 90°$
N CONTINUOUS

DISTANCE
$D > 0$
D CONTINUOUS

$N \propto \nabla D$

A parallel computational model for recovering intrinsic images

FIG. 2.6. Separate visions computations. From (Barrow & Tenenbaum, 1978).

other properties in addition to shape. All of this further weakens the notion of pontifical cells without in any way sacrificing specificity of function in the unit.

Putting Things in Place

Finally, the model must say something about how visual percepts are used in carrying out actions. There is general agreement that people maintain a spatially oriented representation of their environment (probably two—egocentric and allocentric according to O'Keefe & Nadel, 1978) that is used in sensory–motor activities. We suggest that this spatial map is the locus of connections between networks for seeing an object and those for acting upon it. The present model suggests that detailed visual processing (particularly of shape) is mostly done foveally by a network dedicated to recognition. Somehow the results of this analysis must be linked into the spatial model (without any symbols being transmitted). Suppose there were a connection network (cf. Fig. 2.8) that could link the units representing any percept with any unit representing a point in the spatial map (Section 3.3 describes why such a complete interconnection network is not implausible). It is certainly reasonable to assume that the fixation networks also activate (potentiate) the units in the spatial map corresponding to the region of space being examined. Then when the units representing some particular percept win the relaxation contest, we have just the two units active that we would like to be linked. The most obvious way to maintain this connection is (*mirabile dictu*) a mutually activating closed loop, which inhibits its rivals. The dynamic linking of a percept to its place in the mental map is one example of short-term memory (STM). In Section 3.3, we consider the question of dynamic links more carefully and suggest why the capacity of STM is so limited.

The model proposes that various "accidental" properties of the stimulus, like color or texture, could be independently linked to the same unit in the spatial map. Going beyond visual memory, notice also that the contextually correct sense of an ambiguous input to a semantic net will produce more loops than its rivals. We suggest that other conceptual frameworks (e.g., conceptual cases, scripts) provide the same kind of coherent structure with focus of attention playing the role of foveation, but that takes us beyond the scope of this paper (cf. Neisser, 1976; Schank, 1980).

In summary, we postulate a connectionist system of specific units whose computations are best specified directly (the obvious model). The ontological status of pontifical cells and complex concepts are seen to present difficult but not insurmountable problems for such an approach.

Schemas

Many theories of higher mental functions rely heavily on the notion of schemas (frames, scripts, etc.). These are taken either to be cohesive descriptions of situations or to be programlike sequences of activities, often with the distinction blurred. In the present model these two notions of schema coalesce in a natural way; for example, the description of a scene is a way of perceiving it. There is no fixed partition of the network into schemas; rather the collection of nodes active at a given time carry out the behavior attributed to schemas. The "activation" of a schema becomes part of the relaxation process as, for example, in Fig. 2.7. This also suggests that our compound units will sometimes be task specific, with some subunit participating in several compounds at different times. So long as the behaviors are kept separate this creates no major problems for the animal or for our analysis techniques.

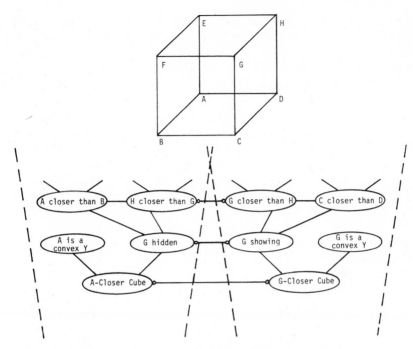

FIG. 2.7. Network fragments for the two readings of the Necker cube.

Visual Memory and Perception

The task of recognizing an isolated cube does not begin to capture the complexity of visual perception. The purpose of this interlude is to suggest how the mechanisms described earlier could be extended to a realistic theory of visual perception, memory, and imagery. The idea is to consolidate the major findings from various disciplines in the uniform framework provided by our distributed information-processing paradigm.

The most obvious simplification in the example was the assumption that a complete image was presented statically to the vision network. But even complete static scenes present major perception problems not dealt with in the example—primarily the body separation problem. The example assumed that each image was relaxed against a single model, but real scenes consist of many objects occluding one another. A great deal of work (particularly in AI) has been devoted to uncovering cues which facilitate the assignment of visual features to separate objects. In the blocks world, certain joint types (like the *T* joints emphasized in Fig. 2.3) provide strong cues for body separation. In general, any discontinuity in depth, color, lighting, etc., provides a potential cue that separate objects are involved. In the extended version of our model, these separation cues would be computed by networks operating on color, reflectance, depth, and other cues as suggested by Fig. 2.6. The total relaxation of the image would involve consistency of separation cues from different sources, assignment of visual features to object-models, and the agreement of the projection of the 3-D reconstructed scene with the image. All of this parallels current developments in machine perception research and appears to present no inherent difficulties.

We know, however, that people do not perceive complete static scenes. Essentially all of our detailed perception of form is done on foveal images of 1–2°. This is, in a way, strongly consistent with the highly elaborated connectionist model suggested above. The massive connectivity required to relax the input against all possible object-models is concentrated in a small part of the visual field. Further reinforcement is provided by the experiments (Kosslyn & Schwartz, 1978) on the fovea of the mind's eye and by the fact that retinotopic foveal mappings extend rather far up the visual system. We propose that images are understood by being mapped onto object-representations in a kind of mind's eye; this is the same notion of spatially coherent frameworks utilized several times before. The detailed fitting of image data to object-models is done foveally by relaxation networks and the results are encoded in a spatial world model and used for further tasks, including goal-oriented perception.

2.3.   LEARNING, REORGANIZING, FORGETTING

The preceding discussion has suggested how visual memory networks might function in visual perception and imagery, given that these networks were already elaborated. We now consider how these networks could undergo change in response to experience. Traditional network models of learning have concentrated on how the weights associated with various connections could change as a function of experience. There are a large number of other issues to be addressed, but adaptation through the changing of weights is a good place to start.

We begin by considering the traditional Necker cube (Fig. 2.7) and ask how one might "learn" to perceive only one of the rival interpretations. In terms of our model, each interpretation would be a network that was self-reinforcing and had inhibitory links to the opposing network at several levels (e.g., vertices getting different interpretations). The perceptual rivalry effect arises because neither network clearly dominates the other. Because there is no third consistent interpretation and the system is hyperconvergent, people experience periodic flips from one interpretation to the other. (One might assume that some kind of habituation causes the break out of a stable interpretation.) Suppose it becomes advantageous to perceive the less common of the readings preferentially (to my knowledge this experiment has not been done). The model predicts that if the mutual inhibition links could become asymmetric the system would exhibit the desired bias toward that reading of the Necker cube.

Change in the weight of connections is universally associated with synaptic plasticity in neurons and there is no reason to question this thesis. Although truly compelling experiments on learning through synaptic plasticity have not been brought off, there is a wide range of evidence of both presynaptic and postsynaptic plasticity as a correlate of behavioral change.

Given that changes in the weight of connections are brought about by modification of synapses, there remains the question of what controls the modification. The most common suggestion is that a connection is reinforced each time that it fires and its unit (cell) also fires. This is almost certainly part of the story, but it omits two important considerations—consequences and importance. If the paired firing gives rise immediately to some dire consequence, strengthening the connection can't be adaptive. At least some key connections will have their strength determined by eventual outcomes of the subnetwork's computations.

It is also true that not everything that is repeated is learned equally. The standard view of this phenomenon is that there is a "second circuit" that innervates the cerebral cortex. Signals in this network specify the value and importance of the overall activity. Once again, there is no definitive evidence that this actually occurs, but there are results from many separate kinds of research that are best explained by a second circuit.

Everyone has had personal experience of the "indelible imprint" of the situations surrounding really crucial life episodes. The most straightforward explanation of how this comes about is the activation of a pervasive importance circuit (Livingston's (1967) "now print"). A detailed anatomical model of how the importance circuits might work in people is presented in Eccles (1978) along with a variety of findings supporting the second-circuit view. Very specific second-circuit mechanisms have been found in invertebrates (Kandel, 1979). Such mechanisms have been postulated to explain detailed findings in animal memory (Thompson, 1976), especially the role of the limbic system. The fact that certain lesions prevent people from being able to learn new things without causing other deficits is also often explained by a second-circuit model (Wickelgren, 1979).

We assume that there is such a network for signaling the importance of ongoing activity in some section of the memory net and rely rather heavily on this assumption. Returning to the Necker cube example, we assume that whatever contingencies caused one interpretation to be preferred are reflected in the value signal. When the Necker-cube perception subnets choose the preferred option, the value signal is positive, and the active connections are reinforced. Notice that the less preferred reading of the Necker cube remains intact and subsequent experience could potentially reverse the dominance relationship. In general, the current model assumes that there are normally several networks representing alternative interpretations of a given situation, arranged with certain dominance relationships. All of these alternatives relax against incoming data (and each other) and can potentially become dominant. These less-preferred networks also participate in reorganization processes (discussed later) and may evolve to be a priori dominant for certain combinations of internal and external signals (cf. Edelman & Mountcastle, 1978).

One could go a good deal further with the notion of learning through changes in the strength of connections. The classical work on perceptrons (Minsky & Papert, 1969) shows that linear adaptive networks with no a priori structure can be made to adapt to a surprisingly broad range of functions by pure parameter learning. Because the visual system has quite a lot of structure and nonlinear computations are present, a great deal can be done with learning based only on the changing of connection strengths. But no one has suggested that there are connections to prespecify exactly the possible concepts arising in human experience; something else must be happening.

There are a number of reasons for believing that there are not preexisting connections for all the new concepts that might arise. For one thing, the entire genome contains only 10^9 bits, which is not enough to specify completely 10^{15} connections. And it is inconceivable that the entire course of civilization has been anticipated. So there is some way of encoding new knowledge in the network. Encoding new knowledge appears to present no difficulties to a symbol-processing theory because everything is interpreted anyway. But we know that new concepts can be integrated into vision, for example, in a way that is not distinguishable from the way older percepts are treated. It does not take significantly more time or effort for an expert shortstop to recognize a double-play ball than to solve standard perception problems. The question becomes one of how new percepts and concepts get integrated into the neural network.

We begin with consideration of a more basic problem, the establishment of connections between similar concepts in different modalities (Fig. 2.2). How does the visual percept *apple* come to be linked to the speech network for saying the word? Although there is some growth of neural connections in adults, it is not nearly fast enough to account for your ability to incorporate the new notion that the Hebrew word for ''apple'' is ''tapooach.'' The appropriate potential connections must already be in place. But we can't believe that exactly the connections needed for linking images (including man-made) with appropriate speech acts are wired in, and there are not nearly enough synapses for total connectivity. This apparent paradox can be resolved quite elegantly by assuming random connections (Fig. 2.8) between units of the visual centers with units of the speech centers.

Figure 2.8 is of course highly stylized, but it does depict what we believe to be the basic situation. If there are layers of units randomly connected through (e.g., two) intermediate levels, the chances of there being a path from any unit on the left (percept apple) to the correct one on the right (speech-act apple) are essentially perfect for realistic choices of numbers. The problem of learning what to say becomes one of strengthening the appropriate synapses.

There are really two problems: the immediate capture of the new linkage (short-term memory or STM) and its permanent integration into the connection structure of the network (long-term memory or LTM). The model assumes that LTM is the result of structural changes representable largely as synaptic weights.

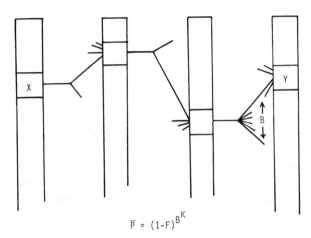

$$\overline{P} = (1-F)^{B^K}$$

$\overline{P}$ = Probability that there is <u>no</u> link from X to Y

N = Number of Units in a "Layer"

B = Number of Randomly Outgoing Branches/Unit

F = B/N (Branching Factor)

K = Number of Intermediate Levels (2 in Diagram Above)

$\overline{P}$ for B = 1000; Different Numbers of Levels and Units

K= \ N=	10^6	10^7	10^8
0	.999	.9999	.99999
1	.367	.905	.989
2	10^{-440}	10^{-44}	10^{-5}

Expected # Paths = $(1-\overline{P}_{K-1}) \cdot B$

FIG. 2.8. Making a connection.

But STM happens much too rapidly to be accounted for by structural change. The model agrees with the conventional wisdom (based on a great deal of evidence [Deutsch & Deutsch, 1975]) that short-term memory is basically an electrical phenomenon relying upon the mutual activation of sets of units. We assume this to be an intermediate step in the formation of permanent structural changes in the strength of connections of the network. Thus STM and LTM are, respectively, electrical activation and structural modification of a neural network for recognition, action, etc.

If we assume that short-term memory is captured as some subnetwork of mutually firing units, one might think that the repetition rule of strengthening active synapses would suffice to solidify long-term memory. One difficulty with this notion is that people's LTM is highly organized and is not just a recapitulation of experience. There are problems even establishing a single link by repetition. Because each neuron sends activation to all of its successors, quite a lot of units in a network like that in Fig. 2.8 will be incidentally potentiated by any ongoing loop. This situation is discussed briefly later and in detail in Feldman and Ballard (1980). It does not appear that pure reinforcement would be adequate to select just the correct paths to be strengthened for the LTM trace with enough speed and reliability. What would work is for the units on the right to transmit some marker chemical backwards through its synapses and for the intermediate layer cells to do the same. (Retrograde transport through synapses is well established and is, in fact, one of the main methods for studying detailed neuroanatomy.) The permanent reinforcement of a synapse would depend on its being both a path from the target and a path to the goal, that is, being on a correct connection link. There would be several correct paths (see the formula in Fig. 2.8), and some of the appropriate synapses on each would be reinforced. The thresholds are presumably an appropriate trade-off between noise resistance and sensitivity depending on the expected number of paths. As mentioned earlier, we also suppose that reinforcement may depend on additional signals that the outcome of the immediate firing pattern was favorable and important (e.g., from a brainstem or frontal network).

Short-term memory appears to be more difficult to capture in a connectionist model. Serious computational problems arise when one tries to implement the notion of a dynamic loop in a network like that of Fig. 2.8. The basic problem is that our units (like neurons) cannot selectively activate only some of their outputs. This means that any activation loop in a network like Fig. 2.8 will, with high probability, activate many units in addition to those desired for the dynamic connection being maintained.

The problem of maintaining dynamic linkages in a connectionist model is a central one and is discussed in detail in Feldman and Ballard (1980). A simplified version of the problem is shown in Fig. 2.9. The figure depicts two layers of units (A–I and a–i), which, as before, could represent images and spoken words. The problem is to arrange intermediate units so that any pairing of units

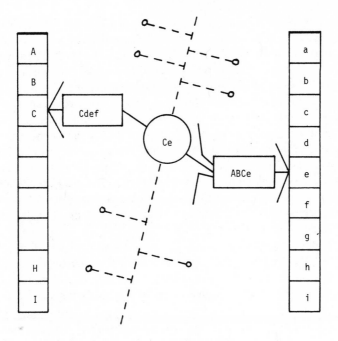

N = Number of Units in a Layer (9 here)

B = Number of Outgoing (Incoming) Branches/Unit (3 here)

Circular Units come one per possible pair, e.g. Ce

Dotted links are inhibition of other circular units
     involving C,e (in this example)

Assuming (unrealistically) 2-way links, this network will
     support any pairing

N^2 intermediate nodes are required for perfect dynamic memory

FIG. 2.9.   Dynamic links, a tiny example.

from the two layers can be dynamically maintained by the network without any cross-talk. The solution presented in Fig. 2.9 is very crude but does seem to be illustrative.

We assume that there are only nine units per layer and that each unit can have at most three inputs and three outputs. We also assume that any active input to a unit will deterministically cause the unit to fire. The requirement of arbitrary pairing is solved by the crude device of having one dedicated unit (the round one) for every possible pairing. The other intermediate cells are needed to meet the fan-in/fan-out constraints. We further assume that each connection is symmetric, representing a link in each direction. With all these assumptions, it works. If *C* and *e* are activated, the loop *C-Cdef-Ce-ABCe-e* will be activated and maintain the association between C and e. If the round unit Ce inhibits totally all other round units involving either C or e, then no other association involving either of these end units could be maintained. Of course, if two pairings tried to get established simultaneously, the network would get confused, but this is inherent in any network that could just as easily have done it the opposite way.

The assumptions about two-way links and unitary thresholds can be relaxed without difficulty. But the problem of N^2 intermediate nodes is serious. Notice, however, that if there are less than N^2 intermediate nodes, then some paths must share intermediate nodes. This guarantees that not all sets of pairings can be learned without interference. There are a number of possible intermediate networks between the concise Fig. 2.8 and the maximally flexible Fig. 2.9, and it is not yet clear how to choose among them. But even the crude arguments presented here are suggestive of why so few new associations can be dynamically retained in short-term memory.

The preceding discussion concerns how a connectionist path from one "center" to another might be selected from a randomly interconnected network by bidirectional tagging for reinforcement. We suggest that the *recruitment* of units to represent new concepts comes about in essentially the same way. Any new concept is perceived as some activation pattern of networks representing existing concepts. If we assume—and there is good reason to do so (Szentágothai, 1978b)—that there are large areas of units that are randomly connected, it will turn out (by the properties of randomness) that certain cells respond much better than their neighbors to the new combination. The network whose activation is the new concept will be mutually potentiating, and the *reciprocal firing* of the units of the network constitutes the short-term memory of the concept. If the new concept is worth learning, the importance signal causes the units that happen to resonate to the new concept to reinforce their active connections. Thus some new units are recruited to help represent the new concept. Notice that the new units will be connected to their constituents and consequences just as semantic net models would like. Wickelgren (1979) suggests that this recruiting ability (which he calls "chunking") is distinctive to birds and mammals and is the main thing lost in amnesia. There are a large number of unresolved issues in representing knowledge as networks. These appear to be neither harder nor easier in the current framework than in traditional AI and information-processing psychology, but a somewhat different set of problems comes to the fore. For example, the active network is a very fast pattern matcher; the problem is to decide how the "pattern" enters and leaves the network.

Deferred Outcomes (More Speculative)

Very primitive animals have some ability to remember not to re-ingest some noxious substance. The evolutionary advantage of this is striking and it is obvious that animals with a complex metabolism might not know for some time whether something ingested was noxious. Rats can do one-trial avoidance learning of tastes with effects delayed several hours (Bureš & Burešová, 1979), and many studies of animal memory are based on this finding. Any model of memory must make some assertions about how short- and intermediate-term memory work and how they interact with long-term memory.

It was suggested earlier that the mutual potentiation at various levels needed for relaxation could also lead to a kind of reverberatory short-term memory. Short-term memory is much stronger, decays rapidly, and has easy access (is, in fact, unavoidable).

Intermediate memory on the order of hours is hypothesized to be the basis for deferred learning and long-term memory reorganization. The model proposes that intermediate memories are reactivated (perhaps during sleep) and the consequences of each significant activity evaluated by *simulation*. The integration and reorganization of long-term memory is hypothesized to be part of this procedure. Things that work well in the simulation get reinforced as described previously and things that seem to go badly get reduced weights.

This discussion slips by so many long-standing issues that even I am a little abashed. But all of its essential steps are known to be plausible. Intermediate-term memory can be affected chemically and electrically as evidenced by disruption studies. Dreams do (at least sometimes) have the nature of a simulation (Jouvet, 1978; Neisser, 1976). Memory does seem to be consolidated during sleep (Bloch, Hennevin, & Leconte, 1979). And the computational requirements for the model to do all this are not excessive. Unless Lashley was right and memory is impossible, something along these lines is really happening, and we should be able to reason about it.

On Forgetting

Let us begin with "remembering." This usually means being able to reconstruct some outcome (e.g., speech) from a partial specification. In the model, if the specification (plus the context) were sufficient to evoke the right response (judged internally or externally), we would say that something was remembered. Recognition, as opposed to recall, refers to cases where a great deal of input is provided as well as those requiring only a binary answer. The familiar phenomena of blocking and tip-of-the-tongue can be viewed as failures of the relaxation process to converge properly. Trying too hard continues to raise the activation levels of the potentiated undesired units.

The difficulty of reconstructing an activation pattern sufficiently like an old one will depend on many factors in the present context and in the histories of the units involved in that memory. If all units were immortal, then there would be a sense in which nothing committed to long-term memory would be totally lost. Weak memories would be those whose units had become involved in other networks and couldn't effectively inhibit alternative organizations. But because new concepts are constantly being built using already committed units and recruiting others, we would literally have no way to determine just what was "remembered" and what was "reconstructed" (Anderson & Bower, 1973; Neisser, 1976). This is bad news for many experimental paradigms but seems to be quite good as a way of coping with the world.

Fitting the Data

Any professional psychologist who has gotten this far will be terribly upset by the paucity of experimental data that have been brought to bear on the model. And with good reason. There have been thousands of relevant experiments and several robust findings that must be accounted for in any serious attempt to explain visual memory. The model as presented is really more of a modeling paradigm; it suggests a class of models that is claimed to be useful. It is not difficult (for a computer scientist) to design a particular model of our kind to compute exactly like any particular detailed model (e.g., HAM by Anderson and Bower (1973) in the literature, and this model will, of course, equally fit the experimental data. Models of the sort suggested here also appear to be a natural way to encode probabilistic processes like those of Ratcliff (1978). The experiments mentioned in the introduction to this chapter could be explained by the assumption that any interesting aspect of the previewed image is enough to throw the forced-choice relaxation in the right direction.

The challenge is to come up with a uniform collection of mutually compatible models that fit as many as possible of the best-established findings. For example, a number of studies (Anderson & Bower, 1973; Collins & Loftus, 1975) suggest that the relaxation time should be proportional to the number of alternatives. The main claim of this chapter is that this enterprise is possible (at least conceivable) in the framework described earlier. I am convinced that such an effort would at least uncover many interesting problems and interrelationships. There does not appear to be another framework that presents the same opportunities, but a parallel enterprise with a different theoretical base could be very exciting as well.

What Experiments Does it Suggest?

Thousands of them, of course. Interesting questions arise at all levels, from detailed neurochemistry to the abstract mathematics of relaxation nets. Most of these are old questions under active study by people far more capable than I of formulating experiments. The hope would be that the model will help some investigators frame their questions in interesting and useful ways.

There also seem to be a number of new issues that arise from this study. A key question is the status of abstract symbols in the brain. If anything nearly as simple as the model is present in animal brains, some indication of relaxation cones should be detectable. Neuroanatomical evidence will be highly relevant; the model predicts changes in unit responses with stimulation of higher centers.

One could imagine raising kittens in a blocks-world and looking for detectors of vertex types or other higher visual constructs. Behavioral tests of particular assumptions using interference, perceptual rivalry, and reaction time paradigms appear to be feasible. The relaxation model predicts that spreading activation with quenching such as that found in Swinney (1979) will be ubiquitous. The spatial coherence assumption should also be amenable to behavior testing.

There is a growing body of work dedicated to explaining visual perception in terms of relaxation models. In our laboratory, current efforts are focused on an implementation of Origami world (Kanade, 1978) and an attempt to describe relaxation networks that combine intrinsic images (Barrow & Tenenbaum, 1978), top-down influences, and optic flow. The problems of integrating multiple views and of treating moving images in this framework lie ahead.

Going beyond the theory of visual memory, one would want to attempt the same level of formulation for other modalities (e.g., speech) and for higher mental functions. Obviously there would be a great need for the study of the properties of networks like ours and how they could function, develop, adapt, and evolve. Both mathematics and computer simulation could be used in this work (cf. Hinton, 1977). Another set of issues involves the application of these ideas on (very!) distributed computing to computer science, particularly VLSI.

The most attractive feature of the model is that it allows results from many different experimental paradigms to be described in a uniform framework. The hope is that the various experimental findings will constrain the space of *models* to the point where we can hope to set forth *theories* of visual memory and other mental functions.

APPENDIX: THE SYMBOLIC NEURAL UNIT

The body of the paper assumes that one can develop a uniform modeling scheme for describing visual memory at many different levels of detail. We present here a brief description of such a modeling scheme, based on the use of communicating finite state machines as the unit of computation.

The first chapter of this book provides a brief overview of the main neurophysiological findings that must be taken into account in any attempt to build biologically plausible models of visual memory. Even that abbreviated presentation makes the case for humility in this enterprise compelling—why not despair of the effort altogether? We will try to outline briefly why the abstract modeling of neurons and neural nets is not unreasonable and why we have chosen the model that is being employed here. More details can be found in Feldman and

Ballard (1980). The crucial question of the scientific usefulness of the model cannot be addressed in advance, of course.

First, there is every reason to believe that the information-processing abstraction captures at least some of the behavior of living systems. When the lateral giant axon of the crayfish fires, its tail flips—always. There is general agreement that the evolution and life of the crayfish contain elements that maintain this cause-and-effect relationship over a considerable range of conditions. Slightly more complex information-processing models have had considerable success in helping to explicate rhythmic functions like the swimming of the leech (Friesen & Stent, 1978). In higher animals the situation is much more complex, but information-processing abstractions are commonly used in describing particular experiments, especially in sensory systems.

Whatever the abstraction of a single neuron, the problem of describing the behavior of collections of neurons remains a central one. One would like to develop a formalism in which a subnetwork of abstract neurons can be replaced by a single element that represents the behavior of that subnetwork. If the formalism can deal with the single elements and collapsed subnetworks uniformly, we have the makings of a recursive structure that will support the modeling of a wide range of systems at varying levels of detail.

For us, an abstract neural element is represented as a finite-state machine that communicates with other such machines. The internal states of the machine are associated with meaningful interpretations (given meaningful names in the diagrams). At the simplest level these might be, for example, Firing, Refractory, or Idle. A simple example of such an element is given in Fig. 2.10. The table representation of the finite-state machine has the states listed along the side and the inputs to the element (i.e., finite-state machine) along the top. The unlabeled column describes what the unit will do in the absence of input. The entries in the table represent the state transitions. Computations of the element may involve any or all of the following three outcomes: (1) change of internal state; (2) change of potential (explained later); and (3) generation of output signals (also explained later).

The circuit of Fig. 2.10 is the simplest stable generator of cyclic patterns and is believed to underlie the control of rhythmic behavior in invertebrates (Friesen & Stent, 1978). Each unit is assumed to be a spontaneous generator of output unless inhibited (the [?] entry says we don't know how soon fatigue would set in). The cycle time of the network is determined by the recovery time of each unit. This can be fixed or can be governed by external input to the subsystem. Notice that the subsystem has only 3 (out of 27) stable states and could itself be modeled as a unit with 3 states: A, B, or C firing. It appears that this kind of encapsulation is not only needed for our understanding of these subsystems but is close to what the rest of the animal's nervous system interacts with.

At higher abstraction levels state names take on situation and task-specific meanings such as Swimming Ahead, Stopped, and Activated. Neuronal units

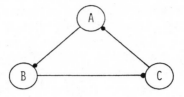

STATE-MESSAGE TABLE FOR A, B, C IS IDENTICAL

	INHIBITORY MESSAGE	——
INHIBITED	INHIBITED	RECOVERING
RECOVERING	INHIBITED	(REC. TIME) FIRING
FIRING	INHIBITED	[?]

SYSTEM STATE:

A	B	C	
F	I	R	A FIRES
I	R	F	C FIRES
R	F	I	B FIRES
F	I	R	.
I	R	F	.
.			.

FIG. 2.10.   Table representation of neuronal timing loop.

also have a numerical value, *potential,* associated with the state of the element. At the lowest level this can be identified with the instantaneous membrane potential of a neuron. More interestingly, at higher levels this can represent the overall level of receptivity of a subnetwork or neural module. The result can be seen as selective potentiation (priming) of units, as used in the body of this chapter.

The output signal from an element will have a symbolic name and a single parameter representing its strength. The signals are not physically distinct: The labels come from our outside interpretation of system function, like the labels on an electric circuit diagram. Depending on the context, the strength of a signal could model a firing frequency, an ion flow, or a volley from a compound unit. For the simple example of Fig. 2.10 neither the potential of a unit or the strength of output signals are assigned numerical values. In the cube example of Fig. 2.4, the strength of output would reflect the confidence of a unit, and the potential could be the result of the algebraic sum of inputs.

The other main point concerns the complexity of the computations associated with the states of the table. The relation between the strengths of signals directed towards a cell and the strength of input that it sees can be very complex. There are issues of signal leakage, spatial summation, temporal summation, dendritic interaction of signals, among others. For an individual modeling task, the scientist will have to make use of a variety of techniques available within the framework. For example, one can choose to model a section of the dendritic tree as a separate element. For complex units, capturing the effect of simultaneous signals to different subunits involves a major open problem in the related areas of computer science. The important point is that it is at least conceptually feasible to model the information-processing behavior of the nervous system at many different levels of abstraction within the same theoretical framework. It is this framework that is implicitly used in discussing the various aspects of memory in the text. A more detailed presentation of the model with connections to biology and computer science is given in Feldman (1979), and a quite technical consideration of the subject, in Feldman and Ballard (1980).

ACKNOWLEDGMENTS

The preparation of this paper was supported in part by the Alfred P. Sloan Foundation under Grant No. 78-4-15.

There is no single idea in this paper for which I would be ready to press a claim for originality. It is a pleasure to acknowledge the contributions made by the students in my seminars while on leave at Stanford and back home at Rochester. In addition to the students, several colleagues have suggested improvements over earlier versions of the paper, including: James Allen, Paul Coleman, David Feldman, Lynn Goldsmith, Pat Hayes, Geoff Hinton, Peggy Meeker, David Taylor, and David Zipser. And the current version could clearly benefit from your suggestions.

REFERENCES

*Anderson, J. A. A theory for the recognition of items from short memorized lists. *Psychological Review,* November 1973, *80*(6), 417–438.

Anderson, J. R., & Bower, G. H. *Human associative memory.* Washington, D.C.: V. H. Winston and Sons, 1973.

Ballard, D. H. Generalizing the Hough Transform to detect arbitrary shapes. University of Rochester: Computer Science Department, TR55, October 1979.

---

*not explicitly referenced in chapter

*Ballard, D. H., & Brown, C. M. *Computer vision.* Englewood Cliffs, New Jersey: Prentice Hall Inc., 1981.

*Ballard, D. H., Brown, C. M., & Feldman, J. A. An approach to knowledge-directed image analysis. In A. R. Hanson & E. M. Riseman (Eds.), *Computer vision systems.* New York: Academic Press, 1978.

Barlow, H. B. Single units and sensation: A neuron doctrine for perceptual psychology? *Perception,* 1972, *1,* 371–394.

Barrow, H. G., & Tenenbaum, J. M. Recovering intrinsic scene characteristics from images. In A. R. Hanson and E. M. Riseman (Eds.), *Computer vision systems.* New York: Academic Press, 1978.

Bloch, V., Hennevin, E., & Leconte, P. Relation between paradoxical sleep and memory processes. In M. A. B. Brazier (Ed.), *Brain mechanisms in memory and learning: From the single neuron to man.* International Brain Research Organization Monograph Series (Vol. 4). New York: Raven Press, 1979.

Bureš, J., & Burešová, O. Neurophysiological analysis of conditioned taste aversion. In M. A. B. Brazier (Ed.), *Brain mechanisms in memory and learning: From the single neuron to man.* International Brain Research Organization Monograph Series (Vol. 4). New York: Raven Press, 1979.

*Buser, P. A., & Roguel-Buser, A. (Eds.). *Cerebral correlates of conscious experience.* Amsterdam: North Holland Publishing Co., 1978.

Collins, A. M., & Loftus, E. F. A spreading-activation theory of semantic processing. *Psychological Review,* November 1975, *82,* 407–429.

Cooper, L. A., & Shepard, R. N. Chronometric studies of the rotation of mental images. In W. G. Chase (Ed.), *Visual information processing.* New York: Academic Press, Inc., 1973.

Deutsch, D., & Deutsch, J. A. *Short-term memory.* New York: Academic Press, 1975.

Eccles, J. C. An instruction-selection hypothesis of cerebral learning. In P. A. Buser and A. Roguel-Buser (Eds.), *Cerebral correlates of conscious experience.* Amsterdam: North Holland Publishing Co., 1978.

Edelman, G., & Mountcastle, V B. *The mindful brain.* Boston, Massachusetts: MIT Press, 1978.

Feldman, J. A. A distributed information processing model of visual memory. University of Rochester: Computer Science Department, TR52, December 1979.

Feldman, J. A., & Ballard, D. H. Computing with connections. University of Rochester: Computer Science Department, TR72, 1980.

*Feldman, J. A., & Nigam, A. A model and proof technique for message-based systems. *SIAM Journal on Computing,* 1980.

*Feldman, J. A., & Yakimovsky, Y. Decision theory and artificial intelligence I: A semantics-based region analyzer. *Artificial Intelligence,* 1974, *5,* 349–371.

Freedman, J., & Haber, R. N. One reason why we rarely forget a face. *Bulletin of the Psychonomic Society,* 1974, *3*(2).

Friesen, W. O., & Stent, G. S. Neural circuits for generating rhythmic movements. *Annual Review of Biophysics and Bioengineering,* 1978, *7,* 37–61.

Haber, R. N. Perception of visual space in scenes and in pictures. In L. D. Harmon (Ed.), *Interrelations of the communicative senses.* 1979. National Science Foundation 8–51.

Hanson, A. R., & Riseman, E. M. (Eds.). *Computer vision systems.* New York: Academic Press, 1978.

Hinton, G. E. Relaxation and its role in vision. University of Edinburgh: Doctoral dissertation, December 1977.

Jouvet, M. Does a genetic programming of the brain occur during paradoxical sleep? In P. A. Buser and A. Roguel-Buser (Eds.), *Cerebral correlates of conscious experience.* Amsterdam: North Holland Publishing Co., 1978.

Kanade, T. A theory of origami world. Carnegie-Mellon University: Computer Science Department, September 1978.

Kandel, E. R. Cellular aspects of learning. In M. A. B. Brazier (Ed.), *Brain mechanisms in memory and learning: From the single neuron to man*. International Brain Research Organization Monograph Series (Vol. 4). New York: Raven Press, 1979.

Kosslyn, S. M., & Schwartz, S. P. Visual images as spatial representations in active memory. In A. R. Hanson and E. M. Riseman (Eds.), *Computer vision systems*. New York: Academic Press, 1978.

Kuffler, S. W., & Nicholls, J. G. *From neuron to brain: A cellular approach to the function of the nervous system*. Sunderland, Massachusetts: Sinauer Associates, Inc., Publishers, 1976.

Livingston, R. B. Reinforcement. In G. C. Quarton, T. Melnechuk, & F. O. Schmitt (Eds.), *The neurosciences: A study program*. New York: The Rockefeller University Press, 1967.

*Marr, D. Representing visual information. In A. R. Hanson and E. M. Riseman (Eds.), *Computer vision systems*. New York: Academic Press, 1978.

*Milner, B. Clues to the cerebral organization of memory. In P. A. Buser & A. Roguel-Buser (Eds.), *Cerebral correlates of conscious experience*. Amsterdam: North Holland Publishing Co., 1978.

*Minsky, M. K-Lines: A theory of memory. *Cognitive Science*, 1980, *4*(2), 117-133.

Minsky, M., & Papert, S. *Perceptrons: An introduction to computational geometry*. Cambridge, Massachusetts: The MIT Press, 1969.

Neisser, U. *Cognition and reality: Principles and implications of cognitive psychology*. San Francisco, California: W. H. Freeman and Company, 1976.

Newell, A. Physical Symbol Systems. *Cognitive Science*, 1980, *4*(2), 135-183.

O'Keefe, J., & Nadel, L. *The hippocampus as a cognitive map*. Oxford: Clarendon Press, 1978.

Paivio, A. Imagery and long-term memory. In R. A. Kennedy and A. Wilkes (Eds.), *Studies in long term memory*. New York: John Wiley and Sons, 1975.

*Piaget, J., & Inhelder, B. *Memory and intelligence*. New York: Basic Books, 1973.

*Pick, H. L., & Saltzman, E. (Eds.), *Modes of perceiving and processing information*. Hillsdale, New Jersey: Lawrence Erlbaum Associates, Publishers, 1978.

*Pribram, K. H., & Gill, M. M. *Freud's project reassessed: Preface to contemporary cognitive theory and neuropsychology*. New York: Basic Books, 1976.

Ratcliff, R. A theory of memory retrieval. *Psychological Review*, March 1978, *85*(2).

*Rumelhart, D. E., & Norman, D. A. The active structural network. In D. A. Norman and D. E. Rumelhart (Eds.), *Explorations in cognition*. San Francisco, California: W. H. Freeman, 1975.

Schank, R. C. Language and Memory. *Cognitive Science*, 1980, *4*(3), 243-284.

*Shepard, R. N., & Metzler, J. Mental rotation of three-dimensional objects. *Science*, 1971, *171*, 701-703.

Standing, L. Learning 10,000 pictures. *Quarterly Journal of Experimental Psychology*, 1973, *25*, 207-222.

Swinney, D. A. Lexical access during sentence comprehension: (Re)consideration of context effects. *Journal of Verbal Learning and Verbal Behavior*, December 1979.

Szentágothai, J. Specificity versus (quasi-) randomness in cortical connectivity. In M. A. B. Brazier and H. Peutsch (Eds.), *Architectonics of the cerebral cortex*. International Brain Research Organization Monograph Series (Vol. 3). New York: Raven Press, 1978.

Thompson, R. F. The search for the engram. *American Psychologist*, 1976, *31*, 209-227.

*von der Malsburg, Ch., & Willshaw, D. J. How to label nerve cells so that they can interconnect in an ordered fashion. *Proceedings of the National Academy of Science, USA*, November 1977, *74*(11), 5176-5178.

*Waltz, D. L. A parallel model for low-level vision. In A. R. Hanson and E. M. Riseman (Eds.), *Computer vision systems*. New York: Academic Press, 1978.

Wickelgren, W. A. Chunking and consolidation: A theoretical synthesis of semantic networks, configuring in conditioning, S-R versus cognitive learning, normal forgetting, the amnesic syndrome, and the hippocampal arousal system. *Psychological Review*, 1979, *86*(1), 44-60.

*Wilson, H. R., & Bergen, J. R. A four mechanism model for threshold spatial vision. *Vision Research*, 1979, *19*, 19-32.

Winograd, T. *Understanding natural language*. New York: Academic Press, 1972.

*Zucker, S. W. Vertical and horizontal processes in low level vision. In A. R. Hanson and E. M. Riseman (Eds.), *Computer vision systems*. New York: Academic Press, 1978.

3 Holography, Associative Memory, and Inductive Generalization

David Willshaw
National Institute for Medical Research, United Kingdom

3.1. INTRODUCTION

In this chapter I review the work on the theory of associative memory that was carried out by myself in collaboration with O. P. Buneman and H. C. Longuet-Higgins at the Theoretical Psychology Unit, Edinburgh University, between 1967 and 1972. We were interested in the basic mathematical problems encountered in designing associative memory devices that would store their information in a nonlocal fashion. We were particularly interested in the design of memory models that could be implemented in neural tissue. Some of this work has already been published (Willshaw, 1972; Willshaw & Buneman, 1972; Willshaw, Buneman & Longuet-Higgins, 1969), but no overall review exists and many of the results in my thesis (Willshaw, 1971) have not been previously published.

Our task is to design structures for the storage and retrieval of items of information, which are called *patterns*. Each pattern to be stored must be identified with a second pattern, to be used as a *cue* or *address* to retrieve the first from store. We are therefore properly concerned with an *associative memory*, a device that stores *pairs* of patterns in such a way that presentation of one member of a pair will elicit the other from store. In fact the two members of a pair need not be distinct. If both were part of the same pattern, the device would be functioning as a *content-addressable* memory.

The technological advances made in the development of the hologram in the 1960s had led people to suggest that the brain functioned on holographic principles. It had long been thought that the brain might store information in a manner resistant to local damage and that allowed for correct retrieval even when an inaccurate cue was presented, and the hologram seemed to possess these properties. The key factor here is the notion of *nonlocal* or *distributed* storage: Each element of the memory contributes to the storage of more than one pair of patterns.

The logical structure of a *local* memory, such as a conventional computer store, is straightforward. Each piece of information is stored in a separate location and can be retrieved with perfect accuracy, and the quantity of information that can be stored is simply given by the number of available locations. The design of a *distributed* memory presents problems. By definition each memory location is to store a number of pattern pairs, all intermingled, and each pattern pair is distributed over more than one memory location. Thus the retrieval process involves more than just the reading out from a sequence of memory locations. One may ask, "How should information be stored in a distributed memory so that it can be retrieved accurately? Are some methods of distributed storage and retrieval better than others? How efficient is the holographic method?"

It was to answer these sorts of questions that we undertook an analysis of distributed memories. The work fell into two parts. Firstly, we investigated (Willshaw, 1971; Willshaw et al., 1969) the conditions under which distributed memories would store their information efficiently (in terms of utilization of the available memory locations) and retrieve that information with high accuracy. Holographic models were examined first, followed by other systems, some of the matrix type, which seemed to have many of the advantages of the hologram without its disadvantages. There is a simple way of classifying all the models discussed, as I explain in Section 3.5.

The second stage of the work (Willshaw, 1972; Willshaw & Buneman, 1972) examined the question of whether a memory can respond appropriately when presented with a cue to which no stored pattern corresponds. This problem can only be attempted satisfactorily if the relations between the cue and the patterns already in store are well defined. It was shown that in this case a matrix memory called the *inductive net* acts as a content-addressable memory: It supplements incomplete descriptions supplied to it on the basis of the information it has in store. Where it is logically possible for it to do so, it can supplement information with which it was not previously provided, by inductive generalization over the patterns already in store.

3.2.   HOLOGRAPHIC MODELS

Holography is a method of information storage employing coherent beams of electromagnetic radiation. It was invented by Gabor (1948, 1949, 1951) and achieved technical importance with the arrival of the laser (Leith & Upatnieks, 1962; Stroke, 1966).

In this context, a *hologram* is a permanent record of the pattern of interference between two light waves, *A* and *B,* in a localized region of space. Subsequent illumination of the hologram with one of the waves effectively unlocks the pattern from store: The incident wave, B, acts so as to cancel out the version of B previously recorded in combination with A, thus producing an approximate reconstruction of A.

Here the hologram is functioning as an associative memory. A record of A and B is stored, and information about B is used as an address to retrieve information about A. Information about A can be used similarly to retrieve information about B. Each portion of the hologram contains information about each part of A and B from which it receives light. Furthermore, if it were possible to record information about more than one pair of objects by exposing the hologram in turn to different sets of interfering waves, the hologram would be functioning as a distributed memory.

3.2.1. The Mathematics of Holography

The holographic process can be formulated mathematically by considering the following example (Collier, 1966; Stroke, 1966).

Two objects, A and B, are illuminated by monochromatic coherent light from a laser by means of a split-beam arrangement (although these remarks refer to optical systems, holograms can in principle be constructed using electromagnetic waves of any frequency). Light is reflected diffusely at the surface of the objects and interferes in a photosensitive solid whose transmittance at any point is assumed to change in direct proportion to the intensity of light at that point (Fig. 3.1). Let the complex amplitudes of the waves diffracted from objects A and B at the point x in the solid be F_A and F_B. Then the change in transmittance, Δt, at x is given by

$$\Delta t = \lambda(F_A + F_B)(F_A^* + F_B^*) \tag{3-1}$$

where λ is a numerical constant and * denotes a complex conjugate. Because F_A and F_B are complex quantities they specify the magnitude and the direction of the waves diffracted from A and B to the point x. Time variation factors have been omitted.

Object A is now removed, the photosensitive solid (the hologram) is treated so that its transmittance does not change further in response to incident light, and it is now illuminated by light reflected from object B, care being taken to maintain the spatial relationships between the parts of the apparatus. Assuming that initially the transmittance, t, is uniform throughout the hologram, the electric field amplitude, G, at x is given by

$$\begin{aligned}
G &= (t + \Delta t)F_B \\
&= tF_B + \lambda \, (F_A + F_B)(F_A^* + F_B^*)F_B \\
&= tF_B + \lambda \, [(F_A F_A^* + F_B F_B^*)F_B + F_B F_A^* F_B + F_A F_B F_B^*]
\end{aligned}$$

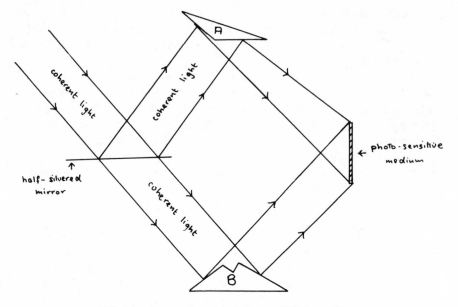

FIG. 3.1.   Construction of the hologram (Willshaw, 1971).

$$\frac{G}{\lambda} = \left(I_A + I_B + \frac{t}{\lambda} \right) F_B + I_B F_A + F_B F_A^* F_B \qquad (3\text{-}2)$$

where $I_A = F_A F_A^*$ and $I_B = F_B F_B^*$ are the intensities due to objects A and B, which are assumed constant over the hologram.

This expression contains a term proportional to F_A and one proportional to F_B, which represent the wave fronts from A and B respectively. Thus, as *both* wave fronts have been reconstructed, on looking through the hologram from the right in the direction of B and then in the direction of the original position of A (Fig. 3.2) *both* images are seen. That of B is brighter than that of A, and the picture is marred by the presence of the wave fronts represented by the term $F_B F_A^* F_B$ in Eq. (3-2). As different parts of the hologram transmit these waves in different directions, the effect of this term can best be regarded as that of introducing noise into the picture.

3.2.2. Development of Holographic Models

A number of authors have drawn the analogy between holograms and the brain viewed as a distributed memory store. Van Heerden (1963a, 1963b) seems to have been the first to do so. He discussed the similarities between the method of optical information storage in solids using coherent light and Beurle's suggestions as to how associative learning could take place in a nerve net by means of modifiable thresholds (Beurle, 1956). Van Heerden pointed out that such systems are able to store large amounts of information, and he stressed the necessity for a calibrating system of pulses in the brain in order to maintain exact phase relations between waves. Other people have discussed the importance of holography in its relationship to the experimental findings of Lashley, who had been led by them to infer that memory traces are not localized in the cerebral cortex (Lashley, 1929), and some have produced holographic brain models (Pribram, 1966; Westlake, 1968).

Longuet-Higgins extended the holographic analogy when he invented the *holophone* (Longuet-Higgins, 1968a, 1968b), which is a distributed memory working in time rather than space. In essence, the holophone is a bank of finely tuned filters, connected in parallel to a common input channel and also connected through variable gain amplifiers to a common output channel. The gains of the amplifiers make up the holophone's memory. The signal to be recorded is passed through the holophone, and the power transmitted by each of the filters is recorded. The gain of each filter is then increased in proportion to the power measured. The net result is to change the response function of the holophone so that when a small portion of a previously recorded signal is fed in, the holophone will produce an approximate rendering of the whole signal. Further signals are stored in an identical fashion.

For a detailed description of the holophone, the reader should consult the original papers of Longuet-Higgins. Its relevance to the present discussion is that it provides a simple, one-dimensional illustration of the holographic principle,

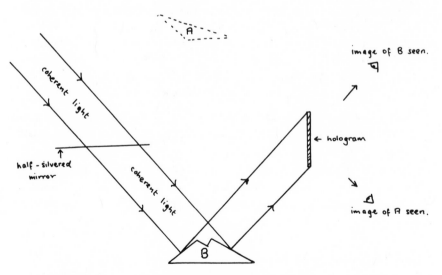

FIG. 3.2.   Use of the hologram and *B* to produce an image of *A* (Willshaw, 1971).

and the mathematics derived for it are typical of other holographic memory models.

The overall computation performed by the holophone (and for that matter, other holographic devices) is relatively simple. It turns out that the effect of storing a signal in it is to change its response function by the autocorrelation function of that signal. Because, by definition of the response function, the output is the convolution of the response function with the input, the entire computation carried out by the holophone is a combination of convolutions and correlations.

The fidelity of recall was investigated by examining a discrete analog of the holophone (Willshaw and Longuet–Higgins, 1969). R patterns are stored, each represented by a sequence of N numbers. The cue is a sequence of L members of one of the stored patterns.

When each pattern value is chosen to be $+1$ or -1 with equal probability, the signal-to-noise ratio, ρ (the ratio of the square of the mean amplitude to the variance), of a component of the recalled pattern is approximately given by

$$\rho = L/NR. \qquad (3\text{-}3)$$

In other words, the signal-to-noise ratio is equal to the length of the cue divided by the total length of all the patterns in store. The performance of the holophone is therefore not very good. The validity of this expression was checked by computer simulation.

This analysis of the holophone raised two questions. Firstly, holographic models of memory, requiring well-tuned filters for temporal patterns or the strict maintenance of phase relations between patterns in the spatial domain, are very complicated systems for the comparatively simple computations that they perform. Are there, therefore, simpler memory models that can mimic a holographic system? Secondly, the fidelity of retrieval of information from holographic models is very low. Are there models that can perform better? To try to answer these two questions we embarked on the work described in the next section.

3.3.   NONHOLOGRAPHIC MODELS

In a search for simpler representations of holographic models of memory we took up the observation of Gabor (1968a, 1968b, 1969) that a system that computes cross-correlations or convolutions can mimic the performance of a Fourier holograph.

3.3.1. The Linear Correlograph

Fig. 3.3(a) shows such a system, called a *linear correlograph* (Willshaw, 1971). Two transparencies, *A* and *B,* are illuminated by a diffuse light source, *D.* Light

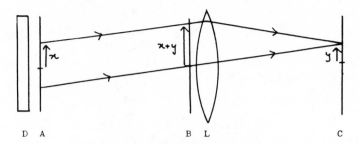

FIG. 3.3(a).   Construction of the linear correlogram.

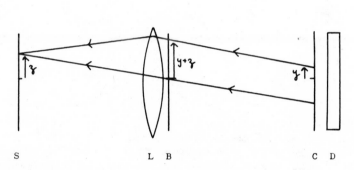

FIG. 3.3(b).   Retrieval of pattern A using the linear correlogram and pattern B (Willshaw, 1971).

transmitted through B is focused onto a photographic plate C by means of lens L. A and C are separated by a distance equal to twice the focal length of the lens and B is placed halfway between them. After exposure, plate C is developed, converted into a positive transparency, which is called a linear correlogram, and then replaced. It is supposed that the transmittance at each point on plate C was modified in proportion to the intensity of the light that fell on it. The retrieval process involves illuminating the linear correlogram by the diffuse source, shifting the lens to the other side of plate B and looking at the pattern of light falling on the screen S which has replaced plate A (Fig. 3.3(b)). By recording other pairs of patterns on the same plate C, it can be made to function as a distributed memory store.

To illustrate the computations performed by this device, a simple one-dimensional case will be considered. $A(x)$ and $B(x + y)$ refer to the intensities of light transmitted through transparencies A and B at points x and $x + y$, which contribute to the intensity, $C(y)$, at point y on C. The distances x, $x + y$, and y are measured perpendicular to the principal optic axis of the lens.

The total intensity falling at point y, and thus the amount by which the transmittance is modified at this point, is given by

$$C(y) = \int A(x)B(x + y)\, dx. \tag{3-4}$$

Retrieval also involves cross-correlations. The intensity at a point z on the viewing screen S, $S(z)$, is (disregarding numerical constants)

$$S(z) = \int C(y)B(y + z)\, dy$$

$$= \int \int A(x)B(x + y)B(y + z)\, dy\, dx. \tag{3-5}$$

Now, if R patterns $[(A^r, B^r), r = 1, 2, \ldots, R]$ are stored, the memory function C has the form

$$C(y) = \sum_{r=1}^{R} \int A^r(x)B^r(x + y)\, dx, \tag{3-6}$$

and the response to cue B^q is

$$S^q(z) = \sum_{r=1}^{R} \int \int A^r(x)B^r(x + y)B^q(y + z)\, dy\, dx. \tag{3-7}$$

This device performs the same computation as the holophone, and has therefore the same poor performance. The expression for the signal-to-noise ratio already quoted for the holophone can be readily derived if we change to discrete notation. It is supposed that each of the N components of a pattern is given equiprobably the value $+1$ or -1 and that the cue $\mathbf{b}^q$ used for the recall of $\mathbf{A}^q$ comprises L components of the vector $\mathbf{B}^q$.

The above equation can be rewritten as

$$S_{kq} = \sum_{r} \sum_{i} \sum_{j} A_{ir}\, B_{i+j,r}\, b_{j+k,q} \tag{3-8}$$

where the discrete quantities i, j, and k have replaced the continuous variables x, y, and z. If recall is accurate, S_{kq} should be proportional to A_{kq}.

This expression for S_{kq} is a sum of NRL products, each with value $+1$ or -1. Now L of these products each has value A_{kq} (when $r = q$ and $i = k$). Each of the other terms can, to a first approximation, be supposed to take the value $+1$ or -1

with equal probability. Thus S_{kq} has a mean value of LA_{kq} and a variance of approximately $NRL - L$. The signal-to-noise ratio is therefore

$$\rho = (LA_{kq})^2/(NRL - L),$$

or

$$\rho = L/NR \quad \text{for large } N. \tag{3-9}$$

3.3.2. The Correlograph

The linear correlograph can be radically improved by adding threshold devices to make a nonlinear system (Willshaw et al., 1969).

We now regard A and B as black cards on which are punched patterns of pinholes. These when illuminated by the light source D produce a pattern of spots on card C. Information is stored by punching a hole through C at every point where a spot appears. For example, suppose that A has 2 holes and B has 3. 6 spots will appear on C, some of which may coincide (Fig. 3.4).

On reconstruction of A, 18 rays strike S; 6 of these retrace the path of rays that originally passed from A through B onto C, and the other 12 strike S at spurious points, points that were not originally pinholes in card A (Fig. 3.5). Consequently, pattern A is seen amongst a background of noise. However because genuine points on S (those which correspond to pinholes on card A) receive 3 rays while spurious points receive fewer than 3, a threshold detector set at a value of 3 will produce a faithful reproduction of pattern A.

Other pairs of patterns are then added by punching holes in card C at the relevant points. In fact, some of these holes will have already been made in the storage of previous pairs. Provided that the number of stored pattern pairs is kept below a certain level, retrieval is excellent, as I now demonstrate.

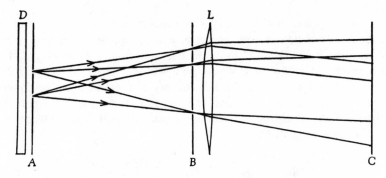

FIG. 3.4. Constructing a correlogram. D is a diffuse light source, L is a lens, and C is the plane of the correlogram of A with B (Willshaw, et al., 1969).

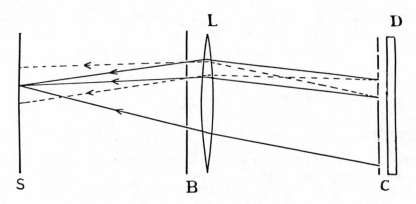

FIG. 3.5. Reconstructing a pattern. Full lines are paths traversed in Fig. 3.4; broken lines are paths not traversed. There are 18 rays that travel from C to S; 5 of these are shown here (Willshaw et al., 1969).

To investigate the conditions for good recall, we adopt an abstract discrete representation. A, B, and C are discrete spaces, each of N points. The N^2 point-pairs formed by linking one point from A with one from B are mapped onto C in the following manner. Point-pair (a_i, b_j) maps onto c_k if $k = (j - i)$ or $(j - i + N)$. Thus the N^2 point-pairs are distributed equally amongst the N points of C. Conversely, in the retrieval process (c_k, b_j) is mapped onto a_i if the same condition is met.

There are R pairs of patterns, each comprising a selection of M of the members of A and M of the members of B. There are therefore RM^2 pairs of points spread out at random amongst the N points of C. The probability, p, that a point c_k is identified with at least one of these pairs is given by

$$1 - p = e^{-RM^2/N} \tag{3-10}$$

The number of points in C identified with the R pattern pairs is therefore pN.

In the reconstruction process, one B-pattern, comprising M points, is combined with the correlogram C to produce a number of rays striking S. Each genuine point on S will receive M rays, so that a detector set to respond to M or more rays will sort out these points from the noise. There is, however, a chance that other positions on S will receive M rays and so register a false report. This will happen with probability p^M, so that the mean number of spurious points in the retrieved pattern will be

$$(N - M)p^M.$$

Good retrieval will be ensured if this number is no greater than 1. A slightly safer upper limit is

$$Np^M = 1,$$

or

$$M = -\log N/\log p. \tag{3-11}$$

We are now in a position to determine the conditions under which the system works optimally. In the retrieval of R patterns, each made up of a selection of M out of N points, the information gained is

$$I = R \log_2 \binom{N}{M} \text{ bits}$$

$$\simeq RM \log_2 N \text{ bits.} \tag{3-12}$$

Using Eq. (3-10) and (3-11), which are expressions for R and M, it follows that

$$I = N \log_2 p \log_e (1-p) \text{ bits,} \tag{3-13}$$

which has a maximum at $p = .5$,

$$I/N = \log_e 2 \text{ or } 0.693$$

and

$$M = \log_2 N. \tag{3-14}$$

Therefore this device works most efficiently when the number of points M in a pattern is related logarithmically to the number of possible points N and when half of the N points of the correlograph have been converted into pinholes. Furthermore, because the correlogram C is effectively a binary store of N bits, under these conditions this device works 69% as efficiently as a conventional store with no associative capability.

3.4. THE ASSOCIATIVE NET

In the previous section I described how the essentials of the holographic memory can be distilled into a simpler model called the correlograph. Its information is stored in a distributed fashion, and with the addition of threshold detectors it can be used almost as efficiently as a conventional local store.

The correlograph has another property, however, which poses a difficulty when one considers how it could be represented in the nervous system. This is the fact that it can cope with displaced patterns. In the reconstruction mode, if the pattern B to be used as a cue is a spatially displaced version of one previously stored, the output will be the appropriate A-pattern, also displaced. The reason for this is that in the construction of the correlogram there is a many-to-one mapping of the point pairs (A, B) onto C: Each point C is identified with N of the N^2 point pairs made by combining members of A with members of B.

This facility is absent in a memory system where each storage location is identified with a unique point pair. Such a system, called an *associative net* (Willshaw, 1971; Willshaw et al., 1969) can be represented by a lattice (Fig. 3.6). The N_A vertical lines and the N_B horizontal lines represent the N_A points of A and the N_B points of B, and the $N_A N_B$ intersections represent the points of C. A particular point in C is regarded as being active if the pair of lines (a_i, b_j) that pass through it have been called into play in the association of at least one of the R pattern pairs. The mathematics of this device is similar to that of the correlograph. Let us suppose that each pair is a selection of M_A of the N_A lines and M_B of the N_B lines. The probability, p, that a given point of C has been activated in the recording process is given by

$$1 - p = e^{(-RM_A M_B / N_C)} \tag{3-15}$$

where N_C is written for $N_A N_B$.

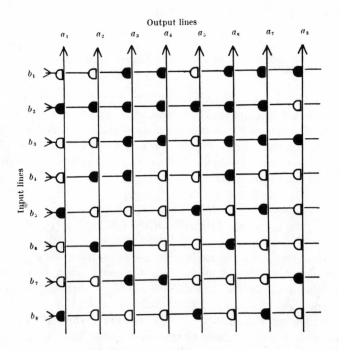

FIG. 3.6.   An associative net. The nodes that have been activated in the storage process are colored black (Willshaw et al., 1969).

When B-patterns are used to recall A-patterns, the threshold detector must be set at M_B units. It will fire in response to spurious outputs with probability p^{M_B}, so that the limit of good recall is set at

$$N_A p^{M_B} = 1. \tag{3-16}$$

It follows that the amount of information stored in the memory is

$$I_A = N_C \log_2 p \log_e (1-p) \text{ bits.} \tag{3-17}$$

As in the correlograph, the efficiency with which the associative net can be made to store information is 69% of the theoretical maximum. I have analyzed the performance of the associative net under a variety of conditions. In some cases I carried out computer simulations to check the analysis. Some of the results are described below; for other results the reader should consult Willshaw (1971).

3.4.1. The Associative Net as a Neural Model

There is a straightforward way of realizing the associative net in nervous tissue. The horizontal lines of Fig. 3.6 are axons of the N_B input neurons, b_1, b_2, ..., and the vertical lines are dendrites of the N_A output neurons, $a_1, a_2. \ldots$ At the intersection of a_i with b_j is a modifiable synapse c_{ij}. This synapse is initially inactive but becomes active after a_i and b_j are made to fire simultaneously, which will occur if an A-pattern containing a_i is presented in association with a B-pattern containing b_j. Thus the synapse functions as a binary switch. If c_{ij} has been activated during the storage procedure, the firing of b_j in the retrieval mode will locally depolarize the membrane of a_i. The output neuron a_i is then supposed to fire if M_B or more input cells depolarize it simultaneously.

The regular network structure of the nerve cells of the cerebellar cortex (Eccles, Ito, & Szentágothai, 1967) might suggest that this part of the nervous system is a form of associative net. But there are important differences between the cerebellum and the associative net that would reduce the efficiency with which the cerebellum could be used in this manner. In particular, the anatomy of the cerebellum dictates that the threshold on the firing of the output lines (Purkinje cells) cannot be set exactly equal to the number of actual input lines but must be determined by a sampling procedure. For a detailed proposal of how the cerebellum might be used as a learning device the reader is referred to the papers by Marr (1969) and Blomfield & Marr (1970). To my knowledge their key proposal, that synapses between the parallel fibers and the Purkinje cells are modifiable, has yet to be confirmed.

One property of the associative net that makes it attractive as a neural model is that good retrieval can be obtained even when some of the storage elements are damaged or when some of the components of the address are incorrect. To achieve this the number of lines to be activated in the storage of a pattern must be greater (and the loading of the net must be lighter) than under optimal conditions (Willshaw, 1971). Resistance to local damage is bought at the expense of storage capacity.

3.4.2. The Associative Net with a Feedback Loop

The nonlinearities of the associative net give it interesting properties when it is equipped with a feedback loop. Here, in the retrieval mode the response to a given cue is used as a new input. This is well illustrated when the associative net is used as a content-addressable memory. Patterns of the type (A, A) are stored and a fragment A' is used to retrieve the rest of A from store. It was found by computer simulation (Willshaw, 1971) that the initial response to a given cue could be improved by feeding the output back into the associative net and continuing until the sequence of outputs so generated converged onto a single pattern.

The same "cleaning-up behavior" was seen when patterns were stored in sequence. Pattern A was associated with B, B with C, C with D, and so on, the last pattern being stored with A. When a fragment of A was used as a cue and then the output used as the next input, after a few passes the sequence of retrieved patterns converged onto the stored sequence, even when the initial cue was a very poor representation of one of the stored patterns. Simulation experiments were performed to see what cycle of outputs would result from any arbitrarily selected cue. (Because each input determines the next output and there is only a finite number of possible outputs, the sequence of outputs must eventually lead into a cycle.) It turned out (Willshaw, 1971) that the length of the typical cycle is very small. For an associative net with 64 horizontal and 64 vertical lines, the length of the cycle generated from an arbitrarily chosen input was typically 50. This is of the order of magnitude of the logarithm of the number of different possible output patterns rather than that number itself, which is 2^{64} or approximately 10^{20}. In all cases when the associative net is equipped with a feedback loop, good recall can only be achieved by loading it more lightly than the optimal conditions, derived in Section 3.4, permit.

3.5. A COMPARISON OF CORRELOGRAPHIC AND MATRIX MODELS

Two sorts of distributed memory have been described. The one has a bank of N memory elements to store associations between the points of A and the points of B, each of which has N elements; the other has N^2 memory elements. What is the formal relationship between these two memory systems, and do they represent the main types of distributed memory?

Let us return to our starting point and consider a way of representing the holographic method of storage in matrix notation. The N-dimensional vector

$\mathbf{A}$ specifies the complex amplitude distribution of the light wave, sampled at N points, which is diffracted from object A. In the holographic plane this amplitude distribution becomes

$$\mathbf{\Psi} = \mathbf{MA} \qquad\qquad (3\text{-}18)$$

where $\mathbf{M}$ is the matrix of the Fourier transformation.

A similar equation can be written for the wave diffracted from object B.

$$\mathbf{\Phi} = \mathbf{MB} \qquad\qquad (3\text{-}19)$$

The construction of the hologram involves increasing the transmittance of each of the N points of the holographic plate in proportion to the intensity of light resulting from the interference of the two waves, which is a function of the two vectors $\mathbf{\Psi}$ and $\mathbf{\Phi}$. The changes in transmittance in all the points of the holographic plate can be expressed in terms of the $N \times N$ storage matrix $\mathbf{X}$, which in this case is a diagonal matrix. Subsequent storage of other pairs of patterns leads to further changes in transmittance, and therefore to further alterations to the matrix $\mathbf{X}$.

We can now formulate an equation for the whole process. Given that a number of pairs of patterns have been stored, suppose that pattern $\mathbf{B}$ is used as the cue to recall $\mathbf{A}$. On presentation of $\mathbf{B}$, the amplitude distribution $\mathbf{\Phi} = \mathbf{MB}$ is set up at the hologram. This distribution is then modified by the memory matrix $\mathbf{X}$. Finally, on moving back from Fourier space into object space, the inverse Fourier transform, described by the matrix $\mathbf{M}^{-1}$, is performed. These three steps are described by the equation

$$\mathbf{S} = \mathbf{M}^{-1}\mathbf{XMB} \qquad\qquad (3\text{-}20)$$

This equation describes in the most general terms the class of *linear* nonlocal associative memories. Different devices can be constructed by choosing different nonlocal transformations, $\mathbf{M}$, and different forms for the storage matrix, $\mathbf{X}$. The corresponding class of *nonlinear* associative memories is described by the equation

$$\mathbf{S} = [[\mathbf{M}^{-1} \mathbf{X} \mathbf{M}]\mathbf{B}] \qquad\qquad (3\text{-}21)$$

where the square parentheses [] indicate nonlinear operations.

Two special cases of these equations are now considered.

As already indicated, substituting the holographic forms of $\mathbf{M}$ and $\mathbf{X}$ in equations 3-20 and 3-21 leads to the mathematics of the holophone and the correlograph respectively. In fact, matrix $\mathbf{M}$ need not be the Fourier matrix; using any orthogonal matrix will lead to the same result.

Secondly, let us suppose that the holographic method of calculating the components of the storage matrix $\mathbf{X}$ is applied to each of its components rather than to the diagonal ones only. $\mathbf{X}$ will therefore have N^2 rather than N nonzero components. Then it is straightforward to calculate (Willshaw, 1971) that the response to the cue $\mathbf{B}^q$ is

$$S_{iq} = \sum_{r} \sum_{j} A_{ir}B_{jr}B_{jq}.$$

(3-22)

This is the correlation type of memory, which has also been discussed by Anderson and by Kohonen. In this model, the signal-to-noise ratio of the response to a cue of length L from a memory that has stored R pattern pairs each of length N is

$$\rho = L/R,$$

(3-23)

which is a factor of N greater than the figure for the holophone. Once again, by inclusion of nonlinear operations, this model can be converted into the associative net. Here, too, the form of the matrix, $\mathbf{M}$, is not crucial.

3.6.   THE INDUCTIVE NET

The associative net is able to deal with incomplete and inaccurate information. When a distorted version of one of its stored patterns is presented to it, under certain conditions the correct pattern can be retrieved accurately. We now take the argument a stage further. The question is whether a memory can be designed, which, when given an incomplete description of a stored item, will furnish those details missing from the description; and will also accept a description to which no stored item corresponds and will supplement this description by inductive generalization over the items already in store. This question is meaningless unless the relationships between the items of information to be stored are well defined. Suppose I am given some numbers to memorize. I am then given another number with a few missing digits and am asked to fill in the gaps on the basis of the order in the numbers I have already learnt. I shall only be able to do this if I can infer the rules used in constructing the given numbers; if there are no rules, the task is insoluble.

The ensemble of patterns that we consider is made up of binary vectors of fixed length. Each vector contains a fixed number of binary features, and for each pair of features not all of the four combinations of feature values, "$++$", "$+-$", "$-+$", "$--$", occur amongst the ensemble of vectors. Suppose, for example, that the vectors describe the appearance of wooden blocks and that one feature relates to color, blue or green, and the other to size, large or small. Further, only three of the four combinations are allowed, there being no blocks which are both green and small. Then if we are told that a particular block is small, we can infer that it is blue; and if a block is green, it must be large. Information about one feature can be used to infer information about another. No two features are logically independent of each other; such an ensemble is said to obey the *four-point condition* (Buneman, 1971). It turns out that the members of such an ensemble can be represented by an unrooted tree, each of whose nodes represents a vector. Each link represents a feature, and so separates those vectors with value "+" for this feature from those with value "−". A six-link tree is shown in Fig. 3.7, and this defines an ensemble of seven binary vectors.

When a selection of patterns is made from a four-point ensemble, owing to the logical relations between the various features more information about the ensemble can be inferred than was explicitly given. For example, let us choose from Fig. 3.7 the patterns **A, E, F,** and **G,** which are

A: (+1, −2, +3, −4, −5, +6),

E: (+1, −2, −3, +4, +5, −6),

F: (+1, +2, +3, +4, +5, −6),

G: (−1, −2, +3, −4, +5, −6).

It can be shown that there are two four-point ensembles from which these four patterns could have been drawn. Each ensemble can be represented by a tree; the two ensembles are represented by the superposition of the two trees, called a *multitree* (Fig. 3.8), where the relative positions of links five and six are not determined. Given that the patterns are from a four-point ensemble, the existence of patterns not explicitly stored can be inferred, as shown by the presence of the nodes labeled **C** and **D** in Fig. 3.8.

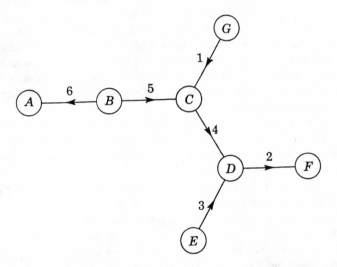

FIG. 3.7. A six-link binary tree. As an illustration of how vectors are assigned to the nodes of a binary tree, the six-dimensional vectors identified with **A** and **D** are: **A**: (+1, −2, +3, −4, −5, +6) **D**: (+1, −2, +3, +4, +5, −6) (Willshaw, 1972).

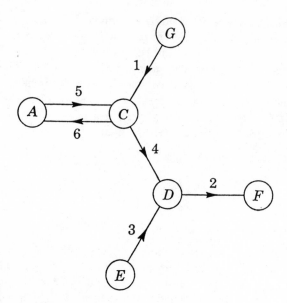

FIG. 3.8. The multitree constructed from the vectors identified with nodes **A**, **E**, **F**, and **G** of Fig. 3.7 (Willshaw, 1972).

The network that can perform inductive generalizations of this kind is similar to the associative net and is shown in Fig. 3.9. This *inductive net* (Willshaw, 1972) is a content-addressable memory, and it is similar in structure and function to the associative net. In the storage of a pattern, the memory elements that are in the inactive state and lie at the intersections of the active horizontal and vertical lines are switched on. In retrieval, activity in the horizontal lines associated with the cue stimulates, through the switches previously turned on, certain (vertical) output lines, and a threshold detector set at the number of active horizontal lines causes some output lines to fire.

In this network there are two horizontal lines associated with each feature, one with each feature value. The vertical lines are also arranged in pairs. Activity in the two vertical lines associated with the same feature is mutually inhibitory, so that there can never be responses from both lines simultaneously.

Let us now see how the inductive net functions. The inductive net of Fig. 3.9 has stored the descriptions of the vectors **A**, **E**, **F**, and **G**. We now present an incomplete description of one of the vectors, say **F**, by activating input line +4. The output is the set of values (+1, +4, +5, −6). Reference to the multitree (Fig. 3.8) shows that this set of feature values is indeed the set common to those vectors that have the value +4. This retrieved set does not specify vector **F** uniquely because there are other vectors that have value +4. The inductive net can therefore supplement incomplete descriptions of stored items, as far as it is logically possible for it to do so.

A more illuminating example is provided by using the cue $(-2, +3, +4)$, which specifies the vector **D**. The output is $(+1, -2, +3, +4, +5, -6)$, a complete description of **D**. What is interesting is that **D** was not explicitly stored. This illustrates the point that the inductive net can generalize, where logically possible, to complete descriptions of items not explicitly stored. Proofs of the theorems specifying the performance of the inductive net can be found in Willshaw (1972).

The capability of the inductive net to generalize becomes an embarrassment when the patterns whose presence are inferred are not in fact members of the chosen ensemble. The general question here is: How does the inductive net deal with ensembles that do not obey the four-point condition? Peter Buneman and I (Willshaw & Buneman, 1972) have considered how to adapt this device to solve the *exact match* problem, which is that of searching amongst a set of stored patterns to find those specified by a given partial description. The system is required to respond only on the basis of the information explicitly stored; there is to be no generalization. We were interested in a content-addressable memory that would work perfectly rather than in the statistical manner of models such as the associative net.

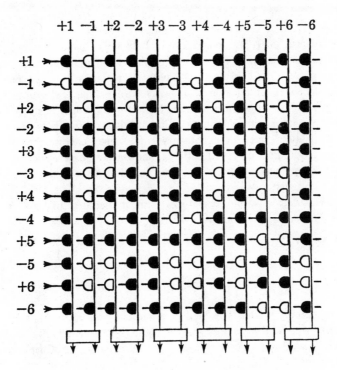

FIG. 3.9.   The inductive net associated with Fig. 3.8 (Willshaw, 1972).

An inductive net can be adapted to deal with ensembles violating the four-point condition by adding extra input lines that respond to *combinations* of feature values; we talk about adding a series of *masks* of various *sizes*. The size of a mask is the number of feature values which must be looked at in order to decide whether the input line should fire. We have shown that the information about the vectors to be stored can be represented on a type of graph that is a generalization of the multitree and that an inductive net equipped with the appropriate extra input lines will be able to supplement incomplete descriptions of the patterns in store. An as-yet-unsolved problem is to find an efficient way of selecting the extra masks. Unless there are very few features it would be inefficient to include all possible masks because the number of possible masks is exponentially related to the number of different features.

3.7. CONCLUSION

It is possible to design nonlocal memory devices that store and retrieve their information efficiently. In considering the various different types of memory, useful distinctions can be made: (1) between the correlographic and the matrix types; and (2) between linear and nonlinear systems, as follows.

1. Matrix versus correlographic memories. In a matrix memory, each storage location is responsible for a different point-pair. Thus pairs of patterns each with N components are stored in a memory with N^2 registers. This system will be therefore expected to have a storage capacity N times that of the correlographic type, which has just N registers. This is certainly true when one compares the associative net with the correlograph. A similar relation exists between the linear versions of the two systems. In both cases the signal-to-noise ratio varies inversely with the number of stored patterns, and for the linear associative net the number of patterns needed to reach a given signal-to-noise ratio is N times that needed for the linear correlograph.

2. Linear versus nonlinear memories. Linear memory models can be described by the matrix equation

$$S = M^{-1}XMB \tag{3-20}$$

and nonlinear models by the equation

$$S = [[M^{-1}XM]B]. \tag{3-21}$$

A particular memory model is defined by a particular choice of M, the transformation matrix, and X, the memory matrix. There is nothing remarkable about the holographic type of model. Indeed it seems to be overcomplex for the computations it performs.

Linear models appear to have disadvantages when used for distributed storage. By its very nature, distributed storage intermingles the stored patterns, and a linear model's response to a given cue will be an average of all stored patterns; even with very few patterns, a retrieved pattern may resemble none of the patterns in store. Linear memories can only be made to work reliably when there are heavy constraints put on the ensemble of patterns to be stored, such as that the patterns form an orthogonal set of vectors.

Nonlinear systems, such as the associative net, can be made to function almost perfectly as long as the memory is not heavily loaded. To use these systems efficiently, however, constraints must be imposed on the type of pattern that can be stored. In the case of the associative net, the number of lines active in storing a pattern must be logarithmically related to the total number of lines available. This constraint is not as severe as those required for the linear model, but it is a constraint nevertheless.

What are the problems in applying the theory of associative memory, either to the design of commercial devices or to the analysis of nervous function? As I see them, the problems are not concerned with the logic of the distributed memory devices as such, but with how to encode the patterns to be stored into a form acceptable to the memory and how to convert the output of the memory back into one of the given patterns. A general-purpose encoding and decoding algorithm, such as one that orthogonalizes the patterns to make them suitable for a linear system, would be very difficult to devise. As far as biological applications are concerned, instead of treating biological patterns as strings of random digits, it would be worth investigating their structure, that is, the logical relations between their component parts. As our work on the inductive net has shown, if the logical relations underlying the data can be isolated, memory systems can be designed that exploit this structure and thereby acquire properties reaching beyond those of a simple memorizing device.

ACKNOWLEDGMENTS

I thank MacMillan Journals Ltd. for permission to reproduce Figs. 3.4, 3.5, and 3.6 and the Royal Society of London for permission to reproduce Figs. 3.7, 3.8, and 3.9.

REFERENCES

Beurle, R. L. Properties of a mass of cells capable of regenerating pulses. *Philosophical Transactions of the Royal Society. Series B* 1956, *240*, 55–94.
Blomfield, S. & Marr, D. How the cerebellum may be used. *Nature*, 1970, *227*, 1224–1228.
Buneman, O. P. The recovery of trees from measures of dissimilarity. In F. R. Hodson, D. G.

Kendall, & P. Tautu (Eds.), *Mathematics in the archaeological and historical sciences*. Edinburgh University Press, 1971.

Collier, R. J. Some current views on holography. *I.E.E.E. Spectrum*, 1966, *3*, 67–74.

Eccles, J. C., Ito, M., & Szentágothai, J. *The cerebellum as a neuronal machine*. Berlin: Springer-Verlag, 1967.

Gabor, D. A new microscopic principle. *Nature*, 1948, *161*, 777–778.

Gabor, D. Microscopy by reconstructed wavefronts. *Proceedings of the Royal Society. Series A* 1949, *197*, 454–487.

Gabor, D. Microscopy by reconstructed wavefronts. II. *Proceedings of the Physics Society*, 1951, *64*, 244–255.

Gabor, D. Holographic model of temporal recall. *Nature*, 1968, *217*, 584. (a)

Gabor, D. Improved holographic model of temporal recall. *Nature*, 1968, *217*, 1288–1289. (b)

Gabor, D. Associative holographic memories. *IBM Journal of Research and Development*, 1969, *13*, 156–159.

van Heerden, P. J. A new optical method of storing and retrieving information. *Applied Optics*, 1963, *2*, 387–392. (a)

van Heerden, P. J. Theory of optical information storage in solids. *Applied Optics*, 1963, *2*, 393–400. (b)

Lashley, K. S. *Brain mechanisms and intelligence*. Chicago: University of Chicago Press, 1929.

Leith, E. N. & Upatnieks, J. Reconstructed wavefronts and communication theory. *Journal of the Optical Society of America*, 1962, *52*, 1123–1130.

Longuet-Higgins, H. C. Holographic model of temporal recall. *Nature*, 1968, *217*, 104. (a)

Longuet-Higgins, H. C. The non-local storage of temporal information. *Proceedings of the Royal Society. Series B* 1968, *171*, 327–334. (b)

Marr, D. A theory of cerebellar cortex. *Journal of Physiology*, 1969, *202*, 437–470.

Pribram, K. H. Some dimensions of remembering: Steps towards a neuropsychological model of memory. In J. Gaito (Ed.), *Macromolecules and Behavior*. New York: Appleton-Century-Crofts, 1966.

Pribram, K. H. The neurophysiology of remembering. *Scientific American*, 1969, *220*(1), 73–86.

Stroke, G. W. *An introduction to coherent optics and holography*. New York: Academic Press, 1966.

Westlake, P. R. *Towards a theory of brain functioning: A detailed investigation of the possibilities of neural holographic processes*. Unpublished doctoral dissertation, University of California, Los Angeles, 1968.

Willshaw, D. J. *Models of distributed associative memory*. Unpublished doctoral dissertation, Edinburgh University, 1971.

Willshaw, D. J. A simple model capable of inductive generalisation. *Proceedings of the Royal Society. Series B*, 1972, *182*, 233–247.

Willshaw, D. J. & Buneman, O. P. Parallel and serial methods of pattern matching. In D. Michie (Ed.), *Machine Intelligence 7*. Edinburgh University Press, 1972.

Willshaw, D. J., Buneman, O. P. & Longuet-Higgins, H. C. Non-holographic associative memory. *Nature*, 1969, *222*, 960–962.

Willshaw, D. J. & Longuet-Higgins, H. C. The holophone-recent developments. In D. Michie (Ed.). *Machine Intelligence 4*. Edinburgh University Press, 1969.

4 Storage and Processing of Information in Distributed Associative Memory Systems

Teuvo Kohonen
Erkki Oja
Helsinki University of Technology

Pekka Lehtiö
University of Helsinki

4.1. INTRODUCTION

4.1.1. A Classification of the Models of Memory Mechanisms

In traditional experimental psychology one of the principal goals of memory research has been to discover the quantitative laws that govern the performance of memory. A universal learning or forgetting curve may be seen as an ideal objective aimed at by researchers who are studying retention of words or letter strings in memory or learning of simple sensory–motor skills. The many stochastic learning models (e.g., Bush & Mosteller, 1955) published in the fifties and early sixties reflect only one facet of this general trend.

The most salient feature in contemporary memory research is the change of goal from the performance of memory to the mechanisms of encoding, retention, and retrieval of information. This gradual adoption of an idea that might be called *the memory mechanism paradigm* has also led to new research strategies. Work in this area has concentrated more and more on the modeling of memory functions; computer simulation models have become indispensable tools of theoretical work.

Although this common interest in memory mechanisms is recognizable in most current research, diversification of the goals has also led to a "balkanization" process (Newell, 1978) typical of different areas of cognitive science. For this reason one of the purposes of this introduction is to classify the various models of memory and to show how they have been motivated.

We divide memory models into two main categories: *physical system models* and *information-processing models*. In the category of *physical system models* we include all those models that try to answer the following question: How is it possible, using a collection of relatively simple elements connected to one another, to implement the basic functions of selective associative memory? Although it is possible to implement memory mechanisms by many different physical systems, we are here interested only in biological mechanisms for which there exists some experimental evidence and that have a plausible principle of operation. The fundamental question, dealt with in this chapter, concerns the mechanism that enables the nervous system to encode associations and subsequently to recall them selectively and independently. In order to explain the function of memory, the following three subproblems must be resolved: (1) What are the variable elements in the neural system capable of accumulating memory traces; (2) which neural events are identified with the reading and writing operations; and (3) what is the addressing mechanism used for memory in the nervous system?

The physical system approach may be contrasted with *information-processing models* that conceive man as an information-processing system executing internal programs for testing, comparing, analyzing, manipulating, and storing information. For an operable information processing paradigm, its propounders had to assume that the *mental processor* had some sort of associative memory capacity.

Within or at the fringe of the Artificial Intelligence community a great number of studies have been published on associative data structures. The aim of these studies has been to develop a representational format that permits the storage of the meaning of a word or a sentence, or more generally, the storage of organized knowledge. Quillian (1968) has formulated the central thesis of his early work on *semantic networks* as follows: "What constitutes a reasonable view of how semantic information is organized within a person's memory [p. 216]?" This is a typical competence question. A more technological approach was, of course, later adopted in the development of data-base software tools. Semantic network models and models of mental processing may be seen as complementary: For instance, in order to explain linguistic abilities, one has to postulate both processing functions and articulated data structures.

4.1.2. Representation of Information by Collective States

An inherent difficulty in the physical modeling of memory obviously arises from the fact that the human mind deals mostly with *concepts* that appear to be distinct and unique items. Attempts to construct abstract structures out of such hypothetical conceptual units are therefore understandable. Nonetheless, it has been pointed out by Simon (1976): "Nothing in contemporary information-processing theories of memory requires that memories be specifically localized; and nothing in those theories is incompatible with a distributed or even holographic theory of physiological basis for memory [p. 80]." In this article an even stronger argument is presented. In fact, because a neural system is an ensemble of a great number of *collectively* interacting elements, it seems more natural to abandon altogether those physical models of memory in which particular concepts correspond to particular spatial locations (nodes) in the hardware. Instead a physically more plausible approach can be based on the assumption that representations of concepts and other pieces of information are stored as *collective states* of a neural network. It then becomes possible to demonstrate the formation of structured *interactions* between these distinct states. Structures of interactions can be made to correspond to *structures of knowledge;* however, they have no direct physical counterparts in the system. *They are realized only through the collective effects and reflected in recall processes.*

The first models of collective memory aimed at an analysis of the accuracy, capacity, and resolution achievable in the basic associative mappings, and they should not be misinterpreted on account of their simplicity. The principal objective in the early models was to show that there exist memory-dependent mappings between patterned sets of signals such that the memory traces can be superimposed on the same substrate in the form of some transformation functions without in any way losing information although the memory traces are superimposed on the same elements. The demonstration of the existence of such selective mappings showed that there may indeed exist distinct representations for pieces of information that nonetheless need not be represented and stored on the memory substrate spatially separated from each other. In the same way as many mathematical or physical entities can have functional expansions, for example, spectral decompositions, it thus became possible to demonstrate that distinct items can be represented as functional components spread all over the memory medium. This kind of collective representation might be called "holographic" or "hololologic," although it need not resemble the usual optical holography that requires coherent wave fronts.

In the memory models advanced in this paper, the answers to questions concerning reading and writing of information, as well as the problem of addressing, follow from the idea that memory is regarded as an *adaptive filter*. When a neural network that implements this filter function is stimulated by signal patterns, each pattern produces adaptive changes in the neuronal interconnections, changes that are equivalent to the writing of information into the memory. Reading from memory can simply be the transformation of input signals in the network, because this transformation is dependent on the previous stimulus sequence. (Detailed description of these transformations as well as the adaptive changes is presented in Section 4.2.) No addressing problem exists because memory traces are spatially distributed and superimposed throughout the network. This approach agrees well with current evidence about the functional structure of the neocortex (Creutzfeldt, 1976).

The very direct analogy between conceptual systems and neural structures was severely questioned at the beginning of the 1970s when several independent articles were published on collective effects as a basis of memory. We review in detail one of the most plausible models, the distributed associative network, in a form that seems to give rise to several fundamental information-processing paradigms in the neural realm.

4.2. ASSOCIATIVE MAPPINGS IN DISTRIBUTED MEMORY SYSTEMS

4.2.1. Associative Recall

A central operation in explaining the functions of distributed memory models is *associative recall*. As stated earlier, if the memorized data contains proper internal relations or links, structures of information can be shown to be reflected in the resulting recall processes, that is, without explicitly being represented in memory. Moreover it is possible to demonstrate processing of semantic data by associative recall as shown in Section 4.4.

In general terms the basic action of associative recall is definable as any process by which an input to the memory system, considered as a "key," is able to evoke in a highly selective fashion a specific *response,* associated with that key, at the system output. Associative recall implies a specific stimulus–response ($S-R$) type of *mapping* in the memory medium, which is able to associate a large number of large-scale activity patterns faithfully and also suppress errors. This mapping may be accompanied by many types of signal feedback and iterative operation.

The fundamental assumption in the approach based on associative mappings or transformations is that both the stimulus and the response are representable as complex, *patterned* sets of parallel signals. The mapping is not defined between individual signals but between these activity patterns as a whole, bringing together and interconnecting the various parts of the patterns. The results of this distributed or "hologic" mode of operation can exhibit many surprising features the existence of which is not obvious at first glance.

The models of distributed associative memory that were published first were primitive in the sense that only direct mappings between pictures or other simple patterns were demonstrated. However it was clear from the beginning that any complex signal representations, even with semantic contents and infrastructure, could have been chosen in place of the pictorial patterns used in simulations. In other words, if the $S-R$ mapping is definable for any sets of signals, then it is also possible to devise a mapping that transforms, for example, the representation of a *statement* into another one. Another fact to emphasize is that, quite intentionally, the $S-R$ model was not loaded with auxiliary functions such as the activity-controlling projections in neural networks or preprocessing transformations of the patterns before they enter the proper memory system. By means of preprocessing operations it is possible to extract any type of features from the primary signals and to use them as a new basis of representation of information; this is already one step towards symbolism, although it too was deliberately neglected in the initial research.

In order to forestall misinterpretation of the network models of distributed memory presented in the following sections, it is necessary to point out that the whole brain is not assumed to be a single uniform network or "matrix" but a complex system consisting of many interacting parts. In the same way as a computer is made of chips of logic circuits, the brain may be composed of a great number of subunits, each one with the properties of a "memory matrix."

4.2.2. Two Structural Paradigms

As a starting point for concrete modeling of associative recall, consider the piece of network or hypothetical neural tissue depicted in Fig. 4.1 (Willshaw, Buneman, & Longuet-Higgins, 1969). The vertical units might represent the dendritic membranes of a set of neurons, and the horizontal lines could correspond to a set of axons or axon collaterals having synaptic connections on the dendrites.

The horizontal lines carry the elements of the *stimulus pattern* in the form of parallel, scalar-valued signals s_j. In a neural network the signal values would be represented by short-term averaged spike frequencies. At the output lines the vertical units send out the *responses* r_i, which similarly are represented by spike frequencies. In this idealized model, there is a *synaptic connection* m_{ij} between every vertical unit i and every horizontal line j. In practice some of the connections may be missing whereas others may be multiple. In the schematic representation the actual locations of connections on the units or the multiplicity of connections have not been shown explicitly.

In order that a given set of stimuli s_j evokes at the output another, predetermined set of response signals r_i, a selective $S-R$ mapping must be encoded into the set of synaptic connections m_{ij}. One may call the array of m_{ij} values the "synaptic matrix." This encoding is adaptively and automatically formed when signals are mutually *conditioned* at the connections as explained below. Selective recall of a given response set from the synaptic matrix can thereby be rendered possible. The conditioned couplings may take many different functional forms. The simplest of them, the linear mapping, as explained in more detail in Section 4.2.3, is suitable as the first approximation. For this conditioning to happen, supervised (and *nonlinear*) learning must take place. For that purpose,

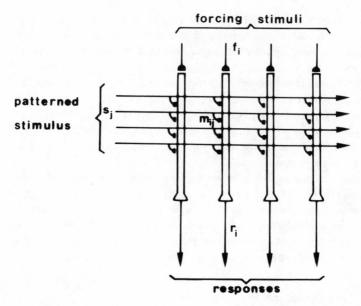

FIG. 4.1. Associative network with a set of connected neurons shown schematically. s_j = elements of the stimulus pattern; r_i = elements of the response pattern; f_i = elements of the forcing stimulus pattern, which are absent during recall; m_{ij} = synaptic connections.

the *forcing stimuli* have been introduced in Fig. 4.1. The forcing stimuli f_i appear as the primary input into the units. In this paradigm they are needed only when learning or *writing into memory* takes place; during learning the forcing stimuli have the same signal values as the desired output responses, which thereby become associated with the conditioning stimulus pattern. During recall there is no input at the forcing stimulus lines. A detailed analysis of the recall and the adaptive processes taking place in the above network, will be postponed to Section 4.2.3.

The system depicted in Fig. 4.1 is highly unsymmetric in the sense that the roles of the conditioning stimulus pattern and the forcing stimuli are strictly differentiated; in recall only the former type of input is used. This paradigm might already serve as a model for some neural structure like the cerebellum where the relation between the different inputs to the Purkinje cells is roughly of this kind. However, this model is unsatisfactory for modeling *cortical* regions of the brain. For instance, in the cerebral cortex there is a rich variety of recurrent activity mediated by axon collaterals and the longer subcortical projections. As a step towards a more realistic paradigm for cortexlike structures, one may replace the network of Fig. 4.1 by that given in Fig. 4.2.

The network of Fig. 4.2 shows two modular subsystems separated by vertical dotted lines. The forcing stimuli in this case comprise the primary patterned input. Each subsystem is characterized by a dense net of interconnections; part or all of the output fibers are *fed back recurrently* into the cortical layer comprised of the parallel neuronal units, where the fibers branch and make redundant connections with the other units of the same subsystem. This simplified scheme neglects the existence of interneurons and other details of the actual topology of the connections; as shown later in Fig. 4.8, a substantial part of the short-range connections may be made subcortically. The network may also seem too homogeneous in that within a subsystem each unit is connected with all the other units. However, as shown in a previous work by one of the authors (Kohonen, 1972), all the connections do not in fact have to exist; if a portion of them is lacking, the system can still be statistically approximated by a complete set of connections.

In addition to short-range recurrent connections, there is a set of long-range connections from one subsystem to another. They introduce other inputs to every subsystem, which will become associated with the activity of the subsystem itself.

The essential feature in Fig. 4.2, referring to connections within a subsystem, is that in the synaptic matrix *every forcing stimulus is conditioned with all the other forcing stimuli of the same subsystem* through the recurrent connections. Within the subsystem there thus exists a complete symmetry with respect to the primary inputs. As a result it becomes possible to use any part of the forcing stimuli as a key. The activity pattern of the rest of the units is reconstructed in the

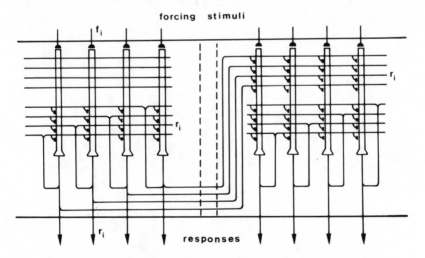

FIG. 4.2.   The modular associative network with recurrent feedback. f_i = elements of the forcing or afferent stimulus pattern; r_i = elements of the response pattern that are fed back into the network at shorter and longer distances. The vertical dotted lines separate the two subsystems shown, and the horizontal solid lines represent the surfaces of the laminar network.

associative recall process through the interconnections. This is the *autoassociative encoding and recall principle* extensively advanced in this chapter.

The paradigms presented in Fig 4.1 and 4.2 represent the extreme and purest cases of $S-R$ mapping, in the sense that Fig. 4.1 has no feedback whatsoever from the response back to the stimulus, but in Fig. 4.2 this feedback within one subsystem has the highest possible degree of completeness. The networks actually existing in the brain probably lie somewhere between these extreme paradigms, and thus their properties can be expected to be a mixture of the properties of these two networks.

In Fig. 4.3, the organization of Fig. 4.2 is shown as a three-dimensional structure. The slabs or subsystems separated by the dotted lines are the areas of the sheet with a high degree of interaction, but the interactions between the subsystems are weaker. The feedback connections mediating these interactions are no longer shown explicitly in Fig. 4.3. The organization depicted is the *laminar network model,* which is later used in the system-theoretical description of distributed memory.

The laminar network model is related (in more detail) to the anatomical and physiological properties of the mammalian brain in Section 4.3. There also, extra features, like the activity control exerted over selected areas, are merged into the model. A feature inherent in the model is that corresponding to the individual subsystems or regions in Fig. 4.2, the sets of input signals and output signals may also be organized into a number of subfields or parts having, for example, different modalities or semantic significance. The data contents of some or all of these subfields may also differ, and there may be neutral areas between them

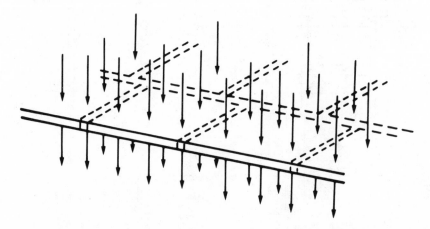

FIG. 4.3.   Three-dimensional view of the modular system. An afferent stimulus pattern enters the top and a response leaves at the bottom. The dotted lines demarcate subfields or subsystems. The infrastructure of the lamina, not shown explicitly, corresponds to that given in Fig. 4.2.

with no signal activity (cf. Fig. 4.10). The important information-processing implications of the infrastructure in the patterns used in models of associative recall is postponed until Section 4.4. In order to describe information processing in such a model, as well as in the simpler associative network model presented earlier in Fig. 4.1, some quantitative analysis of signal transformations must first be presented.

4.2.3. Analysis of Adaptive Transformations

To describe as concretely as possible what kind of interactions between patterned data could be encoded into the networks in distributed form and how selective recall is achievable, we first return to the unsymmetric case of Fig. 4.1. The subsequent considerations of the network should be understood as a *system-theoretical approach* only; no assumptions will be made at this stage about the actual data represented by the patterns of activity.

As a first approximation to the transformations taking place in the network of Fig. 4.1, assume that each response signal, r_i, is a weighted sum of all the stimulus signals s_j and the ith forcing stimulus activity f_i,

$$r_i = \sum_j m_{ij}s_j + f_i, \qquad (4\text{-}1)$$

where the weights m_{ij} stand for the synaptic conductivities. What was said previously about the necessity of a complete set of connections applies here, too: A portion of the connections m_{ij} may be lacking, and the network of Fig. 4.1 then serves as a statistical approximation.

It should further be stressed that the above linear mapping is only one representative in an infinite class of S–R transformations, some of which are derived from the linear models by adding nonlinearities like saturation or threshold triggering to the signal paths whereas others are nonlinear from the beginning. One possible source of misinterpretation of the earlier models of distributed associative memory was the assumed linearity of some approaches: Linearity was never intended to be an essential property but only a first approximation. Nonlinearities can also be introduced in the model as a separate operation, for example, at the output whereby the linear mapping can be assumed as the basic internal mode of operation of the system. In an alternative approach, the neural units are assumed inherently *binary* (Nakano, 1972; Willshaw et al., 1969); if the weighted sum of the binary-valued input signals exceeds a threshold, then the response is 1, otherwise 0. Despite the apparent nonlinearity of this functional form, the integral transformation properties are essentially the same as those explained here using the continuous linear approximation.

Although linearity does not seem to be a necessary property in signal transformation, the near-linearity of neural responses is often a quantitatively justified good approximation (Anderson & Silverstein, 1978).

Assume now that the strengths of the connections m_{ij} in Fig. 4.1 are changed during a learning phase by what is here termed *conjunctive forcing*: m_{ij} is changed only when both of the signals converging on it are active. There seems to be some physiological evidence, treated in Section 4.3, for this type of assumption involving two different signals. If changes (time derivatives) of the values of the m_{ij} are gradual, they are statistically described by a mathematical form in which the conjunction is replaced by the product of the signal values, resulting in the following correlation-type learning scheme:

$$\frac{d}{dt} m_{ij} = \lambda f_i s_j. \tag{4-2}$$

There λ is a scalar determined by the *plasticity* of the connections, which is here assumed constant for simplicity. It might also vary from one connection to another.

Let us now introduce the mathematical conceptualization of *patterns* into the above formalism. At a given instant, there are parallel stimulus signals, $s_1, \ldots,$ s_m, on the input lines of Fig. 4.1. These make up a pattern $\mathbf{s} = (s_1, \ldots, s_m)$, simply defined as an ordered set of simultaneous parallel activities. In a similar fashion, at that same instant there is a forcing stimulus pattern, $\mathbf{f} = (f_1, \ldots, f_n)$, at the input lines and a response pattern, $\mathbf{r} = (r_1, \ldots, r_n)$, at the output lines. For economy of notation only (and without introducing any further mathematical or physiological assumptions) we shall now switch to *matrix algebra* (cf. Bellman, 1960) in the description of associative recall.

The synaptic conductivities m_{ij} can first be arranged into a rectangular array, forming a matrix $\mathbf{M}$ with n rows and m columns. The patterns $\mathbf{s}$, $\mathbf{f}$, and $\mathbf{r}$, being sets of scalar numbers, can be identified with items in a high-dimensional vector space. The term vector here has an abstract meaning, totally different from the conventional two- or three-dimensional vectors used in geometry and field theory; here a vector is simply an ordered set of scalar numbers. It is hereafter assumed that $\mathbf{s}$ is a column vector of m dimensions, and both $\mathbf{f}$ and $\mathbf{r}$ are column vectors of n dimensions.

The pattern vectors $\mathbf{s}$, $\mathbf{f}$, and $\mathbf{r}$ and the matrix $\mathbf{M}$ can now be immediately substituted in Eq. (4-1) and (4-2), so (4-1) becomes

$$\mathbf{r} = \mathbf{Ms} + \mathbf{f} \tag{4-3}$$

and (4-2) becomes

$$d\mathbf{M}/dt = \lambda \mathbf{f}\mathbf{s}^{\mathrm{T}}, \tag{4-4}$$

with $\mathbf{s}^{\mathrm{T}}$ denoting the transpose of vector $\mathbf{s}$.

Imagine now that there is a large number, say p, of different stimulus vectors. They are designated by $\mathbf{s}^{(1)}, \mathbf{s}^{(2)}, \ldots, \mathbf{s}^{(p)}$. Likewise, there are p different forcing stimulus vectors, $\mathbf{f}^{(1)}, \mathbf{f}^{(2)}, \ldots, \mathbf{f}^{(p)}$. The superscript is now used to separate between the different vectors; e.g., each $\mathbf{s}^{(i)}$ is composed of m elements that are the individual parallel signal values making up the spatial activity pattern $\mathbf{s}^{(i)}$, whereas the corresponding m elements of $\mathbf{s}^{(j)}$ ($j \neq i$), may be totally different from these.

Assume that all the synaptic strengths m_{ij} are initially 0, or $\mathbf{M}(0) = 0$; from the instant $t = 0$ onwards the first pair of stimulus and forcing stimulus vectors ($\mathbf{s}^{(1)}$, $\mathbf{f}^{(1)}$) appears at the inputs of the network of Fig. 4.1 and stays constant for a while. According to Eq. (4-4), matrix $\mathbf{M}$ then develops into

$$\mathbf{M}(t) = \lambda t \, \mathbf{f}^{(1)} \, \mathbf{s}^{(1)\mathrm{T}}. \tag{4-5}$$

From this time onwards, the second pair ($\mathbf{s}^{(2)}$, $\mathbf{f}^{(2)}$) appears and so on. If for convenience it is assumed that each stimulus pair is input to the network for a time period whose length is $1/\lambda$, then $\mathbf{M}(t)$ eventually develops into the matrix

$$\mathbf{M} = \sum_{i=1}^{p} \mathbf{f}^{(i)} \, \mathbf{s}^{(i)\mathrm{T}}. \tag{4-6}$$

Matrix $\mathbf{M}$ above takes the form of a *cross-correlation matrix*.

Based on this matrix, it is possible to recall associatively the forcing stimulus patterns using the primary stimuli as keys. It should be stressed that no constraints to the actual form and structure of the $\mathbf{f}^{(i)}$ patterns were given above; theoretically, any set of n scalar signals could appear there. In a concrete example, $\mathbf{f}^{(i)}$ could represent the *classification* of the corresponding stimulus pattern $\mathbf{s}^{(i)}$, in which case the classification of $\mathbf{s}^{(i)}$ would take place very simply by analyzing the response obtained when $\mathbf{s}^{(i)}$ has been used as the stimulus pattern. Of course any other pattern containing some type of information on the primary stimulus can be used as the associated forcing stimulus and then later be recalled associatively.

This becomes evident when the recall operation is defined according to Eq. (4-3) without, however, the forcing stimulus $\mathbf{f}$, which was only necessary during the learning phase. Once the conjunctive learning phase described earlier is over, the specific values given in matrix form by Eq. (4-6) have been *imprinted* into the synaptic connectivities of the network. If now one of the earlier stimulus vectors, say $\mathbf{s}^{(j)}$, is used as the key stimulus in the network, the response becomes

$$\mathbf{r}^{(j)} = \mathbf{M} \, \mathbf{s}^{(j)} = \sum_{i=1}^{p} \mathbf{f}^{(i)} \, \mathbf{s}^{(i)\mathrm{T}} \, \mathbf{s}^{(j)}$$

$$= (\mathbf{s}^{(j)\mathrm{T}}\mathbf{s}^{(j)})\mathbf{f}^{(j)} + \sum_{i \neq j} (\mathbf{s}^{(i)\mathrm{T}} \, \mathbf{s}^{(j)})\mathbf{f}^{(i)}. \tag{4-7}$$

In some cases different stimulus patterns have representations in terms of neural signals that can be assumed to be statistically independent. This independence is often expressable as a mathematical property named *orthogonality;* the key vectors are orthogonal if $\mathbf{s}^{(i)\mathrm{T}}\mathbf{s}^{(j)} = 0$ for $i \neq j$. Moreover, if signal values are standardized, one can assume a metric property such that $s^{(j)T}s^{(j)} = 1$. It then becomes evident that the response $r^{(j)}$ is equal to $f^{(j)}$: the response to $s^{(j)}$ is an *exact recollection* of the forcing stimulus pattern $f^{(j)}$ whose elements became conditioned with the elements of $s^{(j)}$ in the course of learning. It must be emphasized that this is the *optimal* condition; the desired data are recalled completely and without any error. Because the maximum number of orthogonal m dimensional vectors $s^{(j)}$ is m, this is also the maximum number of stimulus-response pairs that can be stored in the synaptic matrix of the network without violating the optimality condition.

If, however, the vectors used as keys above are not orthogonal, then the sum term in Eq. (4-7) will not be 0. It then represents *cross-talk* between the other stored patterns, and the less orthogonal the key patterns are in general, the higher is the cross-talk as compared to the correct recollection.

The occurrence of cross-talk that seems to limit the memory capacity has led to an interesting theoretical question: One may ask whether it is possible to devise a network of the above kind that would implement associative recall with *ideal selectively,* that is, in which, with a hypothetical synaptic matrix **M,** the desired stimulus–response relation would be implementable for *arbitrary* pairs of patterns $(s^{(j)}, f^{(j)})$ such that

$$f^{(j)} = M s^{(j)} \quad \text{for all } j. \tag{4-8}$$

Although information processing implementable by neural functions might quite well employ the powerful property of orthogonality, it is intriguing to find that this problem has solutions that are independent of the orthogonality assumption. This is one of the basic problems studied in linear algebra, and it has a simple answer that can be expressed in the form of a theorem:

Theorem. If all the $s^{(j)}$ are linearly independent (no one can be expressed as a linear combination of the others), then a solution of Eq. (4-8) exists and is given by

$$M = F(S^T S)^{-1} S^T \tag{4-9}$$

where $F = (f^{(1)}, \ldots, f^{(p)})$ and $S = (s^{(1)}, \ldots, s^{(p)})$ are the matrices with the $f^{(j)}$ and $s^{(j)}$ as their columns, respectively, and the superscript T denotes the transpose of a matrix. If the vectors $s^{(j)}$ are not linearly independent, then there exists a unique approximative solution in the sense of least squares

$$\hat{M} = FS^+ \tag{4-10}$$

where S^+ is the *pseudoinverse* of S (Albert, 1972). If vectors $s^{(j)}$ are linearly independent, then in fact $S^+ = (S^T S)^{-1} S^T$; see Eq. (4-9).

Incidentally, $\hat{M}$ has the form of the *best linear unbiased estimator* (BLUE), which is a kind of Gauss–Markov estimator (Lewis & Odell, 1971). Theoretically, even if there were an infinite number of pairs $(s^{(j)}, f^{(j)})$, but they were *clustered,* there would nonetheless exist an approximate solution $\hat{M}$ which defines an "infinite" associative memory in the sense of Eq. (4-8). Matrices of Eq.

(4-9) and (4-10) represent the *optimal linear associative mapping* that has been extensively studied previously by one of the authors (Kohonen, 1977). A demonstration of the use of the optimal linear associative mapping in classification of pictorial patterns is shown in Fig. 4.5 of Section 4.2.7.

4.2.4. Autoassociative Encoding

Very interesting associative recollections are obtained if the optimal linear associative mapping is considered in the case $\mathbf{f}^{(i)} = \mathbf{s}^{(i)}$. Of course, the trivial solution of Eq. (4-8) is $\mathbf{M} = \mathbf{I}$ (identity matrix), but this has no sense; one should set up a more general solution which according to Eq. (4-10) reads

$$\mathbf{M} = \mathbf{F}\mathbf{F}^+ \tag{4-11}$$

Incidentally, this is a so-called *orthogonal projection operator* or *projector* with some interesting pattern-processing properties.

The p different vectors, $\mathbf{f}^{(1)}, \ldots, \mathbf{f}^{(p)}$, all of them n-dimensional, span a *linear subspace* $\mathscr{L}$ in the n-dimensional vector space, that is, the vectors constitute a basis of $\mathscr{L}$. In still other words, $\mathscr{L}$ is the set of vectors that results from all possible linear combinations of the $\mathbf{f}^{(1)}, \ldots, \mathbf{f}^{(p)}$. It is a well-known result from the theory of Hilbert spaces that an arbitrary pattern vector $\mathbf{f}$ with dimensionality n can always be uniquely decomposed into a sum of two component vectors

$$\mathbf{f} = \hat{\mathbf{f}} + \tilde{\mathbf{f}} \tag{4-12}$$

such that $\hat{\mathbf{f}}$, obtained by

$$\hat{\mathbf{f}} = \mathbf{F}\mathbf{F}^+\mathbf{f} = \mathbf{M}\mathbf{f} \tag{4-13}$$

is the *linear regression* of the $\mathbf{f}^{(j)}$ on $\mathbf{f}$ or the best linear combination in terms of least squares, and $\tilde{\mathbf{f}}$ is the residual. In fact, $\hat{\mathbf{f}}$ is contained in the subspace $\mathscr{L}$ whereas $\tilde{\mathbf{f}}$ is orthogonal to $\mathscr{L}$; hence the two vectors are mutually orthogonal, too. We can call $\hat{\mathbf{f}}$ the *optimal autoassociative recollection* relative to the stored information, or the set $\mathbf{f}^{(1)}, \ldots, \mathbf{f}^{(p)}$, and the search argument or key pattern $\mathbf{f}$. Similarly, the matrix $\mathbf{M}$ of Eq. (4-11) is the *optimal linear autoassociative mapping*, which in spite of its simple form will be seen to be capable of processing patterns in rather unexpected ways.

The orthonormality of the stored patterns $\mathbf{f}^{(j)}$ would allow the matrix of Eq. (4-11) to be reduced to another form. For pattern vectors $\mathbf{f}^{(1)}, \ldots, \mathbf{f}^{(p)}$ such that $\mathbf{f}^{(i)\mathrm{T}}\mathbf{f}^{(j)} = 0$ for $i \neq j$ and $\mathbf{f}^{(j)\mathrm{T}}\mathbf{f}^{(j)} = 1$, the corresponding projection operator reads

$$\mathbf{M} = \mathbf{F}\mathbf{F}^T = \sum_{i=1}^{p} \mathbf{f}^{(i)}\mathbf{f}^{(i)\mathrm{T}}. \tag{4-14}$$

The matrix above has the form of an *autocorrelation matrix*. Assume now that a new (independent) pattern vector $\mathbf{f}$ is given as a key input excitation. Its component vectors $\hat{\mathbf{f}}$ and $\tilde{\mathbf{f}}$, can be presented in the form

$$\hat{\mathbf{f}} = \mathbf{Mf} = \sum_{i=1}^{p} (\mathbf{f}^{(i)\mathrm{T}}\mathbf{f})\mathbf{f}^{(i)}, \tag{4-15}$$

$$\tilde{\mathbf{f}} = \mathbf{f} - \hat{\mathbf{f}}. \tag{4-16}$$

Eq. (4-15) shows clearly how $\hat{\mathbf{f}}$, or the optimal autoassociative recollection, is now obtained as a linear combination of the stored vectors, where the coefficients of this expansion are simply the inner products of the stored vectors with the new vector $\mathbf{f}$.

Even in the case of nonorthogonal vectors there exists a mathematical relationship between the optimal autoassociative mapping and the autocorrelation matrix; when matrix $\mathbf{FF}^+$ is presented in the form of a von Neumann expansion (cf. Rao & Mitra, 1971)

$$\mathbf{FF}^+ = \alpha \sum_{k=0}^{\infty} \mathbf{FF}^{\mathrm{T}}(\mathbf{I} - \alpha\mathbf{FF}^{\mathrm{T}})^k \tag{4-17}$$

where $\mathbf{I}$ is the identity matrix, and the matrix series on the right is written out, then the matrix $\alpha\mathbf{FF}^{\mathrm{T}}$ appears as the 0-th degree term. There α is a scalar that lies between predetermined bounds. In this sense, the autocorrelation matrix may be regarded as a 0-th degree approximation of the optimal mapping.

Just as the cross-correlation matrix was imprinted into the synaptic connections of the associative network of Fig. 4.1 by conjunctive forcing, so the autocorrelation matrix, Eq. (4-14), can be shown to be the outcome of a similar learning process in the feedback network of Fig. 4.2. If the modular organization there is approximated by a homogeneous set of mutual feedback connections between the units, then the main difference between mathematical considerations of this network and the one of Fig. 4.1 is that, due to the feedback, the response signals r_i now appear in place of primary signals s_i. This difference becomes clear when the two figures are compared. One horizontal line in Fig. 4.2 carries one response signal r_i, but a corresponding horizontal line in Fig. 4.1 carries an external stimulus signal s_i.

Because of the feedback, however, the signal transmission properties and their mathematical treatment are not as straightforward in this case as in the paradigm considered in the previous Section. This problem has been considered in detail by Kohonen, Lehtiö, Rovamo, Hyvärinen, Bry, and Vainio (1977). First of all, in order to explain the adaptive formation of the optimal linear autoassociative mapping in the laminar network model, one has to take into account *short-range lateral inhibition* between the units or columns. This has the effect of forming weighted sums of neighboring activities locally; in terms of the forcing stimuli f_i appearing at the top of the laminar network, each signal f_i should be replaced by an "effective excitation"

$$f'_i = \sum_j \beta_{ij}f_j \tag{4-18}$$

where the weights β_{ii}, corresponding to direct connectivities, are positive, but the lateral connectivities β_{ij} with $i \neq j$ are predominantly negative or inhibitory; index j runs over a surround of unit i. The numerical values of β_{ij} thus reflect the excitatory and inhibitory penumbrae around a point of afferent excitation. An interesting consequence of lateral inhibition is that, for typical two-dimensional pictorial patterns, the transformation produced by Eq. (4-18) has the effect of orthogonalizing the patterns fairly effectively.

When the orthogonalized input patterns enter the laminar network one at the time and conjunctive learning takes place, the network connections are adaptively changed. Later, when an input pattern is applied, the signals are modified by the network, due to the adaptive effects caused by the earlier signals. This is equivalent to the *reading of stored information from memory*. For details, see Kohonen et al. (1977a).

The autoassociative mapping has the ability to reconstruct any of the stored patterns when only a part of the pattern or a distorted version (e.g., contaminated with noise) is used as the key input. Some demonstrations are shown in Section 4.2.7. There are more far-reaching properties, too, which can be best explained by the subspace formalism of Eq. (4-12). In fact even when the key pattern $\mathbf{f}$ bears no similarity whatsoever to any of the previously stored patterns, $\mathbf{f}^{(1)}, \ldots, \mathbf{f}^{(p)}$, the output or optimal autoassociative recollection $\hat{\mathbf{f}}$ must still reveal some characteristic features common to all the stored patterns, because $\hat{\mathbf{f}}$ is always a vector in the subspace $\mathscr{L}$ spanned by $\mathbf{f}^{(1)}, \ldots, \mathbf{f}^{(p)}$. This implies synthesizing and generalizing abilities, further illustrated by a demonstration in Section 4.2.7.

4.2.5. Extraction of Novelty

In the subspace formalism just presented, it was stated that the projection vector $\hat{\mathbf{f}}$ represented the recollection from memory, and the orthogonal component $\tilde{\mathbf{f}}$ then assumed the role of a *residual*. In regression analysis, the residual would be assumed noiselike and be inversely related to the goodness-of-fit; in the present considerations, however, vector $\tilde{\mathbf{f}}$ is better understood as the result of a particular information-processing operation whose purpose is to *filter out* from the pattern vector $\mathbf{f}$ the component that is explained by the stored data. It is then possible to think of $\tilde{\mathbf{f}}$ as the amount that is "maximally new" in $\mathbf{f}$. It may be justified to call this component the *novelty with respect to the stored vectors,* and the name *Novelty Filter* has been used for a system which extracts $\tilde{\mathbf{f}}$ from input data $\mathbf{f}$ and displays it at the output alone without the $\hat{\mathbf{f}}$ component (Kohonen, 1977; Kohonen & Oja, 1976). The Novelty Filter system has the ability to enhance any nonfamiliar part or features appearing in an activity pattern passing through.

Because $\tilde{\mathbf{f}}$ is obtained from $\mathbf{f}$ by a linear operation, the application of the projection matrix $\mathbf{FF}^+$, where $\mathbf{F}$ is the matrix whose columns are the stored vectors $\mathbf{f}^{(1)}, \ldots, \mathbf{f}^{(p)}$, then it follows immediately that

$$\tilde{\mathbf{f}} = \mathbf{f} - \mathbf{FF}^+\mathbf{f} = (\mathbf{I} - \mathbf{FF}^+)\mathbf{f}. \tag{4-19}$$

where $\mathbf{I}$ is the identity matrix. This shows that $\tilde{\mathbf{f}}$ is the outcome of a linear operation, too, with the matrix

$$\mathbf{P} = \mathbf{I} - \mathbf{FF}^+ \tag{4-20}$$

giving the linear operator. This matrix is the transfer operator of the Novelty Filter. It is a projection matrix, too, because it projects every vector on a subspace $\mathscr{L}^\perp$ which is the orthogonal complement of the subspace $\mathscr{L}$ spanned by the stored vectors $\mathbf{f}^{(1)}, \ldots, \mathbf{f}^{(p)}$.

A network implementation for the Novelty Filter paradigm can be explained in terms of the laminar model with internal feedback, Fig. 4.2. If the separate afferent input signals of the network are again denoted by scalars f_i, the response signals by r_i, and the connectivities of the network by m_{ij}, then the output signals or responses are actually functions of both the afferent input and the other responses of the network, carried by the feedback lines converging on the units. By exact analogy to the mathematical treatment performed earlier in Section 4.2.3., with the same comments applying for the linearity approximation and the completeness of feedback connections, we then have

$$r_i = f_i + \sum_j m_{ij} r_j. \tag{4-21}$$

In vector–matrix form, this reads

$$\mathbf{r} = \mathbf{f} + \mathbf{Mr}, \tag{4-22}$$

which further yields

$$\mathbf{r} = (\mathbf{I} - \mathbf{M})^{-1}\mathbf{f}. \tag{4-23}$$

Thus the *overall* transfer operator for the input patterns is in fact matrix $\Phi = (\mathbf{I} - \mathbf{M})^{-1}$. The crucial difference with respect to the earlier autoassociative network lies in the assumed law for synaptic modification, which in place of Eq. (4-2) now reads

$$\frac{d}{dt} \, m_{ij} = -\alpha r_i r_j. \tag{4-24}$$

In other words, *negative feedback* (mainly due to inhibitory connections) has been introduced, and it will build up adaptively, tending to compensate for the input excitation. Actually the physical implementation of Eq. (4-24) has some extra details not discussed here (Kohonen & Oja, 1976). The laminar model, described by the transfer operator Φ, now becomes equivalent to a very special and selective "habituating filter"; it will display at its output only that component of the input pattern vector which is orthogonal to the subspace already spanned by all earlier inputs, that is, it displays exactly the previously mentioned residual. If each input is applied for a suitably long time, the resulting transfer matrix is in fact $\Phi = \mathbf{P}$, the Novelty Filter projector given by Eq. (4-20). The mathematical form that the learning process takes is describable by a Bernoulli matrix differential equation, whose solutions are intimately related to an algorithm well known in linear algebra, viz. the Gram-Schmidt orthogonalization procedure (Albert, 1972; Oja, 1978). Therefore the term *orthogonalizing filter* has also been used for this system.

Novelty Filtering is a useful fundamental operation in any natural information storing and processing system, because those parts or features of a pattern that are directly expressible in terms of the stored data are rejected, but the filter system is transparent to the most interesting components of new data.

4.2.6. Recollection of Temporal Sequences

The purpose of this section is to demonstrate that *temporal associations* are easily obtainable from an associative memory provided with minor extra features, namely, *delayed feedback*.

Imagine that a sequence of input patterns $\{A(t)\}$ that all share the same *background*, or *context*, **B** shall be stored. Context **B** may now be regarded as a specific part of the input field; however a characteristic of signals applied in this part is that *they are always held constant during a particular sequence* $\{A(t)\}$. On the other hand, different context signals can be used for different sequences. Due to the introduction of context the same pattern $A(t)$ may thus be associated with several different output patterns using different contexts. The role of context has become very central in the temporal mode of operation; by its virtue it becomes possible to identify the different sequences directly and to select one of them for recall.

Consider the sequential machine depicted in Fig. 4.4 (Kohonen, 1977, 1980). The central block is some kind of autoassociative distributed memory network, for example, a laminar memory model discussed earlier. The system receives two types of input: the external input, consisting of **A** and **B,** and feedback input **D.** The feedback is obtained from the output of the system through a delay that, for simplicity, is assumed to have unit length. It may be assumed that if **A** represents a forcing input, then during the input process (writing into memory) **C** is a response that is a replica of **A.** During recall, however, there is no forcing input and **C** is recalled by (**B, D**) used as the key. Assume now that a sequence of inputs $\{[A(1), B], [A(2), B], \ldots , [A(N), B]\}$ is received and stored autoassociatively. When the first input pattern $[A(1), B]$ arrives, the feedback input **D,** due to delay, does not receive any signals yet from **C;** it consists of an empty subpattern $\wp$. When the second pattern $[A(2), B]$ arrives, the previous output $A(1)$ has already been transmitted through the delay, and it is assumed to appear synchronously with $A(1)$. According to the above considerations, the *effective* input sequence of the autoassociative memory is then

$$S = \{[A(1), B, \wp], [A(2), B, A(1)], \ldots , [A(N), B, A(N-1)]\}. \quad (4-25)$$

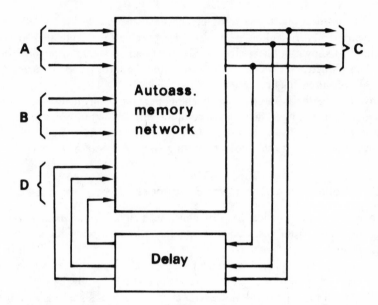

FIG. 4.4. A system for the associative recall of sequences. **A** = forcing input vector; **B** = constant background or context pattern; **C** = response pattern, the recollection from autoassociative memory; **D** = feedback pattern, equal to the response at a previous instant, with the time difference given by the delay.

In order to recall the $\{A(t)\}$ sequence, the reading is started at time $t = 0$ by applying a key input $[A(1), \mathbf{B}, \emptyset]$. Hereafter, no other members of the sequence are needed because they are automatically produced by the memory. At $t = 1$, the input pattern is now $[\emptyset, \mathbf{B}, A(1)]$ where $A(1)$ appears because of the feedback. The memory recalls the missing part $A(2)$ of this activity pattern associatively and produces it at the output. In this manner a continued autonomous process will retrieve the whole sequence $A(2), A(3), \ldots, A(N)$ associated with the background $\mathbf{B}$.

A problem arises if the same state occurs in several places in the sequence and it has a different successor state each time. It should then be realized that the system of Fig. 4.4 is the simplest model containing feedback loops. If there are several feedback paths with different delays, then the model will be able to recall more complicated sequences; in fact, a machine with k different feedback paths is needed to recall correctly a sequence that contains several identical subsequences of length $(k\text{-}1)$.

4.2.7. Some Demonstrations of the Pattern Processing Properties of Optimal Associative Mappings

The simple demonstrations reported in this section are only intended to illustrate pattern-transforming effects of the basic optimal associative mappings; processing of structured information needs a more developed organization as delineated, for example, in Section 4.4. Nor is it claimed that the well-known problem of invariances in perception would be completely solved by the interpolation that takes place in linear transformations. However, even though this experiment does not simulate the operations of the complete visual system, the pictorial material (human faces) is justifiable as test data because it has an inherently natural statistical structure and allows direct inspection of the recollections. The actual neural patterns would look quite different because they are transmitted through many preprocessing stations.

Pattern Classification. As a first demonstration, consider a classifier based on the optimal linear associative mapping for pattern pairs $(\mathbf{s}^{(j)}, \mathbf{f}^{(j)})$; see Eq. (4-9). Here the $\mathbf{s}^{(j)}$ are *prototype* vectors that belong to various *classes;* each $\mathbf{f}^{(j)}$ is a unit vector that has as many components as there are classes of patterns. To every class there corresponds a unit vector with the value 1 in a particular component and 0 elsewhere. For every class, a small number of prototypes is collected; if $\mathbf{s}^{(j)}$ is one of the prototypes, then

$$\mathbf{f}^{(j)} = \mathbf{M} \, \mathbf{s}^{(j)} \quad \text{for all } j \qquad\qquad (4\text{-}26)$$

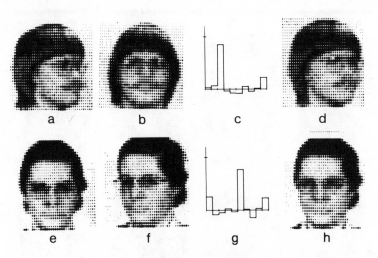

FIG. 4.5. Demonstration of classification by optimal associative mapping. Each of the 10 pattern classes employed consisted of pictures of one person photographed from five different angles, ranging from $+45°$ to $-45°$. Image vectors with components consisting of discrete picture elements were used as pattern vectors; eight intensity levels were defined for each picture element. A distinct unit vector was associated with each person. Parts (a) and (b) show two prototypes from one pattern class (no. 3), and Parts (e) and (f) show two prototypes from another pattern class (no. 6). Part (d) shows a test image of the person in (a) and (b), taken from an angle not used among the prototypes. In the histogram of the recollection, (c), the position of the largest component correctly reveals the number of the class. Parts (g) and (h) repeat the same with another class.

holds exactly. If, however, a vector **s** to be classified has only varying degrees of similarity with the prototypes of different classes, the matrix-vector product **Ms** (associative mapping) produces an output vector **f** that has the same dimensionality as the unit vectors $\mathbf{f}^{(j)}$ but in which each component only describes a "weight" by which **s** belongs to the various classes. The largest component, or weight, is assumed to indicate the classification.

In the demonstration of Fig. 4.5, 10 persons were viewed from different angles, and these images were used as the prototypes of 10 classes, each class corresponding to one person (Kohonen, Lehtiö, Oja, Kortekangas, & Mäkisara, 1977). These prototypes were associated with unit vectors corresponding to different persons. An associative mapping of the images onto unit vectors is seen to be able to interpolate between the representations so as to yield a correct recognition of a person from a viewing angle not occuring in the contents of the memory.

Autoassociative Recall. In order to demonstrate the autoassociative mapping given in Eq. (4-11), the patterns $\mathbf{f}^{(j)}$ that were stored in memory were facial images of different persons; there were 100 pattern vectors stored ($p = 100$). Four of the images are shown in Fig. 4.6 (a-d). An incomplete or noisy version of

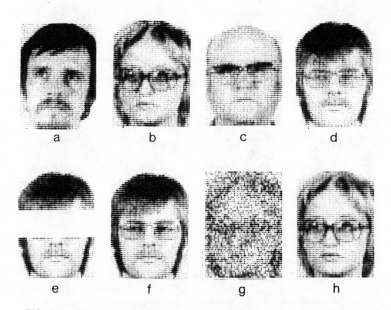

FIG. 4.6. Demonstration of autoassociative recall. Parts (a) through (d) show 4 of the 100 prototype images used to construct the autoassociative projector. When an incomplete or noisy version of a prototype, (e) and (g), respectively, served as the key pattern, the recollection resulting in the optimal autoassociative mapping is then shown to reconstruct the original appearance in (f) and (h), respectively.

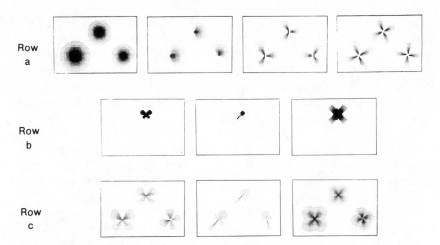

Row
a

Row
b

Row
c

FIG. 4.7. Demonstration of generalization and synthesis by an autoassociative mapping. Row a shows 4 of the 21 different prototypes, each one composed of 3 subpatterns with invariant relations of size, location, and orientation. Row b displays new subpatterns never occurring among the prototypes. Each subpattern is located in the same place as the uppermost subpattern in the prototype images, but the rest of the picture field is empty. In Row c each pattern is the recollection from the autoassociative mapping, computed from the 21 prototypes, when the pattern above it was used as the key. The autoassociative mapping is shown to synthesize new subpatterns exhibiting the same invariance of size, location, and orientation as the prototypes.

one of the stored images, Fig. 4.6(e) or 4.6(g), respectively, is now taken as the key f. The optimal recollection or projection $\hat{f}$ is shown to reconstruct the original appearance, at least approximately, in Fig. 4.6(f) and 4.6(h), respectively.

Another demonstration of autoassociative mapping, emphasizing its synthesizing and generalizing properties, is shown in Fig. 4.7. The prototype patterns were defined as two-dimensional functions on the image field. The field consisted of 3128 points, but in this experiment only 21 different stored patterns were used. Every stored pattern consisted of three subfields each containing a subpattern, whose relations of location, size, and orientation were *invariant* in all prototypes. The *microstructure* in each subpattern, expressed in polar coordinates, consisted of bell-shaped functions in the radial direction and sinusoidal functions with varying frequency and phase in the angular direction. The subpatterns of each prototype were so constructed that the prototype patterns, considered as 3128 component vectors (read from the picture field column by column, with vector elements being the gray scale values of the picture elements), were all linearly independent, in fact orthogonal. Orthogonality is, however, not necessary in principle, but it simplifies computing algorithms because the autocorrelation matrix (cf. Eq. (4-14)) can now be used instead of the autoassociative mapping.

Four of the 21 stored prototype patterns are shown in Row *a* of Fig. 4.7. Various test patterns were used as key patterns, each consisting of some form of subpattern in the same location as the uppermost subpattern in all the prototypes but with the rest of the picture field empty. Three such test patterns are seen in Row *b* of Fig. 4.7. The results of the demonstration, the recollections in Row *c* of Fig. 4.7, show that the invariances in the stored patterns, that is, their internal structure, have become an inherent property of the space of linear expansions and are thus implicitly contained in the elements of the memory mapping. The recollections exhibit in every case the same relations of size, location, and orientation as the prototypes but with the three subpatterns in the recollection similar in form to the one in the key. Even with such a small set of basis functions the autoassociative mapping has achieved the ability to synthesize the two new subpatterns, resembling in form the one used in the key, and also to generalize the structure of the prototypes to hold between these subpatterns of the recollection. It might be expected that with a larger and more representative set of prototypes the recollections would comply even better to the key patterns.

4.3. THE NEURAL IMPLEMENTATION OF ASSOCIATIVE MEMORY

4.3.1. The Laminar Model

Distributed associative memory seems to be implemented in the brain as laminar networks with internal and sublaminar connections. In a fairly homogeneous lamina, it is easy to see how the operation of the network might be mathematically described by a matrix, which may be sparsely occupied.

How does this simplified system-theoretical view accord with the physiological and anatomical reality of the complicated neural machinery comprising the mammalian brain, and what might be the neural embodiment of such a distributed adaptive memory system? These are questions that should be answered before trying to explain mental information processing by the distributed associative paradigm. First of all, the histological analysis of the brain lends support to the idea that neurons are organized into horizontal sheets. This laminar organization is found in neocortex, allocortex, cerebellum, and in many areas of midbrain. (For an extensive collection of empirical results on different laminated structures, see Creutzfeldt, 1976.) The recent findings on these histological structures seem to point to a type of functional organization, whose overall behavior might be approximately described by the mathematical apparatus reviewed earlier. The structure of neocortex is used in the following description as a prototype of all cortical laminated structures.

Although it is morphologically possible to distinguish several layers in the cortical lamina, physiological studies on the mammalian cortex have revealed that the responses are similar in all cells that are confined within vertical columnlike aggregates of cells extending from pia to white matter (Hubel & Wiesel, 1974; Mountcastle, 1957). It is generally accepted that such columns (or slabs) are organized around specific afferent axonal inputs, which they seem to analyze. Teleologically we may think that the columnar organization arises from the necessity to represent different stimulus qualities upon a two-dimensional surface, at the same time preserving the topological organization. Consider the schematic view of cerebrocortical modular organization given in Fig. 4.8(a). This view has been grossly simplified by presenting the net as a ''skeleton cortex,'' omitting most of the cell types and taking into account only the prin-

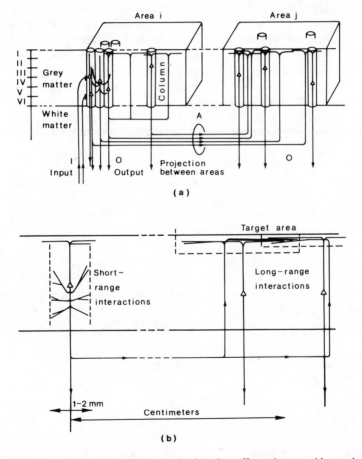

FIG. 4.8. (a) Cortical modular organization. I = afferent inputs, with actual termination not shown explicitly; O = outputs; A = association or commissural fibers mediating a projection between cortical areas. b) Short- and long-range interactions.

cipal neurons, which are pyramidal cells (Shepherd, 1974). The two block-like structures depicted in Fig. 4.8a are cortical modules or areas defined by their cortico-cortical connections. These connections are mediated by the subcortical axons of the pyramidal cells, which, after passing the white matter, ascend vertically through the cortical lamina up to its uppermost two layers, thereby ramifying with a great number of branches and extending over an area with a diameter of 2–3 mm (Szentágothai, 1978). Pyramidal cells have a similarly branching tree of apical dendrites in these layers, which allows a high degree of horizontal interconnectivity between cells. As every pyramidal cell has further axon collaterals that branch within the cortex, one may distinguish between the following three types of horizontal connectivity: (1) intracortical excitatory connections made by axon collaterals at a distance up to 100 μ; (2) intracortical inhibitory connections, possibly mediated through interneurons, which extend to a distance of 500 μ, and depend strongly on distance; and (3) cortico-cortical excitatory connections that may extend over any distance within the cortex. If these connections are made within the same area, then connectivity is independent of distance, and its obvious purpose is to provide the nonspecific interactions between cells. If these cell connections project from one area to another they are scattered over the target area. The commissural fibers between the cortical hemispheres also belong to the class of long-range connections but with specific connectivity. The two latter types of interaction are further shown schematically in Fig. 4.8(b).

It is assumed that the connections of type (3) carry out the memory-dependent interaction of columns. The integrated memory effects are therefore mediated by apical dendrites, which are known to have weaker but numerous excitatory synapses (Shepherd, 1974). The synaptic conductivities m_{ij} (Section 4.2) are used to describe the behavior of these contacts.

The spatial spread of the apical dendrites and the axons terminating at layer I increases the number of synapses and thus ensures a high degree of connectivity. It should be noticed that even if each column is integrating the activity of an area far beyond its dimensions, the response is generated locally by the column itself. There is therefore no lack of resolution in the output activity of the network.

4.3.2. Processing of Information by Interconnected Cortical Areas

It is proposed here that information is processed in interconnected cortical areas. This type of organization emphasizes the fact that each column may have inputs from different processing levels or from different auxiliary areas. Although it is possible to have a sequence of processing levels in certain parts of the brain, the modules may as well have a more parallel organization. A diagram outlining some organizational possibilities is presented in Fig. 4.9.

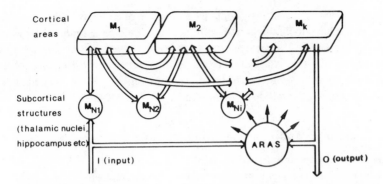

FIG. 4.9. Simplified organization of processing stations, assumed as "matrices," in the brain. The figure is a functional scheme, not showing the true geometry of areas or fibers, the crossing of sensory tracts from the other hemisphere, etc. Mainly those parts are designated that are close to input and output. I = representatives of sensory and other ascending input; O = representatives of descending output to muscles, glands, etc.; ARAS = ascending reticular activation system in the brain stem, which controls the cortical areas.

The interconnected cortical areas are represented in our model by associative memory mappings M_i. It must be understood that these have different degrees of plasticity and memorizing capacity, probably with the plasticity in an adult brain increasing as one moves from the primary sensory areas upwards in the hierarchy. Some or all of the mappings receive afferent inputs of various strengths, although in the schematic figure the inputs have been represented by only one arrow. The afferent input reaches the neocortical areas through thalamic nuclei, depicted in Fig. 4.9 by circles. These contain some mappings M_{Ni}, whose plasticity, if any, is probably much lower than in the cortical areas. Other subcortical units taking part in information processing, like the limbic system, have also been represented by similar circles. The cortical and subcortical units are interconnected in both directions. The efferent cortical outputs are designated by an arrow, again without specifying from which parts of the interconnected net they actually come.

An important subcortical feature in the model is the ARAS, or ascending reticular activating system, located in the brain stem. Its function is to exercise control over the activities in the cortical areas and over the incoming sensory information. It has been empirically shown that the consolidation of memory traces is affected by the activity of ARAS (Bloch, 1976). It thus has the effect of increasing the selectivity and optimizing the resources of the information-processing units by suppressing some activities and enhancing others. This also implies that the plasticity of the network depends on its chemical state or on some other global property.

This description obviously contains a number of gross oversimplifications, which would have to be taken into account in a more detailed model. However it is not the purpose of the present chapter to build a structural model of the brain that precisely fits the available anatomical data but to try to find out what the general ways are in which information processing can be organized using a distributed associative mode of operation.

4.3.3. Synaptic Modification and Learning

Inherent in the laminar network model is the assumption that memory is encoded in the vast number of junction strengths of the interconnections of the network. To be able to write new data into the memory, these junction strengths must be modifiable; to gain selectivity, the modification must depend in some way on the actual signals that are passing through the junction. The convergence of axonal inputs in the cortical lamina ensures that in each column there are synapses signaling the activity of the majority of other columns in the interacting areas. The information needed for cooperative functioning is thus locally available. The selectivity of the memory function is attainable in the network if and only if the synaptic change is limited to some combination of the signal activity. Probably the simplest mechanism proposed to explain the selective synaptic modification is the principle stated by Hebb (1949) in a general nonmathematical form, according to which an individual synaptic junction may increase its efficacy if it is repeatedly activated simultaneously with the triggering of the postsynaptic cell. This hypothesis was presented at a time when the physiological embodiment of learning was thought to be the formation of new stimulus–response connections. Later this hypothesis was expressed as the *conjunction theory* of learning (Eccles, 1978; Marr, 1970): A synapse strengthens if both the presynaptic and the postsynaptic neuron are active at the same time.

One may ask why there has not been a conclusive experimental verification of the existence or nonexistence of conjunction type learning during the thirty years between the appearance of Hebb's book and the present day. The answer lies in the very nature of the conjunction theory. One must realize that this theory does not presuppose that the memory traces are encoded in strong changes in some individual synapses or even in an increasing heterogeneity in the strengths of a number of synapses; the integrated change even in a small population of neurons may be zero due to positive and negative individual changes (cf. Eq. 4–27). The phenomenon is more subtle. It can best be explained by mathematical correlation, which is the macroscopic implication of conjunction learning in individual synapses on the level of the whole network.

It is as impossible to infer the contents of the entire memory from a few junction strengths as it would be to compute, say, the eigenvectors of a large matrix from a few matrix elements. To carry the analogy a bit further, subtle and almost unnoticeable changes in a large number of synaptic strengths can strongly affect the overall properties of the memory filter just as small selective variations in suitably chosen matrix elements may radically alter the linear mapping whose numerical counterpart is the matrix.

For this reason the prospects of a direct experimental breakthrough in favor of the conjunction hypothesis may not be good. This applies especially to large networks, like those of the mammalian cortex. In small systems of neurons the problem may be easier to solve. In fact the most important advances in this area have been made in the study of small neural systems like that of *Aplysia* (Kandel, 1979). This work has revealed some of the laws governing presynaptic sensitization. In the study of higher organisms most of the results are connected to long-term potentiation phenomena in the hippocampus (Eccles, 1979).

If the conjunction assumption is accepted as a working hypothesis, there are still several possibilities for the actual mechanisms involved. Some of these are growth and regression of presynaptic endings; changes in the transmitter concentrations; and redistribution or activation and passivation of postsynaptic receptors of the cell. These may be accompanied by other more permanent changes in the synapses or in the postsynaptic membrane, in which the memory traces become consolidated.

One of the more detailed and plausible models, although by no means the only one producing conjunction-type learning, is the redistribution of receptors between the synapses of a cell according to demand (Huttunen, 1973; Stent, 1973). This explanation has the advantage of being able to produce very quick changes, which may later be consolidated by a fixation of the receptor molecules onto the cell membrane.

This model has been discussed in detail by one of the authors (Kohonen, 1977). The ensuing equation for synaptic change is

$$\frac{d\mu}{dt} = \alpha\eta(\xi - \xi_0) \tag{4-27}$$

where μ is the efficacy of the synapse, η is the postsynaptic activity given on a frequency scale, ξ is the corresponding presynaptic activity, and ξ_0 is an equilibrium value, the input frequency causing no changes in the value of μ. The scalar α is a constant determined by the level of plasticity of the synapse. The above law applies both to excitatory and to inhibitory synapses and explains both weakening and strengthening, depending on whether ξ is below or above the equilibrium level ξ_0. In fact, the term $(\xi - \xi_0)$ may be considered as the effective presynaptic signal, attaining both positive and negative values (Kohonen, 1977).

The term $\eta(\xi - \xi_0)$, which is the product of postsynaptic and presynaptic signals, gives rise to a correlation matrix appearing in the learning equations, as explained previously in Section 4.2.3. Based on the conjunction form of synaptic plasticity, several typical functional units may be *adaptively* formed depending on the wiring of the network. Some such systems were reviewed in Sections 4.2.3.–4.2.6.

4.4. INFORMATION PROCESSING IN DISTRIBUTED ASSOCIATIVE MEMORY

4.4.1. Sensory Experiences as Patterns of Activity Over Memory Fields

As stated in earlier sections, the brain is an interactive system in which the activity of every part is affected by many other parts. Accordingly the associative mapping that takes place in one hypothetical functional unit can only describe an elementary operation in a complex sequence of processes. It is pointed out in the following discussion that these basic operations may, nonetheless, operate upon semantically meaningful representations of occurrences.

For every part or functional unit in the brain that contains memory we shall use a representation that we henceforth call a *memory field*. (A similar approach was taken by Nakano, 1972.) In its simplest form a memory field corresponds to a lamina of memory elements (cells or tightly connected agglomerates of cells such as columns) that have a great number of mutual connections, assumed to be distributed uniformly over the field (cf. Section 4.3.). The memory field can be identified with the top view of an area of cortex. There is sensory or other primary input to every element in this field. This input is assumed to originate at some prior processing stations (e.g., nuclei or other cortical areas) with the result that different locations in the memory field already have differentiated roles; signals representing particular features are clustered in particular locations. Some locations may be thought to receive input from subcortical structures, so these signals may have an emotional significance.

In the modeling approach it is thus possible to assume that within a memory field certain local areas, which we schematically distinguish by circular regions in Fig. 4.10, have a well-defined modality and meaning. *A region is now identified with an attribute, and the spatial pattern of activity within the region represents the value of that attribute.* (In reality, of course, these areas may be more or less diffuse.) There are good experimentally verified reasons to assume

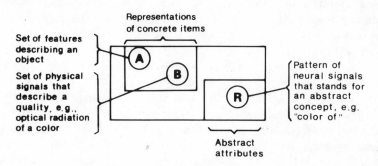

FIG. 4.10.   Hypothetical example of a memory field.

that for a particular sensory experience or other occurrence the pattern of activity over the complete memory field consists of only a few activated local areas (attributes) (Barlow, 1972) whereas the rest of the elements in the field are silent, having effective signal value zero (or rather, being regarded as signalless). This theory of representation now makes it possible to compare the memory field model directly with an abstract relational representation.

Assume for simplicity that there are only three active local areas as in Fig. 4.10, labeled A, R, and B. The signals at A and B may stand for features that make up the representations of two items, for example, one being the representation of an object and the other some concrete physical observation, whereas the region for R might contain neural signals that represent an abstract, relational attribute. Notice that the memory field model would allow an arbitrary number of such attributes to be present in one occurrence. It is also important to notice that attributes are bound to a particular location in the memory field.

This model, which uses patterns in memory fields, can now be contrasted with the traditional way of representing relations in data structures by triples of symbolic items, which may be traced back to the use of predicate calculus in early question-answering systems (McCarthy, 1959). If A, B, and R are symbolic (distinct) *items*, then (R, A, B) is a *relational triple:* For example, R = color of; A = an apple; B = is red; (R, A, B) = color of an apple is red. It is possible to question the generality of this formalism in the description of brain functioning. We feel that linguistic expressions have an extremely high degree of coding based on (implicit) assumptions and conventions, like the assignment of a particular meaning to prefixing, suffixing, and other formats. Expressions like (R, A, B) only *look* simple; in fact their treatment in the brain might need complicated processing, probably augmenting the representation of the arguments by contextual information that indicates their role. The concept of a memory field, in which regions are identified with attributes and the values of attributes correspond to spatial patterns within regions, provides a more realistic view of the representation of information in a neural network. The network is then able to process, for example, semantic triples or other tuples of symbolic items, but this is to be regarded as a secondary process rather than its natural mode of functioning.

4.4.2. Generation of Answers to Implicitly Defined Queries Presented to the Laminar Memory Model

It is frequently stipulated that genuine models of memory should be able to generate answers to complex queries or to perform searches for pieces of memorized information that are only implicitly defined by their relational structure. For this reason there has been considerable interest in memory models defined in certain artificial intelligence languages; the answers are found by a series of list-structure processing operations. In these, tolerance to errors in names, labels, and data structures is poor when compared with the performance of biological memory, nor can this type of memory structure generalize over clustered representations without adding considerable extra apparatus to inspect the memory structures.

Because the associative mappings implemented in the "matrix" memories have the ability of representing and retrieving patterned information that may also be clustered, it would be interesting to develop these models in a direction in which they too could be made to search for implicity defined memorized information on the basis of separately given cues. Contrary to what is generally believed, such processes are implementable by rather simple mechanisms, thereby preserving the ability to deal with data that have statistical properties (i.e., not bound to occur in a unique form). It is even possible to demonstrate some elementary forms of thinking and problem-solving processes, although we are still a long way from implementing real thought processes.

As it might be rather difficult to pick up an exemplary system which is general enough and at the same time reflects powerful information-processing abilities, we would like to rest content with a rather simple example that is still demonstrable with the aid of a few illustrations and a little text. First of all we revert to the field representation introduced in Section 4.4.1. Notice that because there exist interactions (associative connections) between all areas of the memory field, the active areas of the field can also be viewed as distinct functional "units." In this way *the operational units can be regarded as virtual ones,* allocated from the memory "field" according to need by an activation and selection system. It is then possible to consider the autonomous computing processes as taking place in a system of these virtual units or "virtual processors," in a series of iterative recall processes.

It seems that a search task in which the target item is implicitly specified by multiple relationships always involves multiple computations that are *separated in time.* Thus, although the memory network from which associative recall is possible is distributed and the operations in it are fully parallel, nonetheless there must exist a phase in the operation in which intermediate results are collected, compared, and collated. It can now be shown that there is no need to devise a complicated processor for this purpose. In many cases the system that carries out this collection and thus assumes the role of a a short-term memory (STM) can be extremely simple. Some sort of retention of the output signals from a functional unit with a duration of, say, several seconds is necessary, and the easiest way to implement this is by some kind of *"leaky integrator,"* (Shiffrin, 1976). We shall not try to specify a physical or chemical mechanism to make this retention possible. Notice, however, that even dynamic reverberation of signals between two units in a point-to-point fashion is a possible STM, and such point-to-point circuits are known to exist between the cortex and the thalamus of a mammalian brain.

In order to collate signal values obtained in matching separate incomplete patterns, the outcomes must first be normalized. This does not mean simply standardization of signal amplitudes to, say, two discrete levels but rather that the *time integrals* of the output signals from the laminar memory ought to be standardized. This is possible if temporal differentiation of the patterns takes place at the input to the matrix itself, or at its output. Again we shall not specify a particular mechanism more closely. One possible effect would be a short-term habituation, but this process might take on rather complex and at the same time intriguing forms (e.g., Kohonen & Oja, 1976).

One further operation in the collating process is carried out by a *threshold trigger*. The threshold might be adjustable by slow adaptation so that the triggering may be made to occur after two or more accumulated output signals have been obtained in successive matches to incomplete search patterns.

An Example of a Searching Process.   Consider the data structure shown in Fig. 4.11, which is supposed to represent the contents of a semantic memory; this structure is formed of relational triples (A, P, B), (A, Q, C), etc, in which the middle elements always comprise the *link labels,* and the two others the associated items. Assume that item C had to be retrieved on the basis of two incomplete search patterns (A, Q, X) and (E, R, X) with X unknown. The normal search procedure would first determine the set of solutions for X for each search pattern separately, and then find the value $X = C$ as the intersection of these two sets.

Let us now study how the same task would be solved by distributed memory. The data structure would be stored in terms of triples, which would be represented as patterns defined over the memory field, for example, of the type of Fig.

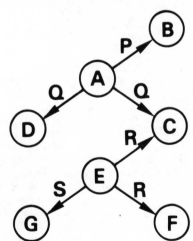

FIG. 4.11. The abstract data structure used in the simulation of Fig. 4.12. Vertices *A* through *G* represent items; edges *P* through *S* represent link labels.

4.12(a). It is noteworthy that there may be similar local areas in two different patterns, but the areas which are similar will vary from one pair of patterns to the next.

Assume now that two cues, two incomplete key patterns, are given as shown in Fig. 4.12(b) and 4.12(c). If either of these were separately applied as inputs to an autoassociative memory network, the responses from the latter, being mixtures of stored patterns, would be defined by Eq. (4–13) and delineated as in Fig. 4.12(d) and (e). Due to the assumed standardization of output signals, these recollections would remain subliminal. If, on the other hand, the two key patterns were applied one after the other, with a delay that is less than the time constant of the STM, then the component pattern C would be recalled with approximately double the intensity of the other components, and it would therefore exceed the threshold. Figure 4.12(f) displays only the above-threshold signals that now constitute the solution of the search task.

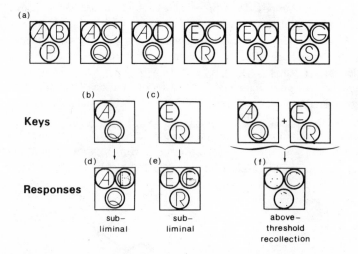

FIG. 4.12. Generation of an answer to an implicitly defined query by the distributed memory model. Part (a) displays in pattern form the relational triples contained in the data structure of Fig. 4.11. The elements of the triples are represented as spatial subpatterns of activity over the memory field. These six patterns have been stored in associative memory. Parts (b) and (c) show two cue patterns applied to the inputs in recall, and (d) and (e), respectively, show subliminal responses that are mixtures of selected images; for example in the upper right-hand subfield of (d), mainly a superposition of C and D is recalled in response to the key pattern (A, Q). When cue patterns (b) and (c) are shown subsequently with a time delay not exceeding the time constant of STM, a superposition of the standardized response patterns (d) and (e) takes place, producing the above-threshold recollection shown in (f). At the upper right-hand subfield of (f), an answer to the query (i.e., C) has thus been produced.

The search problem does not become much more complicated even if significantly more local areas (regions) than three are included in the patterns and if several of them are left unspecified in the keys. Although the internal relations in the patterns would be more complex in this case, nonetheless the phases of associative recall, and the recollection of results by the STM, would take place in essentially the same way as described. On the other hand, such a problem would need much more complicated handling by conventional query languages.

There is an intriguing explanation of the interaction of short-term memory (STM) and long-term (LTM), based on the previous model. As there obviously exist several types of memory effects with different time constants in the nervous system, one might assume that the integrated and processed outcomes from the STM become autoassociatively memorized in this or another network. In a later *recall* process this information can be recalled associatively, etc. This allows rather complicated information structures to accumulate in memory with time, without all of these structures being explicitly present at the same time.

4.4.3. Self-Controlled Operation of the Distributed Memory

Organized computing devices can be built of chips containing only logic gates. Similarly we can imagine an *associative processor*, consisting of many distributed memory units interconnected by bundles of signal lines over which they pass cue patterns and recollections to each other. If the system had closed signal circuits, this passing and transformation of information would proceed recurrently or iteratively with each module adding such information to the patterns as was earlier stored in it. These modules could also standardize their output signal values and extract certain features at their inputs, thus compressing information that was present in the transmitted patterns. Unlike digital computers, such distributed memory systems do not need a highly sophisticated control that opens and closes every signal path in a programmed sequence. If any gating of signal paths exists, it can be of a more or less general nature, comparable to the control of arousal or attention in the nervous system. Coarse spatial control could be achieved by context signals, which activate a subset of units for a particular task. The self-controlled operation of this kind of system should be compared with that of a conventional *analog computer*, especially a *differential analyzer*. The operational units of the latter transform signals internally and pass the results to each other in an asynchronous and highly parallel fashion without external control. The analog computer can be envisioned as an autonomous dynamical system in which computation involves continuous change of the state variables over time.

Although the distributed memory system is assumed to behave in a way grossly similar to an analog computer, there exist some characteristic features that distinguish it from a conventional differential analyzer:

1. The system parameters (the weights) change adaptively due to the occurring signals; that is, *memory traces* are collected that facilitate associative recall.

2. The state variables and the input–output signals between the units are not scalar valued. Processing of information within the units as well as communication between them occurs simultaneously and in parallel over a great number of state variables that constitute the patterns.

3. The outcomes from computations in a memory system are usually not trajectories of signal variables in time as in a differential analyzer. Instead the final state of a memory field can be a stationary pattern, in which case the resulting values of some state variables represent the sought information. Alternatively, the system may run through a sequence of states that represent a dynamic recollection of a memorized occurrence.

4.5. DISCUSSION OF CERTAIN PROBLEMS WHICH ARISE WITH PHYSICAL MEMORY MODELS

4.5.1. The Data-Switching Problem

Conventional information-processing models contain implicit assumptions about computational procedures and underlying programs. Current AI research has most often resorted to procedural models that are directly implementable by present computer hardware and languages developed for it. If these models are also advanced in the context of theoretical psychology, one may easily be misled into assuming that intellectual and especially verbal activities require this type of computation. Very little attention has generally been paid to what digital computation actually means.

In conventional digital computers processing operations are concentrated around central arithmetic–logic circuits and associated registers into which the operands have to be *multiplexed* from the memories. Multiplexing and time-sharing of the computational operations is a natural solution for devices that are based on logic circuits. However it also means extensive data transfers between the operational units during which the format of data must be preserved with high fidelity. Moreover, each particular type of datum must then be guided into a particular destination according to its *role*, which imposes extra requirements on its representation and control. It is highly improbable that this kind of multiplexing or data switching occurs in the neural structures where signals are transmitted at relatively low speeds through more or less fixed pathways and *transformed* during their passage from one processing station to another. It is thus implausible that the representation of information in the central nervous system is based on relational triples where items are ordered by their role.

Instead of assuming that the representations of signals in the central nervous system carry with them some specification of their roles and are thus freely transferable, it would be more natural to assume that *the semantic role of a signal explicitly follows from the particular part of the brain and region in the memory field into which it converges.* This becomes possible because of some degree of genetic predisposition in the gross connectivity, although, as pointed out in Section 4.4, the actual forms of signal patterns within an area may vary with individual experiences.

If brain mechanisms are viewed as highly parallel computing circuits, then ideal parallelism means representation of information that is distributed all over the system. It is then no longer proper to think of information as composed of a great number of more or less independent *records,* a view that has been inherited from serial computers. An occurrence could rather have a representation that occupies the whole system, as the activity patterns over the memory fields do.

The difficulties arising from the data-switching problem with corresponding restrictions set to neural implementation seem to favor memory models that are based on memory fields, that is, the distributed associative memory, as well as the connectionist view.

A particular type of memory field can be made to represent a "connectionist" memory directly. If it is assumed that the *memory elements* of the field (not activity patterns over areas) directly represent items, abstract attributes, etc., then these elements might be named *nodes* as in semantic networks. "Associations" would in this view correspond to direct links between nodes. Obviously this model represents an extreme case in which every single element of the memory field has a semantic interpretation. This is a standpoint adopted by some earlier psychological models of memory (Norman, 1968). Not only must the signals corresponding to every sensory experience then be guided to the nodes with perfect spatial resolution and selectivity, but one must also assume that the location of such a node was determined from the beginning, independently of any sensory experiences.

In fact, in the example of information processing by a laminar network as discussed in Section 4.4, operations were performed by a "hazy connectionist network" in which the local areas corresponded to nodes, and their interactions were mediated through the adaptive lateral connections.

4.5.2. Automatic Formation of Symbols in Associative Mappings

It has been a common view that the central nervous system processes information in symbolic form (Newell & Simon, 1972). This was obviously postulated for the following reasons:

1. Symbols can be made *unique* whereby they facilitate long and complex operation sequences.

2. Symbols can be associated with *concepts*, which in the simplest form are representations of *clusters* in more or less variable occurrences.

3. As the concepts can be defined on different levels of abstraction, a more accurate *meaning* can be given to an occurrence at an increased economy of representation.

An extreme form of symbolism would be a "brain code," the existence of which, however, has never been verified experimentally. Now it has to be emphasized that a symbolic representation need not be identified with a code. It seems sufficient that any substitute pattern that is simpler and more invariant than the original occurrence can be associated with the latter; we have tried to delineate in this paper some possibilities for the embodiment and processing of structured relations between such representations (Sections 4.2.6 and 4.4.2).

A trivial and also common way to define a concept is as supervised association of a symbol to a pattern. However, a much more important and intriguing problem concerns mechanisms by which a symbolic representation could *automatically* be formed in an adaptive system. One possibility, formation of certain discrete states in the system corresponding to distinct statistical "eigenfeatures" of the input information is discussed elsewhere in this book (Anderson & Mozer, Chapter 8, this volume). Sometimes such discrete states are formed by simplification, for example, by amplitude discrimination of signals and dropping of weak segments from sequences. Classification, especially false identification with earlier prototypes, is obviously one process which assigns names to new occurrences.

As to the remaining problem, formation of symbols referring to different levels of abstraction, it is useful to observe that regions in scenes which are more *general* are often also more *constant* and vice versa. This may allow differentiation between hierarchical levels on the basis of conditional probabilities of the subpatterns.

4.5.3. Interdependence of Different Operations in Neural Information Processing

A comprehensive theory of neural information processing has to explain many known phenomena not covered in this chapter. How do we recognize a person on the basis of a scratched old photograph never seen before? How do we allocate attention to different parts of a scene full of objects? What is the basis of the perceptual invariances?

The analytical models in this chapter are the results of the study of basic learning paradigms in the nervous system. They try to explain how the associative storage and recall may be implemented in a neural network. Their ability to explain perceptual invariances or complex mental processes is limited. We feel, however, that even if all cognitive processes are tightly interrelated complex processes, there exist subproblems that may be tackled separately.

The brain, which is the most effective adaptive system, is obviously optimized at all levels, in organization as well as in details. Therefore, because representation of organized perceptions and structured knowledge is a demanding task, it seems reasonable to assume that there exist information-processing stages in the brain that can extract invariant primitives of information from signal patterns. Effective feature extraction and standardization functions are known to exist at least in the primary sensory systems, and they have been subject to many theoretical studies; similar standardizing transformations may be found at higher levels of neural hierarchy, too. At least in theory it then seems profitable to separate the modeling of preprocessing from that of memory functions, which allows a more lucid discussion of the latter.

SUMMARY

The major theme in this chapter has been processing of information in distributed associative memory systems that serve as models of adaptive neural systems. This approach provides an answer to one of the most intriguing problems in neuroscience: How may the neural tissue, which is rather uniform over the cortex, be adaptively specified to carry out the highly differentiated functions found in it.

The chapter was divided into three main parts: We first presented in Section 4.2 some models to explain the basic functioning of the distributed associative memory in system-theoretical terms, using optimal associative mappings. It was shown that items of information can be made to correspond to distributed transformation functions that, although not being stored in spatially separate locations, still preserve the distinctness of representations in the recall process. In Section 4.3 the biological feasibility of these system-theoretical ideas was studied in connection with a laminar network model of the neocortex. In this model information is processed in interconnected cortical areas that make it possible to represent the known specificity of different cortical areas and still apply the principle of distributed associative memory. In Section 4.4 the problem of representing semantic data and generating answers to implicitly defined queries in distributed memories was approached and a solution was outlined in terms of laminar memory fields.

REFERENCES

Albert, A. *Regression and the Moore–Penrose pseudoinverse*. New York: Academic Press, 1972.

Anderson, J. A., & Silverstein, J. W. Reply to Grossberg. *Psychological Review,* 1978, *85,* 597–603.

Barlow, H. B. Single units and sensation: A neuron doctrine for perceptual psychology? *Perception,* 1972, *1,* 371–394.

Bellman, R. *Introduction to matrix analysis*. New York: McGraw-Hill, 1960.

Bloch, V. Brain activation and memory consolidation. In M. R. Rosenzweig & E. L. Bennett (Eds.). *Neural mechanisms of learning and memory*. Cambridge, Mass.: MIT Press, 1976.

Bush, R. R., & Mosteller, F. *Stochastic models for learning*. New York: Wiley, 1955.

Creutzfeldt, O. (Ed.) Afferent and intrinsic organization of laminated structures in the brain. *Experimental Brain Research, 1976, Supplementum 1.*

Eccles, J. C. An instruction-selection hypothesis of cerebral learning. In P. Buser & A. Buser (Eds.), *Central correlates of conscious experience*. Amsterdam: Elsevier, 1978.

Eccles, J. C. Synaptic plasticity. *Naturwissenschaften, 1979, 66,* 147-153.

Hebb, D. O. *Organization of behavior*. New York: Wiley, 1949.

Hubel, D. H., & Wiesel, T. N. Sequence regularity and geometry of orientation columns in the monkey striate cortex. *Journal of Comparative Neurology, 1974, 158,* 267-297.

Huttunen, M. O. General model for the molecular events in synapses during learning. *Perspectives in Biological Medicine, 1973, 17,* 103-108.

Kandel, E. R. Small systems of neurons. *Scientific American, 1979, 241,* 60-70.

Kohonen, T. Correlation matrix memories. *IEEE Transactions on Computers, 1972, C-21,* 353-359.

Kohonen, T. *Associative memory—A system-theoretical approach*. Berlin: Springer-Verlag, 1977.

Kohonen, T. *Content-addressable memories*. Berlin: Springer-Verlag, 1980.

Kohonen, T., & Oja, E. Fast adaptive formation of orthogonalizing filters and associative memory in recurrent networks of neuron-like elements. *Biological Cybernetics, 1976, 21,* 85-95.

Kohonen, T., Lehtiö, P., Oja, E. Kortekangas, A., & Mäkisara, K. Demonstration of pattern processing properties of the optimal associative mappings. *Proceedings of the International Conference on Cybernetics and Society,* Washington, D.C., Sept. 19-21, 1977, 581-585. (b)

Kohonen, T., Lehtiö, P., Rovamo, J., Hyvärinen, J., Bry, K., & Vainio, L. A principle of neural associative memory. *Neuroscience, 1977, 2,* 1065-1076. (a)

Lewis, T. O., & Odell, P. L. *Estimation in linear models*. Englewood Cliffs, N.J.: Prentice-Hall, 1971.

Marr, D. A theory for cerebral cortex. *Proceedings of the Royal Society (London), 1970, B176,* 161-234.

McCarthy, J. Programs with common sense. In D. V. Blake & A. M. Uttley (Eds.), *Proceedings of the Symposium on Mechanization of Thought Processes,* 1959. London: H. M. Stationery Office.

Mountcastle, V. B. Modality and topographic properties of single neurons of cat's somatic sensory cortex. *Journal of Neurophysiology, 1957, 20,* 408-434.

Nakano, K. Associatron—A model of associative memory. *IEEE Transactions on Systems, Man, and Cybernetics, 1972, SMC-2,* 380-388.

Newell, A. Reasoning, problem solving, and decision processes. A paper presented at Attention & Performance VIII Conference, Princeton, 1978.

Newell, A., & Simon, H. A. *Human problem solving*. Englewood Cliffs, N.J.: Prentice-Hall, 1972.

Norman, D. A. Toward a theory of memory and attention. *Psychological Review, 1968, 75,* 522-536.

Oja, E. S-orthogonal projection operators as asymptotic solutions of a class of matrix differential equations. *SIAM Journal on Mathematical Analysis, 1978, 9,* 848-854.

Quillian, M. R. Semantic memory. In M. Minsky (Ed.), *Semantic information processing*. Cambridge, Mass.: MIT Press, 1968.

Rao, C. R., & Mitra, S. K. *Generalized inverse of matrices and its applications*. New York: Wiley, 1971.

Shepherd, G. M. *The synaptic organization of the brain*. New York: Oxford University Press, 1974.

Shiffrin, R. M. Capacity limitations in information processing, attention, and memory. In W. K. Estes (Ed.), *Handbook of learning and cognitive processes, Vol. 4,* New York: Wiley, 1976.

Simon, H. A. The information-storage system called "Human Memory". In M. R. Rosenzweig & E. L. Bennett (Eds.), *Neural mechanisms of learning and memory*. Cambridge, Mass.: MIT Press, 1976.

Stent, G. S. A psychological mechanism for Hebb's postulate of learning. *Proceedings of the National Academy of Sciences*, 1973, *70*, 997–1001.

Szentágothai, J. Specificity versus (quasi-) randomness in cortical connectivity. In M. A. B. Brazier & H. Petsche (Eds.), *Architectonics of the cerebral cortex*. New York: Raven, 1978.

Willshaw, D. J., Buneman, O. P., & Longuet-Higgins, H. C. Non-holographic associative memory. *Nature (London)*, 1969, *222*, 960–962.

5 Representing Implicit Knowledge

Scott E. Fahlman
Carnegie-Mellon University

5.1. AI, PSYCHOLOGY, AND NEUROSCIENCE

The papers in this book represent three very different approaches to understanding the mystery of human thought and memory: the approach of neuroscience and neuroscience-inspired models, the approach of cognitive psychology, and the approach of Artificial Intelligence (AI). All of these approaches are fundamentally mechanistic: They assume that intelligence can be understood, at some level, as the operation of a physical mechanism upon signals representing information. This information is accepted through various input transducers (senses), processed, and stored and ultimately results in signals to muscles and other output transducers. The assumption is that there is no magic here, nothing that is fundamentally beyond human understanding or physical law. Of course that is not to say that the processes of intelligence are simple or that a comprehensive understanding of them is close at hand.

Within this broad assumption that intelligence can be understood in mechanistic terms there is considerable divergence of approach and tradition. The workers in neuroscience and neural modeling attempt to understand the mechanism by understanding its parts and how they are connected and by trying to characterize mathematically the kinds of useful computation that such assemblies can perform. The workers in cognitive psychology attempt to gather meaningful data on human cognitive processes and activities and to develop models that fit their data. Both of these approaches tend to concentrate on particular small areas of cognition at any one time, often with very limited tasks or sets of stimuli; only in this way can the data be separated from the noise. It is not surprising, then, that the models arising from work in these two areas tend to be rather simple and local and that the models can often be expressed in terms of well-understood and elegant kinds of mathematics: continuous linear functions, simple feedback systems, simple statistical dependencies, and so on.

Workers in Artificial Intelligence take a rather different approach, often more synthetic than analytic, more engineering than science. The goal here is to create *and implement* systems that exhibit various aspects of intelligence. It might or might not be part of the goal that these systems accurately model the way the human mind works; it is often enough that *some* precise, mechanistic way has been found to create (and therefore to understand) the abilities in question. The focus in AI tends to be on much broader areas than one finds in the analytic approaches: We study the problem of vision in a noisy real-world context rather then through the discrimination of lines and simple features, the organization of memory to aid problem solving rather than the memorization of nonsense syllables, the understanding of connected speech rather than the classification of sound patterns. This emphasis on integrating local pieces into a more comprehensive whole makes the task harder, of course, but it also helps us to avoid local dead ends. It is not surprising that the models coming out of AI are substantially more complex than the models used in other areas and that complex sets of rules, instructions, and conditionals tend to dominate them in place of the smooth linear mathematics of the simpler models.

This ability to generate and test very complex models of cognitive mechanisms, covering rather large areas of cognitive behavior, is the unique contribution that AI can bring to the study of the mind. Just as the psychologists and brain scientists provide AI with useful constraints, at least for the type of intelligent device they study (which might be the only possible type), AI can provide them with ideas for new kinds of models and also with a bit of perspective, reminding them that there is more to be explained than today's pile of data and that a model of the whole is a very different thing from the sum of the models of the parts.

In some areas, the interaction among these diverse approaches has been fruitful. Not surprisingly, these areas are the ones in which AI has come closest to meeting its own goals: the study of various kinds of abstract problem-solving behavior, the kinds of tasks that people do consciously. Included in this category are tasks such as chess, puzzle solving, and various kinds of symbolic mathematics. As Newell and Simon (Newell & Simon, 1972) have shown, the behavior of certain AI models in such areas is in rather good accordance with data gathered from protocols with human subjects. The serial, computerlike models that have been prominent in most recent AI research seem well suited to modeling conscious intellectual tasks of this kind.

In other areas, however, AI has been less successful both in meeting its own goals of producing intelligent behavior and in generating plausible models for use by students of human intelligence. These areas include the problems of representing and effectively using large bodies of knowledge and also many kinds of recognition problems. The serial, single-processor models of computation have some real difficulties here; and where they have achieved some measure of success, the resulting AI systems have seemed very implausible as models of how a human approaches the same problems. A possible explanation of the difficulty is that in these specialized, unconscious areas of thought the brain makes extensive use of parallel processing, whereas AI models have tended to emphasize ways of making serial machinery do the job. This bias is understandable because AI researchers have not had parallel machines to work with, and it is very hard to develop complex models on gedanken machines. Of course, we in AI cannot expect our colleagues studying human cognition to share this hardware-inspired bias.

This difference between parallel and serial processing is not a fundamental one. Basic automata theory shows that a serial machine of the familiar type can, in principle, compute anything that its parallel cousins can, given enough time. Time, however, can have a tremendous effect on the style of computing that is chosen: There are many operations and algorithms that make perfect sense on a parallel machine but would never be seriously considered on a serial machine because they would take too long. One such operation is the intersection of large stored sets: On a serial machine we go to great lengths to avoid this operation, as it takes time proportional to the size of the sets; on some parallel machines, as we later see, it takes only a constant few cycles, regardless of the set size. If this operation were important in some task like recognition (and I argue later that it is), it is little wonder that the serial and parallel theories have developed differently.

The fact that parallel theories have been neglected in AI, at least in the recent past, does not imply that it must always be so. In fact there has recently been a considerable resurgence of interest in parallel approaches to recognition and the representation of knowledge. In part this is due to the sudden availability of cheap, powerful microprocessor chips from which parallel machines can be built; in part it is due to the gradual realization among some AI researchers that the serial approaches are up against fundamental limits. We can always turn to faster serial machines, but the human brain provides us with a nagging reminder that there must be *some* way to build an intelligent machine out of millisecond-speed components, if we can learn to use parallelism properly.

As yet there is no real consensus among AI researchers as to how much parallelism (if any) is a good thing or what form that parallelism should take. People are exploring in many directions: the actors of Hewitt (Yonezawa & Hewitt, 1977); the society theory of Minsky and Papert (Minsky, 1977); the parallel-matching production systems being developed at Carnegie-Mellon University (Forgy, 1979); and the parallel semantic network systems that are the subject of this paper. Among the advocates of parallelism in AI there is, I think, a feeling that the linear models coming out of neuroscience, although right in their insistence on a parallel basis for recognition, tend to be too simple to capture many phenomena of interest and that a more flexible symbolic approach is needed.

In the remainder of this paper I describe one of these new parallel models being developed in AI: a parallel semantic network system that I call NETL. This system was developed in response to what I felt was a general failure in AI to deal adequately with the problems of representing and using large bodies of real-world knowledge. This system depends on the extensive use of parallelism rather than raw speed to accomplish the necessary searches and deductions. Because of their parallel nature, NETL and the other new AI theories may prove to be a better source of models for students of human cognition than were their serial predecessors.

5.2. IMPLICIT VERSUS EXPLICIT KNOWLEDGE

The human mind can store a tremendous quantity and variety of knowledge— millions of stored descriptions and episodes of many shapes and sizes—and can access whatever knowledge it needs very quickly and flexibly. An AI system, if it is to serve as a model for human knowledge-handling abilities, must exhibit comparable size, speed, and flexibility. This is more difficult than it seems to be at first glance because much of the information that we use in everyday life is not stored explicitly but must be deduced from other information. A seemingly simple query may give rise to a very substantial amount of deduction and search.

Suppose, for example, that I am telling you about a particular animal named Clyde. Clyde is an elephant. As soon as I have told you this one simple fact, you will know a great deal more about Clyde than I have told you explicitly. You can tell me (with a fair degree of certainty) what color Clyde is, how many legs he has, whether he would be a good pet for someone living in a small walk-up apartment, what would happen to him if you held him under water for an hour (and what might happen to you if you tried to), and so on. It is impossible to believe that much of this knowledge about Clyde is stored in explicit form; to believe this, we would have to believe that we had asserted it all (and thousands of comparable facts) as soon as we learned the nature of Clyde. Our only alternative then is to believe that we have such knowledge stored for elephants in general, and that the addition of something like "Clyde is an elephant" to the data base somehow gives us a way of getting to and using this general knowledge without having to copy and index each of these facts explicitly for Clyde and for every other elephant.

Clearly, what is going on here is some form of deduction. If we know the facts "every elephant is gray" and "Clyde is an elephant," that gives us the right to deduce that Clyde is gray. If we know in addition the facts "every elephant is a mammal" and "every mammal needs air," then we may deduce that Clyde needs air. Note, however, that having the right to deduce something is a very different thing from having the job done. In order to answer some apparently simple question about Clyde—what color he is, for example—we might have to perform a large amount of search and deduction. But people, with brains built from elements that are very slow by computer standards, are able to answer such questions very quickly with none of the apparent mental effort that one feels, for example, in adding up a column of numbers.

The search is especially costly if the network of IS-A relations is allowed to branch in the upward direction as well ad downward. In Fig. 5.1, for example, we see that Clyde is not only an elephant, a mammal, an animal, and a physical object but is also a male, a herbivore, a quadruped, a circus performer, and a veteran of the Punic wars. Each of these categories is not only a label but also a description, containing many items of information about members of the class in question. If we want to know whether Clyde is pulled on by gravity, we must look at the PHYSICAL-OBJECT description; if we want to know about his sex life we must look at the MALE description; if we want to know about his pension, we must look under VETERAN. Of course, this diagram is highly simplified; many categories and individuals would have their information scattered over hundreds or perhaps thousands of descriptions as the IS-A tree branches out at many levels.

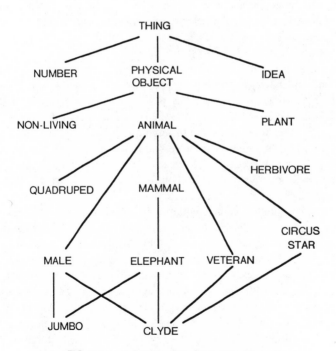

FIG. 5.1.: A Portion of the IS-A Hierarchy

And so, to answer a seemingly simple query about Clyde, we might have to visit many hundreds of nodes in our data base, attempting to retrieve the desired information for each superior class. There is in general no a priori way to know where in the tree to look. Search-guiding heuristics, of the type seen often in AI, can help a bit, but they must be carefully handcrafted for each new body of knowledge, and they often miss what they are looking for. In this case the system must either fail to find the item it is seeking or fall back on exhaustive search. Associative and pseudoassociative storage schemes, of the kind seen in "AI languages" like Planner, Conniver, and QA4, do not help much either; they can reduce the query at each node of the tree to a unit-cost operation, but one must still visit every superior node until the answer is found. It would seem that if retrieval of information from such a system is to be as quick and easy as it seems to be for humans, some parallel scheme must be employed to bring this search under control. The larger the knowledge base is, the more critical this becomes.

Before examining possible parallel solutions to this problem of unmanageable search, let us explore some other guises in which it appears. Suppose that you already know that Clyde is an elephant, and now I tell you that he is also a male. You have no problem with this because you know that there is nothing inconsistent about being in both of these classes at once. But if instead I try to tell you that Clyde is an elephant and also a cabbage, you immediately reject this statement, at least in its literal interpretation. Once again this is very quick and apparently effortless for people, but if we analyze the processing involved, it can require a large amount of searching.

Obviously we cannot afford to store explicitly the fact that no elephant is a cabbage, and that no aardvark is an artichoke, and so on. Instead, we store the fact that no plant is an animal, and classes and individuals below PLANT and ANIMAL in the tree must inherit this prohibition along with all of the other descriptive information from these classes. When new information is added to the knowledge base, we must search through the IS-A hierarchy looking for such prohibitions. Humans are never aware that this search is going on, but if a problem is found we know it at once. If we are looking for humanlike performance, this search need not discover subtle contradictions, but glaring clashes of the elephant–cabbage type must be handled well.

Recognition is another area in which very substantial searches arise in tasks that people have no trouble with. In any recognition task, whether the domain is speech, vision, medical diagnosis, or a problem solver trying to classify a situation, there comes a time when the recognizer has a list of observed features and has to locate the stored description that most closely exhibits all of these features. Suppose, for example, that we are in the Everglades and that we see something moving in the water. It is six feet long, greenish gray, four legged, with little bumps on its back, long pointy teeth, and so on. We have to determine whether we know of anything which exhibits all or most of these features. If we were using a serial machine to perform this processing, we would have a serious problem. We could, of course, scan each stored description looking for a winner, but if our knowledge base holds many descriptions, this could take a very long time (not healthy in the situation described). We need a faster way to perform this search that people often describe as a "flash" of recognition.

The traditional AI answer to this problem is again to use domain-specific heuristics to reduce the search. One common technique is to specify certain prominent features and combinations of features as "triggers," which, when seen, will suggest the associated description for further consideration. These triggers must be carefully chosen for each stored description, for if the triggers are not seen, the description will not be considered. On the other hand, if too many triggers are used, the search becomes as bad as it was under exhaustive search. And even if the trigger features are carefully chosen, the resulting system is brittle. If the triggers for an elephant are its trunk and its big ears, there will be no way to recognize an elephant whose head is behind a bush. What we really need is a system that can find any stored description, given any set of features that is sufficient to uniquely identify it, without scanning the candidates one by one. Of course, there is much more to recognition in real-world domains than the simple search process described above—finding the features, for example, can be a complex recognition task in its own right—but the search described above is an essential element of recognition, and some efficient search technique must be found.

In all of the above problems, two mathematical operations emerge as key components of a humanlike knowledge handling system: transitive closure and set intersection. In inheriting properties from more abstract classes, for example, we need to locate all of an individual's superiors, as indicated by the stored network of transitive IS-A relations. On a serial machine this must take time proportional to the number of superior nodes; on some parallel machines it can be done in time proportional to the length of the longest chain of IS-A links. If the IS-A network is short and bushy, this difference can be tremendous. Intersection is a key element in the recognition task noted above: We can locate a set of descriptions that exhibits each of the observed features individually (often using transitive closure to obtain the full set), and then we must intersect these description sets to find a winner. On a serial machine this takes time proportional to the size of the sets; on some parallel machines, as we later see, it can be done in unit time. Both of these operations are well defined mathematically, but they happen to be very costly to do on a serial processor. If they are indeed key operations in intelligent knowledge handling, it is little wonder that serial AI approaches have had little success in this area.

5.3.   NETL: A PARALLEL MODEL FOR KNOWLEDGE REPRESENTATION

In the previous section I described a number of areas in which the flexible handling of large quantities of real-world knowledge requires so much search and deduction that some sort of parallel approach seems to be necessary. In this section I describe a parallel-processing model that handles these problems very quickly and effectively. The approach described here was inspired by some of the easily observable features of human knowledge-handling abilities—the speed and flexibility with which certain operations are performed, even by relatively slow hardware elements—but this is essentially an AI model. There has been no real effort to fit the details of this scheme to any particular body of data from experimental psychology. The scheme has been more strongly influenced by current or forseeable computer technology. Because this scheme takes the form of a network representing the system's explicit knowledge, I call it NETL. I am able to present only a few aspects of the model in this paper; for a more complete treatment see Fahlman (1979).

The basic components of the NETL system can be seen in Fig. 5.2. In NETL, concepts are represented by very simple hardware elements called *nodes;* relations among these concepts and simple assertions about them are represented by additional hardware elements called *links*. The nodes and links are all attached via a shared, party-line bus to an external controller, a simple serial computer of

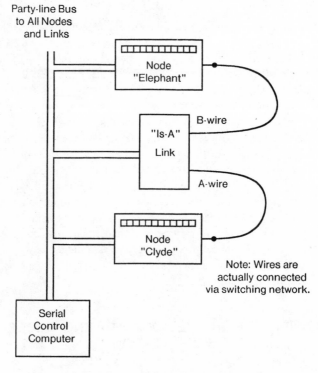

FIG. 5.2:   NETL Hardware Components

the familiar kind. The controller is able to shout simple commands to all of the nodes and links together, or to specified subsets of them, or to individual nodes and links for which it knows the name or serial number. Selected nodes and links are able to reply by placing their own name or serial number on the shared bus. If several elements try to do this at once, there is a mechanism by which they can be lined up and made to report in order of their serial numbers.

Each node contains its serial number, an optional name, a few bits of information about the type of entity the node is representing (an abstract type, an individual, etc.), and some small number of one-bit memory cells (flip-flops) that can be used to mark the nodes. If bit number 1 is set, the node is said to be marked with marker 1, and so on. The exact number of marker bits in each node is not too important; recently we have been using 18. Note that a given marker can be present on many nodes at once. Each node has, in addition to its bus connection to the controller, a terminal to which wires from any number of links can be tied.

The link units are also very simple hardware devices. Each link has a few bits of type information, indicating which of the basic types of link it is, and some number of wires (currently up to six) that can be connected to the terminals on various nodes. An IS-A link, for example, has type bits indicating that it is an IS-A and two wires that can be tied to nodes in the network. One wire (designated "A") goes to the node representing the thing being described; a second wire ("B") goes to the node representing the class into which this object is being placed. To represent "Clyde is an elephant" we locate an unused link; set the bits indicating that this is to be an IS-A link; connect the B wire to the ELEPHANT node; and connect the A wire to the CLYDE node, creating this node if necessary.

Obviously we cannot anticipate all of the relations that will be of interest in the lifetime of the system, so we assign type codes for just a few of the more important relations (IS-A, EQUALS, EXISTS-IN, and a few others). Additional relations are produced by creating a node in the network to represent the new relation and by connecting a wire from each link representing an instance of that relation to this *parent* node. For example, we might want to create links representing the COLOR-OF relation. To do this we first create a COLOR-OF node with an IS-A link to the RELATION category. Now, to say that elephants are gray, we simply select an unused node; mark its type bits to indicate that it is a GENERAL link; and connect its wires to the ELEPHANT, GRAY, and COLOR-OF nodes. Additional mechanisms exist for building up more complex relations, for tying statements to contexts, for creating exceptions to general statements, and many other things; these complexities need not concern us here.

The commands sent out by the controller consist of a prefix and an action. It might, for instance, specify in the prefix that the command is for the CLYDE node only, or for all nodes with markers 1 through 5 turned on, or for all TYPE nodes. The command might be to set marker 6, or to clear all markers, or for the selected nodes to queue up and report their serial numbers over the bus. In giving a command the controller can sense whether any recipient is prepared to respond. In commands to links the controller can specify the types of links that are to respond and can order that the links sense or alter the marker-state of the nodes that they are attached to. A typical order might specify that all IS-A links are to sense whether marker 1 is set on the node attached to their A wire, and if so, they are to set marker 1 in the node attached to their B wire.

Now, how can all this machinery help with the problem of search and deduction? Consider the network of Fig. 5.3, and suppose we want to determine the color of Clyde. First, the control computer tells the CLYDE node to set marker-bit 1. Next, all IS-A links that sense marker 1 on their A-wire node are told to place a copy of marker 1 on their B-wire nodes. In this single operation, we have marked all the nodes that are one level above Clyde in the IS-A hierarchy. This same command is repeated until no further action takes place. At this point we have placed marker 1 on all of the nodes above Clyde in the IS-A hierarchy—that is, on all the nodes from which Clyde is supposed to inherit properties. We now send a command to all COLOR-OF links with marker 1 on their A wire, telling them to set marker 2 in the node tied to their B wire. Finally, we tell all nodes with marker 2 to place their serial numbers on the bus. If all has gone well, there will be only one such node, GRAY, the desired answer.

Note that the above process involves taking the transitive closure of the IS-A relations above CLYDE. We have done this in time proportional to the length of

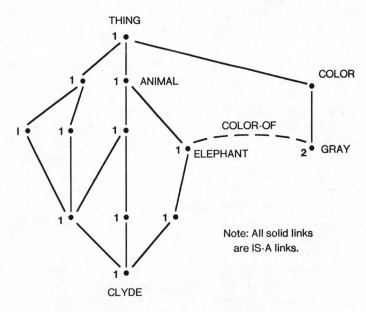

FIG. 5.3:   Finding the Color of Clyde

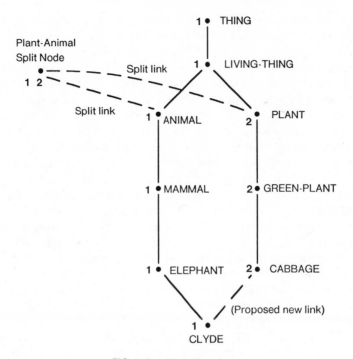

FIG. 5.4: Clash Detection

the longest IS-A chain that must be followed; the time does not depend on the total number of nodes that must be marked due to branching. Because in most applications IS-A hierarchies seldom grow to depths greater than 10, we can quickly answer questions about Clyde's properties even if the basic propagation operation takes a millisecond or more. We need never know exactly where in the IS-A hierarchy the color property is attached; we simply know that Clyde is gray. And because we are, in effect exhaustively searching the descriptions above Clyde in the IS-A hierarchy, we have no need for search-guiding and search-limiting heuristics with the brittleness that they imply. To represent a new domain of knowledge, you just add the knowledge itself; the parallel hardware handles the search.

In Fig. 5.4, we see a NETL representation of the elephant–cabbage clash problem. The node labeled SPLIT indicates that each of the type-nodes to which it is connected (with a special SPLIT link) represents a class of objects that has no members in common with other classes under the same split. In this case the class of living things is divided into animal and plants. If some object is known to be an animal, directly or indirectly, any attempt to make it a member of the plant class should be detected as a clash. If we encounter an exceptional case—a

Euglena, for example—that does belong in both categories, a mechanism is available for making explicit exceptions to the split.

In the diagram we already have Clyde represented as an elephant. The dotted link is a new IS-A link we are proposing to add, which will state that Clyde is a cabbage. Before actually adding this link we check for clashes. First, we mark with marker 1 all of the type-nodes above Clyde. This is essentially the same operation we saw before, and it takes only a few cycles to mark this set. Then, with marker 2, we mark all of the classes above elephant, but we do not allow 2-markers to propagate into or through nodes marked with marker 1. Again this takes only a few cycles. Now we have 1s on all of Clyde's existing superiors, and 2s on those nodes that will become new superiors if we add the new link. We now order that all 1 and 2 markers are to propagate across any SPLIT-links to the attached SPLIT-nodes. Any SPLIT-node that receives both of these markers is being violated and is told to report its identity to the controller via the common bus. And so, in two quick sweeps up the IS-A hierarchy and a constant few additional cycles, we are able to detect any clashes that the new link will cause.

In recognition problems the ability of the network to perform set intersections in parallel becomes critical. To mark all gray things in the network, we first place marker 1 on the GRAY node, then send it backwards across all COLOR-OF links to type-nodes representing objects known to be GRAY. This might mark ELEPHANT, BATTLESHIP, CONFEDERATE-UNIFORM, and many other nodes. We then propagate this marker down all IS-A links to subtypes and individuals that are gray by inheritance: AFRICAN-ELEPHANT, CLYDE, etc. Once again, this takes only a few cycles. For the other features that we want to factor into the recognition, we perform the same process, using a different marker for each feature. Suppose we have six features, and have placed markers 1–6 on the respective sets of objects. We now broadcast a call for any node marked with all six of these markers to report in—it is the description we are seeking.

If more than one node is found, we accept the one that is uppermost in the IS-A hierarchy—that is, we take ELEPHANT rather than many individual elephants. If there are many winning nodes that are uppermost in their respective subtrees, then the identification is not complete and we need to add additional features. If there are no descriptions with all six markers, then either the item being identified is not one that the knowledge base knows about or one of the features is in error. Erroneous features occur often in vision and other real-world recognition domains: What is large, gray, four-legged, floppy-eared, with a long cylindrical nose and a tree growing from its back? In this sort of case we can broadcast a call for nodes with five out of the six markers, then four out of six, and so on until we get some approximation to the best match.

Once again we have a very fast scheme with no need for triggers and other search-guiding heuristics. We made use of transitive closure to mark each set and then intersected the marked sets in a single command. A few extra cycles are needed if we need to resort to partial match, but still this operation is very fast. The time of perform these operations does not depend on the amount of knowledge present in the system. Note that the best match done here is not the familiar weighted average in multidimensional space but is a more Boolean sort of operation depending on the presence or absence of well-defined features.

The NETL system is able to perform many additional operations that I do not have space to describe here. In addition to the IS-A hierarchy it is often useful to mark parts of the hierarchies for PART-OF, BEFORE-AFTER, LARGER-SMALLER, and other transitive relations. Complex context structures, both temporal and spatial, can be marked, and these marks can be used to activate or deactivate subsets of the system's knowledge. This give us an elegant way to indicate changes of state in the network as a function of time. In addition the system can represent multiple worlds without confusing them. This is essential for representing desires, dreams, hypotheses, and works of fiction. All these facilities depend critically on NETL's ability to propagate markers in parallel.

At this point, it might be worthwhile to compare NETL's abilities to those of the linear filter models proposed elsewhere in this volume. These models are also rich in parallelism because all of the filters operate simultaneously, but the parallelism is of a rather different sort. The filter systems, in general, are able to perform intersections in unit time and can even perform complex weighted partial matches that NETL cannot. But these systems cannot easily perform the transitive closure operations that are so important in NETL in the inheritance of information through the IS-A hierarchy. A limited form of inheritance can be performed by certain matrix models (see Hinton Chapter 6, this volume) but only with a fixed predefined set of superior classes. The filter systems also appear to have problems with exceptions, multiple contexts, and other operations that are necessary in representing and using high-level knowledge. Unless some way can be found to overcome these limitations, I believe that the linear filter systems will be of value only for the lowest level of sensory feature detectors, with high-level processing being modeled much more closely by NETL-like parallelism or some sort of hybrid system.

5.4. FUTURE DIRECTIONS

For several years I have been working on NETL without any real hope of implementing the system in true parallel hardware. The problem was not in the expense of the nodes and links—with current integrated circuit techniques we can put a thousand or so of these elements on a single chip. The real difficulty lies in having to wire together new nodes and links as new knowledge is acquired. The link-to-node connections must be private lines, not shared buses, because many signals are transmitted at once over these wires. What is needed is a switching network capable of connecting millions of link-wires to millions of specific nodes, all at once: a sort of huge telephone switching network, capable of handling millions of calls at once.

In the past few months I have developed a type of switching network that makes it possible to build a million-element NETL system at a reasonable cost. The key element in this scheme is a *selector cell* which is able to connect its single input to any of 15 or so outputs. By arranging these selector cells in layers, with the outputs of one layer connected to randomly selected inputs of cells in the next, it is possible to build networks that can connect each input to any of a very large number of outputs independently. It is impossible to guarantee that a given connection can be made, but the probability of failure can be made vanishingly small. In fact this layered arrangement of switching elements was suggested to me by the layered arrangement of neurons in many parts of the cortex, though I appreciate that neurons are more complex than the simple 15-way switches used here. It would be very interesting to see if this model is of more than metaphorical value in explaining the neural mechanisms of memory. Details of this interconnection scheme can be found in (Fahlman, 1980).

I hope to begin design and construction of a million-element hardware NETL system in the next year or two. For economy this machine will use the interconnection scheme described above in conjunction with 1000-way time-sharing of the components. Even with this time-sharing it should be possible for this machine to propagate markers one level in a few milliseconds, comparable to the propagation time of a neuron. A network of a million nodes and links is not nearly enough to build a human-sized knowledge base, but it should be capable of holding substantial bodies of expertise in limited domains.

In the meantime developmental work continues with NETL systems simulated on serial computers. On a PDP-10, such systems are limited to about 10,000 elements—not enough for real-world applications but more than enough for development of the system. With several students I have been trying to develop the NETL representation language to make it easy for users to represent all of the concepts that are easily expressed in English. We are also exploring applications of NETL and NETL-like parallelism to the understanding of natural language and to speech recognition. Once the representation system becomes more stable we intend to explore a number of issues related to learning new information and reorganizing old information in NETL.

I believe that, in its broad outlines, NETL provides an interesting and possibly accurate model of how the human knowledge base system might be organized. NETL is almost unique among current AI systems in that it performs the necessary search and deduction without depending on very fast processing operations. It will, of course, require careful psychological investigation to confirm or refute this conjecture.

It seems much less likely to me (though not impossible) that the computer-inspired NETL elements have any direct relationship to the neural structure of the human brain. A troublesome aspect of NETL is its extreme locality: There is exactly one ELEPHANT node, and if this node is damaged it will be very hard to reconstruct the associated information. In a computer made of fragile neurons one would like a scheme in which component failures are less important. This might just mean that the information must be stored redundantly, but it also suggests that we should search for schemes in which concepts and assertions map into patterns rather than objects. A related problem is the locality of the central control computer. Although we would like the control activities of the knowledge base to be functionally unified, it is both unreliable and inefficient to put the controller in one physical location, with control buses running to everything else. No such controller has been seen in real brains. The problem, then, is to develop a more distributed scheme without giving up the precision and special abilities of NETL.

REFERENCES

Fahlman, S. E. *NETL: A system for representing and using real-world knowledge.* Cambridge, Mass.: MIT Press, 1979.

Fahlman, S. E. *The hashnet interconnection scheme.* (Tech. Rep.). Pittsburgh, Pa.: Carnegie-Mellon University, Department of Computer Science, 1980.

Forgy, C. L. *on the efficient implementation of production systems.* (Tech. Rep.). Pittsburgh, Pa.: Carnegie-Mellon University, Department of Computer Science, 1979.

Minsky, M. L. *Plain talk about neurodevelopmental epistemology.* 5th International Joint Conference on Artificial Intelligence, Vol 2, Cambridge, Mass., 1977.

Newell, A., & Simon H. A. *Human problem solving.* Englewood Cliffs, N.J.: Prentice-Hall, 1972.

Yonezawa, A., & Hewitt, C. *Modeling distributed systems.* 5th International Joint Conference on Artificial Intelliegence, Vol 1, Cambridge, Mass., 1977.

6
Implementing Semantic Networks in Parallel Hardware

Geoffrey E. Hinton
M.R.C. Applied Psychology Unit
Cambridge, England

6.1. INTRODUCTION

There are two very different ways of implementing semantic networks (see Fig. 6.1) in networks of simple hardware units. The obvious approach is to make different nodes in the semantic net correspond to different hardware units and to make links between semantic nodes correspond to hardware links between units. This type of direct implementation is advocated by Fahlman (Chapter 5, this volume) and Feldman (Chapter 2, this volume). It is also implicit in models that talk about "activation" spreading from one semantic node to another (Collins & Loftus, 1975; Levin, 1976).

A radically different approach is to make each node in the semantic net correspond to a particular pattern of activity on a large assembly of units. Different semantic nodes may then be represented by different patterns of activity on the same set of units. The parallelism provided by the multiple hardware units is used to give a rich microstructure to the individual concepts that correspond to semantic nodes rather than being used to allow many concepts to interact simultaneously. The semantic net formalism can then be seen as a crude description of the interactions between complex patterns of activity. The formalism captures the way in which concepts interact, but it ignores the microstructure of the concepts that is provided by the particular patterns of activity used to represent them in the hardware.

I argue that the second approach is a more promising model of how concepts are represented in the nervous system and that an understanding of the particular patterns of activity used for particular concepts (their microstructure) is important because the interactions between concepts that are formalized as a single link in a

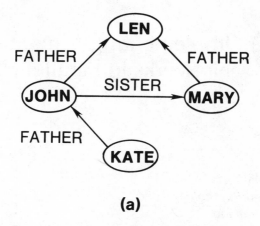

(a)

(JOHN FATHER LEN)
(MARY FATHER LEN)
(JOHN SISTER MARY)
(KATE FATHER JOHN)

(b)

FIG. 6.1.   Two formalisms for representing relational information. In (a) the roles of the constituents of a relationship are determined by their positions at the head, tail, or side of an arrow. In (b) the position in a string determines the role.

semantic net are actually generated by millions of simultaneous interactions at the level of their microstructures. An understanding of these microcomputations is the key to understanding how existing concepts are recalled appropriately, how relationships between concepts change, and how new concepts arise.

It is important to realise that the behavior of any network of hardware units can be described either at the level of activities in individual units or at a higher level where particular distributed patterns of activity are given particular names. This is illustrated in Fig. 6.2. Figure 6.2(a) depicts a set of units and the physical interconnections between them. This set is intended to be merely a part of a larger parallel machine. For simplicity each unit is assumed to have two possible states of activity, and Fig. 6.2(b) shows a hypothetical sequence of states of activity of all the units. Figure 6.2(c) shows the sequential relationships between the patterns of activity of the units in Fig. 6.2a. Notice that although the diagramatic formalism is the same in Fig. 6.2(a) and 6.2(c) the interpretation of that formalism is quite different. In Fig. 6.2(a) the nodes correspond to different parts of the machine; links correspond to particular physical connections; and many different nodes can be active at once. None of these descriptions applies to Fig.

6.2(c). Here the different nodes are implemented in the machine as mutually exclusive, distributed representations, that is, different patterns of activity on the same set of units.

We have seen that the very same physical events can be described at two quite different levels. It is an open question as to which level of description is being used when a psychologist uses the semantic net formalism to describe a person's knowledge.

6.2.   A PROGRAMMABLE PARALLEL COMPUTER

Artificial intelligence differs from experimental psychology or neurophysiology in its criterion for what counts as a good model. Instead of being primarily concerned with explaining behavioral or neurophysiological data, it aims to produce working programs that can demonstrably perform a task. In domains like

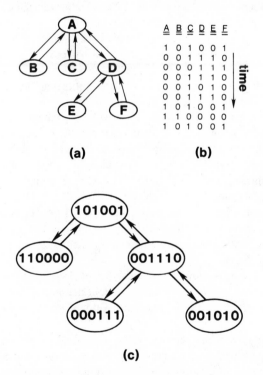

FIG. 6.2.   (a) The physical interconnections between some units that form part of a parallel machine. (b) A hypothetical sequence of states of activity of the units in (a) as a result of mutual interactions and input from the rest of the machine. (c) A graphical representation of the transitions between states shown in (b). Although this graph looks like the graph in (a), it has a quite different interpretation.

language understanding or visual perception, this approach has led to many insights about nonobvious difficulties that any information-processing system must overcome. Because of the prevailing technology, however, the goal of generating a working model has typically meant generating working models on existing digital computers. These computers are very different from the brain, and the differences affect the models. This problem can be circumvented by using a digital computer to simulate a different kind of computer that is much more like the brain. The methodology of building working programs can then be preserved, but now the programs are to be designed for the brainlike, simulated computer.

The simulated computer must be similar enough to the brain so that it is reasonable to expect that the computational techniques that work well on it will also work well in the brain. It is probably not necessary, however, to mimic all the details of the neural hardware exactly in order to discover higher-level, software principles that are applicable to a wide range of highly parallel computers composed of many simple computing elements with rich hardware connectivity.

In order to investigate a particular idea about how the semantic net formalism might be implemented in neural nets, a simple but powerful parallel computer was defined and simulated. The computer consisted of a number of perceptron-like units (see Chapter 1, Section 1.2.2). Each unit had an input line from every unit (including itself). At any moment each input line was either active or inactive (1 or 0). Each line had an associated real-valued weight, and a unit produced a 1 as its output at the next moment of time if the sum of the weights on its active input lines exceeded its threshold. Otherwise it produced a 0. The output of a unit determined the states of activity at the next moment of all the input lines emanating from that unit. This type of computer is a particular example of a matrix model (see Chapter 1, Section 1.2.3). The current states of all the units define a binary state vector. The next state vector is generated by multiplying the current one by the matrix of weights and comparing each component of this vector with the corresponding component in the vector of thresholds, as shown in Fig. 6.3(a).

External input to the system was achieved either by setting the initial states of the units or by giving each unit an external input that could have any real value. This value was added to the sum of the weights on the active lines before thresholding.

In programming a computer of this type to perform a given task, several different kinds of decision must be made. First, the total set of units must be conceptually divided into subsets for representing different entities in the task domain. If local representations are used, there will be a single unit for each entity. If distributed representations are used, different states of activity of the same subset of units will represent different entities, and it will be necessary to choose a particular pattern of activity to represent each entity.

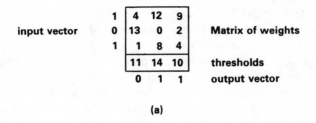

	4	12	9	
input vector	1			
	0			Matrix of weights
	1			

input vector
1 | 4 | 12 | 9
0 | 13 | 0 | 2   Matrix of weights
1 | 1 | 8 | 4

11 | 14 | 10   thresholds
0 | 1 | 1   output vector

(a)

before

1 | 4 | 12 | 9
0 | 13 | 0 | 2
1 | 1 | 8 | 4

11 | 14 | 10
(1) | (1) | (0)

(b)

after

1 | 8 | 12 | 6
0 | 13 | 0 | 2
1 | 5 | 8 | 1

7 | 14 | 13
1 | 1 | 0

(c)

FIG. 6.3.   (a) The matrix of weights for a system containing three units. Each column corresponds to a unit. The output of a unit is generated by adding up all the weights in its column that are in rows that have a 1 as input. This sum is then compared with the threshold. (b) A system that is required to give the output shown in parentheses when it gets the input vector shown. It does not do so, so the weights and thresholds must be changed. (c) The set of weights and thresholds that would be obtained by applying the perceptron convergence procedure if the correct outputs are required to be achieved by a margin of at least 6. The first unit in (b), for example, has active weights of 4 and 1 and a threshold of 11, so it fails to "fire" by 6. It is therefore failing to achieve the required margin by 12. So each of the three relevant quantities is changed by 4 in the appropriate direction.

Once these decisions about representations have been made, it is necessary to select the weights in the matrix so that they cause the appropriate sequences of representations (i.e., binary state vectors). This sounds like a tedious and tricky task, but it can be done automatically if the required sequences of binary state vectors are known. The requirement that one state vector should be succeeded by another is equivalent to a set of separate requirements on each unit; namely, that the state of the unit specified by the second state vector should be caused by the inputs to the unit specified by the first state vector. Thus, requiring a set of sequences of state vectors amounts to requiring each individual unit to respond to some patterns of activity of its input lines with a 1 and to other patterns with a 0. The perceptron convergence theorem (see Chapter 1, Section 1.2.2) specifies a way of finding a set of weights that will achieve any required set of responses to input patterns, provided any such set of weights exists. Figure 6.3 gives a simple example of how the matrix of weights would be changed to make one binary state vector succeed another.

Although the individual units are perceptrons and the perceptron convergence procedure is being used to set the weights, the whole approach is very different from the way perceptrons were originally used. The units "look" at the internal state of the machine not at a perceptual input, and the convergence procedure is used not for learning but for achieving sequences of internal states that have been specified by the programmer.

6.3. FROM SEMANTIC NETS TO STATE VECTORS

The information in any network consisting of nodes connected by labeled, directed arcs is equivalent to a set of triples, each of which consists of two nodes and an arc label. Any device that can produce the missing component of a triple when given the other two elements can be said to contain the information in the semantic network. Cases in which the third component of a triple is not uniquely determined by the other two are particularly interesting and are considered later.

The method that was used for implementing a semantic net in the associative computer defined earlier involved dividing the hardware units into four groups (called assemblies). The first three assemblies were called ROLE1, REL (short for relation), and ROLE2. The states of activity of these assemblies were used to represent the identities of the two nodes and the arc label involved in a relationship. The associative computer could be queried about a particular triple by putting it into an initial state in which two of the first three assemblies had patterns of activity representing two components of the triple, and the remaining assemblies started off with all their units inactive. The computer would complete the triple by settling down into a state in which the missing component of the triple was represented by the state of activity of the relevant assembly.

The fourth assembly was called PROP (short for proposition). For each particular triple stored by the associative computer there was a corresponding particular state of the proposition assembly. Recall of triples from two of their components was achieved by making these states of the PROP assembly have the following properties:

1. Any two of the components of a triple would cause states of the PROP assembly similar to the state that represented the complete triple.

2. States of the PROP assembly that were similar to a state representing a complete triple would cause subsequent states even more similar to the state representing that triple.

3. A state of the PROP assembly representing a particular triple would cause the appropriate states of the ROLE1, REL, and ROLE2 assemblies.

How these three properties of the PROP assembly were achieved is described in the next section after the behavior of a system having these properties has been demonstrated.

Figure 6.4 shows the output of a two-part computer program consisting of a simulator, which simulates a parallel computer, and a handler, which handles the interactions between the user and the parallel computer. The handler translates the first instruction into a set of operations (explained later) that modify the weights of the parallel computer so as to store the three triples (JOHN FATHER LEN), (JOHN SISTER MARY), and (KATE FATHER BILL). The second instruction, (RECALL '(JOHN FATHER O)), tells the handler to set up a particular initial binary state vector in the parallel computer and to print out a description of each subsequent binary state vector. The description is generated by comparing the state of each assembly with a stored list of binary states that have been assigned particular names. If there is no perfect match, the name of the nearest match is used with a numerical suffix indicating the number of places where the match failed. The particular PROP state that represents a complete

```
*(STOREALL '( (JOHN FATHER LEN)
              (JOHN SISTER MARY)
              (KATE FATHER BILL) ))

*(RECALL '(JOHN FATHER O))
```

ROLE1	REL	ROLE2	PROP
JOHN	FATHER	0	0
JOHN	FATHER	0	JOHNFATHERLEN4
JOHN	FATHER	LEN	JOHNFATHERLEN
JOHN	FATHER	LEN	JOHNFATHERLEN

```
*(RECALL '(JOHN O LEN))
```

ROLE1	REL	ROLE2	PROP
JOHN	0	LEN	0
JOHN	0	LEN	?
JOHN	FATHER	LEN	JOHNFATHERLEN2
JOHN	FATHER	LEN	JOHNFATHERLEN

FIG. 6.4. The output of a program that simulates a parallel computer. The STOREALL instruction causes modifications to the interactions between the hardware units. Each RECALL instruction sets up an initial binary state vector for the parallel computer, which then settles down into a stable state that includes a representation of the initially missing component of the triple. In order to make the input and output intelligible, a separate program translates binary state vectors into words and vice versa. Numerical suffixes on words indicate imperfect matches between the actual binary state vectors and ones with known names (see text).

triple is printed out by concatenating the names for the constituents of the triple. This is just a convention for naming the binary state vector and has nothing to do with the way the simulated parallel computer works. Similarly, the stored lists of named binary states are not part of the simulated computer and are not available to it.

Figure 6.4 shows that an initial state vector representing two components of a triple causes a subsequent PROP state close to the one for that triple, which subsequently settles into exactly the PROP state for that triple. Notice that, in this example, even an imperfect PROP state is sufficient to cause the missing component of a triple.

6.4. CONTEXT-SENSITIVE ASSOCIATIONS AND HIGHER-LEVEL UNITS

In order to store triples effectively in an associative computer, it is necessary to make the relational term of the triple act as a context to which the association between the other two terms is sensitive. Suppose, for example, that we wish to store the four triples shown in Fig. 6.5. It is clear that the first term in the triple does not determine the third term. It all depends on what the relational term is. It is also clear that the relational term by itself does not determine the third term either.

It is fairly easy to show that, in a system of the kind presented here, such context-sensitive associations cannot be achieved if the direct effects of two patterns combine to produce a third pattern. In the example in Fig. 6.5, the required third term is either "one" or "two." The patterns for these two terms must differ somewhere, so let us focus on one unit that is, say, on when the third assembly has the pattern for "one" and off when it has the pattern for "two." Consider how the patterns in the other two assemblies influence this unit. The effect of a pattern in one assembly on a unit in another assembly is simply the sum of the weights on the lines coming from the active units in the pattern. So the patterns for "one" or "two" in the first assembly and the patterns for "same" or "different" in the second assembly will contribute fixed amounts, Q_1, Q_2, Q_s, and Q_d, respectively. For the unit to behave correctly it is necessary that:

(ONE	SAME	ONE)
(ONE	DIFFERENT	TWO)
(TWO	DIFFERENT	ONE)
(TWO	SAME	TWO)

FIG. 6.5.   Given this set of four triples, any two components of a triple uniquely determine the remaining component, but simply adding together the effects of the two known components cannot correctly determine the missing one (see text).

$$Q_1 + Q_s > \theta \tag{6-1}$$

$$Q_1 + Q_d \leq \theta \tag{6-2}$$

$$Q_2 + Q_s \leq \theta \tag{6-3}$$

$$Q_2 + Q_d > \theta \tag{6-4}$$

Combining (6-1) with (6-4) yields:

$$Q_1 + Q_2 + Q_s + Q_d > 2\theta \tag{6-5}$$

but combining (6-2) with (6-3) yields:

$$Q_1 + Q_2 + Q_s + Q_d \leq 2\theta \tag{6-6}$$

Hence there is no way of choosing the weights to achieve the desired interactions. This is essentially the same as the proof that a perceptron cannot compute an exclusive-or (Minsky & Papert, 1969).

The importance of this proof is that it shows that simply combining the effects of two patterns does not provide context sensitivity. The only way to achieve this property is by having extra units, which are not used to represent the constituents of a triple and which respond to conjunctions of active units in at least two assemblies. For example, an extra unit might respond to the conjunction of the patterns for "one" and "same" in the first two assemblies. This unit could then cause the pattern for "one" in the third assembly.

The PROP assembly consists entirely of these extra units. The set of patterns to which a unit responds positively can be called its "receptive field." The number of possible receptive fields is extremely large, even for units with a fairly small number of inputs; thus it is out of the question to have all possible receptive fields represented by the units in PROP. Ideally the receptive fields of the extra units should be chosen so as to make the units as helpful as possible in causing the required completions of triples. We return to this issue of selecting helpful receptive fields in Section 6.8. For the simulation, the receptive fields were chosen randomly by assigning random weights to the input lines of the units in PROP.

When a particular triple was coded by the patterns in the ROLE1, REL, and ROLE2 assemblies, it caused a particular pattern of activity in PROP. The mapping from triples to patterns in PROP was random, and the process of storing a particular set of triples in the associative computer did not change this mapping. What did change was the inverse mapping from states of the PROP assembly to states of the other three assemblies. Using the perceptron convergence procedure, the weights that determined this inverse mapping were modified until the three assembly states representing the constituents of each triple were caused by the particular PROP state that those three states gave rise to. This made each triple correspond to a "resonant" state of the whole system because the states of the first three assemblies caused a state of the remaining assembly, which, in turn, caused them.

The resonance was further increased by using the perceptron convergence procedure to modify the weights between units within the PROP assembly until each PROP state that corresponded to a stored triple caused itself as its own successor (in the absence of any input from other assemblies). The result of associating each PROP state with itself in this way was that states similar to one of the autoassociated PROP states tended to become even more like that state. The reason for this effect is that the state of each unit is jointly determined by the effects of all the other active units, so that if a few units have their states changed, the unchanged active units will tend to change them back again.

The way in which states of the PROP assembly are used in storing triples has similarities to a standard computational technique called *hash coding*. To associate social security numbers with names, for example, one first applies a hashing function to the string of characters that make up the name. The function returns a number that is then used as the address for the memory location in which the associated social security number is to be stored. The way in which states of the first three assemblies are randomly mapped onto states of the PROP assembly is reminiscent of hashing, but there is one major difference. Small changes in the character string typically cause the hashing function to return a totally different address; thus hash coding does not work when the key (the character string) is imperfect, unless, of course, all possible imperfections are considered ahead of time, and the information is separately associated with every variation of the key.

The mapping from triples to PROP states, on the other hand, has the property that similar combinations of states for the first three assemblies lead to similar PROP states. The reason for this is that some of the units in PROP will be driven either far above or far below threshold by the states of the first three assemblies. Therefore although small changes in these assemblies will slightly alter the input to these nonmarginal PROP units, the alterations will be insufficient to change their states. When only two of the constituents of a triple are represented in the first three assemblies, the ensuing PROP state will be somewhat different from the state caused by the complete triple, but it will be more similar to it than to the PROP states corresponding to other triples. It will, therefore, tend to be "captured" by the autoassociated PROP state for the whole triple.

We have now seen how the three properties of the PROP states that were described in section 6.3 were achieved. Figure 6.6 shows the various different ways in which the simulation treated the weights determining the effects of one assembly state on another. The units in the first three assemblies have high thresholds but are also self-excitatory. This causes them to act like flip-flops, so the initial states of activity of these assemblies tend to remain stable during the settling process.

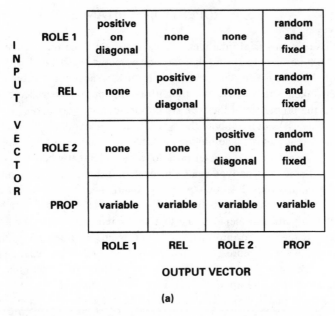

		ROLE 1	REL	ROLE 2	PROP
I **N** **P** **U** **T**	**ROLE 1**	positive on diagonal	none	none	random and fixed
	REL	none	positive on diagonal	none	random and fixed
V **E** **C** **T** **O** **R**	**ROLE 2**	none	none	positive on diagonal	random and fixed
	PROP	variable	variable	variable	variable

OUTPUT VECTOR

(a)

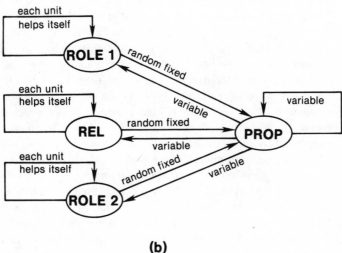

(b)

FIG. 6.6. (a) The matrix of weights arranged for the system that stores triples. Many of the submatrices are null. For the three assemblies that code the constituents of a triple, the submatrices determining the effect of an assembly state on itself have all 0 weights except for the leading diagonal. This makes these assemblies retain whatever patterns they are given. The thresholds (not shown) are all positive. (b) An alternative representation of the way in which the weights are initialized and altered.

6.5. PROPERTY INHERITANCE

A major issue in artificial intelligence is how to relate the representations of a token and a type so as to ensure that facts or properties associated with the type are inherited by the token. One method is to make a new copy of the type each time a new token is required. This straightforward approach is space-consuming because all the properties of the type are duplicated for every token. Also if any new knowledge is acquired about the type, it must be explicitly added to all the tokens that already exist. The obvious alternative to making a full copy of the type is to give each token a pointer back to its type, so that whenever a question arises about the token, the type can be inspected. This approach is currently the generally accepted one. It allows property inheritance in hierarchies in which type/token relationships hold between adjacent levels. Suppose, for example, that Clyde is a particular elephant and that the system needs to know how many legs he has. If there is no information about this attached directly to the Clyde representation, then the representation of Clyde's superordinate type, elephant, is checked. If the answer is not attached to the elephant representation, then its superordinate type, quadruped, is examined, and so on.

Property inheritance appears to be a basic characteristic of human conceptual representations, and consequently the ease with which it is achieved by a representational scheme is a measure of the adequacy of the scheme as a model of human knowledge structures. An approach such as Fahlman's (Chapter 5, this volume), which uses local representations in a parallel machine, needs to have specific hard-wired connections between the representations of types and tokens in order to allow property inheritance. If new connections can be created as required (See Feldman, Chapter 2, this volume), Fahlman's scheme is a neat solution to property inheritance. However there is also a solution which does not require specific connections. If distributed representations are chosen appropriately, property inheritance just drops out.

Suppose that the pattern of microfeatures (individual active units) that represents a type is simply the set of microfeatures common to the patterns that represent the tokens of that type. Any effects that are caused by the pattern for the type will automatically transfer to the patterns for the tokens, unless they are overridden by the effects of the additional microfeatures in a particular token. Thus property inheritance is automatic and there is also a way of preventing it in exceptional cases. Furthermore, generalization will be a basic system property, because type patterns will automatically acquire any effects possessed by all their token patterns.

Automatic generalization is not always desirable. For example, the property of being an individual elephant should not be allowed to transfer to the representation of the type ''elephant'' even though it fits all the tokens. The pattern for the type must be more complex than just the intersection of the microfeatures in the patterns for the tokens. However, the naive idea that abstraction is just the ommission of the microfeatures that vary within the class seems to have some very useful computational consequences in an associative computer of the type presented here.

Figure 6.7 shows the input and output of the computer program when it is instructed to store three triples and then to complete two of them. Figure 6.8 shows what happens if the program is then asked to complete triples that have not been explicitly stored. Remarkably, it gets the right answers. Figure 6.9 shows why. The pattern for CLYDE contains the pattern for ELEPHANT, so the effects of this pattern are inherited by CLYDE. Similarly, the pattern for BILL contains the pattern for PERSON. Figure 6.10 shows what happens if four triples are stored, including one in which a token, SCOTT, behaves differently from its type, PERSON. The two recall tests show that the exception is learnt and that this does not prevent BILL from inheriting his color from PERSON, though the inheritance becomes slightly shaky.

In a sense, distributed representations finesse the property inheritance problem by making the representation of the type be a constituent of the representation of each token. This solution would lead to wasteful, multiple representations of the type in any system that stored individual representations separately, but this problem does not arise in systems where the ability to recreate an active representation is not achieved by storing that representation or anything like it.

```
*(STOREALL '((ERNIE COLOR GREY)
             (ELEPH COLOR GREY)
             (PERSON COLOR PINK)))

*(RECALL '(ELEPH COLOR 0))
```

ROLE 1	REL	ROLE 2	PROP
ELEPH	COLOR	0	0
ELEPH	COLOR	0	?
ELEPH	COLOR	GREY	ELEPHCOLORGREY4
ELEPH	COLOR	GREY	ELEPHCOLORGREY1

```
*(RECALL '(PERSON COLOR 0))
```

ROLE 1	REL	ROLE 2	PROP
PERSON	COLOR	0	0
PERSON	COLOR	0	PERSONCOLORPINK4
PERSON	COLOR	PINK	PERSONCOLORPINK1
PERSON	COLOR	PINK	PERSONCOLORPINK

FIG. 6.7. Three triples are stored and recall is tested for two of them.

*(RECALL '(CLYDE COLOR 0))

ROLE 1	REL	ROLE 2	PROP
CLYDE	COLOR	0	0
CLYDE	COLOR	0	?
CLYDE	COLOR	GREY	?
CLYDE	COLOR	GREY	ELEPHCOLORGREY2

*(RECALL '(BILL COLOR 0))

ROLE1	REL	ROLE 2	PROP
BILL	COLOR	0	0
BILL	COLOR	0	?
BILL	COLOR	PINK	PERSONCOLORPINK2
BILL	COLOR	PINK	PERSONCOLORPINK

FIG. 6.8.   After storing the colors of elephants and people, the system is asked about the colors of CLYDE and BILL. It completes the triples correctly, even though these facts have not been explicitly stored. Figure 6.9 shows why.

*(SHOWSTATES 'ROLE 1)

000000	000000	0
111000	000000	ELEPH
000111	000000	PERSON
111000	111000	CLYDE
111000	000111	ERNIE
000111	101010	SCOTT
000111	010101	BILL

FIG. 6.9.   The patterns of activity used to represent various objects in the assembly ROLE 1. The states of the first six units code the type of object (elephant or person). The remaining six units are used to code a particular token by further specifying a type. The similarity between the patterns for a type and a token cause them to have similar effects on the PROP assembly. This causes appropriate generalization.

6.6.   TWO TYPES OF CONCEPTUAL STRUCTURE

In order to store a semantic net in the manner described above, it is necessary to choose a particular pattern of activity (i.e., a set of microfeatures) to represent each node in the semantic net. A simple first approach is to choose a random pattern for each node and to ensure that no two nodes are too similar. This allows associations between patterns to be implemented, but it fails to capture the similarities of nodes to one another. For example, the method of achieving property inheritance demonstrated in the previous section relies on a particular

*(STOREALL '((ERNIE COLOR GREY)
                (ELEPH COLOR GREY)
                (PERSON COLOR PINK)
                (SCOTT COLOR WHITE)))

*(RECALL '(SCOTT COLOR 0))

ROLE 1	REL	ROLE 2	PROP
SCOTT	COLOR	0	0
SCOTT	COLOR	0	?
SCOTT	COLOR	WHITE	SCOTTCOLORWHITE1
SCOTT	COLOR	WHITE	SCOTTCOLORWHITE

*(RECALL '(BILL COLOR 0))

ROLE 1	REL	ROLE 2	PROP
BILL	COLOR	0	0
BILL	COLOR	0	?
BILL	COLOR	PINK	?
BILL1	COLOR	?	PERSONCOLORPINK4

*(SETTLEMORE)

BILL1	COLOR	?	PERSONCOLORPINK2
BILL1	COLOR	PINK	PERSONCOLORPINK3
BILL1	COLOR	PINK	PERSONCOLORPINK3

FIG. 6.10.   An exception to the rule that people are pink is included in the list of triples to be stored. This does not prevent the system from correctly answering a query about the color of BILL. However the interference caused by the exception makes the system take longer to settle, and it slightly degrades some of the patterns in the final state.

kind of similarity in which the set of microfeatures for a token contains, as a subset, the microfeatures for the type. This example makes it clear that the "direct content" of a concept (its set of microfeatures) interacts in interesting ways with its "associative content" (its links to other concepts). The reason for this interaction, of course, is that the associative content is *caused* by the direct content. Each association is implemented by the process of completing a triple, and this process involves creating a resonance which depends on the direct contents of the concepts being associated.

The distinction between direct content and associative content may be an important contribution of this approach to psychology. There is good evidence (Mandler, 1980) that human memory for items involves two separate components, which Mandler has called "integrative" and "elaborative" structure. The essential idea is that an item has internal coherence as well as external relations to other items. Within the traditional semantic net framework, it is hard to model this distinction. If, however, integrative structure is interpreted as direct content, and elaborative structure as associative content, it is easy to see that the two are qualitatively different.

The semantic net formalism captures an aspect of conceptual structure (the associations between concepts) that subjects are able to make verbally explicit. It also captures the higher levels of our perceptual representations, which seem to involve structural descriptions in which scenes or objects are decomposed into their constituents (Hinton, 1979; Palmer, 1977; Reed, 1974). These structural descriptions are just semantic nets in which the relationships are spatial. A quite different formalism, in which a concept is only a large set of features, is important in explaining similarity judgments (Tversky, 1977). It is also common in models of pattern recognition, which typically assume that a shape can be represented as a set of features. A battle has raged between these two formalisms. Both sides seem to have assumed that the two formalisms are competing to explain the same phenomena.

It is clear that both formalisms are applicable to the computer simulation presented above. Concepts are patterns of activity (sets of microfeatures), and associations involve interactions between these patterns. The semantic net formalism is a high-level description of the associative content and the feature-set formalism is a low-level description of the direct content. There is no conflict.

Neither formalism alone can capture the way in which direct content influences associative content and vice versa. The property inheritance example shows that the interaction between these two types of content can provide a neat solution to a major problem for semantic nets. The next section shows how another major problem may have a similarly neat solution.

6.7.   MEMORY SEARCH AS A CONSTRUCTIVE PROCESS

It is a commonplace in Artificial Intelligence that data structures alone are not enough. There must also be effective search procedures which can find pieces of data that satisfy descriptions (Norman & Bobrow, 1979). A particular node in a semantic net, for example, might be described by saying that it is in relation R to node A and relation S to node B. If many different nodes satisfy each part of the description separately, but only one node satisfies the whole description, then it is nontrivial to find this node.

An obvious but inefficient method is to store separate lists of the nodes satisfying each part of the description and then to find the intersection of the relevant lists. This method requires a lot of extra storage, for the lists, and also involves computing intersections every time a memory search is performed. An obvious use for parallel hardware is to facilitate memory search. How can this be done in an associative computer?

Scott Fahlman (Chapter 5, this volume) shows how the search problem can be solved efficiently in a parallel computer in which there is a hardware processor for each node in the semantic net. Each part of a complex description is used to place a specific marker on all the nodes which satisfy it. A message is then broadcast to all the nodes telling each of them to report back if it has all the markers. I shall outline a method that is similar in spirit to this marker-passing algorithm but is a natural development of the idea that concepts correspond to patterns of activity rather than to particular hardware units. The method resembles Fahlman's in its use of discrete markers, but it differs in that it dedicates particular pieces of hardware to particular markers rather than to particular semantic nodes. In fact a concept becomes nothing more than a particular bundle of markers (i.e., microfeatures).

Given any semantic net, it would be possible to choose patterns of activity to represent the individual nodes in such a way that every triple was implicitly coded by the presence of specific "relational" microfeatures within the patterns for the relevant nodes. For example, if there was a triple $(A\ R\ B)$, the pattern for A would include a microfeature that it shared with all the other concepts that stood in relation R to B. Similarly, the pattern for R would have a microfeature that it shared with all other relations holding between A and B. Each triple would then be coded in two very different ways, once in the interactions between whole assembly states, and once in the direct contents of each of its constituent concepts.

Given this dual encoding, a node satisfying the patterns $(?\ R\ B)$ and $(?\ S\ C)$ could be found in three sequential stages. First, an attempt would be made to complete the triple $(?\ R\ B)$, and this would cause a particular microfeature in the ROLE1 assembly. Next, an attempt would be made to complete $(?\ S\ C)$, using as the initial state of ROLE1 the pattern caused by the previously attempted completion. The combination of S and C would cause another particular microfeature in ROLE1, and the search problem would than have been reduced to a pattern completion problem within ROLE1. This subproblem has its own difficulties, but the aim of this section is merely to show how a problem of one type, finding an implicitly specified node in a semantic net, can be reduced to a problem of a different type that an associative computer handles well.

There is one major difficulty with the search scheme as it stands. It requires that each assembly contain a specific unit for each combination of states of the other two assemblies. So although concepts do not require their own units, combinations of pairs of concepts do. This is unacceptable. Fortunately, it is also unnecessary. Instead of using a single microfeature within A to code the triple $(A\ R\ B)$, a small pattern of microfeatures can be used, provided that the microfeatures are carefully chosen.

A semantic network can be said to contain implicit regularities if the nodes and arc labels can be divided into subsets that satisfy constraints. Suppose, for example, that in a particular network, any relational triple that has a concept from the subset S_1 in ROLE1 and a relational concept from the subset S_r in REL, has a concept from the subset S_2 in ROLE2. In this network there is an implicit constraint on the third constituent of any triple whose first two constituents are from the subsets S_1 and S_r, respectively. If the patterns of activity used to represent particular concepts are chosen carefully, this constraint will show up as a simple microinference at the level of the microfeatures. All that is necessary is that for each relevant subset there should be a specific microfeature that is only possessed by the concepts in that subset. If, for example, the members of S_1, S_r, S_2 have the microfeatures f_1, f_r, f_2, respectively, then f_1 in ROLE1 and f_r in REL will imply f_2 in ROLE2. The system can implement this microinference by having a unit in PROP that responds to the conjunction of f_1 and f_r and causes f_2

Notice that f_2 in this example is a more general case of the kind of relational microfeature described above. Instead of coding that a specific other concept is related by a specific relation, f_2 codes the more general constraint that the concept containing it is related to a concept in the set S_1 by a relation in the set S_r. If there are many implicit regularities in the semantic net, there will be many of these more general constraints, and specific conjunctions of them will code specific relations to specific other concepts. This method of encoding specific relationships as conjunctions of more general constraints is much more efficient than using specific relational microfeatures.

The problem of finding a concept that satisfies both (? R B) and (? S C) can now be solved in essentially the same way as before, but instead of causing a single relational microfeature in the ROLE1 assembly, the combination of R and B will cause a number of more general relational microfeatures, corresponding to many different set memberships that can be inferred from the set memberships of R and of B. Similarly, the combination of S and C will cause further microfeatures corresponding to set memberships that can be inferred from those of S and C. If there is a unique answer to the search problem, the two lots of inferred microfeatures should be sufficient to allow microinferences within an assembly to complete the remaining microfeatures of the answer. If there is no unique answer, the inferred microfeatures, and any more that can be inferred from them, will act as a representation of the set of objects that would satisfy the description.

The central idea underlying this search technique is that a particular concept is just a conjunction of set memberships, and that it is possible to infer some set memberships from others. A ''search'' is performed by using a part of a description to infer some of the set memberships of the desired concept, and then completing the concept by inferring its remaining set memberships. Because the representation of the concept is just this conjunction of set memberships, there is no need for any comparison stage in the search. The idea that remembering involves retrieval of items that are stored as explicit wholes, or that retrieval descriptions need to be matched against such items is entirely inappropriate to this way of implementing remembering.

Kohonen and his co-workers (Chapter 4, Section 4.4.2, this volume) suggest a rather different method of finding items that satisfy complex descriptions. Each part of the description is used to give subthreshold activation to all the nodes satisfying it, and a threshold is chosen such that only the node that satisfies all parts of the description receives enough activation to exceed the threshold. This is a version of the spreading activation approach (Collins & Loftus, 1975). It is like Fahlman's marker-passing algorithm in that it requires a separate hardware node for each item, but it is not as powerful. Instead of having collections of markers at a node, there is a single number, the activity level, which is a much less informative representation. What we know about the brain makes it seem very probable that human thought involves activation spreading between hardware units, but the whole thrust of this chapter is that the psychological level of description is at a higher level than the hardware, and therefore models that are appropriate at the hardware level may be inappropriate at the psychological level. A single activity level, for example, is incapable of representing an intermediate stage in memory search when some but not all of the microfeatures of a concept have been constructed.

Many of the phenomena that are taken to support a spreading activation model (see Ratcliff, Chapter 10, this volume) are also predicted by the model in which remembering involves constructing the appropriate concept by activating its microfeatures. For example, the constructive model predicts that when errors occur they should be similar concepts, because these share many microfeatures. It also predicts that a concept should prime more general concepts of which it is an instance because the representations of these more general concepts are simply a subset of the microfeatures for their specific instances.

6.8.   LEARNING

Within the deliberately restrictive framework of storing and searching sets of triples, there are two rather different learning problems. In order to add a new triple it is necessary to modify the way in which the patterns for the constituents of that triple interact with units in the PROP assembly. The training scheme used by the current computer program is one way of doing this. However, this type of associative learning in which the direct content of the concepts remains unaffected is relatively uninteresting. The major learning problem is to discover how to represent concepts as patterns of activity in such a way that the implicit regularities in the associations between concepts can be captured by microinferences between their microfeatures.

Discovering appropriate microfeatures for a concept is an enormous task because there are so many possible regularities. Given n nodes and r relations, there are $2^n \cdot 2^r \cdot 2^n$ ways of choosing three subsets between which there might be a simple microinference. For more complex inferences involving more than three microfeatures the number is even greater. If one considers that a really useful microfeature will be one that enters into many different microinferences, the problem becomes even more horrendous.

In conventional implementations of semantic nets learning typically requires extra processes that inspect the representations and notice regularities and exceptions (e.g., Winston, 1975). The approach presented here suggests a very different way of implementing learning. Instead of having a separate system that observes the behavior of the units and adjusts their weights so as to "improve" the microfeatures, each unit can be allowed to alter its own weights so as to become a better microfeature (i.e., one that is involved in more strong microinferences). To do this, each unit must have a measure of how useful its current set of weights makes it as a microfeature. It can then change its weights so as to improve this measure. There is not space here to give a detailed account of how this can be done; and I have not yet applied this kind of self-improvement to the aforementioned program, but I shall give a brief outline of the method in order to dispel the common notion that it is impossible for a local unit to improve its behavior unless it receives a second kind of input that explicitly tells it how well it is doing.

As a concrete example, consider the units in the PROP assembly of the program for storing triples. These units were given random weights on their input lines. This was adequate for a simple demonstration program, but it meant that some of the units in PROP were either always on or always off and were thus useless. The behavior of the system would have been better if the units in PROP had changed their weights so as to be more helpful. What that means, in this context, is that they should have come to respond to common combinations of microfeatures from which microinferences could be made.

Whenever there is an inference of the form: $a \ \& \ b \rightarrow c$, the joint probability of all three events, $p(a \ \& \ b \ \& \ c)$, is higher than the product $p(a \ \& \ b) \times p(c)$, which is the expected joint probability assuming that c is independent of a and b. This means that a unit in PROP will be useful for implementing microinferences if it comes to respond to combinations of microfeatures that occur more often than would be expected from their separate probabilities of occurrence. It is possible to make a unit change its weights so as to latch onto such combinations. All that is necessary is to modify the weights continually so as to "hill-climb" in an appropriate measure of the extent to which the unit is responding to the non-independence among its inputs.

One such measure is the difference between the actual frequency, A, with which the unit is on and the expected frequency, E, with which the unit should be on if its inputs were statistically independent. This measure may be clarified by the following example. Consider a unit with 10 input lines each of which has a probability of 1/2 of being active in any particular trial. Suppose that the first 5 lines are perfectly correlated so that on half the trials they are all on and on the other half they are all off. If the unit develops a threshold of 4.5, and weights of 1 on each of the first five lines, and 0 elsewhere, it will actually "fire" on half the trials. Because, however, it can only fire if all the first 5 lines are active and because each line has a probability of 1/2 of being active, the expected probability of firing, *assuming independence,* is only 1/32. Therefore, A = 1/2, and E = 1/32. There is a large difference between *A* and *E* because the particular weights and the threshold cause the unit to respond to a very strong regularity among its inputs.

There are reasons for believing that the optimal measure is neither A − E nor A/E, but this need not concern us here. The main point is that it is possible to estimate *A* and *E* and their partial derivatives with respect to the individual weights on the basis of information that is available locally at the unit. This means that there is enough information available locally to hill-climb in a measure that is a function of *A* and *E*. Thus by continually making small changes in the weights, the unit can increase the extent to which it responds to regularities among its inputs. I have implemented an algorithm of this kind in several very simple domains and it seems to work well, though the convergence rate is rather slow. This type of weight modification rule is considerably more complicated than the simple correlational synapse suggested by Hebb (1949) and others, but it appears that something of this kind is necessary to allow the direct content of concepts to evolve on the basis of the regularities among their associations.

There are some interesting consequences of making direct content evolve as a result of associative content. If the system has already assimilated a set of concepts and has had enough practice at their associations so that the implicit regularities have become embodied in the microfeatures and microinferences, then a concept that obeys the same implicit regularities will be easy to assimilate. Its associations with existing concepts will allow the existing microinferences to determine a suitable direct content for the concept, and this, in turn, will lead to appropriate generalization.

When an entirely novel set of concepts is introduced, there are serious problems. If the concepts do not contain perceptually specified microfeatures, then there may be a vicious circle. There is no good way to choose the initial direct contents, because the appropriate microfeatures and microinferences cannot evolve until enough associative content has been specified to reveal the implicit regularities. But to enter the associative content, it is necessary to have patterns of activity to represent the concepts. If arbitrary patterns are used to begin with, there will be considerable interference between the various facts. Also, it will be hard to search for concepts satisfying multiple partial descriptions because the search process depends on having appropriate microfeatures.

It is possible to avoid the vicious circle if a new system of concepts is isomorphic to one that has already been thoroughly assimilated. The microfeatures of an existing concept can be used to provide most of the direct content for the corresponding new one. The existing microinferences will then transfer, so that once some of the correspondences have been specified, the remaining new concepts will receive the appropriate direct content as a result of their associative content and the existing microinferences.

6.9.   EXTENSIONS OF THE MODEL

The aim of this chapter is to present a novel way of implementing relational data-structures in parallel hardware. The particular example used is unrealistic in many respects, and the aim of this section is to point out these deficiencies so that the simplifications and ad hoc details in the example are not confused with the principles that it is intended to illustrate. I also indicate the directions in which the model could be extended to cope with some of its major limitations.

6.9.1. Multiple Roles

It is clear that people can represent propositions like "the hippy kissed the debutante in the park," which contain more than three constituents. It would be a trivial extension of the program to allow multiple roles like "location" and "time of occurrence". So long as there is a fixed and relatively small set of discrete roles, it is possible to set aside an assembly for each role. However, this simple approach is inadequate if there are a large number of roles and if some are similar but not identical to others. Consider, for example, the two sentences: "Mary beat John at tennis," and "Mary helped John with his sums." It seems wasteful to have an assembly that is permanently set aside for whatever role the "at tennis" is occupying, and it is unclear whether the sums play the same role in the second sentence as the tennis does in the first. It seems that each relation (verb) has an associated role structure, and that the roles in one structure may be similar to, but not identical with, the roles in another.

It would be possible to extend the program to allow the set of available roles to be determined by the relation involved and to allow two roles in different relations to be similar without being identical. Currently, activity in a unit in a particular role assembly represents that there is an object from a specific set in this particular role. The "receptive field" of the unit therefore covers a number of possible objects but only one role. The extreme specificity of a unit with respect to role is what allows the units to be divided into separate assemblies for the purposes of a higher-level description. This specificity could be relaxed so that activity in a unit represented the three-way conjunction of an object-type, a role-type, and a relation-type. The unit would then respond to any object from a specific set occupying any role from a set of similar roles in the context of any relation from a set of similar relations. It is harder to give a simple higher-level description of the representations in such a system, but it would allow much more flexibility in the role structures. If two relations had similar roles, the set of units that would be activated by filling a role in one relation with a specific object would be similar to, but not identical with, the set of units activated by filling the similar role in the other relation with the same object.

6.9.2. Procedures and Control Processes

There has been no attempt to model procedural knowledge. All the examples that have been presented of the simulated parallel computer involve a separate conventional program that sets up the initial assembly states and makes the parallel system run for a few iterations. The only thing the parallel hardware does is settle into a stable state, part of which represents the answer to a query. This is a very limited kind of processing. Clearly, a real system would need to have organized sequences of computations. The process of settling into a stable state would then correspond to a single step of a larger computation. In other words, a more complex parallel system would be organized to perform computations by a sequence of settlings. Each such settling would involve a great deal of parallel computation so that the individual settlings in the sequence could implement properties like content-addressable memory. The next section outlines a way of implementing more complex computations that would involve a sequence of settlings at the level of individual proposition representations.

6.9.3. Inference

Memory must allow inference as well as simple retrieval of the facts that were explicitly stored. If, for example, we store the facts (JOHN has FATHER LEN) and (LEN has BROTHER BILL), we should be able to complete the triple (JOHN has UNCLE ?). This requires an inference schema of the form $(X$ FATHER $Y)$ & $(Y$ BROTHER $Z) \rightarrow (X$ UNCLE $Z)$. One way of implementing this in parallel hardware is to duplicate the structure used for storing and retrieving propositions but at a higher level. A specific proposition would fill one role in an inference schema in much the same way as an object fills a role in a proposition. There would need to be separate assemblies for simultaneously representing several different proposition/role combinations. However if these assemblies were filled sequentially, it would be unnecessary to duplicate the apparatus for representing individual propositions. The very same apparatus could be used sequentially for retrieving the various individual propositions used in the inference and also for "unpacking" the representation of the inferred proposition into its separate constituent objects. Section 6.10 shows how object roles can be filled sequentially in creating the representation of a proposition, and the same method can be used at a higher level in constructing an inference.

There are, of course, many unsolved problems in implementing inferences in this way. The appropriate inference schema needs to be invoked, and there must be microinferences at the level of the inference schema that implement the constraints between the bindings of the variables in the constituent propositions. Quantifiers pose problems that have not even been explored in this context. Nevertheless there seems to be no reason to suppose that explicit inference presents an insuperable problem to the kind of memory being proposed.

6.10. LOADING ASSEMBLIES WITH PATTERNS

The program for completing triples requires the known components of a triple to be represented as patterns of activity in the appropriate assemblies. Currently the loading of particular patterns into particular assemblies is performed by the conventional program that handles the parallel simulation. In a more complete parallel system it would be necessary for the loading to be done by the parallel system itself. Suppose, for example, that a query was presented to the system as a sequence of pairs of patterns, one of which represented a component of the triple and the other of which represented the role of that component within the triple. How could the pattern of activity representing the role be used to direct the pattern representing the component to the correct assembly? Kohonen et al. (Chapter 4, Section 4.5.1, this volume) refer to this as the data-switching problem, and they point out that it is hard to solve in the matrix models.

Figure 6.11 shows the output of a program that simulates a parallel machine composed of eight assemblies. The first two are used to represent a component of a triple and its role within the triple. The next three form a filter that is used for solving the data-switching problem. The last three are used to accumulate the serially presented constituents of a triple, and they correspond to the first three assemblies of the previous model. Figure 6.11 shows that the pattern in the OBJECT assembly is copied, after two iterations, into whatever assembly is specified by the contents of the WHROLE assembly. Figure 6.12 shows that if the constituents of a triple are known, the pattern in the WHROLE assembly determines which constituent gets copied into the object assembly.

The program works by using the assemblies TROLE1, TREL, and TROLE2 as a "skeleton" filter. The units in these assemblies have high thresholds, but a particular pattern of activity in WHROLE provides enough excitatory input to all the units in one of the assemblies in the filter so that further excitatory input from other assemblies is enough to turn particular units on. Units in the other two assemblies of the filter do not receive excitatory input from WHROLE. They therefore remain so far below threshold that none of them are turned on by the effects of the patterns of activity in the other assemblies. Each of the assemblies in the filter acts as a selective channel that allows mutual interaction between the object assembly and one of the last three assemblies. The pattern in the WHROLE assembly has the effect of opening up just one of these channels.

The interactions between units are set up so that a pattern in the object assembly will tend to cause a corresponding pattern in each of the filter as-

*(ZEROALLASSEMBLIES)
*(INPUTPAIR '(JOHN ROLE1))
*(SETTLE)

OBJECT	WHROLE	TROLE 1	TREL	TROLE 2	ROLE 1	REL	ROLE 2
JOHN	ROLE 1	0	0	0	0	0	0
JOHN	0	JOHN	0	0	0	0	0
JOHN	0	0	0	0	JOHN	0	0
JOHN	0	0	0	0	JOHN	0	0

*(INPUTPAIR '(MARY ROLE2))
*(SETTLE)

OBJECT	WHROLE	TROLE 1	TREL	TROLE 2	ROLE 1	REL	ROLE 2
MARY	ROLE 2	0	0	0	JOHN	0	0
MARY	0	0	0	MARY	JOHN	0	0
MARY	0	0	0	0	JOHN	0	MARY
MARY	0	0	0	0	JOHN	0	MARY

*(INPUTPAIR '(MOTHER REL))
*(SETTLE)

OBJECT	WHROLE	TROLE 1	TREL	TROLE 2	ROLE 1	REL	ROLE 2
MOTHER	REL	0	0	0	JOHN	0	MARY
MOTHER	0	0	MOTHER	0	JOHN	0	MARY
MOTHER	0	0	0	0	JOHN	MOTHER	MARY
MOTHER	0	0	0	0	JOHN	MOTHER	MARY

FIG. 6.11.   The first instruction puts all eight assemblies into the null state. The instructions following fix the initial states of the first two assemblies and cause the system to iterate until it reaches a stable state. States of the OBJECT assembly and the last three assemblies are stable because the units in these assemblies have high thresholds but are strongly self-excitatory. States of the other assemblies are transitory because the units are not self-excitatory.

semblies and vice versa. Also, a pattern in any of the filter assemblies will tend to cause a corresponding pattern in one of the last three assemblies and vice versa. Thus the pattern in WHROLE can direct the flow of information between the first assembly and the last three by selectively opening one of the three channels provided by TROLE1, TREL, and TROLE2.

The mechanism is called a skeleton filter because it works by enabling a skeleton subset of the units in the filter. It is similar in spirit to the more sophisticated filter described by Sejnowski (Chapter 7, this volume).

Figure 6.13 shows that the system can handle sequential input as fast as it can be presented. Although it takes two iterations for input to pass through the filter, successive inputs can be "pipelined" so that a sequence of N inputs only requires $N + 1$ iterations.

```
*(SETINITIAL '(0  0  0  0  0  JOHN  MOTHER  MARY))
*(INPUTPAIR '(0  ROLE1))
*(SETTLE)
```

OBJECT	WHROLE	TROLE 1	TREL	TROLE 2	ROLE 1	REL	ROLE 2
0	ROLE 1	0	0	0	JOHN	MOTHER	MARY
0	0	JOHN	0	0	JOHN	MOTHER	MARY
JOHN	0	0	0	0	JOHN	MOTHER	MARY
JOHN	0	0	0	0	JOHN	MOTHER	MARY

```
*(INPUTPAIR '(0  REL))
*(SETTLE)
```

OBJECT	WHROLE	TROLE 1	TREL	TROLE 2	ROLE 1	REL	ROLE 2
0	REL	0	0	0	JOHN	MOTHER	MARY
0	0	0	MOTHER	0	JOHN	MOTHER	MARY
MOTHER	0	0	0	0	JOHN	MOTHER	MARY
MOTHER	0	0	0	0	JOHN	MOTHER	MARY

FIG. 6.12. If a triple is present in the last three assemblies, the initial state of the WHROLE assembly determines which component of the triple is transferred to the OBJECT assembly. It does this by temporarily opening one of the three channels provided by TROLE1, TREL, and TROLE2.

```
*(INPUTSEQUENCE '((JOHN ROLE 1)  (MARY ROLE 2)  (MOTHER REL)))
```

OBJECT	WHROLE	TROLE 1	TREL	TROLE 2	ROLE 1	REL	ROLE 2
JOHN	ROLE 1	0	0	0	0	0	0
MARY	ROLE 2	JOHN	0	0	0	0	0
MOTHER	REL	0	0	MARY	JOHN	0	0
?	0	0	MOTHER	0	JOHN	0	MARY
?	0	0	0	0	JOHN	MOTHER	MARY

FIG. 6.13. The INPUTSEQUENCE instruction causes a particular sequence of pairs of states in the first two assemblies. This sequential input causes the components of a triple to be accumulated in the last three assemblies.

6.11. SUMMARY

In our attempts to understand how information is stored and processed in the brain we are limited by our knowledge of the brain's hardware, by our knowledge of what people can do, and by our ideas about possible ways of organizing information processing in parallel hardware. This chapter has tried to add to the repertory of ideas about information processing by demonstrating a novel way of storing and searching complex, flexible data-structures in highly parallel hardware.

Current digital computers implement flexible data-structures by using pointers. One data-structure is given a link to another by being given its address. This scheme depends on the addressing mechanism and the storage of different data-structures in different places. An alternative scheme which has been proposed by Minsky (1980), Fahlman (Chapter 5, this volume), and Feldman (Chapter 2, this volume) is to replace the addresses by real hardware connections. This removes the need for an addressing mechanism, but it makes it hard to see how new connections can be established rapidly. A third possibility is that concepts are represented by large patterns of activity, and that data-structures are stored by modifying the interactions between these patterns. The aim of this chapter has been to show that this idea is feasible by building a very simple working model.

ACKNOWLEDGMENTS

I would like to thank Eileen Conway, Ed Hutchins, Don Norman, Chris Riesbeck, and Dave Rumelhart for their help. The preparation of this chapter and the research reported in it were performed while I was a Visiting Scholar with the Program in Cognitive Science, at the University of California, San Diego, supported by a grant from the Sloan Foundation.

REFERENCES

Collins, A. M., & Loftus, E. F. A spreading activation theory of semantic processing. *Psychological Review*, 1975, *82*, 407–428.

Hebb, D. O. *Organization of behavior*. New York: Wiley, 1949.

Hinton, G. E. Some demonstrations of the effects of structural descriptions in mental imagery. *Cognitive Science*, 1979, *3*, 231–250.

Levin, J. A. *Proteus: An activation framework for cognitive process models (ISI/WP-2)*. Marina Del Rey, California: Information Sciences Institute, 1976.

Mandler, G. Recognizing: The judgment of previous occurrence. *Psychological Review*, 1980, *87*, 252–271.

Minsky, M. K-lines: A theory of memory. *Cognitive Science*, 1980, *4*, 117–133.

Minsky, M., & Papert, S. *Perceptrons*. Cambridge, Mass.: MIT Press, 1969.

Norman, D. A., & Bobrow D. G. Descriptions: An intermediate stage in memory retrieval. *Cognitive Psychology*, 1979, *11*, 107–123.

Palmer, S. E. Hierarchical structure in perceptual representation. *Cognitive Psychology*, 1977, *9*, 441–474.

Reed, S. K. Structural descriptions and the limitations of visual images. *Memory & Cognition*, 1974, *2*, 329–336.

Tversky, A. Features of similarity. *Psychological Review*, 1977, *84*, 327–352.

Winston, P. H. Learning structural descriptions from examples. In P. H. Winston (Ed.), *The Psychology of Computer Vision*. New York: McGraw-Hill, 1975.

7

Skeleton Filters in the Brain

Terrence J. Sejnowski
Department of Neurobiology
Harvard Medical School

7.1. LOOKING AT THE BRAIN

The human brain is a dull gray and glistening white tissue having the texture of stiff pudding. Under high magnification the brain looks like an intricate three-dimensional maze, as shown in Fig. 7.1(a). Each component is being studied in painstaking detail, but despite our increasing knowledge of the brain's structure our ignorance of how the brain works remains almost complete. However, neuroscientists have an advantage that workers in Artificial Intelligence do not yet have: a working model and an existence proof that problems in perception and cognition have at least one solution. If we knew how to look and what to look for, we might be able to see in Fig. 7.1(a), for example, a part of an algorithm for some problem in visual perception.

The fundamental design principles of a machine must be understood before its function can be deduced from its structure. For example, the piece of integrated circuit in Fig. 7.1(b) is a meaningless abstract design without knowing the principles of digital logic. Neuroanatomy is similarly meaningless without knowing how the signals that carry meaningful information are transformed by each component. Quite possibly we do not yet know the signals in the brain that encode thought, thus making the physiological study of cognition nearly impossible. We do have some understanding of how sensory information and motor commands are encoded, and a similar form of coding is probably exploited for central functions as well.

Peripheral sensory codes depend on labeled lines: The central nervous system "knows" where each input originates just as a central telephone exchange "knows" the origin of each telephone line. Are neurons in the central nervous

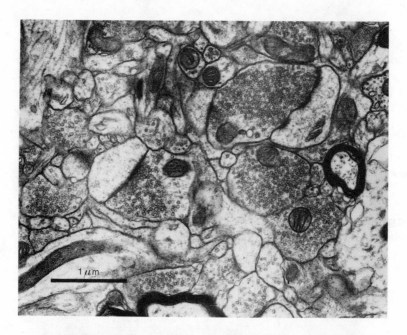

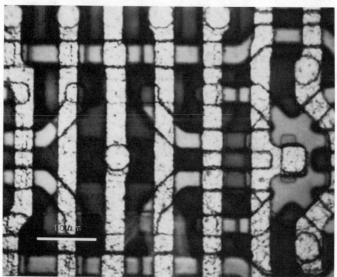

FIG. 7.1. (a) Highly magnified view of a cross section through the visual cortex of a rat using an electron microscope. The vesicle-filled profiles are presynaptic terminals. Several synapses, characterized by a presynaptic accumulation of vesicles and a postsynaptic thickening, are visible (courtesy of Simon LeVay). (b) A 16K Random Access Memory manufactured by MOSTEK. The magnification is about ten times less than in (a). Because silicon chips are essentially two-dimensional, the number of wires that can interconnect logical units in a large-scale device is severely limited.

system similarly labeled; that is, does the response of a neuron "mean" the same thing and represent a fixed address for a particular piece of information? Primary sensory areas of the brain appear to respond to sensory input in this way. For example, a visual scene is represented in the primary visual cortex by the subset of neurons that respond to particular features in the scene (Hubel & Wiesel, 1977). At higher levels of the nervous system, information may be represented by neurons that respond to a different set of primitive features—ones that are perhaps closer to the primitive components of perception. Are different perceptual states at some high level represented by the activation of different populations of neurons? The extreme possibility that small nonoverlapping populations represent percepts is called a localized representation, or sometimes a "grandmother cell" or "pontifical cell" theory (Barlow, 1972; Feldman, Chapter 2, this volume). The other extreme possibility that only large completely overlapping populations of neurons represent percepts is called a distributed representation. Both extremes are parallel models, but the essential information in one case is spatially separated and in the other case is spatially mixed.

These possibilities could be tested by mapping the electrical activity of a large number of neurons during different perceptual states. Although this type of experiment is not feasible with current physiological techniques, an anatomical technique using a radioactively labeled sugar analog, [^{14}C]-2-deoxyglucose, has been used for qualitatively mapping functional activity in the brain with a resolution of about 50 μ (Des Rosiers, Sakurada, Jehle, Shinohara, Kennedy, & Sokoloff, 1978; Hubel, Wiesel & Stryker, 1978; Sokoloff, Reivich, Kennedy, Des Rosiers, Potlak, Pettigrew, Sakurada, & Shinohara, 1977). Recent improvements in the technique now make it possible to measure the functional activity of single neurons with 1 μ resolution (Sejnowski, Reingold, Kelley, & Gelperin, 1980).

The implications of a distributed representation are explored in this chapter. Although different perceptual states are initially represented by overlapping populations of neurons, a new type of representation emerges, called a skeleton filter, which is intermediate between a localized representation and a distributed representation.

7.2.   LISTENING TO THE BRAIN

Take a fine tungsten wire, etch its tip to about 1 μ, slowly lower it through a small hole made in the back of a cat's skull, and amplify the microvolt potentials from the microelectrode. Many neurons in the brain produce a brief signal that sounds like a pop when played through a loudspeaker. If the microelectrode is properly positioned in the cat's visual cortex, a burst of firing occurs whenever a bar of light moves in a particular direction at a particular position in the cat's visual field. The specificity of the response was a surprise to David Hubel and

Torsten Wiesel, who first performed this experiment, and it is surprising today how much they subsequently learned about the architecture of the visual cortex by recording from one cell—out of billions—at a time.

Although the average response of a neuron in the visual cortex from a dozen trials is a reasonably repeatable measurement, the firing pattern varies from trial to trial, as shown in Fig. 7.2. Stochastic variability is found not only in the cerebral cortex, but as well at every level of the nervous system, including the sensory receptors. One of the chief sources of noise in the brain occurs at synapses where a chemical neurotransmitter is used to signal between neurons.

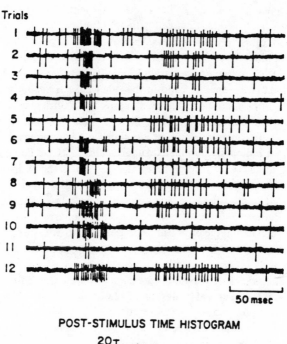

50 msec

POST-STIMULUS TIME HISTOGRAM

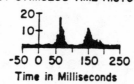

Time in Milliseconds

FIG. 7.2.   Extracellular recordings from a single neuron in cat visual cortex. This neuron responded best to a slit of light obliquely oriented in a particular part of the visual field. Twelve successive responses of the neuron to 50 msec exposures of light are shown above, and the average response for 20 trials is shown below. Although the pattern of firing varied from trial to trial (and some parts of the response drop out entirely, such as in trials 5, 10, and 11), the average over the ensemble of trials, called the poststimulus time histogram, is a repeatable measurement (Morrell, 1972).

The neurotransmitter is stored in small packets called vesicles, visible in Fig. 7.1(a), and released from the presynaptic terminal in discrete units. For example, at the junction between a motor neuron and muscle in the frog, approximately 300 vesicles are released with each synaptic activation. A statistical variation of about 17 vesicles, or 6 percent of the total, can be expected during a normal activation of the synapse. Many central synapses are believed to release fewer vesicles and consequently have greater variation. Even in the absence of activation vesicles are released spontaneously, producing miniature synaptic potentials.

Quantal fluctuations at synapses is just one of several sources of noise in the nervous system. How is the brain able to function reliably with so much intrinsic variability? Perhaps the variability is not as serious as it appears (Bullock, 1970), or perhaps redundancy allows a reliable response from a population of neurons (Cowan, 1973); perhaps too we are asking the wrong question, being misled by the digital computer as a model of reliability. Could the apparent variability in the response of single neurons provide us with a clue to a basic design principle of the nervous system?

Let us take a closer look at the data in Fig. 7.2. By concentrating on the response of the neuron to the stimulus, we have overlooked another interesting feature. The neuron is active even before the stimulus and maintains an apparently random background firing. This so-called spontaneous activity is common in the nervous system although the average background firing rate varies from neuron to neuron. In the retina, for example, ganglion cells, which send signals from the eye to the brain, have spontaneous activity in complete darkness, which may increase, decrease, or remain unchanged when the retina is exposed to a steady background illumination.

Spontaneous activity is generally regarded as a bias against which inhibitory as well as excitatory signals can be imposed. Because an impulse-producing neuron has a threshold below which it can transmit no signal or information, a neuron is most sensitive to input changes when maintained near threshold. If a neuron is too far above threshold, then the signal gets swamped by the background. Threshold is, of course, an unstable region, so the price of high sensitivity is high susceptibility to noise. The high levels of spontaneous activity in the brain and the apparent variability in the response of single neurons are indications that many neurons operate near threshold much of the time.

Although the large-scale electrical activity of the brain was explored long before single-cell recording was perfected, relatively little has been established about brain mechanisms from gross recordings. One qualitative feature of EEG recordings, however, is so common that its implications are sometimes overlooked: Widespread rhythms occur throughout the cerebral cortex and subcortical structures with frequencies between 5–100 Hz. The fact that any signal survives averaging over millions of sources, is coherent over large areas of the brain, and changes with the behavioral state of the animal strongly suggests significant temporal synchronization and spatial correlation among the sources of the EEG, one of which is believed to be the potentials generated at synapses. The possibility that synaptic events are correlated and synchronized is at present beyond the limits of experimental verification, but its consequences are worth exploring.

These three features—stochastic variability, spontaneous activity, and correlated electrical events—lead to a view of the brain that is probabilistic rather than deterministic, inherently distributed rather than local, and dynamic rather than static. Unfortunately, our experience with probablistic, distributed, dynamic systems is limited. Even simple examples and models would help us grasp the brain's complexity.

7.3.   SIMPLIFYING THE BRAIN

A successful model in physics is often a caricature, extracting only a few essential features from a complex phenomenon but allowing these to be studied with clarity and precision. For example, the two-dimensional Ising model of the ferromagnetic phase transition, although unrealistic, is nonetheless important because it has an exact analytic solution and demonstrates a phase transition qualitatively similar to experimental measurements. Could a similar approach be useful in studying the brain? A simple but effective model of the brain does not yet exist, in part because its essential design features have not yet been identified. Nevertheless the strengths and limitations of simple models based on our present knowledge should be carefully examined. New ideas are more easily evaluated in comparison with already well-understood if inadequate models.

Consider a neuron, or some part of it, as a processing unit with several inputs and an output. In some models the processing is assumed to be linear: The output of each unit is proportional to the sum of its inputs. However, if a processing unit has a threshold or any other departure from proportionality, then the model is nonlinear. The class of all linear models is mathematically well understood, but each nonlinear model requires a difficult individual analysis. Linear models, such as those discussed by James Anderson and Geoffrey Hinton (Chapter 1, this volume) and Teuvo Kohonen, Pekka Lehtiö and Erkki Oja (Chapter 4, this volume) are useful for analyzing distributed properties of general networks. In nonlinear models localized computations must be studied in specific networks, such as the model of stereopsis by David Marr and Tomaso Poggio (1976) and the model of visual cortex by George Ermentrout and Jack Cowan (1979). Geoffrey Hinton (Chapter 6, this volume) demonstrates a nonlinear model of associative memory.

None of the models mentioned thus far explicitly takes into account the variability and randomness observed in the nervous system. A new approach is required based on probabilistic rather than deterministic mathematics. Fortunately, powerful tools from probability theory are available and have been applied to a wide variety of problems in control and communication by electrical engineers. A simple probabilistic model of interacting neurons is presented in this section that provides an unexpected unification of the linear and nonlinear models.

A Simple Nonlinear Model

A cell maintains ionic gradients across its surface, which produce a potential difference between the outside and the inside of the cell. An incoming signal at a synapse, by altering the ionic conductance of the membrane, can change the membrane potential. A simple model for a single passive neuron, which to a first approximation behaves like a leaky capacitor, is given by

$$\tau \frac{d}{dt} \phi(t) + \phi(t) = B\eta(t), \tag{7-1}$$

where $\phi(t)$ is the membrane potential at time t and $\eta(t)$ is a single input with coupling strength B. The left side of Eq. (7-1) provides temporal integration of the input with a time constant τ. An excitatory input produces a sudden increase in the membrane potential, which then exponentially decays. The general solution of Eq. (7-1) for an arbitrary time-varying input is

$$\phi(t) = \int_{-\infty}^{t} e^{-(t-t')/\tau} B\eta(t') \, dt'. \tag{7-2}$$

A generalization of this linear model to a linearly interacting population of N neurons with membrane potentials $\phi_1, \phi_2, \ldots, \phi_N$ and M inputs $\eta_1, \eta_2, \ldots, \eta_M$ is given by

$$\tau \frac{d}{dt} \phi_a + \phi_a = \sum_{b=1}^{N} K_{ab}\phi_b + \sum_{c=1}^{M} B_{ac}\eta_c, \tag{7-3}$$

where K_{ab} is the strength of coupling from the bth neuron to the ath neuron, and B_{ac} is the strength of coupling between the cth input and the ath neuron. The general solution of this model is:

$$\phi_a(t) = \int_{-\infty}^{t} \sum_{b=1}^{N} T_{ab}(t - t') \sum_{c=1}^{M} B_{bc}\eta_c(t') \, dt', \tag{7-4}$$

where $\mathbf{T}(t - t')$ is the impulse response and depends only on $\mathbf{K}$. The network of neurons behaves like a multidimensional linear filter of the type used by electrical engineers to filter signals from noise. The network is especially sensitive to inputs with particular frequencies, given by the eigenvalues of $\mathbf{K}$, and to particular input patterns, given by the eigenvectors of $\mathbf{K}$.

The completeness with which the linear model can be analyzed is of great advantage when applying it to concrete cases. For example, Halden Hartline and Floyd Ratliff in 1957 using a linear model with lateral inhibition were able to successfully predict the response of the *Limulus* lateral eye to steady-state patterns of light. More recently, Bruce Knight Jr., Fredrick Dodge Jr., and their colleagues have extended the model to predict the response of the *Limulus* retina to arbitrary time-varying illumination, thus making it the best-understood piece of nervous tissue. Details of the *Limulus* model can be found in a review (Knight, 1975) and a volume of collected papers (Ratliff, 1974).

A Simple Nonlinear Model

Signals propagated down the thin dendrites of neurons exponentially decrement with a typical length constant of 250μ. Long-distance communication is accomplished with active regenerative channels in the membrane that produce a brief all-or-none impulse, the action potential. Above threshold the rate of impulse firing increases monotonically with input and saturates at some maximum, as shown in Fig. 7.3. Some general qualitative properties of nonlinear models are already found in a single neuron which synapses onto itself. If the average effect of impulses at the synapse is assumed to be proportional to the firing rate, then the steady-state membrane potential of the neuron should satisfy

$$\phi = K \rho (\phi) + B \eta, \tag{7-5}$$

where η is an external input, B is the coupling strength of the input, K is the coupling strength of the neuron with itself, and $\rho (\phi)$ is the firing rate of the neuron, as shown in Fig. 7.3. The dependent variable in Eq. (7-5) is ϕ, the effective membrane potential, defined as the membrane potential that the neuron would have in the absence of impulses. Unlike the linear model, for which there is a unique solution for any input, the nonlinear model can have more than one steady-state solution to a single input, as shown in Fig. 7.4. The past history of the neuron determines which of the multiple states is obtained. As the input slowly changes, new solutions may appear and old ones disappear: The critical input at which a transition between solution branches occurs is called a bifurcation. (The nonlinear one-neuron model is by coincidence formally identical to the Curie–Weiss mean-field theory of magnetism, with ϕ playing the role of magnetization and η identified with the externally applied magnetic field.)

The number of multiple states and the complexity of transitions between them increases with the number of interacting neurons. A nonlinear model for N neurons with membrane potentials $\phi_1, \phi_2, \ldots, \phi_N$ and M inputs $\eta_1, \eta_2, \ldots, \eta_M$ is given by

$$\tau \frac{d}{dt} \phi_a + \phi_a = \sum_{b=1}^{N} K_{ab}\rho_b(\phi_b) + \sum_{c=1}^{M} B_{ac}\eta_c, \tag{7-6}$$

where B_{ac} is the coupling strength from the cth input to the ath neuron and K_{ab} is the coupling strength between the bth neuron and the ath neuron. Note that

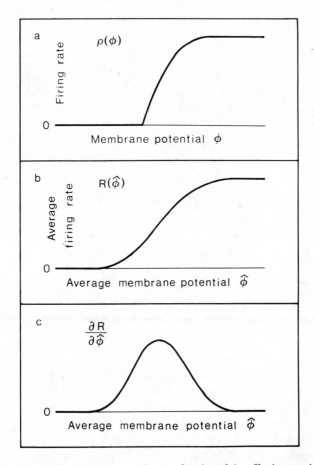

FIG. 7.3. (a) The firing rate, $\rho(\phi)$, as a function of the effective membrane potential ϕ for a typical neuron. (b) The average firing rate $R(\hat{\phi})$, defined in Eq. (7-8), as a function of the average membrane potential $\hat{\phi}$ holding all higher-order moments of ϕ fixed. (c) The partial derivative of $R(\hat{\phi})$ with respect to $\hat{\phi}$, which appears in Eq. (7-10).

the only difference between the linear model in Eq. (7-3) and the nonlinear model in Eq. (7-6) occurs in the nonlinear transduction, $\rho(\phi)$. For an impulse-producing neuron, the transduction between its input and output has a sigmoidal shape, as in Fig. 7.3, but in general the transduction can be an arbitrary nonlinear function. The model then applies equally well to neurons that do not produce impulses and to parts of neurons that are functionally independent processers (Shepherd, 1978).

Multiple perceptual states evoked by a single stimulus are common in the visual system, particularly in the perception of depth. A simple example is an

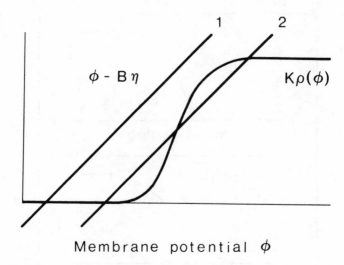

Membrane potential ϕ

FIG. 7.4. Graphic solution of the nonlinear one-neuron model, Eq. (7-5). The intersection of the straight line ϕ - B η (shown for two different values of the input η) and the sigmoidal ρ (ϕ) are solutions of the model. For input η_1 there is a unique solution, but for the input η_2 there are three solutions of which the middle is unstable.

outline of a box, called the Necker cube, which can be seen in two stable three-dimensional configurations. Bela Julesz (1974) has emphasized that the properties of binocular depth perception, such as a sharp transitions and hysteresis between stable states, are characteristic of some nonlinear systems. David Marr and Tomaso Poggio (1976) have demonstrated a nonlinear model similar in form to Eq (7-6) that can detect depth in random dot stereograms. A nonlinear model of the visual cortex has been studied by George Ermentrout and Jack Cowan (1979) who found that the symmetries of solutions near a bifurcation point resemble the visual patterns reported by subjects during drug-induced visual hallucinations. The nonlinear model in Eq. (7-6) has a rich mathematical structure that we are only beginning to understand.

A Simple Probabilistic Model

The response of a neuron is the visual cortex to a pattern of light on the retina varies from trial to trial despite efforts to control experimental conditions strictly. By averaging the response over a number of trials, the variability in the response not related to the stimulus is reduced. The counterpart of experimental averaging in probability theory is called the ensemble average. Rather than model an input, for example, as a single function of time, an ensemble of inputs is chosen, the members of the ensemble differing from one another by random variations. The solution of an equation for an ensemble of inputs is a corresponding ensemble of solutions. A great deal of information can be obtained from the ensemble in addition to the average solution, such as the average square variation or variance from the average. The average over an ensemble should not be confused with the average over time although under certain conditions the two may agree.

The nonlinear model in Eq. (7-6) can be made probabilistic by including noise with the inputs on the right side. Corresponding to an ensemble of inputs, each with a different random noise component, there is an ensemble of membrane potential responses derived from Eq. (7-6). Define the ensemble average of the membrane potential as

$$\hat{\phi}_a (t) = E \; \phi_a (t), \tag{7-7}$$

where E, the ensemble average or expectation operator, takes all the membrane potentials in the ensemble at a particular time and produces a single function, the average membrane potential $\hat{\phi}_a (t)$. Similarly, the ensemble average firing rate for an impulse-producing neuron is defined as

$$R_b (t) = E \; \rho_b (\phi_b (t)). \tag{7-8}$$

The ensemble average firing rate corresponds technically to the limit of the experimental poststimulus time histogram for an infinite number of trials.

A probabilistic analysis of the nonlinear model has been given elsewhere (Sejnowski, 1976b, 1977b). The strategy in the analysis is to set up a hierarchy of equations governing the statistical moments and to make reasonable simplifying assumptions to study each tier in the hierarchy. Although the equations in the hierarchy are coupled, each tier can, to some extent, be analyzed separately.

The lowest tier deals with first-order moments: the averages of single variables. The average membrane potentials satisfy an equation similar in form to the model itself, with $\rho_b (\phi_b)$ replaced by $R_b (\hat{\phi}_b)$, a somewhat smoother nonlinear function as shown in Fig. 7.3. The properties of the deterministic model in Eq. (7-6), which have already been discussed, hold as well for the equation that governs the average membrane potentials.

The second tier of the statistical hierarchy concerns second-order moments: the averages of squared variables and products of two variables. The average firing rate on the first tier is known to carry sensory information to the central nervous system and motor commands to muscles. Relatively little experimental effort has been devoted to measuring second-order moments, such as the variance of the firing rate, or correlations between membrane potentials, so it is not clear what information, if any, is carried on the second tier. An analysis of the second tier is nonetheless important for two reasons: First, the variances of the membrane potentials feed back to affect the first-order equations; and second, it is worth knowing what to look for if the nervous system does make use of higher-order moments.

Correlations between the spike trains of nearby neurons have been measured throughout the brain (e.g., retina:Rodieck, 1967; Mastronarde (in press); lateral geniculate nucleus: Stevens & Gerstein, 1976; cerebellum: Bell & Kawasaki, 1972; auditory cortex: Dickson & Gerstein, 1974). Relatively few experiments have been designed to measure changes in correlations in response to sensory stimulation. One intriguing example of stimulus-dependent correlations between two neurons in visual cortex is shown in Fig. 7.5. Because the membrane potential in a neuron is often below the spiking threshold, correlations between

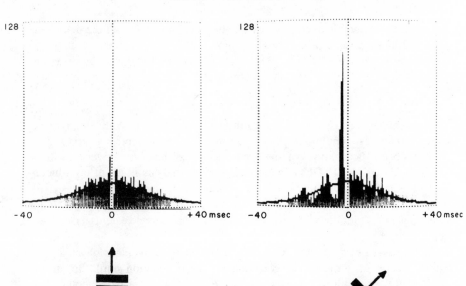

FIG. 7.5.   Cross-interval histograms of impulse firing from two simultaneously recorded neurons in visual cortex of a cat. Each stimulus bar was 2° wide at the cat's eye and the pattern of bars (shown below each histogram) was moved sinusoidally through 20° every 6 sec in the direction indicated by the arrows. The histogram was computed by measuring the time difference from every impulse in one train to the nearest preceding and succeeding impulse of the second train. If the impulses in the two neurons were occurring independently, the histogram should agree with the solid line. The left histogram agrees well with the control calculation, but the right histogram shows a series of peaks at approximately 3, 11, and 22 msec, indicating that one neuron tended to follow the other with those intervals. Thus the correlations between the two neurons depended on the stimulus. (Gerstein, 1970)

membrane potentials should be at least as prominent as correlations between spike trains.

A second-order correlation that has been normalized to remove the influence of first-order averages is called a covariance and is defined as

$$\text{cov} [\phi_a (s), \phi_b (t)] = E [\phi_a (s) \phi_b (t)] - E \phi_a (s) E \phi_b (t). \qquad (7-9)$$

The covariance is positive when the two membrane potentials fluctuate together more often than by chance, negative when they fluctuate oppositely more often than by chance, and zero when they are completely independent.

A neuron in cerebral cortex, such as the pyramidal cell in Fig. 7.6, continually receives an extremely large number of synaptic events along thousands of inputs. By the central limit theorem in probability theory, the sum of a large number of independent random signals has an approximately Gaussian distribution. Hence

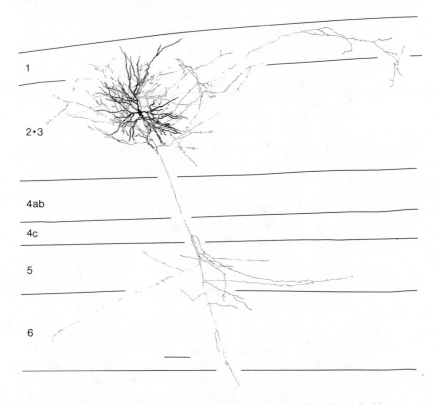

FIG. 7.6. Pyramidal cell in visual cortex of the cat. The cell was impaled with an intracellular electrode, and after its response to visual stimuli was determined, an enzyme, horseradish peroxidase, was injected into the cell. The neuron's axonal tree (thin processes) was as extensive as its dendritic tree (thick processes). (Gilbert & Wiesel, 1979)

it is reasonable to assume that the membrane potential of a typical neuron in cerebral cortex is Gaussian, an assumption that can be checked experimentally. This assumption can be rigorously proved as a limit theorem in some related dynamical systems (Stuart Geman, unpublished). An unexpected simplification occurs in the analysis of the covariance if the membrane potentials are Gaussian: Although the model is highly nonlinear, the covariance between membrane potentials satisfies a linear equation identical in form to Eq. (7-3). However, the coupling strength in the equation for the covariance is not K_{ab} but

$$K'_{ab} = K_{ab} \; \frac{\delta R_b(\hat{\phi}_b)}{\delta \hat{\phi}_b} \qquad (7\text{-}10)$$

The multiplicative factor in the effective coupling strength K'_{ab} has a simple intuitive explanation. As shown in Fig. 7.3, this factor is small when the average membrane potential is far below or far above threshold and is largest when the average membrane potential is near threshold. The covariance is a signal contained in the fluctuations of the membrane potential: The neuron will not transmit information in the fluctuations if the membrane potential is below threshold or if the neuron is saturated above threshold but will transmit information in the fluctuations if the neuron is poised near threshold. As a consequence, only a skeleton network of neurons near threshold significantly affects the covariance. The processing of covariance is linear even for large fluctuations as long as the Gaussian assumption remains valid.

The probabilistic analysis summarized here unifies two classes of models with very different character. On the first tier, the average membrane potentials are governed by a nonlinear equation identical in form to those in the nonlinear class, Eq. (7-6). On the second tier, the covariance between membrane potentials satisfies a linear equation, Eq. (7-4). The coupling between the nonlinear and linear equations suggests a novel and flexible way to control the processing, storage, and retrieval of distributed information.

7.4. MODELING MEMORY

Models of memory are uncomfortably abstract: first, because cognitive processing is several stages removed from the physical representation of sensory information; and second, because no one knows where or how thinking takes place. What then is the value of modeling an unidentified brain area that processes undetermined information? There is, perhaps, something to be learned about the adequacy of the model for studying qualitative properties of the functioning brain.

The best-studied model of associative memory is the linear matrix model (Anderson, 1970; Kohonen, 1972; Steinbuch, 1961). In the simplest example, the interactions between neurons in Eq. (7-3) are ignored and only static inputs are studied. The output of a neuron, ϕ_a, then satisfies

$$\phi_a = \sum_{b=1}^{M} B_{ab}\eta_b, \qquad (7\text{-}11)$$

where the B_{ab} are the coupling strengths of the branching inputs η_b. How should the B_{ab} be chosen so that a specific input pattern will produce a desired output pattern? What happens as we increase the number of paired associations? Is there a simple algorithm for computing the optimal B_{ab}? All of these questions have precise answers, as discussed by Kohonen et. al. (Chapter 4, this volume). The same techniques can be applied to the static solutions of the linear model in Eq. (7-3), which includes interactions,

$$\phi_a = \sum_{b=1}^{N} K_{ab}\phi_b + \sum_{c=1}^{M} B_{ac}\eta_c, \qquad (7\text{-}12)$$

where the coupling strengths between neurons, K_{ab}, are altered to store input-output associations rather than B_{ab}. A review of this model, including useful demonstrations, is given by Kohonen (1977).

The matrix model resembles memory in the same way that a toy glider resembles a bird. It does fly, in a rigid sort of way, but it lacks dynamics and grace. The input and output vectors in the matrix model are purely spatial, but as we know from common experience, associations have a temporal flow. Furthermore, associations depend overwhelmingly on context, which is entirely missing from the model. Can the matrix model be suitably generalized to overcome these shortcomings? In the case of dynamics the answer is yes, as shown shortly. No linear model, however, can ever be constructed to include context or contingencies: Like a toy glider a linear model always "flies" in a straight line.

Time

Most of us have a reasonably good memory for temporal sequences. Given the first few bars of a familiar tune, we can usually identify, if not reproduce, the rest of the tune. Christopher Longuet-Higgins (1968) proposed a model of temporal memory that he called the holophone in analogy with the distributed storage of spatial information in the holograph. The holophone can record temporal associations to a given input and respond with the associated signal whenever the input reoccurs. The original model of the holophone suggested by Longuet-Higgins involved banks of filters and variable amplifiers, that is, a realization in the frequency domain. Because the holophone is a linear filter whose output is of the form given by Eq. (7-4), the linear model in Eq. (7-3) is an equivalent state-variable realization of the holophone if only a single input and a single output are condidered. David Willshaw (Chapter 3, this volume) discusses extensions of the original holophone model and some of its limitations.

The time-dependent linear model, by virtue of the first term in Eq. (7-3), adds a rich temporal dimension to the static model in Eq. (7-11). Moreover, the analytic solution is explicitly known: The filter matrix in Eq. (7-4) has the form

$$T_{ab}(t) \sim \sum_n \sum_k t^k e^{-\lambda_n t} \sin (\omega_n t) P_{ab}(n, k), \qquad (7\text{-}13)$$

where λ_n and ω_n are derived, respectively, from the real and imaginary parts of the eigenvalues for the coupling matrix K, and P (n, k) are a set of matrices doubly indexed by (n, k) and derived from the eigenvectors of K.

The filter matrix T (t) is the response of the model to a sudden burst of action potentials along the inputs. If for convenience we assume that the inputs do not branch (B is diagonal), then by Eq. (7-4) the response of the time-dependent model is

$$\phi_a(t) = \sum_b T_{ab}(t) \eta_b, \qquad (7\text{-}14)$$

where η_b is proportional to the number of action potentials along the bth input. Thus the membrane potential of each neuron is the sum of many exponentially damped, sinusoidally varying components indexed by n. However, the envelope of the kth term in the second summation has a peak that appears later as k increases. Each term has a separate matrix P (n, k), that transforms the input into a different spatial output, and these successively unfold in time. Rather than give rise to a single output as in the case of the static model, a single input in the dynamic model produces a doubly indexed set of associated outputs, one set indexing the frequency spectrum and the second set indexing the sequence in time. Further details about the output pattern are given elsewhere (Sejnowski, 1976b).

Synaptic Plasticity

The physical basis of learning and memory is unknown. Alteration in the strengths of synapses between neurons has been shown to underlie habituation of a simple reflex in *Aplysia,* a marine mollusk, and similar mechanisms may underlie more complex forms of learning (Kandel, 1976). The matrix model and filter model of memory predict the conditions under which synaptic strengths should change in order to store new associations optimally (Kohonen, 1978; Sejnowski, 1977a). New experimental techniques are needed to test these predictions in the vertebrate central nervous system.

One of the best-studied areas of the brain is the cerebellum, an area that receives inputs from both motor and sensory systems and is intimately involved in motor coordination. Experiments on the vestibulo-ocular reflex indicate that the cerebellum may be involved in motor learning (Ito, 1975; Robinson, 1976). Following the suggestions of Brindley (1964) and Szentágothai (1968), Marr (1969) and Albus (1971) have proposed detailed theories for associative motor learning in the cerebellum that predict plasticity for synapses between parallel fibers and Purkinje cells (Fig. 7.7). According to Marr (1969) the synapses should be "facilitated by the conjunction of presynaptic and climbing fiber (or postsynaptic) activity". Some conjunctions, however, take place purely by chance; because accidental coincidences are unrelated to an animals's experience, they can have little or no adaptive value. Moreover, unless means exist for weakening the plastic synapse, continual random coincidences inexorably push it to maximum strength. A plastic synapse whose strength can be flexibly adjusted within its range should therefore be capable of long-term depression as well as

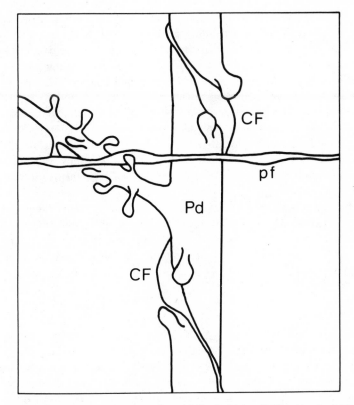

FIG. 7.7. Schematic illustration of a cerebellar Purkinje cell *Pd* (with a dendritic branchlet), a climbing fiber *CF* (entwining the dendritic trunk), and a parallel fiber *pf* (passing through the dendritic tree), based on Palay and Chan-Palay (1974). Climbing fiber varicosities make numerous synaptic contacts with spines on the dendritic trunk. (Sejnowski, 1977*a*)

long-term facilitation, and the condition for weakening the synapse should be as specific as that for strengthening it—otherwise the information stored as the synaptic strength is lost.

Without proposing an all-encompassing theory for the cerebellum, the probabilistic model in the previous section can be applied to the specific problem of plasticity in the cerebellar cortex (Sejnowski, 1977a, 1977b). The result overcomes some of the shortcomings of previous predictions. If K is the strength of a plastic synapse, then the learning algorithm derived from the dynamic filter model of memory is

$$\frac{d}{dt} K = \gamma[p(t)c(t) - \hat{p}(t)\hat{c}(t)], \qquad (7\text{-}15)$$

where the constant γ determines the rate of change of the synaptic strength, $p(t)$ is the presynaptic input (a parallel fiber in the cerebellum), $c(t)$ is the "teaching" input (a climbing fiber in the cerebellum), and $\hat{p}(t)$ and $\hat{c}(t)$ are their average values. Thus the algorithm predicts that the strength of the synapse should increase whenever the parallel fiber and climbing fiber are activated together more often than by chance, decrease in strength whenever they are activated together less often than by chance, and maintain a constant average strength when the two inputs are uncorrelated. This covariance storage algorithm has two advantages: First, the problem of saturation from chance coincidences is overcome; and second, the entire dynamic range of synaptic strength is always available. One problem that the algorithm does not solve is deviation from the average strength owing to random fluctuations. However, this problem can be minimized by limiting the time during which a synapse is sensitive to modification.

A similar algorithm was independently proposed by Leon Cooper, Fishel Liberman, and Erkki Oja (1979), who used it to model the acquisition and loss of neuron specificity in the visual cortex during development. The convergence and stability of a wide class of learning algorithms has been studied by Élie Bienenstock (1980).

Skeleton Filters

The linear filter model for memory viewed as a processing unit has two types of terminals—inputs and outputs. Recall from memory, however, depends not only on sensory inputs but on expectation and context as well. How can these influences be accounted for in the model? Adding a second input for context does not help: The new output is simply a linear superposition. A new type of input is needed, one that can change the processing of other inputs.

The probabilistic model discussed in the previous section provides the required flexibility. The linear filtering of the input on the second tier depends on the skeleton network determined by the first tier. Two types of input can therefore be distinguished: (1) inputs that affect the average membrane potentials, and hence by Eq. (7-10) the skeleton network for the filter; and (2) inputs that affect the correlations between membrane potentials. (Both types of inputs may, of course, be carried by a single set of input fibers.) Contextual information, represented by the average firing rates of neurons in the filter, could completely alter the correlated output associations evoked by correlated inputs. Consequently, the probabilistic model allows many different skeleton filters to be embedded in the same population of neurons. For example, each different visual pattern excites a different subset of neurons in the visual cortex, which could in turn serve as a different skeleton filter for processing correlations.

Our sensitivity to a particular sensory signal can be greatly enhanced when our attention is properly focused. The cue can be physical, grammatical, meaningful, or any other perceivable dimension. A skeleton filter with internally generated inputs rather than sensory inputs driving the background firing rates is a candidate model for selective attention. The type of information to which the skeleton filter could be made sensitive depends on where the filter is placed in the processing stream. Evidence exists for filtering on all levels, from early sensory selection to late conceptual selection (Norman, 1976).

Items in human memory which are associated with each other can be related in many different ways. A table and chair can be related by color, style, function, or any other conceivable dimension. In a semantic network, relationships are graphically summarized as a set of items joined by relational arrows, as Scott Fahlman discusses in chapter 5 of this book. How is the discrete representation of knowledge in a semantic network related to the analog representation of information in distributed filters? The simplest unit of knowledge in a semantic network is a triple of two items and a relation between them. A relation cannot be included in a linear filter because, as we have seen, there is no way for a linear filter to account for a contingency in the association between two items. In a skeleton filter, however, contingency is represented by the background firing rates, as illustrated in Fig. 7.8. If the firing rates in an area were to represent a relation, then the skeleton filter could generate output associations to input items relative to that relation.

The skeleton filter viewed as a processing unit has three types of terminals, one of which can be used to represent contextual and relational information. Skeleton filters could, in principle, be used selectively to store and retrieve associations in long-term memory, to attend sensory information, and to manipulate relational knowledge. The selectivity of a skeleton filter does not depend on the details of the particular network model analyzed here. Any model composed of nonlinear threshold devices will exhibit transitions between different processing states. If the nonlinearity is strong, such as the step functions that Geoffrey Hinton uses in the model he discusses (Chapter 6, this volume), then the transitions between states is sharp and the control of the "skeleton" will be "tight". Weaker nonlinearities, such as a linear device with a threshold, allow more

a

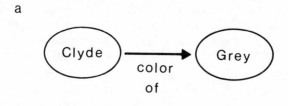

b

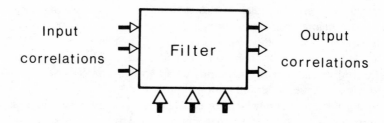

Average firing rates

FIG. 7.8.   (a) Example of an elementary triple from a semantic network. The item "Clyde" (an elephant) is linked with the item "grey" by the relation "color of." (b) Schematic diagram of inputs and outputs for a skeleton filter. Input correlations are transformed by the filter matrix $T(t)$ given by Eq. (7-13). The filter matrix and hence the output correlations depend on the average firing rates R_b through the effective coupling matrix in Eq. (7-10).

gradual transitions and "softer" control. The probabilistic model in this chapter starts with an arbitrary sigmoidal nonlinearity, which includes step functions and linear threshold devices, and derives an exactly linear skeleton network embedded in the full nonlinear model. Thus, control of the skeleton can be "tight" in one area and "soft" in another, and the processing is linear in both cases.

7.5.   THEORY AND PRACTICE

Three theoretical traditions have independently contributed to our present understanding of distributed information processing. Workers in two traditions were inspired by distributed processing in the brain: those interested in associative memory concentrated on linear models (Anderson, 1970; Kohonen, 1972; Longuet-Higgins, 1968) while those who emphasized cooperative properties developed nonlinear models (Ermentrout & Cowan, 1979; Julesz, 1974; Marr & Poggio, 1976). A third tradition, inspired by machines rather than man, deals with the control of complex physical systems and the communication of information. The probabilistic tools developed by systems engineers were applied in this chapter to a nonlinear model that previously had only been treated by deterministic techniques. A surprise occurred during the analysis of the model: If a reasonable assumption is made then the linear and nonlinear models become unified in a single probabilistic one. In addition to being theoretically attractive the unification has experimental implications that are directly testable.

The primary variable in most network models is the average firing rate, which is known to code sensory and motor information in the central nervous system. In the probabilistic model the membrane potential is taken as the primary variable, and the average firing rate appears as a derived statistical variable. In most linear network models the average firing rate of a neuron is assumed to vary linearly with total input, but this is only a valid approximation over a small part of a typical neuron's operating range, as shown in Fig. 7.3. Linearity appears in the probabilistic model not at the level of the average membrane potential or average firing rate but at the level of correlations between membrane potentials, a higher-order statistical variable that is just beginning to be explored experimentally.

Correlations are signals contained in the fluctuations of the membrane potentials from their average values, a component that is usually ignored in most experiments. Whether large-scale correlations exist and are related to sensory processing can be directly tested by intracellular recording from neurons in cerebral cortex. Charles Gilbert and Torsten Wiesel (1979), for example, have used intracellular recording in the visual cortex to identify the class of a neuron from its average response and to determine its morphology following injection of a marker (Fig. 7.6). An ensemble of responses contains information beyond the average response, such as the ensemble correlation, which may also depend on the stimulus. An ensemble of intracellular recordings from a pair of neurons responding to a controlled sensory stimulus could be used to determine the ensemble correlation between the membrane potentials and to test the key assumption that membrane potentials have a Gaussian distribution. These experiments are difficult and might seem unpromising: Only in a few areas of the cortex, such as the primary visual cortex, is enough known about the first-order average response to justify looking at second-order signals. However, the importance of higher-order processing cannot be properly assessed until data are available from carefully controlled experiments. A probabilistic model may be useful in suggesting worthwhile measurements and in analyzing the data.

The unification of the linear and nonlinear models by a single probabilistic model provides a rigorous basis for a new device, the skeleton filter, which combines the advantages of linear filters from systems engineering with the flexibility of nonlinear control. A skeleton filter is a skeleton network of neurons in an area that linearly filters correlations along incoming spike trains. The subset of neurons in the skeleton network, and hence the filtering characteristics of the network, can be adjusted by changing the average firing rates of the neurons. In principle a skeleton filter could be used to implement selective attention, to provide for the selective storage and retrieval of information from associative memory, and to manipulate relational knowledge, which is not possible in a strictly linear model.

The aim of the probabilistic model summarized in this chapter is to provide a bridge between neural "hardware" and behavioral "software." If the model is a good first approximation to information processing in the central nervous system, then the parallels with communications and control engineering could prove useful not only in interpreting experimental data but in understanding the brain's design principles as well. In particular, linear systems theory, which has important applications in signal detection and spacecraft guidance, can be considered the machine language for a "chip" of highly interconnected neurons in a skeleton filter. Many chips, perhaps many millions, may be required for each sensory system and each level of cognitive processing. The "columns" (Mountcastle, 1979) and "dendritic bundles" (Roney, Scheibel, & Shaw, 1979) that have been found in the cerebral cortex are candidates for such skeleton filter chips.

The brain contains the solutions to numerous problems in control and communication that faced our distant ancestors. Despite the brain's formidable complexity, its design principles need not be complicated, just as the biochemical complexity of the cell does not obscure the simplicity of life's design principle, the replication of DNA. Future workers may uncover some of the brain's design principles.

REFERENCES

Albus, J. S. A theory of cerebellar function. *Mathematical Biosciences,* 1971, *10,* 25–61.

Anderson, J. A. Two models for memory organization using interacting traces. *Mathematical Biosciences,* 1970, *8,* 137–160.

Barlow, H. B. Single units and sensation: A neuron doctrine for perceptual psychology? *Perception,* 1972, *1,* 371–394.

Bell, C. C., & Kawasaki, T. Relation among climbing fiber responses of nearby Purkinje cells. *Journal of Neurophysiology,* 1972, *35,* 155–169.

Bienenstock, É. L. *A theory of development of neuronal selectivity.* Unpublished doctoral dissertation, Brown University, 1980.

Bullock, T. H. The reliability of neurons. *Journal of General Physiology,* 1970, *55,* 565–584.

Brindley, G. S. The use made by the cerebellum of the information that it receives from sense organs. *International Brain Research Organization Bulletin,* 1964, *3,* 80.

Cooper, L. N., Liberman, F., & Oja, E. A theory for the acquisition and loss of neuron specificity in visual cortex. *Biological Cybernetics,* 1979, *33,* 9–28.

Cowan, J. D. The design of reliable systems. In M. A. B. Brazier, D. O. Walter, & D. Schneider (Eds.), *Neural Modeling.* Los Angeles, Calif.: Brain Information Service, 1973.

Des Rosiers, M. H. Sakurada, O., Jehle, J., Shinohara, M., Kennedy, C., & Sokoloff, L. Functional plasticity in the immature striate cortex of the monkey shown by the [^{14}C]deoxyglucose method. *Science*, 1978, *200*, 447-449.

Dickson, J. W., & Gerstein, G. L. Interactions between neurons in auditory cortex of the cat. *Journal of Neurophysiology*, 1974, *37*, 1239-1261.

Ermentrout, G., & Cowan, J. D. A mathematical theory of visual hallucination patterns. *Biological Cybernetics*, 1979, *34*, 137-150.

Gerstein, G. L. Functional associations of neurons: Detection and interpretation. In F. O. Schmitt (Ed.), *The Neurosciences: Second Study Program*. New York: The Rockefeller University Press, 1970.

Gilbert, C. D., & Wiesel, T. N. Morphology and intracortical projections of functionally characterized neurones in cat visual cortex. *Nature*, 1979, *280*, 120-125.

Hubel, D. H., & Wiesel, T. N. Functional architecture of macaque visual cortex. *Proceedings of the Royal Society (London)*, 1977, *B198*, 1-59.

Hubel, D. H., Wiesel, T. N., & Stryker, M. P. Orientation columns in macaque monkey visual cortex demonstrated by the 2-deoxyglucose autoradiographic technique. *Science*, 1978, *269*, 368-330.

Ito, M. Learning control mechanisms by the cerebellum flocculo-vestibulo-ocular system. In D. H. Tower (Ed.), *The Nervous System* (Vol. 1). New York: Raven Press, 1975.

Julesz, B. Cooperative phenomena in binocular depth perception. *American Scientist*, 1974, *62*, 32-43.

Kandel, E. R. *A cell-biological approach to learning*. Bethesda, Md.: Society for Neuroscience, 1978.

Knight, B. W. The horseshoe crab eye: A little nervous system whose dynamics are solvable. *Lectures on Mathematics in the Life Sciences*, 1975, *5*, 111-144.

Kohonen, T. Correlation matrix memories. *IEEE Transactions on Computers*, 1972, *C-21*, 353-359.

Kohonen, T. *Associative memory*. Berlin-Heidelberg-New York: Springer-Verlag, 1977.

Longuet-Higgins, H. C. Holographic model of temporal recall. *Nature*, 1968, *217*, 104.

Marr, D. A theory of cerebellar cortex. *Journal of Physiology*, 1969, *202*, 437-470.

Marr, D., & Poggio, T. Cooperative computation of stereo disparity. *Science*, 1976, *194*, 283-287.

Mastronade, D. N. Correlated firing of cat retinal ganglion cells. *Journal of Neurophysiology*, in press.

Morrell, F. Integrative properties of parastriate neurons. In A. G. Karczmar & J. C. Eccles (Eds.), *Brain and Human Behavior*. Berlin-Heidelberg-New York: Springer-Verlag, 1972.

Mountcastle, V. B. An organizing principle for cerebral function: The unit module and the distributed system. In F. O. Schmitt (Ed.), *The Neurosciences: Fourth Study Program*. Cambridge, Mass.: MIT Press, 1979.

Norman, D. A. *Memory and attention*. New York: Wiley 1976.

Palay, S. L. & Chan-Palay, V. *Cerebellar cortex: Cytology and organization*. Berlin-Heidelberg-New York: Springer-Verlag, 1974.

Ratliff, F. (Ed.) *Studies in excitation and inhibition in the retina*. New York: The Rockefeller University Press, 1974.

Robinson, D. A. Adaptive gain control of vestibulo-ocular reflex by the cerbellum. *Journal of Neurophysiology*, 1976, *39*, 954-969.

Rodieck, R.W. Maintained activity of cat retinal ganglion cells. *Journal of Neurophysiology*, 1967, *30*, 1043-1071.

Roney, K. J., Scheibel, A. B. & Shaw, G. L. Dendritic bundles: Survey of anatomical experiments and physiological theories. *Brain Research Reviews*, 1979, *1*, 225-271.

Sejnowski, T. J. On global properties of neuronal interaction. *Biological Cybernetics*, 1976, *22*, 85-95. (a)

Sejnowksi, T. J. On the stochastic dynamics of neuronal interaction. *Biological Cybernetics*, 1976, *22*, 203–211. (b)

Sejnowski, T. J. Statistical constraints on synaptic plasticity. *Journal of Theoretical Biology*, 1977, *69*, 385–389. (a)

Sejnowski, T. J. Storing covariance with nonlinearly interacting neurons. *Journal of Mathematical Biology*, 1977, *4*, 303–321. (b)

Sejnowski, T. J., Reingold, S. C., Kelley, D. B., Gelperin, A. Localization of [^{3}H]-2-deoxyglucose in single molluscan neurons. *Nature*, 1980, *287*, 449–451.

Shepherd, G. M. Microcircuits in the nervous system. *Scientific American*, 1978, *(2)*, 93–103.

Sokoloff, L., Reivich, M., Kennedy, C., Des Rosiers, M. H., Potlak, C. S., Pettigrew, K. D., Sakurada, O., Shinohara, M. The [^{14}C]deoxyglucose method for the measurement of local glucose utilization: Theory, procedure, and normal values in the conscious and anesthetized albino rat. *Journal of Neurochemistry*, 1977, *28*, 897–916.

Steinbuch, K. Die Lernmatrix. *Kybernetik*, 1961, *1*, 36–45.

Stevens, J. K., & Gerstein, G. Interactions between cat lateral geniculate neurons. *Journal of Neurophysiology*, 1976, *39*, 239–256.

Szentágothai, J. Structural–functional considerations of the cerebellar neuron network. *Proceedings of the IEEE*, 1968, 56, 960–968.

8 Categorization and Selective Neurons

James A. Anderson
Michael C. Mozer
Brown University

> *. . . from discrimination between this and that a host of demons blazes forth.*
>
> —Huang Po

8.1. INTRODUCTION

Much of the power of human cognition arises from the fact that it resides in both a conceptual world and a physical world. The interface between these two worlds is accessible to study and is of great importance and interest. Perhaps the most frequently used word to describe this interface is *categorization*.

The physical world is composed of objects which can vary in a number of ways, some important for cognition and some less so. To use a simple example, the number of photons reaching the eye from an object may go up and down considerably as the ambient light intensity increases or decreases. Yet within well-studied limits the object is recognized as the same object. At the same time we can often detect physical differences such as intensity, wavelength, and so on. Cognitive psychology generally ignores these aspects of reality as being of only secondary interest.

It seems true that the highest levels of cognition are independent of many physical parameters either in the environment or in the details of the process observed. A table is a table, no matter how many photons it reflects. More interestingly, a table is a table even though it can differ widely in physical structure, being made of metal, mahogany, or marble but still a table. This

213

presents a classic philosophical problem going back to the time of the Greeks. It can be convincingly argued that there is no absolute defining property of "tableness" shown by tables and by nothing else. On the contrary, a table consists of a bunch of correlated attributes relating physical form, functionality, location, and many other properties. There seems to be no simple, adequate, rule-bound definition of table.

Let us note that much of the power of human cognition, especially of language, is that it operates at a level of abstraction removed at least one step from the simple physical properties of the environment. There are enough similarities among tables to allow the useful submergence of what may actually be quite gross differences.

There are several aspects to categorization. In the real world events do not repeat exactly. Given the amount of internal noise in our nervous system, even if events did repeat exactly, the internal representations of them might not. Elementary entities in most "cognitive" models are typically assumed to be something called *ideas* or *concepts*. Although there are complications, what is required is the notion of an equivalence class that can contain examples that are not identical with other class members but that are somehow "like" them. In any case we are working with a noisy, probabilistic process, trying to form equivalence classes of things which are not really equivalent.

This may not be a satisfactory epistemology; but the *practical* virtue of this ability is undeniable; and our success as a species seems partial proof of its usefulness, though as is true of most biological adaptations, there are numerous untidy aspects to the process.

Aims of This Chapter

What we do in this chapter is threefold, and modest compared to the general problem of categorization. First, we sketch an approach to a simple kind of categorization that is consistent with, and an outgrowth of, the kinds of distributed parallel models using state vectors that are discussed in Chapter 1 of this book. Second, we apply this model specifically to the categorization of capital letters and describe the results of a test of the model. Third, we make some comments about brain organization that, somewhat surprisingly, the simulation makes relevant.

We specifically do *not* review the psychological literature on categorization. We have discussed this elsewhere (Anderson, 1977; Anderson, Silverstein, Ritz, & Jones, 1977). We recommend the collection of papers contained in Rosch and Lloyd (1978) as a good entry to modern psychological thought in this area. Here, we are concerned only with a simple formal model and its implications for neuroscience.

8.2.   VECTOR MODELS

State Vectors

The fundamental, active entities in some of the models that are discussed in Chapter 1 and the approach discussed here use "state vectors." Elements of the vectors are generally considered to be neurons or something closely related to neurons, and the magnitude of activity is proportional to firing frequency or something derived from firing frequency, such as deviation from spontaneous activity level. The evolution of the state vector with time describes the behavior of the system.

To give a hypothetical physiological example, the input state vector might represent the input to the cortex from a specific sensory nucleus, the projection to Area 17 from the lateral geniculate nucleus, for example. Further along, one region of cortex might project to another region of cortex. Here both input and output would be far removed from the direct sensory representation of the original stimulus, having been subjected to many other influences as well as the initial input. The models we propose are for modules that represent only an elementary processing unit of the brain, a chip, as it were, only one stage of a large organization. The maximum size of a module might be approximately that of a Brodmann area; more realistically a single cortical area might contain several such modules, intertwined and interacting. The class of layer 5 pyramids in Area 17 might be given as an example of a set of cells of this kind. The same cortical area might contain several other units of the kind we discuss. There certainly are very many cells in one module, hundreds of thousands at the least, but this is only a small fraction of the cells present in the brain.

Because we are emphasizing the centrality of state vectors, let us mention one more important theoretical property that we would like to see and that our models can provide. It is the property of *reconstruction* that is discussed in Chapter 1 in relation to the linear associative model and that is also discussed and demonstrated by Kohonen, Lehtio, and Oja in their contribution to this book.

Suppose we wish to classify a particular input as an example of one thing or another. There are two fundamentally different approaches we could take. We suspect that the brain may use both. First, we could view the categorization problem like a detection problem. An output, a single number or decision, is delivered depending on the result of a computation on the input. The output of the system bears no physical relation to the input. Second, we observe that in the associative matrix models discussed elsewhere in this book, the output is not anything like a single value but is a state vector just as is the input. If the input is noisy, or only partially present, or if there is noise or damage in the memory matrix, then the desired output should be resistant to this as much as possible.

We should like to be able, for instance, to reconstruct the entire output vector, or a close approximation to it, from a degraded or partially absent input vector.

In this case we actually repair the state vector. Perhaps we can assume a similar process takes place in categorization: In some sense we want to *construct* the category as the output or have as output a noise-free state vector that directly represents the category. The output vector is of importance in itself. It corresponds to a physical pattern of electrochemical events that might drive other sets of neurons, eventually leading to motor neurons and muscle activity. We actually want to construct a pattern and not improve the signal-to-noise ratio of the detection statistic.

It is hard to overemphasize the importance of this property. We are talking about a nervous system where state vectors are *things*. In the motor system this is obvious. A pattern of nervous activity causes diverse muscles to contract forming a coordinated movement. The state vector, which at one place in the nervous system might be usefully interpreted at a cognitive level, now elsewhere in the brain is the actual effective output, executing physical action. The state vector is not *representing* anything.

Neuronal Selectivity

As mentioned in Chapter 1, there is compelling evidence that cortical organization is partially parallel, certainly so at the level of the modules of the system, and partially distributed. By this we mean that individual cells may respond to a range of stimuli and are not as finely tuned as "grandmother cells," which respond to a single "wordlike" item and, presumably, to nothing else. A completely distributed system where every cell responds to some degree to every input is equally unrealistic. It is a fact that most neurons are selective, responding to only a small fraction of the potential events in the world. Figure 8.1 shows the two extreme hypotheses. There is a flow of information from top to bottom. At the top might be a parallel sensory receptor layer, a retina, for example, where a complex stimulus can affect almost any cell, but a cell is affected by only a particular aspect of the stimulus. At the bottom might be the set of motor neurons, where any motor neuron can potentially have its activity altered by any sensory input. There are activity patterns of large dimensionality and low single-unit selectivity, in terms of the complex input, at both input and output.

What happens in the middle? The grandmother-cell hypothesis suggests at the point of maximum cell selectivity something rather like Fig. 8.1(left), an hourglass, where at some set of internal elements, neurons or synapses, only one element is activated and the rest are silent. Conversely the fully distributed models suggest something like Fig. 8.1(right) where there is no "necking down," and at each and every point distribution is total with all cells responding in some way to all stimulus patterns. The nervous system, as a matter of experimental

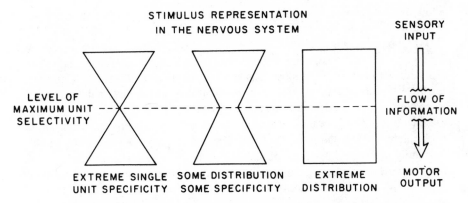

FIG. 8.1. Schematic description of three hypotheses for selectivity of single neurons in the central nervous system. At the sensory input side a complex stimulus may be, and in fact usually is, coded by many sensory receptors. Similarly at the motor output a complex stimulus may potentially affect the discharge of any or all motor neurons. In between, extreme single-unit selectivity (grandmother cells) assumes there is a level where, of many possible cells, only one responds to the complex stimulus. This is the point of maximum selectivity. A completely distributed model (e.g., a Fourier transform hologram) may have many or all cells change their discharge in response to a sufficiently complex stimulus. To us the evidence suggests that an intermediate position is correct. Cells show, even at the point of maximum selectivity, modest distribution coupled with considerable single-unit selectivity. A guess would be that perhaps a few percent of cells in a relevant region of cortex might change their discharge when a complex stimulus appeared.

fact, seems to have chosen an intermediate position biased toward selectivity, perhaps something like the diagram in Fig. 8.1(center), where a small fraction, not one and not all, of the cells at the point of maximum selectivity change their activity for a complex stimulus.

Determining the value of this fraction is one of the most interesting neuroscientific problems we can think of. Barlow (1972) has suggested that it is very small, perhaps 1000 active cells out of 70,000,000 in the primary visual cortex. Our feeling is that it is considerably bigger than this and might lie in the range of from 1–10% for a given sensory system and for a complex stimulus associated with significant learned behavior. For example, a meaningful visual stimulus might cause about this fraction of cells to modify their discharge rates in the inferotemporal cortex, an advanced but visual area of the cortex that seems to be responsible for some of our more complex visual functions. At present this estimate is only a conjecture, but it will not be so for long. Current anatomical techniques, in particular the 2-deoxyglucose mapping technique and its refinements, could eventually allow us to get a firm estimate on this number by allowing us to take a snapshot of cell activation over the entire brain when the system is responding to a meaningful stimulus.

We should emphasize one implication of this estimate. A nervous system where only 1% of the cells in a given cortical area was activated would appear to be extremely selective with most cells not responding to most stimuli. Considering the difficulty and tedium of single-cell recording, a system with this degree of selectivity would be difficult to work with using single-unit techniques. Yet for a reasonable chunk of cortex containing tens of millions of cells, a million or so cells might be responding to a given stimulus if only they could be found, indicating in fact a high degree of distribution in the representation. Cells in this area might have selectivities far removed from grandmother cells but might easily be interpreted as being such.

8.3.   ABSTRACTION AND CATEGORIZATION

Abstraction

Let us now return to the questions related to categorization. One of the things required for categorization is an equivalence class that can contain examples that are not identical with other class members but that are somehow like them. There are many ways this could be accomplished. Next we discuss an approach that arises from the state-vector approach to cognition.

Two related models are involved. In the first we ask how it is possible to develop the idea of a "category" when all that are presented are examples of the category, which may differ in detail. The association model discussed in Chapter 1 and in Chapter 4 by Kohonen et al. then has represented within it terms containing the sum of state vectors. Suppose we have a number of examples of the same category. Denote the category by the state vector $\mathbf{g}$ and the different examples by $\mathbf{f}_1, \mathbf{f}_2, \ldots, \mathbf{f}_k$. Form the association of each $\mathbf{f}_i$ and $\mathbf{g}$. Each incremental synaptic connectivity matrix, $\Delta \mathbf{A}$, assuming the simplest generalized Hebbian synaptic modification scheme discussed in Chapter 1 and by Kohonen et al. is given by

$$\Delta \mathbf{A}_i = \mathbf{g}\mathbf{f}_i^T \tag{8-1}$$

The overall synaptic connectivity matrix $\mathbf{A}$ is given by

$$\mathbf{A} = \mathbf{g} \sum_i \mathbf{f}_i^T \tag{8-2}$$

where $\mathbf{f}^T$ is the transpose of $\mathbf{f}$. Note that the expression contains the sum of the $\mathbf{f}_i$. As we have discussed elsewhere (Anderson, 1977) this term acts like an average response computer, a commonly used signal-processing technique of great simplicity and power. If the inputs, $\mathbf{f}_i$, are correlated, as they must be in many cases of interest the central tendency of the $\mathbf{f}_i$ will be extracted. The associated response will then be most vigorous to the central tendency. There is also an automatic measure of belongingness in this model (nearness in a geometrical sense) that is consistent with models of categorization such as those of Rosch (Rosch & Lloyd, 1978), where most natural categories are held to contain "prototypes," or best examples, and a distance metric, giving distance from the prototype of a particular example. Here we constructed the prototype, and the distance metric is generated during operation of the system. Some experiments (Knapp, 1979; Posner & Keele, 1968, 1970) are consistent with the simplest form of this model.

Categorization

Many simple categories do seem to have a structure of this kind. However many useful cognitive categories need to have much sharper "edges" and flatter "centers," particularly in language where words often seem to be either something, or not something, with a very small transition region.

The models we have discussed here have been more or less linear. Vector multiplication and addition are linear; the synaptic modification assumed is nonlinear. This assumption is unrealistic because we know there are important and essential nonlinearities at all levels of the nervous system. Linear systems obey, indeed it is their defining property, the principle of superposition. This means if associations are formed between two different inputs and outputs, and an input is provided that is the sum of the original two inputs, the output will be the sum of the two associated outputs. We used this property as the basis for the averaging abstractor. However if we wish, as we surely must, to make finer categorizations, making discriminations between inputs that are close together, this system will not work well.

We need a stronger categorizer. More, to work usefully with some categories we would like to proceed, once the sensory input has been processed, at a level of abstraction where all examples are represented by the same state vector. This does not necessarily mean that the properties that are peculiar to one instance are lost. What we desire is a separation of those particular properties from the representation of the type. We have observed that the concept "table" permutes in a way that is to a first approximation independent of the details of the particular tables involved. We may not have lost track of the particular details of the table under discussion. But it is the ability to operate at this higher level that allows the serious proposal of psychological and computational models, such as semantic networks.

We need a way of taking a particular example of a category and representing it by some standardized state vector, which is the same for all members of the category. This does not mean that the entire state vector must be the same for every example. Details need not be lost, merely some portion; perhaps a specific part of the system contains a categorizer as we propose. For our simple model system, however, we lose detail to obtain greater generality. This is exactly the kind of desirable result that follows from the theory of perception, generally accepted, called *feature analysis,* where features, a small set of perceptually salient entities, are detected, and the input is then represented in terms of this simplified set. This technique allows for fast, efficient processing because it discards irrelevant information at an early stage. We try to capture this aspect of categorization here.

8.4. FEEDBACK MODELS: WHAT IS A MACROFEATURE?

Simple nervous system models for feature analysis and categorization usually assume a high degree of single-unit specificity with features essentially corresponding to selective single units. It has been argued elsewhere that this assumption is both incorrect, based on the physiological data, and unnecessary because there may be more interesting ways to accomplish the same thing. Our suggestion (Anderson, Silverstein, Ritz, & Jones, 1977) was to make use of the properties of a set of neurons which projects to itself. The neuroanatomical inspiration for this model was the recurrent collateral system of cortical pyramids. This collateral system is not a simple lateral inhibitory system, but on the contrary seems to be at least partially excitatory. (See Chapter 1.) Figure 8.2 presents a schematic version of the anatomy assumed.

Let us make the unsupported assumption that this system shows the same kind of simple Hebbian synaptic modifiability that was used there. Because the set of neurons projects to itself, we have a powerful feedback system. A pattern of activity will learn itself. The synaptic change for each component $a(i, j)$ of the feedback matrix $\mathbf{A}$, where η is a learning parameter, is given by

$$a(i,j) = a(j,i) = \eta \, f(i)f(j). \tag{8-3}$$

$\mathbf{A}$ is a symmetric matrix with real and orthogonal eigenvectors. Symmetry need only hold statistically; the model is formally quite insensitive to this result. The matrix, $\mathbf{A}$, is related to the sample covariance matrix of principle component analysis. The eigenvectors with the largest positive eigenvalues contain the largest amount of variance. If a set of items is learned, these eigenvectors are the most useful for making discriminations between members of the set; this is what makes principal component analysis useful for representing data. Because our feedback system contains the potential for excitation, we must consider its properties with respect to the eigenvectors. (Eigenvectors are vectors that have the property that when they are multiplied by the matrix $\mathbf{A}$, the resulting vector is unchanged in direction. That is, if $\mathbf{f}$ is an eigenvector of the matrix $\mathbf{A}$, then,

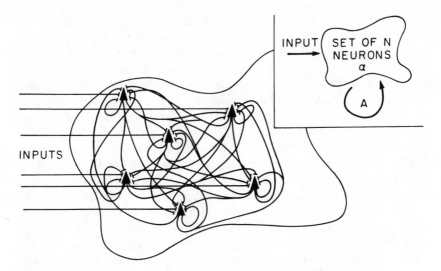

FIG. 8.2.   A group of neurons feeds back on itself through modifiable connections of the type described in the text. This is a six-dimensional system. Note that each cell feeds back to itself as well as to its neighbors. (Anderson, Silverstein, Ritz, & Jones, 1977.)

$$\mathbf{Af} = \lambda \mathbf{f} \qquad\qquad (8\text{-}4)$$

where λ is a constant.)

When an activity pattern appears at the input to the set of neurons, it will be fed back. By a process somewhat like resonance, with time the eigenvectors with the largest positive eigenvalues will be increasingly strongly represented in the activity pattern on the set of neurons. (Remember, eigenvectors are not changed in direction, merely in amplitude, by passage through the feedback system.) These particular eigenvectors are also the most useful for making the discrimination. If we were to call the eigenvectors with large positive eigenvalues *features,* then we would have a system that has some similarities to what feature analysis is supposed to do but where features are now represented by large patterns of activity rather than by selective neurons.

Let us construct two ugly new words from one good, but ambiguous, old one. Let us call "macrofeatures" the activity pattern we have just discussed. They are eigenvectors of the connectivity matrix. Let us call "microfeatures" the kinds of selectivity actually shown by single neurons. For example, oriented line segments with details that vary from cell to cell are the microfeatures displayed by Area 17 neurons. Microfeatures are related to, and may be components of, macrofeatures, but the connection need not be simple. We claim that macrofeatures are what perception and feature analysis actually use and are the psychologically salient entities. In the discussion following, it should always be clear from context or from usage which kind of feature we are talking about.

Our example also demonstrates the powers of a parallel system for perceptual analysis. If this kind of relative weighting is desired, the parallel system realizes it in a way that is fast, straightforward, and reliable. However, at no point are the macrofeatures themselves available, only their weighted sum. The macrofeatures themselves may be very difficult to characterize even though they are formally completely defined.

This example lets us make another comment about the nature of matrix models. As was mentioned in Chapter 1, we see quite clearly the distinction between an explicit, active part of the system, the state vector, and an implicit part, the connectivity matrix. The bulk of the information-processing power of the system is in the implicit structure and may be extraordinarily difficult to observe. Because of the strong interaction between different events in the implicit structure, rules of behavior may be complex, even paradoxical, yet have lawful genesis, internal consistency, and even statistical optimality. Characterizing the rules of behavior may be far more difficult than might be hoped, and for quite fundamental reasons.

Feedback and Dynamics

We have suggested a scheme for learning, which primarily concerns the implicit part of the system. Now we consider the dynamics of the state vectors, the behavior of the explicit part after the system has learned. Suppose the response to the input pattern and the output of the feedback system have comparable time courses. Here we choose a particularly simple dynamics; a version of this model using trace decay in continuous time has been presented elsewhere. (Anderson, 1977) Let $\mathbf{x}(t)$ denote the state vector at time t. Integer values are taken by t because we use a computer; conversion to continuous time presents no difficulties. We assume decay is small, so the activity of the system at time t is assumed to be the sum of activity at time t and the activity of the feedback matrix at time t; that is, we have the simple expression

$$\mathbf{x}(t + 1) = \mathbf{x}(t) + \mathbf{A} \ \mathbf{x}(t) = (\mathbf{I} + \mathbf{A}) \ \mathbf{x}(t) \tag{8-5}$$

where $\mathbf{I}$ is the identity matrix. This is a positive feedback system.

This presents us with a serious problem because all positive values of eigenvalue lead to activity growing without bound. We must now break with simple linearity.

One way to contain activity is to observe that real neurons have limits on their activity: They cannot fire faster than some limiting frequency, or slower than zero. Suppose we incorporate this in our model. A state vector is a point in high dimensionality space. Putting limits on firing rate corresponds to containing allowable state vectors in a hypercube, leading to the nickname of this model, "brain-state-in-a-box." Our primary interest in this hypercube becomes the 2^n corners. Qualitative dynamics in the system are straightforward. Suppose we start off with an activity pattern receiving positive feedback. The vector lengthens until it reaches a wall, that is, a firing limit for one component. The vector will keep trying to grow but cannot escape the box. It heads for a corner where it will remain if the corner is stable; not all corners are stable. If we allow any of a number of kinds of decay or fatigue, there are stable points outside of corners, but many components of the state vector still saturate. We are not now concerned with the obvious problem of how to "reset" the system, that is, how to get it out of a corner. Discussion of this point along with debate about more cosmic issues can be found in a recent exchange of letters (Anderson & Silverstein, 1978; Grossberg, 1978).

8.5.   A NUMERICAL EXPERIMENT

We have simulated several systems with the "brain-state-in-a-box" model, including a previously described application to spoken Dutch vowels (Anderson, 1977). Here the system learned input vectors whose components represented the amount of energy present in different frequency bands when a vowel was spoken. The system eventually learned to classify vowels so that each input vowel was represented by a single unique corner. The system showed some desirable traits, such as a considerable amount of resistance to input noise, ability to reconstruct damaged or missing parts of the input, and improvement in speed and accuracy with experience. This was a small system with only eight components, perhaps not representative of larger systems. The traditional stimulus set for pattern classifiers is letters, so we felt that when computational resources became available we would try to categorize letters using the model.

We coded uppercase letters into 117-element vectors. The coding was straightforward and was meant to be as like the way the visual system codes stimuli as possible. Part of the vector was a point-for-point excitatory mapping of the visual image with an accompanying inhibitory surround. The letters were placed on a 7 × 7 matrix and letters were drawn in what seemed like a reasonable way, allowing for the surround, which extended the 7 × 7 matrix to 9 × 9. The 81 matrix positions corresponded to the first 81 elements of the input state vector. The other 36 elements were coded by looking for oriented line segments. The 7 × 7 matrix was divided into nine overlapping 3 × 3 subregions. The presence and orientation of line segments in these nine regions was coded by the response of orientation-selective model units, responding to the presence of a line segment oriented at 0, 45, 90, and 135°. The 81 elements in the point-for-point coding, coupled with four possible line orientations in each of nine regions gave us 117-element vectors. Figure 8.3 shows several letters and their vector coding. The coding is straightforward, though tedious, and can be reproduced easily. No

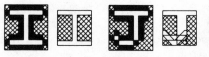

FOUR SAMPLE LETTER CODINGS

FIG. 8.3. Four sample letter codings for the simulations. These pictures are convenient representations of the 117-element vectors used to code the 26 letters. The left part of the coding for each letter contains 81 elements and corresponds to a modified point-for-point simple mapping. Letters were drawn on a 7 × 7 grid. Positive values are represented by white in the figure, negatives by black, and zero by cross-hatching.

    Each grid position containing part of the letter was given a positive value. An inhibitory surround was added by placing minus values in nondiagonal adjacent positions. To accommodate the surrounds, the grid was expanded to 9 × 9, the numerical values involved giving rise to the first 81 positions of the vector. The right-hand representations for each letter show the remaining 36 vector elements that were generated by a simple scheme for line detection. Nine 3 × 3 grids were overlapped on the 7 × 7 grid. Each grid was analyzed for line segments at four orientations: 0, 45, 90, and 135°, which were located on the small grid. The double-width vertical bar of the "J" occurred because of the overlap of the small grids: This line was detected by two small grids. For computation the 117-element vectors were processed further: The mean of the elements in each vector was set equal to 0 by subtracting the element mean from each element. The vector was normalized. For some simulations, the average letter vector, averaged across all 26 letters, was subtracted from each individual letter vector.

particular font was employed; a certain amount of experimenter license was involved. The sum of the elements in each vector was set equal to 0 by subtracting the average element and then the vectors were normalized. We felt that this large vector was at least a first approximation to the rich coding found in the human visual system.

    One further modification of the vectors as a group was made. We summed all the vectors and found the average vector. The average vector was then subtracted, and the resulting vectors were used. The average was not large relative to representative single elements, but it was not negligible either. We also did a simulation using the direct codings.

    In the learning phase of the simulation, letter vectors were presented at random. The feedback matrix was applied according to the formula given earlier,

$$\mathbf{x}(t + 1) = (\mathbf{I} + \mathbf{A})\mathbf{x}(t), \tag{8-6}$$

for seven iterations. The final state was then learned, according to the outer-product learning rule discussed in Chapter 1, that is, the incremental matrix $\Delta \mathbf{A}$ is formed as

$$\Delta \mathbf{A} = \eta \; \mathbf{x} \; \mathbf{x.}^{T} \tag{8-7}$$

We assumed that it was necessary to stop learning at some point. Some variant of this assumption seems essential to avoid domination of the system by the eigenvector with the largest eigenvalue. Our assumption, which we have used in the past, notes the final value of the model cell's firing rate after seven iterations. If it is at the saturation limit then there is no change in the synaptic strength of that cell. If the jth cell saturates then the jth row and column of the incremental matrix, $\Delta \mathbf{A}$, are set to zero. The modified incremental matrix is then added to the overall connectivity matrix, $\mathbf{A}$. We suspect that the exact form of this assumption does not make much difference, but this is a matter for further study.

There is absolutely no instruction in this procedure. The system does not know and does not care if classification is correct or incorrect, fast or slow, or anything else. It seems clear to us that even a slight amount of feedback as to correctness should improve operation.

Behavior of the system is insensitive to the learning parameter, η. Simulations were done using a learning parameter that varied over two orders of magnitude, from 0.0005 to 0.05, with no essential difference in behavior, though the smaller parameter required many more presentations for equivalent learning.

We now discuss a simulation using a learning parameter of 0.05 with the average 117-element vector subtracted, with the input vectors coded as described, and with limits of saturation at plus and minus 0.3. The $\mathbf{A}$ matrix was started from 0.001 $\mathbf{I}$.

The pattern of results we have seen before appeared here also. Initially many letters were confused. The system categorized incorrectly different letters together into particular corners, forming clumps of letters. Then, with more trials, the clumps separated until at 5000 trials, only W and N were categorized together in the same corner. W and N remained together until the simulation was stopped following 10,000 presentations. In our codings, W and N were quite similar. Table 8.1 shows this process. One of the strongest and most obvious predictions of this approach to categorization, as well as one of the most useful, is that the speed of categorization should increase with learning, speed being defined as the number of iterations required for all components of the state vector to saturate. This property was unmistakable in the data; as one example, the average number of iterations required for a letter input to reach its final corner was 12.7 at 1000 trials, when a great deal of learning had already taken place, decreasing to 9.8 at 10,000 trials. Both speed and accuracy of categorization increased in this range.

Many of the most interesting properties of this system are involved with the eigenvectors and eigenvalues of the connectivity matrix for theoretical reasons we have sketched before. We calculated the eigenvectors and eigenvalues every 1000 trials. The eigenvectors form an orthogonal basis set. Because of their expected similarity to the factors of factor analysis (not identical because of the

TABLE 8.1
Equivalence Classes Where More Than One-Letter
Coding Is Categorized In The Same Final State
("clumps"), as a Function of Learning Trials.

No. of Trials	Different Letters Categorized Identically
1000	B, E, G, O
	A, I
	C, K, N, W, X
	D, M, Q, S, T, V, Y
	F, P, R
2000	B, E
	G, O, S, V
	N, W
	K, X
	Q, Y
3000	F, P
	G, S
	N, W
4000	F, P
	G, S
	N, W
5000	N, W
6000	N, W
7000	N, W
8000	N, W
9000	N, W
10,000	N, W

nonlinearity of the system), we would hope to be able to represent letters by weighted sums of only the first few eigenvectors with the largest eigenvalues and neglect the rest. This kind of representation is a commonly used analytical technique. It allows only a few terms of a sum to represent the significant aspects of its behavior while many other terms, adding little to informational content, can be discarded. It is the basis of many practical applications of techniques such as Fourier analysis and factor analysis.

It is easy to calculate the appropriate weighting coefficients. If $(\mathbf{e}_1, \mathbf{e}_2, \ldots, \mathbf{e}_N)$ are the normalized orthogonal eigenvectors of $\mathbf{A}$, then a vector, say $\mathbf{v}$, can be described as the sum,

$$\mathbf{v} = c_1 \, \mathbf{e}_1 + c_2 \, \mathbf{e}_2 + \ldots, + c_N \, \mathbf{e}_N. \tag{8-8}$$

If we wish to know c_i then we need only take the inner product or dot product $(\mathbf{v}, \mathbf{e}_i)$ because

$$(\mathbf{v}, \mathbf{e}_i) = c_i (\mathbf{e}_i, \mathbf{e}_i)$$

$$= c_i. \tag{8-9}$$

When we checked this with the eigenvectors after 10,000 learning trials, we found by representing letters as appropriately weighted sums of the eigenvectors with the first 10 largest eigenvalues that every letter was classified in its own corner. However the speed of categorization of the complete letter was faster and the final corner for the reduced representation was not always identical to that found for the complete letter vector. When letters were represented as appropriately weighted sums of the first 10 eigenvectors, the letters, with 2 exceptions, I and Z, ended in final corners very close to the corner associated with the complete letter. The 2 letters, I and Z, had final states that differed very significantly. About half the values of final state for the representations of these 2 letters were different from those for the complete letter. The other 24 letters differed in an average of 5 elements for the final states between the complete letter and the sum. As we would expect, if we increased the number of eigenvectors that formed the sum, the final state approached that for the complete letter. When the first 25 eigenvectors were used, the final state of the sum differed from the complete letters by an average of slightly over one element and about half the letters did not differ at all. Clearly we can reduce the effective dimensionality of inputs to the system by representing the 117-element vectors as a smaller weighted set of the macrofeatures we have calculated. The coefficients correspond to a smaller dimensionality system.

The eigenvalue spectrum is of great importance in many physical systems. The theoretical analysis indicated that size of eigenvalue is proportional to the "importance" of that eigenvector in representing the input in relation to the set of items learned by the system, a result confirmed by the success of the aforementioned system using a macrofeature representation. There is a serious problem that can arise here. As we have discussed elsewhere, only some corners are stable. If one eigenvalue is very much larger than the others, then this eigenvector will dominate the behavior such that only a pair of corners (in its direction and opposite to it) are stable; that is, all inputs are classified into one or the other corner as a final state. This effect is very pronounced in computer simulations if a learning limitation assumption is not made.

The 10 largest eigenvalues, calculated each 1000 trials, are given in Table 8.2. It can be easily seen from the ratio between the first and the tenth largest eigenvalue that the eigenvalue spectrum is contracting at the upper end of the spectrum. This is to be expected. The learning limitation assures that once a direction is so strongly fed back so as to reach its limits quickly, then eigenvectors with strong components in that direction will grow slowly or not at all whereas directions that do not limit will continue to strengthen.

This behavior has an interesting interpretation. When a stimulus set is first presented, the system rapidly picks up the most salient commonalities of the

TABLE 8.2
Values of 10 Largest Eigenvalues of Matrix After Each 1000 Presentations
During Learning
Average of Letters Subtracted From Letter Vectors
(Learning Parameter 0.05)

1000	2000	3000	4000	5000	6000	7000	8000	9000	10,000
0.317	0.529	0.600	0.656	0.723	0.812	0.832	0.837	0.843	0.894
0.337	0.537	0.643	0.714	0.756	0.822	0.841	0.877	0.893	0.930
0.417	0.563	0.678	0.733	0.794	0.838	0.869	0.881	0.913	0.951
0.458	0.625	0.723	0.766	0.809	0.862	0.896	0.905	0.935	0.967
0.512	0.671	0.752	0.774	0.857	0.931	0.957	0.964	0.980	1.022
0.582	0.700	0.766	0.866	1.022	1.064	1.090	1.091	1.093	1.099
0.647	0.732	0.834	0.948	1.086	1.156	1.177	1.180	1.183	1.197
0.754	0.915	0.992	1.043	1.131	1.177	1.196	1.200	1.205	1.251
0.898	1.016	1.128	1.214	1.422	1.518	1.530	1.537	1.539	1.547
1.113	1.287	1.353	1.371	1.441	1.534	1.547	1.556	1.558	1.570

Ratio Between Largest and Tenth-Largest Eigenvalue

3.51	2.43	2.25	2.09	1.99	1.89	1.86	1.86	1.85	1.76

items, the average, for example. If the stimulus set is actually composed of dissimilar items, then many items are first clumped together, and only the grossest differences are reflected in categorization. But as learning progresses, eigenvectors with smaller eigenvalues grow, relatively, allowing the ultimate separation of items initially together.

As mentioned earlier, we subtracted the average letter from the codings before they were learned. We thought that it would be interesting to try to see if this system could learn to separate unaveraged letters. We should expect initial learning to be tremendously dominated by the average, which proved to be the case. For this simulation we used the learning parameter of 0.001. Table 8.3 lists the two largest eigenvalues and their ratio up to 20,000 learning trials, as far as we let this system go. (Note that the learning parameter is only 1/50 as large as that we used for our other simulation, thus learning occurs much less rapidly.) The domination of the system by the largest eigenvalue is clear. However the spectrum was starting to contract, indicating that the process was at work. At 2000 trials there were only four clumps, but after 20,000 trials there were nine clumps.

Learning speeds up when the DC letter component is subtracted, but the system will still work, albeit more slowly and temperamentally, if this is not done. Interestingly, if the letters without the average subtracted are used as a test set, the matrix formed from letters with the average subtracted categorizes them almost perfectly.

We make one more general comment about the eigenvectors of this system. Many "feature" lists for capital letters have appeared in the psychological litera-

TABLE 8.3
Two Largest Eigenvalues
Given every 5000 Presentations
for Unaveraged Letters
(Learning parameter 0.001)

1000	5000	10,000	15,000	20,000
0.263	0.573	0.603	0.680	0.789
0.822	1.860	1.959	2.058	2.115
Ratio of the Largest to the Next Largest Eigenvalue				
3.13	3.25	3.25	3.03	2.68

ture. It always seemed to us that these feature sets were highly unlikely to be those that a nervous system might actually use. It also seemed most unlikely that the macrofeatures based on our model would have an easy interpretation, a prediction that seems to be the case. The five eigenvectors with largest eigenvalue are presented in Fig. 8.4; we can discern no particular resemblance to anything like the line-and-curve segments that are typical of intuitively derived "feature" sets. We have also presented a representation of the eigenvector with the 12th largest eigenvalue, to show that occasionally one finds macrofeatures that seem to "make sense." Letters that contained a large positive coefficient for this macrofeature were *A, F, H, K, P,* and *R.* Large negative coefficients were seen in *G, I. L, U, Y,* and *Z.* Positive response seemed to consist of something like detection of a horizontal bar in the middle coupled with relative lack of letter in the lower right-hand corner.

It should be pointed out that the coefficients derived as we have described have continuous values and can potentially be present in any amount, as is seen in Table 8.4. They are not binary features and the actual coefficients calculated showed a wide range of values. Also, programs used to calculate eigenvectors are not determined as to sign. Thus the eigenvectors shown in Fig. 8.4 could have equally well been of opposite sign. As far as we can tell, a change in sign of these eigenvectors does not improve meaningfulness. For the record, we present in Table 8.4 the coefficients of the first 10 eigenvectors for all 26 letters. According to the model we are discussing, this corresponds to a "feature decomposition" in terms of the 10 most significant macrofeatures.

Single-Element Behavior

Let us consider the behavior of single elements in this system. Because this model has neural inspiration, if not a neural basis, it might be interesting to look at it in light of our previous discussion of specificity and distribution. Initially the network is completely interconnected, every element connected to every ele-

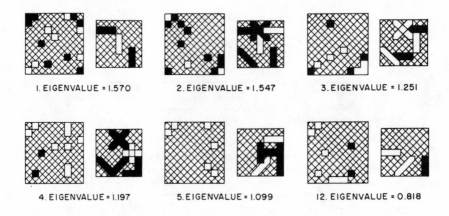

1. EIGENVALUE = 1.570   2. EIGENVALUE = 1.547   3. EIGENVALUE = 1.251

4. EIGENVALUE = 1.197   5. EIGENVALUE = 1.099   12. EIGENVALUE = 0.818

SIX "FEATURE" VECTORS

FIG. 8.4. Representations of the five eigenvectors with largest positive eigen-value plus one additional eigenvector. For display purposes, only significant positive and negative values (> 0.1) are represented as white (positive) and black (negative).

In reality, these vectors are continuous valued. The same coding scheme demonstrated in Fig. 8.3 is used to draw these representations. These vectors correspond to macrofeatures in our model. Note the general lack of immediately obvious interpretation. For example, the eigenvector with the twelfth largest eigenvalue could be interpreted as a "detector of horizontal bars in the middle, coupled with relative lack of letter in the lower right corner," which was about as meaningful as these eigenvectors got. This particular eigenvector was strongly represented in F, P, and R but not in E or G.

ment. The stimulus set, by design, had positive or negative responses from almost every element (75–95%) when a letter was presented. Specificity must develop by learning because it clearly is not built in. Also the final state of the system is fully active with every element full on or full off.

There is almost no selectivity at the input or the output. But as far as we know, no one has seriously proposed a single-letter–single-neuron model of letter perception. What are the responses of our elements, simplified neurons, to features when there is no feedback, or when the features are first presented? There are 117 model neurons. Although the eigenvectors calculated are normalized, a histogram of their values would give us some idea of the relative distribution of immediate element responses to particular features. Table 8.5 gives the histogram of absolute values of the first 10 eigenvectors in bins 0.1 units wide. These data might provide evidence for specificity if turned up by a neurophysiologist. For all the eigenvectors about 100 (85%) of the elements have essentially no

TABLE 8.4
Coefficients of the 10 Eigenvectors with Largest Eigenvalues
in the Expansion of the 26 Letters Computed after 10,000
Learning Presentations
(Learning Parameter 0.05)
Average Letter Vector Subtracted from the Individual Letter Vectors
Before Computation
In the Context of the Model, This Table Gives the
"Macrofeature Decomposition" of the Letters in Terms of
the 10 Most Significant Macrofeatures

	Eigenvalue [1]									
	1.570	*1.547*	*1.251*	*1.197*	*1.099*	*1.022*	*0.967*	*0.951*	*0.930*	*0.894*
A	−0.123	0.025	−0.042	−0.143	−0.126	0.006	0.002	0.171	0.115	0.111
B	−0.129	0.117	−0.190	−0.063	0.055	−0.184	−0.113	0.121	−0.026	−0.053
C	−0.059	0.087	−0.063	0.135	0.034	−0.103	−0.038	0.014	−0.099	0.043
D	−0.122	0.024	0.007	0.083	−0.064	−0.046	0.105	−0.122	0.149	0.098
E	−0.056	0.076	−0.134	0.021	0.032	−0.121	−0.089	0.086	−0.110	0.038
F	−0.036	−0.018	−0.074	−0.072	−0.025	−0.015	−0.067	0.088	−0.057	0.045
G	−0.137	0.079	−0.141	0.044	−0.030	−0.113	−0.035	0.031	−0.073	0.083
H	−0.007	0.012	−0.008	−0.180	−0.092	0.011	0.004	0.118	0.146	0.132
I	0.067	0.094	−0.076	0.134	−0.081	−0.193	0.005	−0.057	−0.174	−0.059
J	0.031	−0.048	0.111	0.058	−0.119	0.115	0.115	−0.010	−0.242	0.039
K	0.017	−0.113	0.109	−0.066	0.076	0.276	−0.137	0.004	0.145	−0.208
L	0.110	0.181	−0.020	0.092	0.085	−0.164	−0.060	−0.055	−0.033	−0.052
M	0.126	−0.026	0.104	−0.096	0.006	0.087	0.001	−0.001	0.194	0.101
N	0.051	−0.051	0.157	−0.045	0.034	0.195	0.132	−0.066	0.136	−0.031
O	−0.103	0.056	−0.040	0.079	−0.014	−0.057	0.028	0.062	−0.069	0.183
P	−0.064	0.018	−0.114	−0.079	−0.019	−0.077	−0.082	0.086	−0.004	0.000
Q	−0.085	0.015	−0.006	0.193	0.031	0.081	0.129	−0.075	0.043	0.007
R	−0.062	0.010	−0.027	−0.026	0.050	0.065	0.040	0.045	0.000	−0.128
S	−0.167	0.030	−0.133	−0.044	−0.015	−0.105	−0.109	0.078	−0.073	0.027
T	0.093	−0.066	−0.078	0.090	−0.124	−0.079	0.069	−0.089	−0.174	−0.057
U	−0.007	0.016	0.075	0.004	0.001	−0.065	0.026	0.002	0.013	0.138
V	0.176	−0.151	0.225	−0.160	0.046	0.110	−0.049	−0.115	0.044	−0.017
W	0.048	−0.084	0.103	−0.036	0.035	0.202	0.112	−0.037	0.165	−0.028
X	0.160	−0.149	0.195	0.013	0.121	0.280	−0.013	−0.142	0.108	−0.277
Y	0.225	−0.160	0.152	−0.041	0.026	−0.062	0.084	−0.137	0.021	−0.135
Z	0.053	0.028	−0.089	0.109	0.078	−0.045	−0.062	−0.001	−0.143	0.001

[1]Note that the eigenvectors are computed in a way that does not necessarily allow for the most meaningful interpretation of sign. Comparisons of sign are not significant between eigenvectors.

TABLE 8.5
Histogram of Absolute Values of Elements of the 10 Eigenvectors with the Largest Eigenvalues
Eigenvectors Were Normalized
Results After 10,000 Learning Trials
(Learning Parameter 0.05)
Average Letter Vector Subtracted from the Presented Letter Vectors

		Absolute Value						
Rank	Eigenvalue	0.0–0.1	0.1–0.2	0.2–0.3	0.3–0.4	0.4–0.5	0.5–0.6	0.6–0.7
10	0.894	105	8	2	0	1	0	1
9	0.930	104	6	4	0	3		
8	0.951	100	13	1	1	1	0	1
7	0.967	104	9	1	2	0	0	1
6	1.022	101	9	4	2	0	1	
5	1.099	103	8	3	1	2		
4	1.197	98	12	2	5			
3	1.251	101	9	5	1	1		
2	1.547	96	12	7	2			
1	1.570	97	12	7	1			

TABLE 8.6
Plot of Absolute Values of Response of Single-Model Neurons to the Presentation of the 10 Eigenvectors with Largest Eigenvalues
Cells Whose Response to All 10 Eigenvectors is Less Than 0.1 Are Not Given to Save Space

Neuron Number[a]	Absolute Value						
	0.0–0.1	0.1–0.2	0.2–0.3	0.3–0.4	0.4–0.5	0.5–0.6	0.6–0.7
1	8	2					
2	4	3	2	1			
9	7	1	2				
10	4	3	2	1			
17	8	2					
20	8	2					
23	5	3	1	1			
30	7	2	1				
34	7	2	1				
35	8	2					
40	7	3					
51	4	2	0	2	2		
52	9	1					
55	6	4					
56	7	2	0	1			

TABLE 8.6
(*Continued*)

Neuron Number[a]	Absolute Value						
	0.0–0.1	*0.1–0.2*	*0.2–0.3*	*0.3–0.4*	*0.4–0.5*	*0.5–0.6*	*0.6–0.7*
58	9	1					
61	2	3	2	2	0	0	1
62	6	1	1	1	1		
63	7	1	1	1			
64	9	1					
67	8	2					
71	9	1					
72	4	5	1				
74	9	1					
75	6	4					
79	7	1	1	1			
80	4	5	1				
81	7	1	2				
			Points				
			Lines				
82	8	2					
83	6	3	0	0	1		
87	9	1					
88	5	1	3	0	1		
89	8	1	1				
90	7	2	1				
94	1	7	1	0	1		
96	4	0	3	2	1		
104	3	4	1	0	0	1	1
107	4	1	3	1	0	0	1
108	3	4	2	1			
111	5	4	1				
112	1	7	1	0	1		
114	9	1					

[a] Model neurons numbered between 1 and 81 had center-surround organization with spatially localized receptive fields and detected presence or absence of part of a letter at a particular point (excitation) or immediately adjacent (inhibition) point in the letter array. Model neurons numbered between 82 and 117 detected oriented line segments in 3 × 3 areas on the letter array.

initial response to a given eigenvector. Some eigenvectors are represented by the vigorous response of only a few elements whereas others have a larger number of more uniformly responding cells. The overall picture is of a moderate amount of specificity in terms of the responses of single model cells to particular eigenvectors. Elements of the system are obviously far more selective in responses to eigenvectors than to letters.

The other question to ask about selectivity involves individual model neurons. Do elements respond strongly to one and only one eigenvector or to several?

Results of this part of the simulation are shown in Table 8.6. With respect to selectivity examples of either extreme or moderate selectivity can be found. Cells 83 and 88 both respond to one feature vector, yet cell 88 also responds to three other eigenvectors at the 0.2–0.3 level. Cell 94 responds strongly to one vector and moderately to eight. Cell 104 responds at a very high level to only two vectors. It is difficult to make firm statements about the degree of selectivity, but it does seem clear that there is always moderate selectivity and occasionally extreme selectivity.

We have let ourselves view this data as a neurophysiologist might. It is natural, and quite reasonable, to be very concerned with large responses of model elements or of real neurons. We should be aware, however, that the combined effects of the many weakly responding cells may in fact be more powerful than the few strongly responding cells. The integrated effect of many weak responses is exceptionally difficult to detect in real brains but is almost certainly of great importance. Also we are assuming for this model a greater symmetry between excitation and inhibition than is found in the real nervous system: We have assumed that the positive limit equals the negative limit, but in reality the potential positive excursion is much greater in almost all cases. Even in our initial letter coding, however, the inhibition was less localized than excitation.

It may seem strange to talk about selectivity in a system which has an output that is fully saturated and with all cells equally active. However if the initial response of the cell could be studied or if the feedback system could be turned off, the cells would show this pattern of selectivity. This makes a prediction for single units found in the real brain.

We would expect to find that if the feedback system was disabled cells would tend to be *more* selective in their responses. Also, the later components of the response should be far more labile, context sensitive, and dependent on the distributed feedback system than the early responses. Speculation is notoriously tricky in this area, but we should expect that feedback, which if we are correct is implicated in fairly high-level cognitive function, should be disabled when a cortex is in deep sleep or under certain kinds of anesthesia (particularly barbiturates). There have been relatively few studies of details of receptive field properties under these conditions. Some kinds of anesthesia, in particular, chloralose, give a pattern of results that can be interpreted as having the opposite effect, actually potentiating converging pathways. (Albe-Fessard & Besson, 1973; Phillips & Porter, 1977)

There seems to be a nearly universal finding that the cortex is more responsive, more labile, and more adaptable in the awake animal than in animals under (barbiturate) anesthesia. There also seems to be general agreement that cortical cells are more responsive when the animal is awake than in deep sleep. A recent abstract by Livingstone and Hubel (1980) found that for Area 17, out of a sample of 76 cells "24 gave stronger evoked responses during waking whereas only 2 gave weaker responses." This has also been found for the inferotemporal cortex where cells are much more responsive during fast than slow EEG (Gross, Rocha-Miranda, & Bender, 1972). An early but direct experiment by Bear, Sasaki, and Ervin (1971) studied Area 17 cells under short-acting barbiturate anesthesia and in the awake state and found that awake animals tended to have much more labile responses, and the early components of the response tended to be much more stable than the more variable later response. The general picture of stable early components and variable later responses that can be abolished with barbiturates seems quite common in other areas of the cortex as well. (See Werner & Whitsel, 1973). A very large part of the evoked response literature in humans is devoted to the highly variable later responses of the evoked response recorded with gross electrodes, which are often of considerable cognitive interest. (See the interesting historical review by Donchin, 1979, for example.)

Although none of this counts as very firm evidence, and equally valid alternative explanations are possible, it is at least qualitatively consistent with the kind of diffuse model, making use of lateral, converging connections, that we presented here. In fact, because the models we have discussed make such strong predictions about the time course of information processing and the neural events underlying them, this may be the most immediately productive way to extend the models. The most significant feature the model currently lacks is a way to reset the system after it reaches a stable point. Incorporating habituation and inhibitory pathways of the appropriate kind might generate a model that would be able to make contact simultaneously with details of some significant neuroscience, and a large body of psychological literature on the time course of information processing.

The pattern of cell selectivities that appears in the simulation is intriguing but cannot be directly compared to the real nervous system, though it is not grossly at variance with what seems to be found. Another direction to extend the model would be to incorporate limited connectivity with spatial structure to the connections of model neurons. It is a little surprising that any selectivity at all arises from a model that initially is completely nonselective. We may be seeing in both the real nervous system and in the model the operation of some vaguely discerned statistical principles involved with the coding and recogition of patterns suitable for use in a noisy world.

ACKNOWLEDGMENTS

We would like to acknowledge the support of the Ittleson Family Foundation, the National Science Foundation (Grant BNS-79-23000), and the use of the facilities of the Brown University Computing Center.

Figure 8.2 was reprinted by permission of the American Psychological Association.

REFERENCES

Albe-Fessard, D., & Besson, J. M. Convergent thalamic and cortical projections—the non-specific system. In A. Iggo (Ed.), *Handbook of Sensory Physiology (Vol. 2). Somatosensory System.* Berlin: Springer, 1973.

Anderson, J. A. Neural models with cognitive implications. In D. LaBerge and S. J. Samuels (Eds.), *Basic processes in reading: Perception and comprehension.* Hillsdale, N.J.: Lawrence Erlbaum Associates, 1977.

Anderson, J. A., & Silverstein, J. W. Reply to Grossberg. *Psychological Review,* 1978, *85,* 597–603.

Anderson, J. A., Silverstein, J. W., Ritz, S. A., & Jones, R. S. Distinctive features, categorical perception, and probability learning: Some applications of a neural model. *Psychological Review,* 1977, *84,* 413–451.

Barlow, H. B. Single units and sensation: A neuron doctrine for perceptual psychology. *Perception,* 1972, *1,* 371–394.

Bear, D.M., Sasaki, H., & Ervin, F. R. Sequential change in receptive fields of striate neurons in dark-adapted cats. *Experimental Brain Research,* 1971, *13,* 256–272.

Donchin, E. Event-related brain potentials: A tool in the study of human information processing. In H. Begleiter (Ed.), *Evoked Brain Potentials and Behavior,* New York: Plenum Press, 1979.

Gross, C. G., Rocha-Miranda, C. E., & Bender, D. B. Visual properties of neurons in inferotemporal cortex of the *macaque. Journal of Neurophysiology,* 1972, *35,* 96–111.

Grossberg, S. Do all neural models really look alike? A comment on Anderson, Silverstein, Ritz, and Jones. *Psychological Review,* 1978, *85,* 592–596.

Knapp, A. G. *Determinants of typicality structures.* Unpublished honors thesis, Center for Neural Sciences, Brown University, Providence, R.I., 1979.

Livingstone, M. S., & Hubel, D. H. Evoked responses and spontaneous activity of cells in the visual cortex during waking and slow wave sleep. *Meeting Proceedings, ARVO,* Orlando, Fla., 1980, 223. (Abstract)

Phillips, C. G., & Porter, R. *Corticospinal Neurones.* London: Academic Press, 1977.

Posner, M. I. & Keele, S. W. On the genesis of abstract ideas. *Journal of Experimental Psychology,* 1968, *77,* 353–363.

Posner, M. I. & Keele, S. W. Retention of abstract ideas. *Journal of Experimental Psychology,* 1970, *83,* 304–308.

Rosch, E. & Lloyd, B. B. *Cognition and categorization.* Hillsdale, N.J.: Lawrence Erlbaum Associates, 1978.

Werner, G. & Whitsel, B. L. Functional organization of the somatosensory cortex. In A. Iggo (Ed.), *Handbook of Sensory Physiology (Vol. 2) Somatosensory System.* Berlin: Springer, 1973.

9 Notes on a Self-Organizing Machine

Stuart Geman
Brown University

9.1. INTRODUCTION

This chapter sets forth a design for a system whose purpose is to discover temporal and spatial regularities in a high-dimensional environment. Whereas the goal of this research is the realization of an "intelligent system," the model is based on principles of organization and self-modification widely believed to be in force in the nervous system. The design is of a parallel-processing machine composed of nonlinear and highly interconnected devices. As it is presented here, the model is a general one in the sense that it is not dedicated to any particular environment or task. A specific implementation of the model requires the specification of two sets of parameters: the "input primitives" and the "direction primitives." The input primitives represent the information about the environment that is available to the system. The direction primitives define what is "good" and what is "bad" relative to the system.

It may help to orient the reader if I briefly describe a particular implementation of the model that is now being developed. In this implementation the environment is the world of numbers, leading to input primitives such as odd, even, prime, sum, exponentiate, etc. Direction primitives specify that a non sequitur, such as attempting to perform a binary operation with only one available argument, is bad, that a conjecture that is well supported (as by trial and error) is good, and so on. The system interacts with a computer, requesting numbers and the results of operations, and attempts to discover regularities among these primitives.

Whereas it is my position that the principles of organization and modification used here are in force in the nervous system, I do not propose that this implementation mimics, in any specific sense, the techniques of a mathematician. This implementation is meant as an exercise toward developing a system that can discover regularities in complicated environements. The point of using numbers is that they provide an extremely convenient world in which to experiment, but the model is in no way dedicated to this world. In fact the presentation in this chapter will rarely refer to this implementation because it is not yet complete and there are few results to report.

Humans learn, and learn to discover, regularities in the complex and high-dimensional environments of the "real world." We cannot reasonably expect to invent another solution to this inference problem, at least not one that will approach the general application of human thought. Therefore it would seem to be expedient to look to the neural and cognitive sciences for clues about the proper architecture, and it is in this spirit that the model here has been developed. However, I am *not* proposing this model as a "neural network" model. It will be clear to the reader with even a rudimentary knowledge of neurophysiology and neuroanatomy that the basic units of information processing used here have little to do with real neurons. In fact I will completely ignore the problem of realizing these units in neurallike machinery, because I do not believe that the specification of such a realization would at this time be a useful exercise. Models have been formulated at the level of neural structure for the realization of a variety of "higher-level" functions presumed to be carried out by some part of the nervous system. Yet we can seriously question whether these models have improved our understanding of human intelligence. The real problem may lie in identifying which functions to realize. We can imagine numerous architectures of nonlinear neuronlike elements, communicating through modifiable connections, for the execution of virtually any well-specified procedure of information processing. But it would be difficult to choose between these architectures based on what little is known of the physiology of higher-level function in the nervous system. The right question now may be *what* to build rather than *how* to build it.

A problem that is fundamental to our understanding of the nervous system, and one that has implications for the design of Artificial Intelligence, is the proper interpretation of "local" activity in the brain. Many authors have argued that little significance can be attached to activity at any particular location; it is the pattern of activity across a neural system that embodies the system's interpretation of a stimulus. This point of view arises mainly as a corollary of the distributed memory hypothesis, which has its roots in the classical experiments of K.S. Lashley (1950). Others have taken the point of view that local activities have a very specific and often "high-level" interpretation. An often quoted paper by H. B. Barlow (1972) argues for the existence of "grandmother cells," whose activities signal the presence of specific stimuli, such as chairs, cars, or particular individuals. The semantic net approach to Artificial Intelligence can be interpreted in this way (see Fahlman, Chapter 5, this volume) if an individual node representing a specific concept, pattern, or operation is identified with an individual hardware unit.

The present model is based on the proposition that both interpretations are, at once, in force. It may be useful to anticipate now the discussion in this regard by outlining an argument for this point of view. It is well demonstrated that the efficacy of synaptic connections can be influenced by the activities of the neurons that communicate through these connections (see discussion in Chapter 1, this volume). It is just such changes that most investigators see as the neurophysiological analog of associative learning. Let us accept the point of view that synapses are, indeed, the site of the engram and that modification of synapses can be described by some function of the presynaptic and postsynaptic activities. Then, at any stage in development, what has been learned can depend only on pairwise relations among the activities of individual neurons. Suppose that these neuronal activities are at all levels as unselective, in terms of "events" and "objects," as the activities at the most peripheral levels. It is then difficult to see how a synaptic memory, based only on pairwise associations, could contain information about highly complex and specific relations among these events and objects, as the human memory most certainly does. It would seem that activities in some neurons need to signal selective events rather than a noninformative mixture that occurs as frequently as the primitives themselves.

It is widely believed that ontological development includes a process by which some cells of the visual cortex, initially not completely specific in their activities, come to signal selective events, or "features," in the environment. Many investigators have suggested that this process continues, in a hierarchical fashion, as one moves to deeper levels of processing in the brain. The system described in this chapter utilizes just such a process to create local activities that signal selective events. Of course, care must be taken as to which events are to be represented because we cannot possibly represent all such "high-order" relationships in an environment that has any appreciable number of dimensions. The precise mechanism used is described in some detail in the sections to come. The point that I wish to make here is that, as a result of this process, a familiar event achieves both distributed and local representation. The representation is distributed at the most peripheral levels, where the event is signaled by the activities in a particular set of primitives, whereas this representation is increasingly localized as we move deeper into the system. It will be seen that the model here continues to utilize all levels of this representation.

Whereas the presentation here is about the design of a system for the organization of information in complex environments, behind this design there is a model for the nature of the information to be processed. I begin in Section 9.2 with an attempt to identify some salient features of real-world environments, and this discussion guides the development of the system as it follows in later sections. Mechanisms for the associative learning and associative recall of spatial[1] relations are described in Section 9.3. It is these mechanisms that suggest the local/

---

[1] "Spatial" refers here to associations among events that occur simultaneously. It is not in specific reference to visual.

global representation scheme referred to earlier. I argue that an associative process will be effective provided that both forms of representation are available. Section 9.4 then outlines the means by which the system develops this representation. It may be seen that this is dependent on the particular experience of the network. The pieces, as they have been described up to this point, are then brought together in Section 9.5. The result is what I will call a *spatial coding module,* one of the three building blocks of the system. Temporal relations are organized and learned by a very similar structure called a *temporal coding module,* which is the topic of Section 9.6. The principles of architecture and function developed for the two types of coding modules are then applied to the problem of organizing and integrating the actions of the entire system. The result, a *control module,* is the main topic of the final section, Section 9.7. Scattered through the atricle are 11 propositions. These statements are intended as informal summaries of the main assumptions on which the design is based.

I do not attempt to describe the system in full detail. Certainly this would be premature. The current implementation already suggests changes in many of the particulars. Still we do expect, and have so far been able, to maintain the essential principles of organization as they are presented in this article.

Finally, let me anticipate two likely, and largely valid, criticisms—first, that the difficult problem of extracting appropriate primitives in real environments has been completely ignored. Perhaps an understanding of what to do with these primitives at "higher" levels will point to an understanding of what constitutes good peripheral machinery. It is possible that the peripheral hardware problem will prove to be more difficult than the problem of higher-level intelligent processing. A second objection is that the idealizations are absurd and that time and features do not have discrete representations in the nervous system. The model here has its generalizations to continuous time and continuous features. The philosophy is to work with a system that can be analyzed and simulated with relative ease and hope that it will suggest the correct generalizations.

9.2. ON THE NATURE OF ENVIRONMENT

This chapter proposes a mechanism for organizing the information of real-world environments, and this mechanism reflects a particular point of view concerning the nature of such information. This section is devoted to a discussion of the assumptions that comprise this point of view. This may appear to be a circuitous route to a description of the system, but the design of this system is, in large measure, based on the formulation developed here.

It is best to start with a discussion of features because it is the purpose of the system to learn relations among features. Actually a precise definition evolves from the description of the design, but for now we can think of a feature in pretty much the conventional "pattern recognition" sense: Features describe the status (present or absent, present in what form or to what degree, etc.) of specific events in the system's environment. Mostly, I refer to "high-level" features. These may, for example, signal specific words, objects in a visual scene, or in medicine the outcome of a diagnostic test. Of course something must be said about the development of high-level features from more primitive features, but a discussion of this aspect of the model is better motivated later. The notion of a feature also includes representations of "actions," analogous to the way in which proprioception represents motor activity as part of our sensory environment. From this point of view learning the consequences of certain actions under certain circumstances is a special case of learning relations among features, for the consequences, the actions, and the circumstances all have a common representation. A good analogy to the "feature" defined here is the "cogit" of the Hayes-Roth (1977) theory.

The values of features form a representation of the system's environment. It is natural to think of all these values as being available at each instant, and this point of view is implicit in the pattern recognition formalism and in many of the current models of memory. The design here is based on a different point of view, one which explicitly recognizes the existence of an "unobserved" state, in which the value of a feature is not available. In a cognitive sense it is clearly not the case that at each instant every feature is examined or appreciated. At any instant we are unaware of most of the complement of sensory information potentially available. Also, features may be unobserved because their values are physically not available. We recognize words with just a subset of the acoustic information that we are capable of using, as when listening over a telephone. A good example, at a higher level, is the result of a test in diagnostic medicine. If the test is not performed, then we have no value for the feature that is the test result. If the test is performed, then we observe this feature, and it may be positive or negative or possibly any of a continuum of values.

My point is that features come in two states: *observed* and *unobserved*. The value of a feature is available only when the feature is in the observed state. The unobserved state generally carries little or no information. This distinction between the observed and unobserved states of a feature is the basis for a definition of "associative recall." Roughly, associative recall in this model is a process of predicting, or "filling in," the values of certain unobserved features. These statements lead then to the first proposition:

Proposition 1. The processing of a feature distinguishes two states: observed and unobserved. In the observed state the value of the feature is available. In the unobserved state this value is not available. In itself the *state* of a feature contains little information.

As a first approximation I usually assume that the state of features carry *no* information with respect to the values of features: The states and values of features are independent.

It is obvious that memory would have no purpose if past experiences could not be taken as evidence towards a correct interpretation of future experiences. Plainly there is a relationship between past observations and the course of events in the future. I have used a model of this relationship to guide the design of the system presented here. Formally this is a Bayesian model, in which the prior distribution (which is only partly specified) is on distributions among features. To speak loosely, the prior determines what relations among features we are likely to encounter. This approach has the advantage that it easily translates assumptions about the nature of evidence into precise statements about the prior distribution. In theory this precision should in turn dictate the details of mechanisms for the processing of information by the system. In fact what I have is only a heuristic connection between the system and this Bayesian model. Therefore I replace a formal description of this model with a looser, more intuitive discussion of its main assumptions.

In this model, the "environment" is a vector-valued random function of (discrete) time.[2] The components of this vector are the features, and the prior distribution is a distribution on the probability law for this process. The most complete possible observation is of the entire vector,

$$f_1(t), \ldots, f_n(t),$$

where $f_i(t)$ is the value of the ith feature at time t. If we use "?" to indicate an unobserved feature, an actual observation looks like

$$f_1(t), f_2(t), ?, ?, ?, \ldots, f_k(t), ?, \ldots, f_n(t),$$

for example. It is assumed that the ?s contain no information about the values of the unobserved features.

There are three main assumptions about this process, and these are formulated as conditions on the prior distribution. These are the assumptions of constancy, continuity, and consistency. Constancy demands that the rules do not change: The process is stationary. If the rules appear to change, then it is because context has changed or because associations were by chance. Memory would serve no purpose in an environment that did not respect some measure of stationarity. (Actually I assume something stronger—a type of ergodicity or mixing to insure convergent behavior of certain estimators introduced later.) By continuity I mean, roughly, that similar events tend to have similar implications. Of course this "rule" is not absolute; but it *tends* to be true; and this is exactly the notion that the Bayesian formulation captures.

It should be easy to appreciate that something like constancy and continuity is in force in the real world. Indeed it is difficult to imagine a model for a learning

---

[2]The reader unfamiliar with probability theory is cautioned against interpreting "random" as meaning "unstructured." Indeed a deterministic model is an example of the more general probabilistic approach.

system that would not anticipate, implicitly, these conditions. Certainly there is a good deal more regularity in real environments. We find evidence in our experience for novel circumstances, and neither constancy nor continuity can account for this. It is easier to learn the diagnosis of a new disease if we are already familiar with other diseases. Why should this be true? The world of medicine allows us to utilize what we have already learned about the relations among symptoms in the context of this new disease. Thus the disease's manifestations can be largely inferred from only a partial description of its symptomatology. Roughly, consistency is the assumption that there is an environmental analog to the perceptual process of "filling-in" and the cognitive process of "stringing together associations":

Proposition 2. The probabilistic relations among features are consistent: It is more likely that A will be evidence for C when A is evidence for B and B is evidence for C.

This proposition may appear so natural that it involves no assumption at all. But the world need not have this property. Given a precise formulation of Proposition 2, it is not hard to demonstrate models that violate consistency. And, as a corollary, a learning machine can fail to take advantage of this presumed regularity.

As a simple example of a world that has the properties of constancy, continuity, and consistency, consider the "circles world," constructed as follows (see Fig. 9.1). Each feature in this world is associated with a circle on the unit torus. These circles are chosen, independently and once and for all, by first randomly choosing a center from the uniform distribution of the torus, and then randomly choosing a radius from some fixed distribution. Features are binary valued, with values $+$ and $-$ indicating the regions inside or outside of the associated circles. The choice of which value will indicate which region is made independently for each feature by a (fair) coin flip. Hence each feature is an independently generated binary-valued function defined on the unit torus. If we now put a uniform probability distribution on this torus, then the features can be viewed as random variables on the resulting probability space. Notice that these are not, in general, independent random variables. (In Fig. 9.1, for example, f_1 $= +$ implies, deterministically, $f_3 = -$; f_1 and f_3 are certainly not independent random variables.)

The process, $(f_1(t), \ldots, f_n(t))$, $t = 1, 2, \ldots$, is generated by first choosing a sequence of independent points, one for each t, on the unit torus using the uniform probability distribution. The values of the features at a given time are then determined by the position of the corresponding point. The observed process is generated at each time, t, by flipping independently for each feature, a (possibly biased) coin, and entering "?" (unobserved) if the result is heads or the value of the feature if the result is tails.

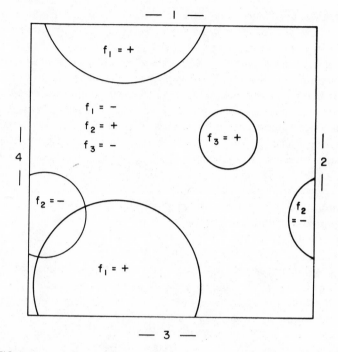

FIG. 9.1.   A "circles world" with 3 features. The surface is a torus: sides 1 and 3 and sides 2 and 4 are identified.

It is clear that the condition of independence between the unobserved state and the values of features is satisfied. It is also true that the circles world satisfies the conditions of constancy, continuity, and consistency. I have found this structure to be a useful conceptual tool as well as a convenient device for creating simulated environments in which to test some of the learning and recall algorithms described in later sections.

9.3.   ASSOCIATIVE LEARNING AND RECALL

Begin with an idealization: Features are to be taken as binary valued. By almost any interpretation, features in fact have many-valued, or continuous-valued, representations in the brain. But it is unlikely that the transition from "feature present" to "feature present at a particular strength or value" is fundamental. In fact, I believe that the binary idealization, because of its simplicity, can often "clear the air," and suggest the proper generalization to a continuous formalization. In any case, most of what is developed has a natural analog for continuous-valued features.

Features, for now, may be at any level of the cognitive hierarchy. They may represent phonemes, edges, words, diagnostic symptoms, or even phrases or thoughts. Section 9.4 attempts to make the connection from primitive to high-level feature. But for now, let us take features as fixed and given, and concentrate on the problem of learning and retrieving their interimplications.

Binary features can be thought of as indicating the presence or absence of some event. As proposed in the previous section the point of view here is that most of the features are most of the time unobserved; there is no direct information available on the presence or absence of the related event. Within this formalism recall has the natural interpretation of being a process by which the values of certain unobserved features are filled in (estimated). I am not suggesting that *all* unobserved features are estimated. Circumstances will define a collection of "target" features whose values are of particular importance at a particular time. In short:

Proposition 3. The purpose of recall is to estimate the values of a particular set (target set) of unobserved features.

We may think of each target feature as a classification. In the binary formalism, for each target feature, recall performs a two-way classification of the observed features, with the categories being the presence or absence of the event associated with that target feature.

A target feature in medicine might be a particular disease. The observed features correspond to observed symptoms (which may be "observed" to be present or absent) or to the results of completed tests. Estimating the values of the target features corresponds to establishing which diseases are present and which are not. Or, given the presence of a disease, certain symptoms may play the role of target features. Given ischemic heart disease, do we expect blockage of a particular coronary artery; do we expect hypertension; etc.? In vision we might think of the "label" as the natural target feature, given the image of an object (a collection of observed features). Or, with a partial observation of an object, we might think of the target features as being those unobserved features that are ordinarily associated with that object. In mathematics, concerning numbers, we may observe a set of features that define the event "odd plus odd" and wish to estimate the value of the target feature "even"—is it present or absent?

Target features are estimated using the information available: the values of the observed features. The straightforward approach is to estimate, individually, the value of each target feature using knowledge, from experinece, of the associations between the observed and target features. This procedure has no limitation if an infinite time of experience is available. The complete statistics between the observed and target features can then be known and an optimal (whatever the criterion) estimator constructed. But experience is finite, and in the most interesting cases, brief; an effective algorithm will anticipate certain structures. What sort of relations do we *expect* to find? In the language of Section 9.1, I am referring to the prior distribution, which determines what worlds we are likely to encounter and about which we have made certain assumptions. Here the relevant assumption is consistency, which suggests that a recall algorithm take advantage of, in a particular way, experience concerning certain of the unobserved features.

If cigarette smoking usually contributes to cardiovascular disease, and cardiovascular disease usually shortens life span; then, with everything else being equal, we take it for granted that cigarette smoking is likely to shorten life span. I want to emphasize that this does indeed involve an assumption; a prior distribution can be constructed so that such reasoning will prove unprofitable, or if we wish, *always fail*.

Let us suppose that we have defined a "local" mechanism for generating an opinion about the value of any particular unobserved feature given an arbitrary collection of observed features. One such mechanism will be discussed in detail presently. For now assume that it is available. Consistency suggests the following mechanism for obtaining the values of the target features: First, fill in those unobserved features about which the local algorithm has a "strong opinion," strong being defined with respect to some threshold value. If the target features are among these estimated features, then the procedure terminates. If not, then utilize the augmented set of observed features (truly observed plus filled-in features) to fill in another generation of unobserved features. Continue until either the target features are filled in or the process terminates by virtue of no further opinions having strength above threshold. In case of the latter, start again with a lower threshold. This is "associative recall," as it is defined in this model. Thus:

Proposition 4. Call a feature *decided* if it has been observed or its value has been estimated (filled in). The values of the target features are estimated by a recursive process that terminates when all target features are decided. A step in this recursion is the calculation of an *opinion* concerning the value of each undecided feature using the (observed and filled-in) values of the decided features. If, for a particular undecided feature, the opinion is above a threshold value, then this feature is filled in and becomes decided.

The relation of this model for recall to the notions of consistency and associative memory is clear. Loosely speaking, if A is associated with B and B is associated with C, then we come to associate A with C through the progression $A \rightarrow A \cap B \rightarrow A \cap B \cap C$, and furthermore the world is such that this association is usually appropriate.

(An appealing alternative way to incorporate information gained about the unobserved features in the estimation of target features is the "projection method": Experience is used to construct the projection operator onto the space spanned by that experience. The response to a stimulus is the action of this operator on that stimulus, and this action selects a combination of experience "close" to the stimulus (c.f. Kohonen, 1977). Although this recall algorithm is not based on a notion of consistency, it does use all of the information in the experience set rather than being limited to what has been learned about the relations between observed and target features. The difficulty, for our purposes, is that there is no apparent way to incorporate the unobserved state effectively. Suppose, for example, that "0" is used to indicate the unobserved state and that each feature has value 1 or 2. Then because of the distortion of patterns by the unobserved state, the span of the experience set will approach the *entire* space. For example, every feature may eventually be observed in isolation of all other features, at which time the experience set spans the entire feature space, and the projection operation returns the stimulus unaltered. Kohonen calls an experience set a set of *samples* and a stimulus a *key*. The point of view taken in this article is that the samples and the keys are of the exact same nature.)

I turn now to a discussion of the local algorithm, the appropriateness of which determines the accuracy of the proposed recall mechanism. The purpose of the local algorithm is to compute an opinion of the true value of an unobserved feature, given the values of a collection of observed features. The "strength" of this opinion should reflect the strength of the evidence available for this opinion.

Let us consider the nature of the information available in the collection of observed features. For this purpose it is useful to make a distinction between what I call *implicit* and *explicit* information. Consider a Venn diagram in which the regions are defined by particular features taking particular values. A point in this diagram can be thought of as a particular stimulus. (For the circles world, introduced in Section 9.1, the unit torus can serve as the Venn diagram when the circles associated with the collection of features have been drawn in.) Suppose that the observed features are f_i and $f_{i'}$, and that these observations define, respectively, the regions A and B in the Venn diagram. These observations contain, *implicitly,* the information that the stimulus is within A ∩ B. However unless there is a third observed feature, $f_{i''}$, such that a particular value of this feature indicates, precisely, the region A ∩ B, this information is not *explicitly* available (unless, of course, it should happen that A ⊂ B or B ⊂ A). The point is this: It is a practical limitation that the great majority of such information can only be available implicitly for a feature set of any appreciable size. If there are only 100 features in the circles world, then there are potentially 3^{100} ($> 10^{47}$) such regions, and even the human brain could not possibly have available an explicit representation for every such region. (This widely appreciated limitation is the focal point for the discussion in the next section.)

In the example we are given an observation of f_i and $f_{i'}$, and we wish to estimate the value of some unobserved feature, say f_j. The message from the previous paragraph is that we cannot reason that the stimulus is in A ∩ B and then ask for the most likely value of f_j because such information will in general not be explicitly available. We must somehow combine the *separate* information contained in the statements "stimulus in A" and "stimulus in B." In other words the problem is one of properly combining the information contained individually in each of the observed features (such as f_i) concerning the value of a particular unobserved feature (such as f_j). Presumably this information is gained from joint observations of features f_i and f_j in the past; that is, evidence concerning the relation between features f_i and f_j is gained each time these features are simultaneously observed, and probably not otherwise. "Probably not otherwise" in part reflects the assumption that there is no information in the fact of the unobserved states and in part reflects the assumption that a filled-in feature is not treated as an observed feature with respect to learning. (The value filled in for an unobserved feature is based entirely on the experience of the system and, as such, contains no new information concerning the relation between f_i and f_j.)

The local algorithm chooses a value for f_j given observations, say, of f_i and $f_{i'}$. On what basis can a "rational" choice be made? It should be emphasized that conventional statistical approaches have very little to offer in the present context. Either a Bayesian or a maximum likelihood estimator would require a knowledge of the joint conditional distribution of f_i and $f_{i'}$, given f_j. But as I have argued earlier, we must for practical reasons assume that higher-order information of this type is not explicitly available. This joint condition distribution could be reduced to a product of individual conditional probabilities with an assumption of conditional independence, but there is no reason for believing that this is even approximately true. (Certainly it is not true, for example, in the circles world.) It should also be recognized that even a knowledge of individual conditional probabilities cannot be assumed because we are interested here in estimation based on finite (and typically "small") samples. On the other hand, the *optimal* (minimum expected error rate) local decision function (based on pairwise observations) could be implemented if there were available a completely specified prior distribution for the Bayesian model developed in the previous section. This would in fact eliminate the motivation for a recursive scheme, the optimal decision being made by a direct application of the local algorithm to the target features. But it would be difficult indeed to argue for any such completely specified prior distribution.

The strategy that I take in developing a local algorithm is to assume first (temporarily) a complete knowledge of all pairwise statistics among features. Even then a "best" decision function is not defined—again because of an incomplete specification of the prior distribution. I argue instead for a particular decision function by virtue of its satisfying certain "commonsense" constraints on its general form. I then move to an approximation of this algorithm when given only partial knowledge of the relevant second-order statistics.

Concerning f_i and f_j, we can, at best, have available a complete description of the joint statistics of these two random variables. Let us say, for definiteness, that each feature, f_i, can have values $+$ or $-$, as in the circles world. Then the most complete possible information is summarized by the joint probability distribution function

$$P\ (f_i = a, f_j = b), \qquad a = +\ \text{or} -, \qquad b = +\ \text{or} -;$$

and this information would be available after an infinite number of joint observations of f_i and f_j. Let us suppose, for the time being, that all joint distributions are in fact known and ask by what function of these distributions would we obtain a local opinion for the value of an unobserved feature, f_j. Let O_j represent the strength of the conviction that $f_j = +$. Because f_j is binary, it will be enough to specify a means for computing O_j. Think of $+\infty$ as representing the strongest possible conviction and $-\infty$ as representing the weakest possible conviction (i.e., the strongest possible conviction that $f_j = -$). Suppose it is observed that $f_i = +$. It is evident that the following ''boundary conditions'' should be in force: If $P\ (f_j = +|f_i = +) = 1$, then O_j is maximal, that is, $O_j = +\infty$; if P $(f_j = +|f_i = +) = 0$, then $O_j = -\infty$, (we know that $f_j = -$); if $P\ (f_j = +|f_i = +) = \frac{1}{2}$, then the observation $f_i = +$ does not contribute to O_j.

Before writing down an expression for computing O_j, which respects these boundary conditions, I need to introduce some new notation. Concerning a feature f_i, a ''+'' will be thought of as signaling the presence of an associated event whereas ''−'' will signal its absence. For each feature, two new variables, y_i and n_i, are defined by

$$y_i = \begin{cases} 1 & \text{if } f_i = +, \\ 0 & \text{if } f_i = -\ \text{or } f_i \text{ is unobserved};\end{cases}$$

$$n_i = \begin{cases} 1 & \text{if } f_i = -, \\ 0 & \text{if } f_i = +\ \text{or } f_i \text{ is unobserved}.\end{cases}$$

In words: y_i indicates that the event associated with f_i is present (yes-activity); n_i indicates that this event is absent (no-activity). If both y_i and n_i are 0, then the ith feature is unobserved. Finally, for any pair, i and j, let $r_{ij}^+ = P(f_j = +|f_i = +)$ and let $r_{ij}^- = P(f_j = -|f_i = +)$.

Given complete second-order statistics, one possible functional form for O_j that is consistent with the preceding discussion is

$$O_j = \frac{1}{m} \sum_{i=1}^{n} y_i \log \left(\frac{r_{ij}^+}{1-r_{ij}^+} \right)$$

$$= -\frac{1}{m} \sum_{i=1}^{n} y_i \log\ (1-r_{ij}^+) + \frac{1}{m} \sum_{i=1}^{n} y_i \log\ (1-r_{ij}^-) \qquad (9\text{-}1)$$

where $m = (\#\ \text{observed events}) = (\#\ \text{features observed to have value } +) =$

$$\sum_{i=1}^{n} y_i.$$

The purpose of the factor $1/m$ is to adjust for the effect on O_j of merely observing more events—which, in itself, should not provide evidence toward the true value of f_j. Thus (9-1) describes a procedure by which all observed events are "polled" and two sets of averaged opinions are computed: the opinion that f_j = + and the opinion that f_j = −. The conclusion, O_j, is the difference between these. Notice that any observed event can itself determine the value of O_j by implying with certainty, f_j = + or f_j = −. Given a threshold T, the local algorithm chooses f_j = + if $O_j > T$, f_j = − if $O_j < -T$, and does not fill in at j if $|O_j| < T$.

Notice that only those observed features with value + (the observed events) contribute to O_j. This asymmetry in the treatment of present versus absent events is mostly for convenience: It allows us to use the present notation without modification to describe temporal recall (first discussed in Section 9.6). There need not be any loss of generality because we can always introduce a new feature such that "+" indicates the *absence* of the event associated with some f_i.

It remains to define the local algorithm for finite experience. Here, of course, the numbers $P(f_j = +|f_i = +)$ and $P(f_j = -|f_i = +)$ are not available. However we may have available functions $r_{ij}^+ (t)$ and $r_{ij}^- (t)$ (t being time) that will, eventually, approximate these conditional probabilities. In this case, O_j can still be computed from Eq. (9-1), with r_{ij}^+ and r_{ij}^- replaced by $r_{ij}^+ (t)$ and $r_{ij}^- (t)$, respectively.

For $r_{ij}^+ (t)$, an obvious choice is

$$r_{ij}^+ (t) = \frac{(\# \text{ simultaneous observations of } y_i = 1 \text{ and } y_j = 1 \text{ up to time } t)}{(\# \text{ simultaneous observations of } y_i = 1 \text{ and } y_j = 1 \text{ up to time } t) + (\# \text{ simultaneous observations of } y_i = 1 \text{ and } n_j = 1 \text{ up to time } t)}$$

and a similar expression for $r_{ij}^- (t)$ would replace $y_j = 1$ by $n_j = 1$ in the numerator. But, for our purposes, these sample estimators suffer a serious flaw. Suppose, for example, that for some i we have so far observed f_i and f_j simultaneously only once. Then either $r_{ij}^+ (t)$ or $r_{ij}^- (t)$ will be 1, and in any future observation of f_i, the computation of O_j will be dominated by the ith term in one of the summations of (9-1).

Intuitively, the opinion of a feature f_i concerning the value of a feature f_j should be weighed against how often f_i and f_j have been observed simultaneously. How experienced is the opinion? If there have been very few joint observations, then the ith terms in (9-1) should not contribute heavily to the computation of O_j. We seek functions $r_{ij}^+ (t)$ and $r_{ij}^- (t)$ that have the two properties:

1. $r_{ij}^+ (t) \rightarrow P(f_j = +|f_i = +)$ and $r_{ij}^- (t) \rightarrow P(f_j = -|f_i = +)$ as $t \rightarrow ,$; and
2. $r_{ij}^+ (t)$ and $r_{ij}^- (t)$ are small when the number of simultaneous observations of f_i and f_j are small.

Notice that the second property would insure that the contribution to O_j by "inexperienced features" is small. One way to achieve these properties is through a realization of the following differential equations:

$$\frac{d}{dt} r_{ij}^+ = \epsilon(n_i + y_i)(n_j + y_j)y_i(y_j - r_{ij}^+)$$

and

$$\frac{d}{dt} r_{ij}^- = \epsilon(n_i + y_i)(n_j + y_j)y_i(n_j - r_{ij}^-). \tag{9-2}$$

ϵ is a small parameter that contributes to the stability of the functions r_{ij}^+ and r_{ij}^-. The factor $(n_i + y_i)(n_j + y_j)$, which appears in each equation, is 1 when f_i and f_j are observed simultaneously and 0 otherwise. Modification, then, only occurs when f_i and f_j are observed simultaneously.

The equations in (9-2) are examples of a class of random equations that can be well approximated (for all time $t \in [0, \infty)$) by a simpler, *deterministic,* system, provided that the sequence of stimuli satisfy a mixing (ergodiclike) assumption (see Geman (1979)). The deterministic system associated with (9-2) is

$$\frac{d}{dt} r_{ij}^+ = \epsilon\{E[(n_i + y_i)(n_j + y_j)y_i y_j] - E[(n_i + y_i)(n_j + y_j)y_i]r_{ij}^+\}$$

$$\frac{d}{dt} r_{ij}^- = \epsilon\{E[(n_i + y_i)(n_j + y_j)y_i n_j] - E[(n_i + y_i)(n_j + y_j)y_i]r_{ij}^-\} \tag{9-3}$$

where E means expected value. The smaller ϵ is, the better the approximation. Recall now the assumption of independence of the *states* (observed vs. unobserved) and *values* (+ or −) of features. One implication is that

$$E[(n_i + y_i)(n_j + y_j)y_i y_j] = pP(f_i = + \quad \text{and} \quad f_j = +),$$

$$E[(n_i + y_i)(n_j + y_j)y_i n_j] = pP(f_i = + \quad \text{and} \quad f_j = -),$$

and

$$E[(n_i + y_i)(n_j + y_j)y_i] = pP(f_i = +)$$

where, for short, I have let p stand for the probability of simultaneously observing f_i and f_j. Hence, (9-3) can be written as

$$\frac{d}{dt} r_{ij}^+ = \epsilon p[P(f_i = + \quad \text{and} \quad f_j = +) - P(f_i = +)r_{ij}^+]$$

$$\frac{d}{dt} r_{ij}^- = \epsilon p[P(f_i = + \quad \text{and} \quad f_j = -) - P(f_i = +)r_{ij}^-], \tag{9-4}$$

which has as solution

$$r_{ij}^+(t) = P(f_j = +|f_i = +) [1 - \exp(-\epsilon p P(f_i = +)t)]$$

$$r_{ij}^-(t) = P(f_j = -|f_i = +) [1 - \exp(-\epsilon p P(f_i = +)t)]. \tag{9-5}$$

The result is intuitive: $r_{ij}^+(t)$ is asymptotically close to $P(f_j = +|f_i = +)$, and the rate of approach is faster the more frequently that $f_i = +$ and the more frequently that f_i and f_j are observed simultaneously. Notice then that a realization of (9-2) achieves, approximately, properties 1 and 2. [If the values of features are *not* independent of the states of features, then the asymptote is $P(y_j = 1|y_i = 1$ and f_j observed) with rate constant $1/\epsilon P(y_i = 1$ and f_j observed).]

In summary I interpret "associative learning" to be a process by which information is gained about pairwise statistics among features. In recall this information is used to evaluate both the *opinion* of a particular decided feature about the value of an undecided feature, and the *experience* of that opinion. Necessarily, then, two pieces of information must be acquired in the learning process. In the design proposed here, the two parameters $r_{ij}^+(t)$ and $r_{ij}^-(t)$ contain the necessary information. Thus:

Proposition 5. Associative learning is a process of gaining pairwise statistics among features. This information is utilized in associative recall to evaluate both the opinion of a particular decided feature and the experience behind that opinion. The net opinion about an undecided feature is influenced more by more experienced features.

9.4. A SECOND FORM OF LEARNING: DEVELOPMENT OF HIGH-ORDER FEATURES.

How effectively does the proposed process for recall estimate values of target features? The main limitations seem to be the absence of explicit representations for potentially important high-order statistics. Using the Venn diagram introduced earlier, we suppose that $f_i = +$ and $f_{i'} = +$ indicate regions A and B, respectively. Suppose further that $A \cap B$ is not explicitly available in the sense of the discussion of the previous section. It may be that for some feature j:

$P(f_j = +|f_i = +)$ is nearly 1,

$P(f_j = +|f_{i'} = +)$ is nearly 1,   but

$P(f_j = +|f_i = +$ and $f_{i'} = +)$ is 0.

Eventually the recall algorithm choses $f_j = +$ whenever the observation is $f_i = +$ and $f_{i'} = +$. There is as yet no mechanism by which this error will be corrected.

The problem is a familiar one in statistics. In regression, for example, an equation involving only linear combinations of the independent variables is sometimes inadequate. The addition of variables that are themselves higher-order functions of the independent variables may considerably improve the performance of the equation. Loosely speaking, in the foregoing example we are attempting to regress the value of the feature f_j onto those of the features f_i and $f_{i'}$. Another way of saying that we do not have explicitly available A ∩ B is to say that second-order functions in the features f_i and $f_{i'}$ are not available. Or perhaps a closer analogy is to the pattern classification problem, if we think of f_j as representing a binary classification. A decision surface derived only from joint statistics between the classification and the individual features proves to be a poor classifier. It is often necessary to make explicit use of higher-order statistics among the features.

I take it for granted that:

Proposition 6. In processing information the nervous system makes explicit use of statistics that are of high order in the most primitive features.

Recall the notation introduced in the previous section: $y_i = 1$ indicates the observation $f_i = +$, and $n_i = 1$ indicates the observation $f_i = -$. Because we can always introduce new features in which the roles of the values $+$ and $-$ have been interchanged, I can without loss of generality assume that the important information is contained in the observations of the random variables y_i, $(i = 1, 2, \ldots, n)$. Then, an *explicit* representation of all potentially available (and important) information is equivalent to having a realization of every function of the form

$$z = y_{i_1} y_{i_2} \cdots y_{i_k} \qquad (9\text{-}6)$$

where $1 \leq k \leq n$ and $1 \leq i_j \leq n$ for each j. In words, an explicit representation of all important information requires the indicator functions of intersections of arbitrary collections of the regions defined by $y_i = 1$, $(i = 1, 2, \ldots, n)$.

It is completely clear that all functions of the form (9-6) cannot be explicitly represented. The number of such functions is enormous in any but the most trivial examples. There are at least two obvious criteria that an indicator function of this type should satisfy before any "machinery" is committed to its explicit representation. One is frequency of occurrence. If an event never occurs there is certainly no purpose in developing for it an explicit representation. It may happen, for example, that the intersection of the sets defined by $f_i = +$ and $f_{i'} = +$ is empty, in which case $f_i = +$ and $f_{i'} = +$ will never occur simultaneously.

Everything else being equal, the events that are represented should be those occurring most frequently. But it is also true that some events are more important than others, and the statistics associated with such events should be given some measure of preference in committing the available machinery. More will be said later about what makes an event "important," but roughly what I mean is that certain events have associated with them a "hard-wired" *value*—they are painful or pleasurable; they may satisfy a particular need; etc. A possible example of such an event, relevant to the discussion found at the beginning of this section, is "prediction error"; it would be natural to assign to this occurrence a (negative) hard-wired value. Such events are specified by the direction primitives referred to in the introduction, and discussed in more detail in the final section, Section 9.6. The point to be made here is that events that are better correlated with important events should be better represented. Thus the event A ∩ B (introduced earlier in this section) would be given some priority as a candidate for explicit representation by virtue of its likely correlation with prediction errors.

These considerations suggest a second form of plasticity, one which is distinct, at least in purpose, from the associative-type modification postulated in the previous section. The purpose of this second form of plasticity is to commit machinery (perhaps cells or functionally grouped collections of cells) to the representation of statistics that are of increasingly high order. It is a common idea that such a process exists in the nervous system, and that, in a hierarchical fashion, units so-far committed form the "primitives" for the commitment of still higher-level units. I propose, in addition, that this process is biased towards more frequent and more "important" statistics, thus:

Proposition 7. There is a form of plasticity whose purpose is the commitment of neural machinery to the representation of high-order statistics. Successive levels in a hierarchy commit themselves to joint statistics among previously committed units of lower levels. At every level of the hierarchy commitment is to those statistics that are, by some measure, most frequent and most important. A statistic's "importance" is its correlation to important events, and these are innately defined.

Thus "importance" acts something like a "now print" (see Livingston, 1967), nonspecifically overweighting those statistics with which it is associated.

The hypothesis is that the commitment is hierarchical, not only in the sense that increasingly higher-order statistics become represented, but, as well, in the sense that the statistics of one stage form the substrates for the statistics at the next stage. One could imagine a hierarchy in which every stage drew solely from the first stage, seeking increasingly higher-order statistics. However in order to preserve the possibility of commitment to any statistic of a given order, one would need an unimaginably rich initial connectivity between the highest levels and the first level. The successive scheme suggested here avoids this difficulty but not without a price. Successive commitment limits the repertoire of a given level by what has already been chosen in the previous levels.

For definiteness, I outline the method of commitment used in our simulations, but I do not mean to suggest that this method is in any sense physiological. The assumption here is that the *result* of commitment is to create a representation of those statistics that are a combination of frequent and important. No assumption is intended about the specific mechanism by which this may be accomplished in the nervous system. (The problem of identifying such a mechanism is closely related to some interesting theoretical work by Bienenstock, 1980; Cooper, Liberman, & Oja, 1979; and von der Malsburg, 1973.)

Think of features as being represented by units consisting of two nodes, a yes-node and a no-node. Activity in the yes-node of the ith unit represents $y_i = 1$; activity in the corresponding no-node represents $n_i = 1$. These units are organized into a series of levels with, say, level 1 at the bottom, level 2 just above this, and so on. (The levels do not necessarily have equal numbers of units.) Initially only level 1 units are active and are participating in associative learning and recall. Following a specified "critical period" (defined as an a priori fixed number of observations at level 1), level 2 units become active, representing newly defined features, which henceforth participate in the associative processes. The result of this commitment is that the yes-node of a level 2 unit signals an event of the form $y_i = 1$ *and* $y_j = 1$, where f_i and f_j are two features represented in the first level. The corresponding no-node signals that either $n_i = 1$ or $n_j = 1$ or both n_i and n_j are 1 (i.e., there is enough evidence to establish that not both f_i and f_j are 1). Formally, the new feature, say f_k, is defined by

$$y_k = y_i\, y_j, \quad \text{and} \quad n_k = n_i + n_j - n_i\, n_j.$$

For each pair of yes nodes in level one, the number of times that these nodes are simultaneously active is recorded. This number is augmented by the observed correlation between such activity and activity in the direction (good/bad) primitives referred to earlier. If level 2 has m units, then, at the end of the critical period, these units are committed to a representation of the m pairs of level 1 units with the largest so-computed indexes. Following the commitment of level 2, over the next critical period, level 3 is committed using pairs of *level 2* with level 1 units. And then, level 4 commits, using pairs from level 2; and then level 5, using pairs of level 3 with level 2; and so on (see fig. 9.2). For illustration, imagine that every level has m units. Then at any given time, we are maintaining a list of only order m^2 indexes, and this is perfectly manageable.

At all times all committed units participate in the processes of associative learning and associative recall. Early in the experience of the system the lowest levels of the committed units will dominate the associative recall process. This is a result of the preference given to experienced units in the calculation of local opinions, as discussed in Section 9.3. Later, higher-level units will exert the greatest influence on recall. This derives from the fact that the yes-nodes as-

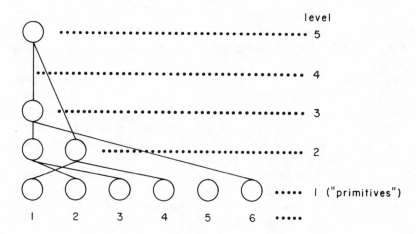

FIG. 9.2.   Example of units committed to high order relations. The first level 5 unit, initially inactive, now indicates the simultaneous occurrence of the events associated with the first level 3 unit and the second level 2 unit (equivalently, the simultaneous occurrence of the events associated with units 1,2,3,4, and 6 of level 1).

sociated with these units represent more selective events (viz. the *intersections* of events associated with lower-level units), implying that the conditional probabilities given activities in these yes-nodes will tend to be closer to 0 or 1. Consequently, the associated r_{ij}s will have asymptotic values that are also closer to 0 or 1, and [by Eq. (9-1)] these coefficients will eventually dominate the calculation of local opinions.

I pointed out in the introduction that this model is based on a compromise between local and distributed representations of information. At the lowest (earliest) levels of processing, a stimulus has a distributed representation; the activities of numerous units each signal the presence of a lower-order event contained in the stimulus. At successive levels of processing the representation becomes better localized; more selective units signal the presence of more complex combinations of events peculiar to the stimulus.

9.5   A SPATIAL CODING MODULE

The discussion so far has been of a model for representing, updating, and retrieving information about those relations among features that may exist at a fixed time. As of yet there is no mechanism in this model for processing temporal relations among features. I call those relations that do not contain a temporal component, spatial relations, and the machinery proposed for processing such information a spatial coding module (SCM, for short). What I say about the processing of *temporal* information is closely patterned after the model for processing spatial information. As an introduction to a temporal coding module, as well as a summary of the model so far, this section briefly reviews the proposed mechanisms for representing, learning, and recalling spatial relationships.

The SCM consists of layers of possibly differing numbers of units. A unit is a pair of nodes: a yes-node and a no-node. Activity in a yes-node signals the occurrence of an event, whereas activity in the corresponding no-node indicates that the event has not occurred. Absence of activity in either node indicates that the event is unobserved—it may or may not have occurred. Initially only the first layer of units participates in information processing. These layer 1 units are primitives of the SCM; they represent the total information available to the module. Layer 2 units become participants in SCM processing by committing to the representation of a new feature over a specified critical period. As a result of the commitment process activity in a yes-node of a layer 2 unit comes to signal the simultaneous activity in two particular yes-nodes of layer 1. Call the units associated with these two yes-nodes the "substrates" of the layer 2 unit. The no-node in this layer 2 unit signals activity in the no-node of at least one of the substrate units. Layer 2 units commit to those pairs of units that, over the critical period, are most frequently observed to have simultaneous activities in their yes-nodes as well as being most highly correlated with activities in the direction primitives. Over ensuing critical periods, layer 3 units commit to pairs consisting of one layer 2 unit and one layer 1 unit; then layer 4 units commit to pairs of layer 2 units; then layer 5 units commit to pairs of one layer 3 unit and one layer 2 unit, and so on.

At all times, those units that are committed participate in the associative learning and recall processes. Associative learning is the calculation of conditional probabilities: Each yes-node in the module computes for every other node in the module (excepting its no-node pair), the conditional probability of activity in that node given that the corresponding unit is active (observed) and that the yes-node itself is active.

Recall is a process of filling in yes-or-no activities at unobserved units. Activity at any given unobserved unit can be filled in by examining the associations to the yes- and no-nodes of that unit from all active yes-nodes. Estimates of the true value (yes or no) of a particular collection of unobserved units (target units) are derived by a recursive process which repeatedly fills in all unobserved units for which the active yes-nodes (observed plus filled-in) strongly suggest a value. The process terminates when all target units are filled in.

Before closing this section, it may be worthwhile to anticipate some of the discussion of Section 9.7, on a control module. Evidently, mechanisms must be developed for the execution of such activities as choosing target units, setting a threshold for the determination of which units are filled in at a particular step in the recall process, deciding when the SCM should be in "recall mode" and when it should be learning associations and committing new units, etc. It is the status of these decisions—decisions that control the activity of the SCM—that form the primitives (level 1 units) for the control module. In the design that I later propose the control module processes the activities associated with these primitives in much the same way as the SCM processes the activities that signal events in its environment.

9.6.   A TEMPORAL CODING MODULE

I make a distinction between two types of memories, those that associate events that tend to occur simultaneously and those that associate events that tend to occur in sequence. Although this separation is largely artificial, it is a useful idealization, and it can be expected to suggest mechanisms that recognize the continuum between "spatial" and "temporal" information. Imagine that time is discrete and that a stimulus occurs at each instant. Stimuli are represented exactly as before: a set of values composing a feature vector with explicit account taken for observed versus unobserved states.

The purpose of the "temporal coding module" (TCM) is to learn, and be able to recall, temporal relations that may exist among the features. The design principles are those of the spatial coding module: the commitment of machinery to high-order statistics, the learning of second-order statistics (conditional probabilities) between nodes, the reconstruction of events by a local filling-in process together with a global recursion process. Given these parallels, and given the detail with which the SCM has been described, an outline of the TCM design will substitute for a complete description.

The nature of the information processed by a TCM is determined by the primitives for the module. As with the SCM these primitives are the layer 1 units, each of which consists of 2 nodes having the same interpretation as in the SCM. Following the previous development, we think of primitive only as relative to the rest of the module. Primitive may refer to the detection of a particular frequency or of a particular type of transition in an auditory signal, or an entire word or even phrase may be primitive. A primitive may be a *top*-level unit of an SCM or of another TCM.

In analogy to the need for an explicit representation of high-order spatial statistics, there is a need here for an explicit representation of high-order temporal statistics. The reasoning is the same: It would appear that learning is the computation of second-order relations—relations among pairs. If neither of these pairs is itself of higher order than the primitives, then the organism ignores forever high-order statistics, and it is obvious that the behavior of the nervous system is not merely a function of second-order relationships. In the SCM, with binary features, "high order" referred to the intersection of a collection of features. Activity in a yes-node of a level 2 unit represented the simultaneous occurrence of activities in the yes-nodes of two level one units. The analog for the TCM is the hierarchical representation of *permutations* of pairs of lower-level units. Hence, a yes-node in the second level will come to indicate the completion of a sequence of activities in two consecutive yes-nodes in level 1. For example, a level 2 unit may have as substrate the (i, j) *ordered* pair of level 1 units. If activity in the i unit yes-node is followed immediately by activity in the j unit yes-node, then the yes-node in this level 2 unit is activated. (In our simulations, the timing is defined such that this level 2 unit is active simultaneously with the completion of the pair, i.e., the level 2 activity coincides with the activity in the second member of the level 1 pair.) If either the i level 1 unit no-node was active at the previous time or the j level 1 unit no-node is currently active, then the no-node in this level 2 unit is currently active. Any other sequence of (i, j) level 1 unit activities produces no activity (unobserved state) in this level 2 unit. Level 3 units represent permutations of level 2 followed by level 1 units; level 4 units represent permutations of pairs of level 2 units; level 5 units represent permutations of level 3 followed by level 2 units; and so on. (Activity in a level p unit is said to *follow* activity in a level q unit if it occurs during the pth period of time after activity in the level q unit. In other words, the sequence of primitives associated with the level q unit must immediately precede the sequence of primitives associated with the level p unit.)

We are again faced with the problem of selecting a small fraction of all possible statistics of a given order to which we will commit machinery. The solution, for the TCM, is the same as for the SCM. Levels commit following successive critical periods, and commitment is to those permutations most frequently observed and most highly correlated with activities in the direction primitives. Eventually activity in the yes-node of a unit in the kth level signals the completion of a particular sequence of k level 1 yes-node activites.

Associative learning in the TCM is by the same mechanism as in the SCM, except that the r_{ij}s update when activity in one unit "follows" (recall definition) yes-node activity in another unit rather than when activities occur simultaneously. Asymptotically, $r_{ij}^+(r_{ij}^-)$ approximates (in the sense discussed in Section 9.3) the probability that activity in the yes- (no-) node at j follows activity in the yes-node at i, given that activity at j is observed.

From the collection of activities in a particular set of units in a TCM, an ensuing sequence is predicted using a mechanism similar to the filling-in process proposed for the SCM. The TCM first chooses that yes-node whose activity is most strongly suggested by the activities present in the network. The decision function for this choice is exactly the one used in the SCM, and I would support its appropriateness by the arguments used there. After a node is chosen the values of all other units are recomputed just as though the sequence of primitives associated with the chosen unit had been observed, and from here the prediction process can continue.

As in the discussion of an SCM, it is worth noting here that a set of primitives of a control (versus environmental) nature have been implicitly defined. These primitives determine the depth of a temporal prediction, perhaps the level from which the filled-in unit is drawn, perhaps which other modules should influence the prediction, and certainly when such a prediction should be attempted. It is primitives such as these that comprise level 1 of the control module.

9.7   INTEGRATION

Temporal and spatial coding modules can be integerated, in a parallel or hierarchical structure, without modification of the mechanisms so far hypothesized. A parallel structure requires a degree of connectivity which will permit the state (set of active units) of one module to influence the local prediction (filling-in) process in the other. A spatial-to-temporal connection associates by the rules of the TCM, computing, asymptotically, the conditional probability that the TCM node "follows" (as defined in Section 9.6) the SCM node, given that the TCM unit is observed. A temporal-to-spatial–type connection associates by the concurrence rule used in the SCM and is asymptotically equal to the conditional probability of the SCM node being active, given that the TCM node is active and that the SCM unit is observed. Of course, full connectivity between modules is, at some point, not practical. Given a constraint on connectivity, it would be natural to use the more selective, and presumably more informative, higher-level units from a given module for communication to another module. A hierarchical structure can be achieved by taking as primitives, for one module, the top-level units of one or several other modules. The processing of information through such a network is well defined whatever the identities (spatial or temporal) of the individual modules. It is the availability of this hierarchy, a hierarchy that demands no new principles of architecture or function, which I believe justifies the notion of feature as it is introduced in Section 9.2, and used throughout this chapter.

Yet the design remains that of an "open" system. There is no mechanism for determining when an SCM begins a recall process, or what threshold is used during this process, or to what depth a TCM search should go. These control-type decisions can be organized by a logical structure that is very much akin to the structures proposed for temporal and spatial coding. Let us represent each available control activity by a unit of the type used in the TCM and SCM. Yes-node activity means that the corresponding action is being executed. For example, such activity may initiate the associative selection of a unit in a particular level of a particular TCM, or the setting of a recall threshold to "high" in a particular SCM. I assume that these primitive actions have their analog in the nervous system:

Proposition 8. There is a special class of motor primitives (*control primitives*) whose activities effect changes in the state of neural machinery.

The *control module* is a layered network of units in which these primitives form the first row. Its purpose is to learn to choose actions that are "appropriate" given the current available information concerning the state of the environment and the state of the network it controls. The principles of operation are analogous to those for the SCM or TCM, with choosing the "next move" (or next sequence of moves) playing the role of filling-in in the SCM or predicting in the TCM.

In the control module, as in the SCM and the TCM, higher-level units come to represent sequences or combinations of level 1 primitives. The argument for the existence of such units is much the same: It is obvious that explicit account must be taken of high-order relations in the control primitives, and it would seem that a local representation of such relations is necessary if it is the connections between pairs of units that ultimately determine how we get from a currently active set of units to a newly activated unit.

I have said that the control module operates in a manner much like the SCM and the TCM. In particular the control module chooses a next move or sequence of moves in a manner analogous to the filling-in or prediction process of the SCM or TCM. The action of the control module, then, is largely determined by the strengths of the r_{ij}s associated with the various connections to its units. If it is the purpose of the control module to choose "appropriate" actions, then we must interpret the strengths of the r_{ij} coefficients in a way which is fundamentally different from their interpretations in the SCM or TCM. In particular, Eq. (9-2) can no longer apply to the updating of these coefficients. It is the control module itself, using these coefficients, that determines the sequence of units which are activated, and therefore these coefficients can not simply reflect the relative frequency with which one node has followed another.

The missing ingredient is, of course, a definition of *appropriate action*. On this point, even a superficial development could consume an entire article. Instead of attempting a proper defense for the way in which "appropriate action" is defined here, I am simply describing its functional realization in the control module and hope that the reader will not find this realization unituitive.

The notion of appropriate action is based on a special class of primitives (*direction primitives*) whose activities, through their influence on the control module, ultimately determine the direction of the network. These premitives model those inputs that can be interpreted as having an *inherently* good or bad meaning to the nervous system. In the system, good or bad meaning is defined operationally; it is the effect of activity in a unit representing a direction primitive that determines the extent to which that primitive is good or bad. Other inputs will come to have good or bad value by virtue of their associations with activities in these units, but the development of such associations requires no new mechanisms; they result from the modification of coupling coefficients situated between SCM, TCM, or control module units and those units representing direction primitives; to summarize:

Proposition 9. There is a special class of primitives (*direction primitives*) that, by virtue of their influence on learning (commitment and associative), can be thought of as having positive or negative meaning to the nervous system.

The particular primitives employed depend on the particular application. Some direction primitives for the numbers world simulation were mentioned in the introduction. Presumably such things as hunger, pain, and perhaps joy, companionship, and the like play the roles of direction primitives for people. (Here, of course, it would be nearly impossible to distinguish what is truly a primitive from what has been associated with a primitive.)

The influence of activity in the direction primitives on the commitment process in SCMs and TCMs has already been described. Activities in direction primitives are also responsible for the development of the coupling coefficients of the control module (i.e., all r_{ij} for which j represents a unit of the control module). Roughly, if the unit i has been "followed" (recall the definition given in Section 9.6) by the unit j, and if there is net positive activity in the set of direction primitives, then r_{ij}^+ is incremented upward and r_{ij}^- incremented downward. If net activity in the direction primitives is negatie, then movement of the coupling coefficients is in the opposite direction.

Proposition 10. In networks of control features (features that derive from control primitives) associative learning is determined by activity in direction primitives rather than by observed correlation. Positive activity reinforces currently active associations; negative activity reinforces the negative of currently active associations.

The actual equations are such that the r_{ij}s remain always between 0 and 1, so that the local decision function, Eq. (9-1), still makes sense. The control module chooses a next move by looking ahead some fixed number of iterations (which number may itself be a control primitive) and evaluating the expected positive or negative consequences of a given sequence. "Looking ahead" means choosing potential paths by the TCM procedure, governed by the r_{ij}s (i may refer to a unit in any of the three types of modules). "Evaluating" means taking a certain average of the associations with direction primitives over the units in a particular path.

Proposition 11. Networks of control features activate new features by a combination of filling-in (guided by connectivities) and a bias towards features strongly associated with positive activity in direction primitives.

The details are not important. What should be emphasized is the position that *declarative* and *procedural* knowledge have essentially the same representation.[3] The structure envisioned for temporal and spatial coding of the environment applies to the problem of organizing an appropriate direction for the network as a

---

[3]For a good discussion of this issue and an example of a model based on the opposite proposition, see Anderson (1976).

whole. Thus units are successively committed to the representation of more and more complex actions, and the choice of new actions is driven by coefficients containing information about the significance of pairwise activities in these units.

My approach has demanded a strict separation of the notions of temporal and spatial associations, a binary notion of feature, and a rigid definition of temporal ordering. The advantage is that the logic of the processing is largely accessible. We can be reasonably sure that certain stability problems are avoided and that the architecture truly lends itself to a hierarchy, that "more is better." But the approach is severely restrictive. There are few environments that respect these conditions of regularity. The approach taken here is based on the expectation that the right generalizations will come from models sufficiently idealized to permit thorough analysis and simulation.

ACKNOWLEDGMENT

Research supported in part by the National Science Foundation through Grant MCS 76-07203 and by the Air Force Office of Scientific Research through Grant 78-3514.

REFERENCES

Anderson, J. R. *Language, memory, and thought*. Hillsdale, N.J.: Lawrence Erlbaum Associates, 1976.

Barlow, H. B. Single units and sensation: A neuron doctrine for perceptual psychology? *Perception*, 1972, *1*, 371–394.

Bienenstock, E. L. A theory of development of neuronal selectivity. Unpublished doctoral dissertation, Div. of Appl. Mathematics, Brown University, June, 1980.

Cooper, L. N., Liberman, F., & Oja, E. A theory for the acquisition and loss of neuron specificity in visual cortex. *Biological Cybernetics*, 1979, *33*, 9–28.

Geman, S. A method of averaging for random differential equations with applications to stability and stochastic approximations. In A. T. Bharucha-Reid (Ed.), *Approximate solution of random equations*. Amsterdam: Elsevier-North Holland, 1979.

Hayes-Roth, B. Evolution of cognitive structure and processes. *Psychological Review*, 1977, *84*, 260–278.

Kohonen, T. *Associative memory, a system theoretic approach*. Berlin: Springer-Verlag, 1977.

Lashley, K. S. In search of the engram. *Society of Experimental Biology Symposium* (*No.* 4): *Physiological mechanisms in animal behavior*. Cambridge, England: Cambridge University Press, 1950.

Livingston, R. B. Brian circuitry relating to complex behavior. In G. C. Quarton, P. Melnechuk, & F. O. Schmitt (Eds.), *The Neurosciences*. New York: Rockefeller University Press, 1967.

von der Malsburg, C. Self-organization of orientation sensitive cells in the striate cortex. *Kybernetic*, 1973, *14*, 85–100.

10 Parallel-Processing Mechanisms and Processing of Organized Information in Human Memory

Roger Ratcliff
Dartmouth College

The main aim of this chapter is to describe research in two areas of cognitive psychology that are relevant to the interests of workers in Artificial Intelligence (AI), cognitive science, and neural modeling. The chapter is divided into two parts: First, a parallel-processing associative model for recognition of independent items is presented. This model can be viewed as an up-to-date example of psychology's contribution to parallel-processing systems. The second part of the chapter presents some experimental results and psychological models concerned with processes and the representation of organized information in human memory.

In the area of neural modeling researchers are usually concerned with developing models that are able to account for behavioral results. Researchers in Artificial Intelligence have two slightly divergent aims: The first is to develop computer programs that perform certain tasks with humanlike or better intelligence. The second aim is to use any insights as theories of human performance and to model behavioral results. For both of these it is necessary to select aspects of human performance for comparison. The neural modeler or AI researcher has to find and select behavioral data that can provide good tests for his or her model but this process can be rather haphazard. For example, the selection may be made on the basis of the last few articles read, or it may be the latest paradigm of the local cognitive psychologist.

In the first section of this chapter I describe a parallel-processing associative model for recognition that accounts for a great deal of data in its domain of applicability and use this model as a case study in examining the relationship between theory and data. In particular several important properties of reaction time data are presented and several major properties of the human processing system are brought into focus and described in terms of the model. It should be made clear at the outset that the model presented is composed of two parts: a mathematical model and a metaphor that is used to elucidate the model and present a particular view of the processing system. Several of the neural network models presented in this book may be quite compatible with the mathematical model, yet may present a different metaphor for the model (see Hinton, Chapter 6, this volume).

10.1.   A MODEL FOR ITEM RECOGNITION

Reaction time has been used as the main dependent variable for developing and testing many models in cognitive psychology. I argue that the statistic, mean reaction time, is almost totally inadequate for such purposes (though it has proved useful in getting some areas of research started). One problem is that certain models of the recognition process, serial scanning models, can be mimicked by several other kinds of models, for example, parallel-processing models and direct-access models (based on strength theory), at the level of mean reaction time. Thus it is difficult to press any claims as to the nature of the processes involved in the tasks under study. Another problem that has arisen is that many models that are quite adequate at the level of mean reaction time have serious problems with the shape of reaction time distributions. Models of processing should account for the overall shape of reaction time distributions, that is, produce distributions that are positively skewed. If such care is not taken, then it is possible to produce models that are falsified by the data that they were designed to fit (see Ratcliff & Murdock, 1976).

Another factor of considerable importance is the relationship between accuracy and reaction time. There is always a relationship between accuracy and reaction time in recognition data: In a condition in which recognition is easy, a response is usually accurate and fast, whereas in a condition in which recognition is harder, a response is less accurate and slower. (This reflects difficulty of retrieval rather than the speed–accuracy tradeoff that will be discussed later.) It is relatively easy to produce a model that deals just with reaction time or just with accuracy, but I believe that it is important for any model of processing to deal with the relationship between accuracy and reaction time. A third factor of considerable importance is flexibility in the processing system. Subjects can choose to respond slower in most tasks in order to gain accuracy, or they can sacrifice accuracy to increase speed. Flexibility should therefore be central to any model of processing.

I now present a model for the process involved in recognizing whether an item is a member of a previously presented list. This model attempts to account for the shape of reaction time distributions, the relationship between speed and accuracy, and the flexibility in the processing system. In a typical procedure, a list of items (words, letters, numbers, or pictures) is presented to a subject. This list is called the memory set. The subject is then presented with a test item and has to respond as to whether that item was in the list. Typically accuracy and reaction time are recorded and form the basic data.

According to the model the test item is encoded and then compared to the representation of each item in the memory set simultaneously (i.e., in parallel). Each individual comparison is accomplished by a random walk process. A decision is made when any one of the comparisons ends in a match or when all of the comparisons end in a nonmatch. When the decision has been made, the appropriate response is initiated. The overall scheme is shown in Fig. 10.1.

This scheme (random walk comparison process: comparisons carried out in parallel, self-terminating for positive responses and exhaustive for negative responses) provides the core of the mathematical model. It is later shown that this model does a good job in dealing both qualitatively and quantitatively with a relatively large amount of data from recognition studies. The metaphor that follows is not the only possible description of the processing system, but it does provide a reasonable way to understand the operation of the mathematical model. In a later section the relationship between the mathematical model and neural network models (providing a different metaphor for the model) is examined.

The metaphor used to describe the interaction between the test item and items in memory is a resonance metaphor. The test item causes memory items to resonate: the greater the resonance, the closer the match; the smaller the reso-

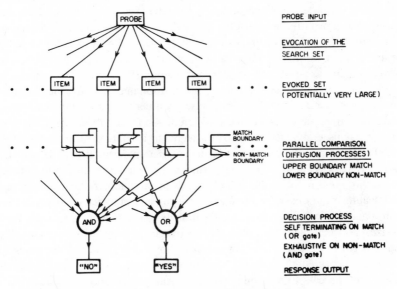

FIG. 10.1.   An overview of the recognition model. Copyright 1978 by the American Psychological Association. Reprinted by permission.

nance, the poorer the match. The resonance metaphor is used to indicate that items outside the immediately preceding memory set are accessed in the comparison process. Atkinson, Herrmann, and Wescourt (1974) have shown that items in a set of instructions enter the comparison process. They presented items from the instructions as negative items in the test list in a recognition experiment. Reaction time to these items was slower than reaction time to control items. Monsell (1978) has traced out the decay function and found that a test item last presented several lists back can influence speed and accuracy of a "no" response. The size or amount of resonance drives the random walk: the greater the resonance, the greater the rate of approach to the match boundary; the smaller the resonance, the faster the approach to the nonmatch boundary.

The size of the resonance is determined by several factors. First, it appears that every kind of similarity enters the comparison; for example, Juola, Fischler, Wood, and Atkinson (1971) performed an experiment with words as study and test items. They looked at three types of negative test items (items to which the correct answer was "no"): homophones and synonyms of stimulus words and neutral words. They found that synonyms were 60 msec slower than neutral words and that homophones were 120 msec slower than neutral words. When homophones were broken down into two classes, visually similar and visually dissimilar, increases in reaction times were 200 msec and 40 msec, respectively. These results show that semantic, visual, and acoustic similarities enter the comparison between a test item and stimulus items. Morin, DeRosa, and Stultz (1967) have shown that the more numerically remote a negative probe is from the memory set, the faster the response (e.g., a negative response to a 1 as a test item is faster than a negative response to a 6 if the study items were 7, 8, and 9). Besides similarity, how recently a study item was presented affects both reaction time and accuracy in many different paradigms.

From this discussion it can be seen that many different kinds of information enter the comparison process. The probe information interacts with memory trace information producing a yes or no response. In order to maintain the notion that the memory trace consists of many different kinds of information, the term relatedness is used to describe the overall amount of match. An example of the way relatedness may be derived independently is given in Rips, Shoben, and Smith (1973). They obtained ratings from subjects for the similarity between pairs of birds and pairs of animals. From these similarity ratings multidimensional scaling solutions were obtained for birds and animals separately. Two-dimensional solutions were adequate; the dimensions were identified as predacity and size. To determine the relatedness between two concepts, the euclidean distance between the two concepts in the two-dimensional space can be assessed. This single-measure relatedness is used as the value of drift that drives the random walk process to determine whether probe and memory items match. If relatedness is high, then drift toward the match boundary is rapid; if relatedness is low, then drift is towards the nonmatch boundary. In the mathematical model relatedness has variability in that two nominally equivalent items (e.g., having the same serial position in the memory set) may have different relatedness values, for example, because they have been learned to different levels.

The comparison process can be illustrated by supposing that the probe and memory items are represented by a vector of features. The comparison then proceeds by a gradual accumulation of feature matches (which could be either a serial or parallel process). Each time a match occurs between a feature in the probe and a feature in the memory item a step is taken toward the match boundary in the random walk. Each time a nonmatch occurs, a step is taken toward the nonmatch boundary. Relatedness represents the overall number of feature matches between the probe and the memory item. In terms of the resonance metaphor the size of the resonance represents the average rate of feature matches.

One source of variability, variability in relatedness, has already been mentioned. It can be seen that there is a second source of variability and that is variability in the rate of accumulation of evidence. Two probe vectors, with the same number of feature matches to a particular memory-item vector, may have differences in the order of matches and nonmatches so that one comparison may have mainly feature matches in the first part of the comparison, and another comparison may have mainly nonmatches in the first part of the comparison. These two processes would have quite different times to reach the match or nonmatch boundary (the processes may even reach different boundaries). Thus we can identify two different sources of variability in the model; variability in relatedness and variability in the comparison process.

In the specific mathematical model, the comparison process is modeled by the continuous analog of the random walk: the diffusion process. The diffusion process is the component of the model that accounts for such factors as reaction time distributions, speed–accuracy relationships, and variable criteria, that is, flexibility in processing. The critical assumption made is that relatedness is proportional to the average drift in the diffusion process. Relatedness between a probe and a memory-set item when the probe matches the memory item is assumed to be distributed normally with mean u and variance η^2 and for a nonmatching probe and memory item, relatedness is again assumed to be distributed normally with mean v ($u > v$ usually) and variance η^2. A criterion is set between u and v such that values of drift on the u side of the criterion are positive (drift towards the match boundary) and values of drift on the v side of the criterion are negative. Figure 10.2 illustrates the relatedness distributions, the random walk process, and the diffusion process.

Reaction time distributions of the usual empirical shape are produced by the diffusion model. Figure 10.3 shows the way in which the normal distribution maps into a positively skewed reaction time distribution. In addition variability in drift works to make the distributions more positively skewed. As can be seen

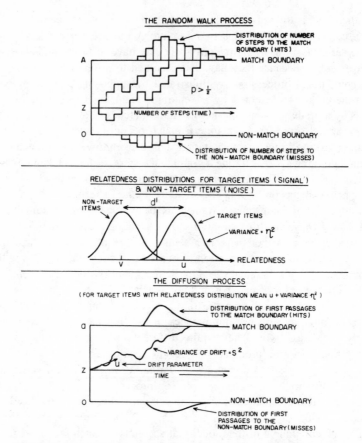

FIG. 10.2.   An illustration of the random walk and diffusion process together with relatedness distributions that drive the diffusion process. Copyright 1978 by the American Psychological Association. Reprinted by permission.

from Fig. 10.3, a prediction of the model is that as relatedness decreases, the mean and mode of the distribution both increase and diverge as is seen in reaction time data.

There are three variable criteria in the model: the zero point of relatedness, and the positions of the two boundaries. It is assumed that all these criteria are to some extent under the subject's control. The way subjects are able to control their speed–accuracy criteria is by adjusting the position of the match and nonmatch boundaries. The criterion in relatedness can be adjusted, in the same way that the criterion in signal detection theory can be adjusted, to vary the relative numbers of false positive responses and false negative responses. These two sets of criterion adjustments are not entirely independent in that adjustments in any of the three criteria produces changes in both speed and accuracy of responses.

From Fig. 10.2, it can be seen that the random walk process integrates both reaction time and accuracy in a single theoretical mechanism. This integration allows speed–accuracy trade-off to be explained in terms of changes in boundary positions. The closer the match and nonmatch boundaries are to the starting point of the random walk, the faster and less accurate are responses; the further away from the starting point, the slower and more accurate are the responses (with relatedness values and relatedness criterion held constant). There are two major ways in which speed–accuracy trade-off may be studied. First subjects can be induced to respond with either speed or accuracy by instructions. This mode of responding can be termed information-controlled processing; the subject determines when to respond based on the amount of information accumulated. The model as described so far is concerned with this mode of responding. Second, the experimenter may determine the time at which the subject will respond using a deadline or signal to respond. In this case, the mode of processing may be termed time-controlled processing. Figure 10.4 shows the way the distribution of evidence spreads in time-controlled processing. Initially the evidence begins at the

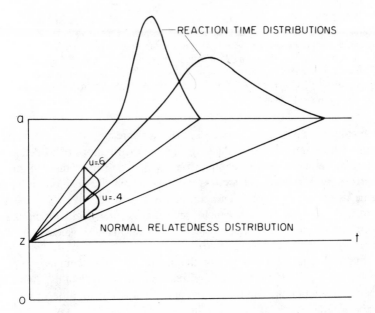

FIG. 10.3. A geometrical illustration of the mapping from a normal relatedness distribution to a skewed reaction time distribution (with variance in drift $s^2 = O$). (Note that as relatedness decreases, the distribution tail skews out. a represents the distance between the bottom and top boundaries of the diffusion process; z represents the distance between the bottom boundary and the starting point; and u represents the mean of the normal relatedness distribution.) Copyright 1978 by the American Psychological Association. Reprinted by permission.

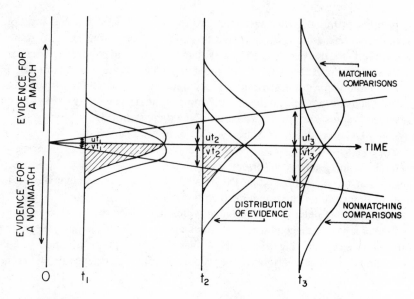

FIG. 10.4.   Spread of evidence as a function of time in the unrestricted diffusion process for one matching and one nonmatching process. (At time t_1, there is a large amount of overlap; at time t_3, the overlap has reached asymptote, with asymptotic $d' = (u - v) / \eta$ [See middle panel of Fig. 10.2]. u is the mean of the match relatedness distribution, and v is the mean of the nonmatch relatedness distribution.) Copyright 1978 by the American Psychological Association. Reprinted by permission.

starting point z; as processing proceeds, evidence spreads out with the variance a function of time (t). At large values of time the distributions of evidence (both for matching and nonmatching comparisons) will tend to an asymptotic form: All comparisons with positive relatedness will have reached a position on the positive side of the starting point, and comparisons with negative relatedness will have drifted negative. Thus it can be seen that accuracy will asymptote as a function of time at the d' value defined by the relatedness values (and this is observed in practice; see Reed, 1976).

From this discussion it can be seen that the random walk comparison process is capable of accounting for the shape of reaction time distributions, the relationship between reaction time and accuracy, and the flexibility of processing evident in speed–accuracy trade-off.

Error Analysis and the Time Course of Evidence Accumulation

If it is possible to investigate the patterns of errors at different signal lags in a deadline or response signal experiment, then it is possible to examine the kind of information that is being used by the subject at different points during the time course of accumulation of evidence. Pachella, Smith, and Stanovich (1978) performed experiments in which subjects were presented visually with one of four stimuli, the letters *B, C, D,* and *E* were required to name the stimulus at certain deadlines. Pachella et al. performed error analyses at each of the deadlines and found that the error patterns could be well fitted by an informed guessing model. The informed guessing model in this application had the following states: *BCDE, BD,* and *CE* (determined by fits of the model to the data; other sets were shown to be unimportant). If subjects had no information they guessed from the set *BCDE;* if they had some information, then they either had information that distinguished the set *BD* from *CE* or total information. As the deadline became longer, the probability of being in one of the confusion sets became smaller. From the results it can be seen that it is possible to trace out the time course of accumulation of evidence and to find out the form of the evidence being accumulated at particular points during the time course.

McClelland (1979) has presented a model for the case where processes operate in cascade; that is, one processing stage can make use of the partial results of a previous processing stage. It is possible to account for the results of Pachella et al. (1978) in terms of this cascade model by supposing that at short lags the response is made on the basis of information from early processing stages in which the subject has little information (i.e., is in a guessing state). At intermediate lags the response is made on the basis of partial information from which the subject can distinguish sets *BD* from *CE,* and at longer lags the subject uses information from later processing stages in which total information is available. Ratcliff (1980) has presented the mathematics necessary to deal with the diffusion process when the rate of information accumulation varies as a function of time. In this case, experiments of the kind performed by Pachella et al. (1978) will provide information that may help identify the processing stages in a cascade-type model or that might identify the type of evidence being accumulated at a particular time in a diffusion model.

The Decision Process

The decision process is conceived of as a process in which the results of many comparisons are combined to produce a single yes/no decision. The process terminates when one comparison ends in a match leading to the production of a positive decision but has to wait for all comparisons to terminate in a nonmatch to produce a negative response.

It may be somewhat difficult to see how "yes" and "no" responses can have about the same reaction time, as is observed experimentally, when negative responses require that all comparisons terminate whereas positive responses require only one comparison to terminate with a match. The model allows the relative speed of yes and no responses to be determined by the relative starting point to boundary distances, and in fits of the model it is found that the starting point to match boundary distance is in general greater than the starting point to nonmatch boundary distance. Because subjects are able to manipulate these boundary positions (in the formulation of the model), they can vary the relative speeds of match and nonmatch processes that lead to yes and no responses (note that accuracy will also covary). A direct analogy can be found in the analysis of detection data and signal detection theory. In signal detection theory the proportions of correct yes and correct no responses are used to compute two measures of performance, a measure of discriminability and a measure of the criterion that subjects set. The criterion setting reflects the relative certainty subjects place on yes and no responses: Subjects can chose to respond "yes" only when very sure thus producing relatively few but very accurate yes responses, or subjects can chose to respond "no" only when very sure, or at any point in between. Ratcliff and Hacker in an unpbulished experiment investigated criterion effects on reaction time by measuring reaction time in two experiments in which subjects were encouraged to be sure when responding "yes" in one condition and to be sure when responding "no" in another condition. In a recognition memory task reaction time was found to covary with accuracy in that when subjects were responding in the sure yes-condition, accuracy for yes responses was high and reaction time for yes responses was 168 msec slower than reaction time for no responses. In the sure no-condition accuracy for no responses was high and reaction time for no responses was 203 msec longer than for yes responses. These data can be modeled by assuming that the random walk boundaries are adjusted so that in the sure yes-condition the match boundary is far away from the starting point and the nonmatch boundary is relatively close to the starting point. This adjustment will lead to the observed pattern of data. The main point to note is that the relative speed of yes and no responses is under the control of the subject and is another indication of the flexibility in processing discussed earlier.

Summary of the Model

The model I present deals with aspects of experimental data that are held to be critical for any reasonable model of item recognition. The relationship between accuracy and reaction time is implicit in the random walk comparison process and the random walk process guarantees reaction time distributions of the correct shape. Flexibility in processing is allowed by the variable (subject-controlled) criteria, and adjustment of these criteria allow the modeling of such things as speed–accuracy trade-off. As well as accounting for the experimental data within any single paradigm, the model accounts for performance on several different paradigms and thus allows comparisons to be made among those paradigms (see Ratcliff, 1978, for details).

Comparison with Anderson's Model

It is easy to see relationships between the above model and certain neural network models. In particular, the model can be related to a recognition model developed by J. A. Anderson (1973). In that model the memory representation of a set of items is a vector of N elements. A particular item is represented by a specific vector of N elements. The memory representation of several traces is then the vector sum of the individual traces. The match between a probe and the overall memory is simply the dot product between the probe vector and the overall memory vector (i.e., each element in the probe vector is multiplied by the corresponding element in the memory vector). In Anderson's model positive and negative evidence (element matches and nonmatches, respectively) are accumulated separately until one of them exceeds a fixed criterion. If this were modified so that positive and negative evidence canceled, then the comparison process would be a random walk. The model suffers the problem, however, that there is no separate record of each memorized item. Thus, on the basis of this memory, subjects would be unable to judge such things as frequency of occurrence of items in a list and would be unable to determine in which list an item had been presented (these arguments are the same as those presented against strength theory, see Anderson, J.R., & Bower, 1972; Wells, 1974).

In contrast to neural network models of the type developed by Anderson, the retrieval model I describe maintains that the representations of items in memory are functionally independent; that is, there are separate representations of the occurrence of individual items. It turns out that in fitting response signal data (Reed, 1976), a model that assumes that all information about the study material is combined in a single vector would not produce adequate fits. The inadequacy of such a fit is one reason that the item recognition model described above maintains separate representations for each item encoded.

General Discussion

For neural modelers whose area of interest is higher cognitive functioning, one of the major aims of modeling is to realize psychological functions such as recognition, association, and categorization in terms of reasonable neural models. There are presently available models that do a good job of representing similarity, partial matching of items, reconstruction of stimuli from degraded probes, recognition, association, and categorization (see Anderson & Mozer, Chapter 7, and Kohonen et. al., Chapter 4, this volume). Each of the models does a good job of mimicking human performance within its domain and has desirable properties from the standpoint of system design.

There are three major problems with these kinds of models. The first is that they seldom add much to our psychological understanding of the structure and processes that they model in that they rarely make strong predictions about how humans will perform in other tasks, they rarely integrate experimental paradigms so as to provide parameter invariance across tasks. The second problem concerns mimicking of the different neural schemes by each other and the difficulty of separating these schemes on the basis of desirable properties or fits to data. The third problem concerns the completeness of such models; each of the models can be considered a building block or an element in an intelligent system, but there seems to be no attempt to develop a control structure that fits these elementary processes together to produce an intelligent system. There are also several more detailed difficulties, and these include problems in modeling semantic networks with labeled relationships that appear to be a prerequisite to representing world knowledge and allowing the system to make inferences (see Hinton's chapter in this volume).

Artificial Intelligence models seem to be complementary in some respects. The main concern is with a whole system (no matter how modest) that in fact performs the tasks it was designed to perform. The notion of control and of fitting elementary processes together is of central importance. In these models (see Fahlman, Chapter 5, this volume) world knowledge and relational information are used in the knowledge base, and such information allows inferences to be made. However, such Aritificial Intelligence models have difficulty in representing similarity (except by relative distance in the network) and in performing partial matching (matching an incomplete probe against memory). It is also difficult to see how such models would be implemented in the nervous system.

Both of these areas of research have insights to gain from psychology. At some point a researcher has to choose some set of phenomena to model. If the choice is made on the basis of what an intelligent system should do, then this often boils down to the use of informal psychological data. Psychology can point to data that may rule out various alternate, intuitively appealing models. For neural modelers, psychological results can often form the basis for the whole modeling effort, and for Artificial Intelligence researchers, psychological results can point to more useful methods of organizing the theoretical processing system. It should be noted that psychology often gains insights from Artificial Intelligence, and some theories developed first in Artificial Intelligence are then taken as psychological theories and subjected to experimental test.

In the next section I present a brief discussion of some psychological research on the topic of the organization of information in memory and processes involved in encoding and retrieval.

10.2. ORGANIZED MEMORY: PROCESS AND STRUCTURE

There seem to have been relatively few attempts by cognitive psychologists to communicate the present certainty of phenomena and theories to groups such as Artificial Intelligence researchers and neural modelers. This section is a small attempt to present some of the more recent findings in the general area of research concerned with the structure of semantic knowledge and the representation of text in memory and with processes involved in manipulating this information. In particular I discuss topics such as the distinction between automatic and strategic processes, a line of research that may allow us to decide whether inferences are made at input or output in text processing and the processing of world knowledge (verification of well-known facts).

Automatic and Strategic Processes

The processes involved in priming have come under considerable scrutiny recently. The main result is that presenting one concept (word or letter) can activate another concept leading to a faster match, lexical decision, or recognition for the second concept. For example, in a letter-matching task (Posner & Snyder, 1975), the subject is to respond as to whether two target letters presented simultaneously are the same or different. The same response is speeded if a prime letter, presented before the target letters, matches the target letters (i.e., a facilitation effect).

Automatic and strategic components of priming can be separated by studying the time course of this facilitation, using a procedure in which the target letters are presented at a variable interval (e.g., at 50, 100, 200, and 400 msec) after the prime. The priming effect appears to have two components. The first component has been called an automatic component; it is characterized by a very rapid onset; in many experiments, prime onset to target onset as short as 100 msec is sufficient to produce facilitation. The second component has been termed strategic facilitation and is characterized by a much less rapid onset, often several hundred milliseconds.

Automatic and strategic processes can also be distinguished by probability manipulations. Automatic processing has no inhibition associated with low probability alternatives whereas strategic processing often has inhibition associated with low probability alternatives. For example, in the letter-matching paradigm, if the prime does not match the test letters (in a condition in which there is a low probability of a prime–target nonmatch) then there is inhibition; that is, the same response is slowed (Posner, 1978, p.100).

Neely (1977) provided a particularly clear example of the separation of automatic and strategic components of facilitation in a lexical decision task. Subjects were presented with a prime word, to which they made no response, followed by a target. The subjects were required to decide whether the target letter string was a word. The prime was one of three category names or a row of *x*s. Subjects were told that if the prime was *bird* then they should expect the target letter string to be a member of the bird category if the letter string were a word. If the prime was *building* then the target word would be a body part with high probability. If the prime was *body* then the target letter string would be a building part with high probability. Subjects were explicitly told to shift their attention when they saw the *building* or *body* prime to the expected category. The time course of processing was examined by varying the prime to target delay. For the categories *building* and *body* there was facilitation for a target that was a member of the prime category at short delays (250 msec). This was interpreted as automatic activation. At longer delays (750 msec) the response to a target that was a member of the prime category in this shift condition was inhibited (a longer reaction time). The expected target (a body part if *building* was the prime) produced facilitation at longer delays but not at short delays. These results were interpreted as supporting the automatic–strategic distinction.

A similar series of questions can be asked about priming in recognition. McKoon and Ratcliff (1980) and Ratcliff and McKoon (1978) have used priming in recognition as a technique for examining the structure of text in memory. For example, Ratcliff and McKoon (1978) presented sentences to subjects for study and then tested single words for recognition. Response time to a word immediately preceded in the test list by a word from the same sentence was 100 msec faster than the response time to a word immediately preceded by a word from a different sentence. The size of the priming effect was found to be greater if the priming pair were from the same proposition than if the priming pair were from different propositions. This result was taken as support for the view that the structure of sentences is propositional. McKoon and Ratcliff (1980) showed that the magnitude of the priming effect varies as a function of the distance between the prime and test words in propositional structure of the paragraph. Thus the technique provides an index of the distance between two propositions in terms of the size of the priming effect. The priming effect in recognition shows that activation is not just reserved for preexisting semantic networks. Accessing a concept that was just studied in text serves to activate concepts related in the text. The amount of activation varies as a function of the relative distance between the concepts in the text. The question arises as to whether the priming effect is automatic or strategic. Ratcliff and McKoon (in press, a) have investigated automatic and strategic components of priming in recognition. In the first experiment it was found that the probability that a priming pair occurred in the test list had no effect on the size of the priming effect. This suggests that the priming effect is automatic in the sense of Tweedy, Lapinski, and Schvaneveldt (1977). In the second experiment the time course of processing was examined. A prime was presented to which the subject was not required to respond. Following this by a variable amount of time (e.g., either 50, 150, 450, 850 msec) the test word was presented for recognition. It was found that facilitation (when the prime and test word were from the same sentence) had been produced by 150 msec. Inhibition (when the prime and test words were from different sentences) occurred later in processing and showed up by 450 msec. The third experiment was designed to investigate strategic priming. Subjects were presented with two sentences and told that if the prime word was from one sentence, then the test word would be from the other sentence with high probability, and they should attempt to switch to that sentence. It was found that it took somewhat longer than 750 msec for subjects to switch—there was little facilitation at 750 msec for words from different sentences, large facilitation at 1800 msec, but large inhibition when the prime and test words were from the same sentence at 750 msec—which indicates that strategic priming in recognition in this paradigm takes considerably longer than automatic processing. Thus we can conclude that the priming effects reported by McKoon and Ratcliff as an index of paragraph structure are automatic priming effects because all intertest intervals were kept less than 200 msec.

The automatic–strategic distinction has implications for the earlier discussion about flexibility of processing. Strategic processes are those subject to flexibility such as changing criteria or selecting among alternative succeeding processes during the course of processing. Automatic processes are those processes that run off no matter what the subject attempts to do strategically. The distinction between automatic and strategic processes has considerable importance for models of human processing (see also Schneider & Shiffrin, 1977 for discussion of the development of automaticity) but as yet has been largely ignored in the areas of Artificial Intelligence and neural modeling. The distinction may prove of help in determining whether a particular kind of inference is made at the time of reading a text or at the time of retrieval of that text.

Semantic Verification Experiments

Recent psychological investigation into the structure of semantic memory originated when Collins and Quillian (1969) performed several experiments to test Quillian's network theory of semantic memory. In this theory, concepts such as *robin, bird, animal,* and *thing* are stored in a hierarchy with *thing* as the root node and other concepts branching off (e.g., *animal* would be one link from *thing, bird* one link from *animal,* and *robin* one link from *bird*). In the experiments, subjects were asked to verify statements such as "a robin is a bird," or "a robin is an animal." The prediction made was that the time required to verify the sentence is a linear function of the distance between the concepts in the memory representation. This prediction was verified and further experiments followed, but several problems were found in attempting to fit data from negative responses. Rips, et al. (1973) developed an alternative model of the representation of semantic information. Their model represents similarity in terms of overlap of semantic features instead of distance in terms of number of links in a network model. See Smith (1978) for a discussion of further properties of feature and network models. Rips et al. performed several experiments in which the variable semantic relatedness was controlled and varied, and they found that semantic relatedness was a much better predictor of reaction time than hierarchical distance (in fact it was even suggested that the variable heirarchical distance had no effect on reaction time). Smith, Shoben, and Rips (1974) developed a feature-matching model that accounted for reaction time differences in terms of feature overlap, where feature overlap was used to represent semantic relatedness. In addition, Smith et al. added a decision mechanism (similar to signal detection theory) that was based on a model for item recognition developed by Atkinson and Juola (1973). This retrieval model predicted that the more related (the greater the feature overlap) are two concepts, the faster and more accurate the positive response, and the slower and less accurate the negative response. Thus, verifying "a robin is a bird" is faster than verifying "a penguin is a bird" and responding negatively to "a bird is a robin" is slower and less accurate than responding negatively to "a bird is a penguin." This prediction is upheld when the relationship tested is of the form category and member, but when the relationship is an antonym relationship, the prediction is contradicted by data (e.g., Glass, Holyoak, & Kiger, 1979). Antonym relationships are verified quite quickly, the more related the terms, the faster. For example, "is a brother a sister?" is responded to negatively more quickly than a more indirect (and less related) antonym such as "is a brother a female?" Holyoak and Glass (1974) have presented data that suggest that production frequency is a better predictor of reaction time in such semantic verification tasks. From their results they developed a model to account for negative decisions that involved production or search then checking. Lorch (1978) has presented data that suggests that the two separate factors, production frequency and semantic relatedness, both have effects on verification reaction time and accuracy.

In order to account for many of the problems found in the original Collins and Quillian model, Collins and Loftus (1975) presented a revision of the model. The model assumes that concepts are stored in a network with the links between concepts labeled (as before) and weighted (i.e., by weights that denote strength of association between the concepts). The mechanism for retrieval consists of two stages: First, activation spreads from concepts represented in the question to activate a portion of semantic memory; second, that active portion is evaluated. This model has two main problems. First, the spreading activation process is probably not able to produce the levels of successful retrieval that humans produce (see Anderson & Hinton, Chapter 1, this volume). Furthermore, Ratcliff and McKoon (in press, b) have shown that the time required for activation to spread through a semantic network is very small, activation spreads too fast to account for any temporal variability in reaction time data (i.e., reaction time differences between conditions). Thus it seems that the spreading activation component of this model is largely unnecessary. Second, the evaluation process is not spelled out in sufficient detail though several different matching processes are described, for example, using counterexamples or distinguishing properties. However it is quite unclear which combination of mechanisms are used to explain experimental data and how all these mechanisms may be coordinated in a processing system.

From this discussion it can be seen that the theoretical interpretation of semantic verification is no longer simple (as it was with the models of Collins & Quillian, 1969, or Rips et al., 1973). We can identify two important variables that affect performance, semantic similarity and production frequency, and we can note that antonyms appear to be processed differently to category-member relationships. But as yet we have no general relatively complete model of semantic verification. It is my guess that no simple elegant model will be developed for the semantic verification task; rather the kind of model developed will incorporate several autonomous subprocesses as in the Collins and Loftus (1975) model.

10.3. CONCLUSIONS

A main concern of this chapter is the relationship between psychological data and theory. In the first part of the chapter, a parallel-processing, associative model for recognition is presented. Besides providing a recent example of psychology's contribution to the theme of this book, the model provides an example of a theory that is general (applies across a range of paradigms) yet also explains and fits data within its domain in considerable detail. At the core of the model is a random walk comparison process that relates accuracy and reaction time, accounts for the shape of reaction time distributions, and allows the flexibility in processing necessary to account for speed–accuracy trade-off and other criterion adjustments. A model such as this can be seen as a replacement for informal data because the model summarizes a great deal of data in its domain so that other modelers need only concern themselves with the predictions of the model as a first step in further development. In a great number of enterprises in cognitive psychology, theories of the generality and detail of the theory presented in the first part of this chapter are not available. The second part of the chapter describes recent developments in two areas of research, each of which is concerned with some aspects of the structure of semantic information and text in memory and the processes involved in encoding, accessing, and retrieving such information. First it is argued that an important characteristic of the human processing system is the distinction between automatic processes that have rapid onset and are not subject to flexibility of processing and strategic processes that have much slower onset and can be adjusted by subjects particular processing strategies. This distinction has not yet entered the areas of neural modeling and Artificial Intelligence. Second an empirical method of studying the structure and process of permanent knowledge, the study of semantic verification, is reviewed. At present it seems that explanations of semantic verification results can no longer be simple but that we can identify two important variables, semantic relatedness and production frequency, and it seems that antonyms are processed differently from category-member relationships. There is a great deal of psychological research into parallel processing and associative memory, and it is hoped that this discussion will prove useful to neural modelers, Artificial Intelligence researchers, and perhaps even psychologists.

ACKNOWLEDGMENTS

Preparation of this chapter was supported by NICHD grant HD 13318-01. Figures were reproduced by permission of the American Psychological Association.

I would like to thank Gary Dell, Gail McKoon, Ben Murdock, and Ed Smith for comments on an earlier draft of this chapter.

REFERENCES

Anderson, J. A. A theory for the recognition of items from short memorized lists. *Psychological Review,* 1973, *80,* 417–438.

Anderson, J. R., & Bower, G. H. Recognition and retrieval processes in free recall. *Psychological Review,* 1972, *79,* 97–123.

Atkinson, R. C., Herrmann, D. J., & Wescourt, K. T. Search processes in recognition memory. In R. L. Solso (Ed.), *Theories in cognitive psychology: The Loyola Symposium.* Hillsdale, N.J.: Lawrence Erlbaum Associates, 1974.

Atkinson, R. C., & Juola, J. F. Factors influencing speed and accuracy of word recognition. In S. Kornblum (Ed.), *Attention and performance* (IV). New York: Academic Press, 1973.

Collins, A. M., & Loftus, E. F. A spreading-activation theory of semantic processing. *Psychological Review,* 1975, *82,* 407–428.

Collins, A. M., & Quillian, M. R. Retrieval time from semantic memory. *Journal of Verbal Learning and Verbal Behavior,* 1969, *8,* 240–247.

Glass, A. L., Holyoak, K. J., & Kiger, J. I. Role of antonym relations in semantic judgments. *Journal of Experimental Psychology: Human Learning and Memory,* 1979, *5,* 598–606.

Holyoak, K. J., & Glass, A. L. The role of contradictions and counterexamples in the rejection of false sentences. *Journal of Verbal Learning and Verbal Behavior,* 1975, *14,* 215–239.

Juola, J. F., Fischler, I., Wood, C. T., & Atkinson, R. C. Recognition time for information stored in long-term memory. *Perception & Psychophysics,* 1971, *10,* 8–14.

Lorch, R. F., Jr. The role of two types of semantic information in the processing of false sentences. *Journal of Verbal Learning and Verbal Behavior,* 1978, *17,* 523–537.

McClelland, J. L. On the time relations of mental processes: An examination of systems of processes in cascade. *Psychological Review,* 1979, *86,* 287–330.

McKoon, G., & Ratcliff, R. Priming in item recognition: The organization of propositions in memory for text. *Journal of Verbal Learning and Verbal Behavior,* 1980, *19,* 369–386.

Monsell, S. Recency, immediate recognition memory, and reaction time. *Cognitive Psychology,* 1978, *10,* 465–501.

Morin, R. E., DeRosa, D. V., & Stultz, V. Recognition memory and reaction time. In A. F. Sanders (Ed.), *Attention and performance I.* Amsterdam: North Holland, 1967.

Neely, J. H. Semantic priming and retrieval from lexical memory: Roles of inhibitionless spreading activation and limited capacity attention. *Journal of Experimental Psychology: General,* 1977, *106,* 226–254.

Pachella, R. G., Smith, J. E. K., & Stanovich, K. E. Qualitative error analysis and speeded classification. In N. J. Castellan, Jr. & F. Restle (Eds.), *Cognitive theory, Volume 3.* Hillsdale, N.J.: Lawrence Erlbaum Associates, 1978.

Posner, M. I. *Chronometric explorations of the mind.* Hillsdale, N.J.: Lawrence Erlbaum Associates, 1978.

Posner, M. I., & Snyder, C. R. Attention and cognitive control. In Solso, R. L. (Ed.), *Information processing and cognition.* Hillsdale, N.J.: Lawrence Erlbaum Associates, 1975.

Ratcliff, R. A theory of memory retrieval. *Psychological Review,* 1978, *85,* 59–108.

Ratcliff, R. A note on modeling accumulation of information when the rate of accumulation changes over time. *Journal of Mathematical Psychology*, 1980, *21*, 178-184.

Ratcliff, R., & McKoon, G. Priming in item recognition: Evidence for the propositional structure of sentences. *Journal of Verbal Learning and Verbal Behavior*, 1978, *17*, 403-417.

Ratcliff, R., & McKoon, G. Automatic and strategic priming in recognition. *Journal of Verbal Learning and Verbal Behavior*, in press. (a).

Ratcliff, R., & McKoon, G. Does activation really spread? *Psychological Review*, in press. (b).

Ratcliff, R., & Murdock, B. B., Jr. Retrieval processes in recognition memory. *Psychological Review*, 1976, *83*, 190-214.

Reed, A. V. List length and the time course of recognition in immediate memory. *Memory & Cognition*, 1976, *4*, 16-30.

Rips, L. J., Shoben, E. J., & Smith, E. E. Semantic distance and the verification of semantic relations. *Journal of Verbal Learning and Verbal Behavior*, 1973, *12*, 1-20.

Schneider, W., & Shiffrin, R. M. Controlled and automatic human information processing. *Psychological Review*, 1977, *86*, 1-66.

Smith, E. E. Theories of semantic memory. In W. K. Estes (Ed.), *Handbook of learning and cognitive processes* (Vol. 6). Hillsdale, N.J.: Lawrence Erlbaum Associates, 1978.

Smith, E. E., Shoben, E. J., & Rips, L. J. Structure and process in semantic memory: A featural model for semantic decisions. *Psychological Review*, 1974, *81*, 214-241.

Tweedy, J. R., Lapinski, R. H., & Schvaneveldt, R. W. Semantic-context effects on word recognition: Influence of varying the proportion of items presented in an appropriate context. *Memory & Cognition*, 1977, *5*, 84-89.

Wells, J. E. Strength theory and judgments of recency and frequency. *Journal of Verbal Learning and Verbal Behavior*, 1974, *13*, 378-392.

Author Index

Subject Index

A

Abstraction, 218–219
Accuracy of response, 266–272, 274, 280–281
Activation, spreading, 26–27, 75, 161, 179, 280
Addresses, addressing, 10–11, 22, 83, 95, 107, 170, 187, 191
Analyzer, differential, 137–138
Artificial Intelligence
    comparison with psychology and/or neuroscience, 29, 51, 145–148, 163, 189, 265, 275–276
    focus and goals of, 146, 265, 276
    hardware considerations in, 31, 138, 147, 164
    implausibility of, 147
    models, 276
Associations
    context-sensitive, 168–169, 203
    pairwise, 15–16, 239
    temporal vs. spatial, 258, 263

B

Behavior
    single-element, 229–235
Brain (*see also* Neocortex, mammalian; Nervous system, mammalian)
    as computer, 9, 54, 139
    cerebellum, 204–205
    "code" of, 140
    electrical activity in, 191–194
    "local" activity in, 238
    models of, 16
        holographic, 87
        simple linear, 195–196
        simple nonlinear, 196–198
        simple probabilistic, 198–202, 206–210
    parallelism of, 9, 147
    skeleton filters in, 189–210
    thalamus, 134

C

Categories, 218–219 (*see also* Categorization)
    and "prototypes," 219
    "edges" and "centers" of, 219
Categorization, 213–235, 275
Cells (*see also* Neurons):
    death of, 62
    "grandmother," 61–62, 191, 216, 218, 238
    individualism of, 17, 37, 42–44
    pontifical, 61–64, 191
    pyramidal, 32–35, 128, 199, 201
    stellate, 32, 34
Cerebellum (*see under* Brain)
Closure, transitive, 151, 154, 156–157
Coding, 189, 262 (*see also* Encoding, autoassociative)
    hash, 170